Rural Tourism and Recreation

Principles to Practice

Dedication

To Laurence and Frances who have borne neglect with equanimity

Rural Tourism and Recreation

Principles to Practice

Lesley Roberts and Derek Hall

Leisure and Tourism Management Department
The Scottish Agricultural College
Auchincruive, Ayr
UK

with additional contributions

CABI *Publishing*

CABI *Publishing* is a division of CAB *International*

CABI Publishing
CAB International
Wallingford
Oxon OX10 8DE
UK

Tel: +44 (0)1491 832111
Fax: +44 (0)1491 833508
Email: cabi@cabi.org
Web site: www.cabi.org

CABI Publishing
10 E 40th Street
Suite 3203
New York, NY 10016
USA

Tel: +1 212 481 7018
Fax: +1 212 686 7993
Email: cabi-nao@cabi.org

A catalogue record for this book is available from the British Library, London, UK.

Library of Congress Cataloging-in-Publication Data
Rural tourism and recreation : principles to practice / edited by Lesley Roberts and Derek Hall.
p. cm.
Includes bibliographical references (p.).
ISBN 0-85199-540-3 (pbk. : alk. paper)
1. Tourism--Europe. 2. Rural development--Europe. I. Roberts, Lesley. II. Hall, Derek, 1948–

G155.E8 R87 2001
338.4'79140456--dc21

2001025123

ISBN 0 85199 540 3

Typeset in 9/11pt Melior by Columns Design Ltd, Reading
Printed and bound in the UK by Biddles Ltd, Guildford and King's Lynn

Contents

List of Tables

List of Boxes

List of Figures

List of Plates

Contributors

J. Bessière, Centre des Etudes Touristiques et des Industries de l'Accueil (CETIA), University of Toulouse le Mirail, Maison de la Recherche, 5 allées Antionio Machado, F-31058 Toulouse Cedex 1, France

S. Boyne, Leisure and Tourism Management Department, The Scottish Agricultural College (SAC), Auchincruive, Ayr KA6 5HW, UK

A. Copus, Rural Policy Group, Management Division, The Scottish Agricultural College (SAC), Craibstone, Aberdeen AB9 2YA, UK

D. Grant, Leisure and Tourism Management Department, The Scottish Agricultural College (SAC), Auchincruive, Ayr KA6 5HW, UK

S. Grimes, Department of Geography, National University of Ireland, Newcastle Road, Galway, Republic of Ireland

D. Hall, Leisure and Tourism Management Department, The Scottish Agricultural College (SAC), Auchincruive, Ayr KA6 5HW, UK

B. Lane, Rural Tourism Unit, Centre for the Historic Environment, University of Bristol, 43 Woodland Road, Bristol BS8 1UU, UK

L. Lumsdon, Department of Hospitality and Tourism Management, Manchester Metropolitan University, Hollings Faculty, Old Hall Lane, Manchester M14 6HR, UK

M. MacLeod, Rural Policy Group, Management Division, The Scottish Agricultural College (SAC), Craibstone, Aberdeen AB9 2YA, UK

V.T.C. Middleton, Charcoal House, Low Nibthwaite, Cumbria, LA12 8DE, UK

M. Nylander, Rural Tourism Working Group, Rural Policy Committee, Maaseutumatkailun teemaryhmä, PL 186, FIN-00531, Helsinki, Finland

L. Roberts, Leisure and Tourism Management Department, The Scottish Agricultural College (SAC), Auchincruive, Ayr KA6 5HW, UK

G. Rognvaldsson, Holar Agricultural College, Holar i Hjaltadal, Saudarkrokur, Iceland

R. Sharpley, Centre for Travel and Tourism, University of Northumbria, Longhirst Campus, Longhirst Hall, Morpeth, Northumberland NE61 3LL, UK

F. Simpson, Land Use Consultants, 21 Woodside Crescent, Glasgow G3 7XH, UK

F. Williams, Rural Policy Group, Management Division, The Scottish Agricultural College (SAC), Craibstone, Aberdeen AB9 2YA, UK

Preface

It is no accident that the publication of this book coincides with the second international conference hosted by the Leisure and Tourism Management Department at the Scottish Agricultural College (SAC), Auchincruive, in September 2001. The restructuring of agricultural industries, evident in attempts to broaden rural economic bases through diversification, requires support that has led to a broadening of scope within many of the institutions that assist Europe's rural industries. This explains the positioning and purpose of the tourism department in SAC, and illustrates the particular focus of its development work. In September 1998, The Leisure and Tourism Management Department held its first international conference. Entitled *Rural Tourism Management: Sustainable Options*, it was dedicated to assisting the formulation of a rural tourism research agenda and to highlighting areas of policy which such research might best inform. The resulting 'Auchincruive Declaration' (Hall, 1999, 2000) set out this agenda.

The conference proceedings (Hall and O'Hanlon, 1998) and the subsequent declaration augmented a number of English language texts on the subject of rural tourism which appeared towards the end of the 1990s, filling a void that almost bordered on neglect of the subject. There were a number of book chapters and academic papers on the subject that attempted to develop frameworks for addressing issues within this area of study (see Chapter 1 and recommended reading). With the exception of Sharpley and Sharpley (1997) and Page and Getz (1997), however, many of the texts, and most of the book chapters and journal papers, were relatively inaccessible, their existence known only to a small community of rural tourism 'specialists': researchers, academics and students.

As well as producing the *Auchincruive Declaration*, the Rural Tourism Management conference pointed to a critical gap between research findings and their application: the 'implementation gap' identified by Butler and Hall (1998a: 106; 1998b: 254), among others. Despite delegates converging from five continents, it was notable that attempts to attract a range of practitioner groups to the conference bore little fruit. Academic conferences, it seems, are for academics. Other professionals – from the consultancy or development sector or from businesses themselves – appear not to consider them to be appropriate (and separate events were later held for them at Auchincruive). Might this help to explain the implementation gap, we wondered? Almost certainly. Much academic research, whether conceptual or empirical, informs development processes and might contribute a great deal to tourism and recreation in rural areas – industries that are far from achieving their development potential. But if ideas get no more than a brief airing in the shadow of an ivory tower before being committed to their place in the relative obscurity of the academic library shelf, their impacts will be minimal, where they are felt at all.

We needed to find a way, therefore, to:

- make research findings more widely available; and
- place more focus on explicit policy and/or commercial relevance.

This book's title directly reflects these two key aims. In its approach to the principles and practice it seeks to bring together, the book has three main objectives:

- to review the work of a wide range of academics and practitioners, presenting it collectively, contextually and in an accessible manner;
- to illustrate the work's policy and commercial relevance and/or application by linking it with policy, planning and markets for tourism and recreational products and services; and
- to adopt a rather different analytical approach through its focus on neither tourism nor the tourist but on the ways in which the one is consumed by the other.

The third objective arises from recognition of a gap in the existing literature. Much analytical research focuses on the supply of tourism and recreation in rural areas as one of the outcomes of agricultural restructuring. This is critical from a policy and planning perspective, and provides practitioners in the fields with a wealth of research to inform development processes. Diversification into tourism and recreation, however, requires a move into highly competitive markets that are largely driven by demand, and are thus subject to different economic laws. In practice, tourism must work alongside or within rural development. In principle, the two are rarely analysed together. Thus the stage was set for a book and a second conference to try to bridge the implementation gap and to bring together those who research issues of tourism in rural areas, and those who work in their development.

In relation to the book, we wondered why such an obvious need had not been met by other authors. Surely others had recognized the gap. Why, then, had no one else tried to fill it? Probably, we realized somewhat later, because the task is such a formidable one.

Writing one publication for more than one audience is not easy. We have tried to produce a concise and informative academic text that will provide appropriate material and perspectives for the constant band of tourism 'specialists' (primarily Chapters 2–5). We have also attempted to provide something of a flavour of this research for the practitioner market (in Chapters 6–8). Chapters 1 and 9 provide an introduction and concluding synthesis, respectively. The work of a number of authorities in their fields is included in the form of 'invited viewpoints', and these add to, and sometimes provide the focus for, the chapters' main debates. Comprehensive cross-referencing makes it possible for each audience to focus on their preferred 'section', dipping into the other as required, thus customizing the research process. The two sections are linked by, and explained through, five key themes that can be traced throughout the book. The pivotal theme of *paradox* reflects complexities such as continuity and change, sustainability and unsustainability, principles and practice, and more. It suffuses the remaining themes that signify the book's central concerns: *change, unsustainability, transparency* and *integration.* Although the themes are embedded within the core concerns, the relative importance of each fluctuates depending on the points in question. Dominant themes are identified at the start of each chapter.

Given its particular aims and focus, however, there are some issues that the book does not address. It has not been possible, for example, to consider all issues relating to rural development and the processes of tourism and recreation within this context. Political processes are only touched upon (although questions of community and policy issues are considered). The subject of economic development relates only to tourism's development and does not extend to issues of relative values and opportunity costs. Moreover, the loaded question of funding for private and public sector ventures is not addressed.

Ironically, problems of language and cultural barriers within Europe – that is the often self-imposed monolingual constraints of native English-speakers – mean that English language texts often barely draw on the substantial literature in other European languages, notably German and French, despite ever-increasing collaboration in research and publication between European partners. Equally, while colleagues from Scandinavia, Iberia and The Netherlands have made important contributions to English language literature, relatively few German and French native speakers have crossed the cultural divide. One exception is the late Martin Oppermann whose considerable contribution to the literature on tourism in rural areas (e.g. Oppermann, 1995a,b, 1996, 1997) is readily acknowledged. The contributions to this volume by Jacinthe Bessière, Mirja Nylander and Gunnar Rognvaldsson represent a small attempt to draw on the European experience, and to begin to redress the imbalance. Thus, one central aim of the book – to make research findings accessible to a wider audience – has been constrained by linguistic accessibility, further reflecting the significance of the book's pivotal theme.

Lesley Roberts
Derek Hall
Auchincruive
January 2001

References

Butler, R.W. and Hall, C.M. (1998a) Conclusion: the sustainability of tourism and recreation in rural areas. In: Butler, R.W., Hall, C.M. and Jenkins, J. (eds) *Tourism and Recreation in Rural Areas.* John Wiley & Sons, Chichester, pp. 249–258.

Butler, R.W. and Hall, C.M. (1998b) Tourism and recreation in rural areas: myth and reality. In: Hall, D. and O'Hanlon, L. (eds) *Rural Tourism Management: Sustainable Options.* The Scottish Agricultural College, Auchincruive, pp. 97–107.

Hall, D. (1999) Rural, wilderness and forest tourism: markets, products and management. In: Arola, E. and Mikkonen, T. (eds) *Tourism Industry and Education Symposium, Jyväskylä, Finland.* Jyväskylä Polytechnic, Jyväskylä, pp. 69–86.

Hall, D. (2000) Rural tourism management: sustainable options conference. *International Journal of Tourism Research* 2, 295–299.

Hall, D. and O'Hanlon, L. (eds) (1998) *Rural Tourism Management: Sustainable Options.* The Scottish Agricultural College, Auchincruive.

Oppermann, M. (1995a) A model of travel itineraries. *Journal of Travel Research* 33(4), 57–61.

Oppermann, M. (1995b) Holidays on the farm: a case study of German hosts and guests. *Journal of Travel Research* 34(1), 63–67.

Oppermann, M. (1996) Rural tourism in Southern Germany. *Annals of Tourism Research* 23, 86–102.

Oppermann, M. (1997) Rural tourism in Germany: farm and rural tourism operators. In: Page, S.J. and Getz, D. (eds) *The Business of Rural Tourism: International Perspectives.* International Thomson Business Press, London, pp. 108–119.

Page, S.J. and Getz, D. (eds) (1997) *The Business of Rural Tourism: International Perspectives.* International Thomson Business Press, London.

Sharpley, R. and Sharpley, J. (1997) *Rural Tourism: an Introduction.* International Thomson Business Press, London.

Acknowledgements

The contributions by Andrew Copus and Marsaili MacLeod, and by Steven Boyne, both in Chapter 2, have drawn upon research which has been part-funded by the Scottish Executive Rural Affairs Department (SERAD), and its predecessor, the Scottish Office Agriculture, Environment and Fisheries Department (SOAEFD), for The Scottish Agricultural College (SAC).

The research on which Fiona Williams's contribution in Chapter 8 is based derives from a project (FAIR-CT96–1827) funded by the European Commission Agriculture and Fisheries Research Programme (FAIR) on 'Regional Images and the Promotion of Quality Products and Services in the Lagging Regions of the European Union' (RIPPLE, 1997–1999). The collaborating laboratories were: the departments of geography at the Universities of Coventry, Galway, Caen and Valencia; the Management Division of the Scottish Agricultural College, Aberdeen; the Welsh Institute of Rural Studies, Aberystwyth; the Rural Economy Research Centre and the National Food Centre, Teagasc, Dublin; CEMAGREF, Clermont Ferrand; the Department of Economics, University of Patras; and the Institute for Rural Research and Training, Helsinki University.

Not least, grateful thanks are due to many supportive friends and colleagues for their patience and understanding, and for their contributions, acknowledged or otherwise. Indeed, many thanks to all the contributors, most of whom submitted their manuscripts on time, and claimed they understood what they were committing themselves to. The authors wish to thank those who contributed less formally to the book's aims by providing case study and other illustrative materials. In particular, they thank Ron Day, ECEAT-Poland, Dan Gamber and David Hughes, Joy Gladstone, Dave Grant, Paul Hodgson, David McEwan, Pandelia Pandeliev, and Scottish Natural Heritage. Thanks also to the commissioning, editorial and production team at CAB *International*: Tim Hardwick and Zoe Gipson.

Abbreviations and Acronyms

ABDC	Argyll and Bute District Council
ADAS	Agricultural and Development Advisory Service (UK)
ADT	Australia Department of Tourism
AIE	Argyll and the Islands Enterprise
ANTREC	Assoçiata Naţionala de Turism Rural, Ecologic şi Cultural
ATLAS	European Association for Tourism and Leisure Education
B&B	bed and breakfast
BEST	Business Enterprises for Sustainable Travel
BTA	British Tourist Authority
CAP	(EU) Common Agricultural Policy
CCS	Countryside Council for Scotland
CEE	Central and Eastern Europe
CETIA	Centre des Études Touristiques et des Industries de l'Accueil (University of Toulouse)
CIS	Commonwealth of Independent States (part of the former Soviet Union)
CLA	Countryside Landowners Association
CRN	Countryside Recreation Network
CTAP	community tourism action plan
CTO	Cyprus Tourist Board
DCMS	Department of Culture, Media and Sport (UK)
DETR	Department of the Environment, Transport and the Regions (UK)
DG	Directorate General (European Commission)
DTI	Department of Trade and Industry (UK)
EAGGF	European Agriculture Guidance and Guarantee Fund
EC	European Commission/European Community
ECEAT	European Centre for Ecological Agriculture and Tourism
ECHP	European Commission Household Panel
ECTARC	European Centre for Traditional and Regional Cultures
EEA	European Economic Area
EIU	Economist Intelligence Unit
EP	European Parliament
ERDF	European Regional Development Fund
ESA	environmentally sensitive area
ESF	European Social Fund
ETB	English Tourist Board

ETC	English Tourism Council
EU	European Union
EUROTER	European Rural Tourism Organization (sponsored by the Council of Europe)
FAIR	European Commission Agriculture and Fisheries Research Programme
FHB	Farm Holiday Bureau
FHG	Farm Holiday Group
FNNPE	Federation of Nature and National Parks of Europe
GDP	gross domestic product
GIS	geographical information system(s)
GNP	gross national product
HIE	Highlands and Islands Enterprise
HORECA	hotel, restaurant and catering sector (for European employment statistics compilation)
IFH	Icelandic Farm Holidays
IST	information society technologies
ITDC	India Tourism Development Corporation
IUCN	International Union for the Conservation of Nature (World Conservation Union)
IUOTO	International Union of Official Travel Organizations
LA21	Local Agenda 21
LEADER	*Liaisons Entre Actions pour la Développement des Economies Rurales*
LFA	less favoured area
MAFF	Ministry of Agriculture, Fisheries and Food (UK)
MAUP	modifiable statistical area problem
MEK	Finnish Tourist Board
MoD	Ministry of Defence (UK)
NACE	European (Eurostat) standard for employment sector statistics
NFU	National Farmers Union
NGO	non-governmental organization
NNP	Northumberland National Park
NNPA	Northumberland National Park Authority
NPDA	national park direction area
OECD	Organization for Economic Cooperation and Development
OTA	Otterburn training area
RIPPLE	Regional Images and the Promotion of Quality Products and Services in the Lagging Regions of the European Union (research project)
SERAD	Scottish Executive Rural Affairs Department
SME	small- and/or medium-sized enterprise
SMTE	small- and/or medium-sized tourism enterprise
SNH	Scottish Natural Heritage
SOAEFD	Scottish Office Agriculture, Environment and Fisheries Department
SSSI	site of special scientific interest
STB	Scottish Tourist Board
STCG	Scottish Tourism Coordinating Group
TER	*L'Association Tourisme en Espace Rural*
TETF	Tourism and Environment Task Force
TFCI	Tourism Finance Corporation of India
TMP	tourism management programme
TTI	Travel and Tourism Intelligence

UNCED	United Nations Conference on the Environment and Development
VAT	value-added tax
VF	visiting friends
VFR	visiting friends and relatives
VR	visiting relatives
WCED	World Commission on Environment and Development
WCS	World Conservation Strategy
WHI	Walking the Way to Health Initiative
WTB	Wales Tourist Board
WTO	World Tourism Organization; World Trade Organization
WTTC	World Travel and Tourism Council
YTS	Youth Training Scheme

1

Prelude

The title of this book is presumptuous, if not contradictory. 'Rural tourism' is at best an ambiguous term, and most likely a chimerical concept, for reasons we hope to explain in subsequent chapters. 'Principles' and 'practice' as two of the most commonly misspelled words in the English language are notoriously regularly employed in the titles of tourism-related texts. Specifically, in the compilation of this volume, its authors have three main objectives; these are to:

- review the work of academics and practitioners concerned with recreation, tourism and rural development issues, and to present an accessible synthesis of key issues arising from the observations and conceptualizations of such work;
- illustrate policy and commercial relevance and/or application by linking the key issues raised by such work with policy, planning and markets for tourism and recreational products and services; and
- adopt a rather different analytical approach by emphasizing a focus on neither tourism nor the tourist but on the ways in which the one is consumed by the other.

As a starting point, this introductory chapter has three basic objectives. These are to:

- examine in outline the (dimensions of) issues relating to, and questions surrounding, recreation and tourism in rural areas;
- evaluate the nature of, and requirement for, definitions of key concepts and terms; and
- outline the structure and purpose of the book, and introduce key themes characterizing the interrelationships between rural development processes and recreation and tourism.

Significance of Tourism and Recreation in Rural Areas

Various estimates suggest that tourism in rural areas makes up 10–20% of all tourism activity, and a EuroBarometer (1998) survey reported that 23% of European holidaymakers choose the countryside as a destination every year. But Lane (1994b), among others, has pointed to the absence of any systematic sources of data on 'rural tourism', since neither the World Tourism Organization (WTO) nor the Organization for Economic Cooperation and Development (OECD) has appropriate measures. Several constraints on accurate and comparatively meaningful data relating to rural tourism and recreation therefore persist:

- differences in national definition and enumeration: one country may include only farm and nature tourism, while another will consider many economic activities outside of urban areas to be part of rural tourism;
- many rural tourists and recreationalists are excursionists (day visitors) rather than those making overnight stays (the extent of whom can to some extent be measured in terms of bed-nights);

- rural tourism's very diversity and fragmentation (e.g. Table 1.1), whereby tens of thousands of enterprises and public initiatives are active across Europe, some of which are listed with local or regional bodies such as tourism boards and authorities, while others are not.

Rural environments have a long history of being managed for recreational purposes, and this symbiotic relationship has had important impacts on both environment and activity. Some rural landscapes have been notably moulded for the recreational enjoyment of particular elites, such as European landed

Table 1.1. Range of tourism and recreation activities in the countryside (adapted from Thibal, 1988; Lane, 1994b: 16).

Touring	*Cultural activities*
Hiking (footpaths, fitness trails, nature parks)	Archaeology
Horse-riding	Restoration sites
Touring in gypsy caravans, wagons	Rural heritage studies
Motorized touring (trail riding, all-terrain vehicles, motoring)	Local industrial, agricultural or craft enterprises
Small town/village touring	Museums
'Adventure' holidays/wilderness holidays	Courses in crafts
Cycling	Artistic expression workshops
Donkey riding	Folk groups
Cross-country skiing	Cultural, gastronomic and other routes
Water-related activities	*Health-related activities*
Fishing	Fitness training
Swimming	Assault courses
River/canal tourism (houseboats, narrow boats, barges)	Spas and health resorts
Canoeing, kayaking and (whitewater) rafting	*'Passive' activities*
Windsurfing	Relaxation holidays in a rural milieu
Speedboat racing	Nature study in outdoor settings, including birdwatching, photography
Sailing	Landscape appreciation
Facilities of the 'aqualand' type	
Aerial activities	*'Hallmark' events*
Light aircraft	Rural sporting festivals
Hang-gliding and micro-light aircraft	Agricultural shows
Hot air balloons	
	Business-related
Sporting activities	Small-scale conventions/conferences
Requiring natural settings:	Incentive tourism short-breaks
Potholing	
Rock climbing	
Orienteering	
Requiring modified/constructed settings:	
Tennis	
Golf	
Low-intensity downhill skiing	
Hunting	

estates of the 17th and 18th centuries (Towner, 1996). Some land management techniques required for shooting 'game' – such beasts as red deer and grouse – have changed little in some parts of Europe for over 200 years. Yet until the late 18th century opportunities to participate in 'tourism' or indeed formal recreation in rural areas were extremely limited. Travel was slow, uncomfortable and frequently dangerous, particularly in upland and forested areas: climate, wild animals and brigands all contrived to generate pejorative images of such places. With an emphasis on romanticism and scenery, the European 'Grand Tour' undertaken by some British upper classes in the mid-16th to 18th centuries embraced an interest in rural environments (Towner, 1985).

While historical patterns of recreational activity have combined to produce or influence a wide range of rural environments, such landscapes are often characterized by the twin forces of continuity of use and constant change. In some of the more urbanized European countries the construction of exclusive rural landscapes for the recreation of affluent elites furthered the trend of restricting general access to the countryside.

Significant numbers of the urban middle classes began visiting the countryside as recreationalists in the 19th century, often encouraged by images portrayed by the popular culture of the time (Constable's painting, Wordsworth's poetry, Hardy's novels). From the 1840s, railway construction began providing easier and safer access to more remote and attractive rural areas. In some countries, the working populations of industrialized regions, as ex-rural migrants or descendants of rural migrants, had regularly visited rural areas not least to visit friends and relatives. In other countries, where rural roots had been severed, urban working families began visiting the countryside. By the early 20th century questions of access to and preservation of valued landscapes were becoming popular issues. This was most dramatically articulated in England by a mass trespass on Kinder Scout in the Derbyshire Peak District in 1932. This act was important in establishing the principle of recreational access in the UK National Parks and Access to the Countryside Act of 1949, and in influencing similar legislative change elsewhere in Europe (Smith, 1983; Jenkins and Prin, 1998).

Because of the substantial changes brought to agricultural and forestry operations during the second half of the 20th century, many landed estates, partly or wholly maintained for recreation and as an escape from urban life, were rendered economically unviable. Many have been broken up; lands have been sold to agribusinesses and often substantial buildings taken over by public and private organizations such as corporations, educational and health bodies. Those remaining discovered that new or revived recreational demand could assist economic survival through conversion into hotel, health, sporting, retirement and other leisure-related accommodation purposes. Grounds have been reinvigorated for such activities as golf, equestrian events, wildlife and theme parks (Cherry, 1993).

An ever-increasing number of smaller, often commercial recreation areas now dot the rural landscape, along with a vastly greater number of small private individual leisure properties, normally centred on a residence, frequently a part-time one. This is not to suggest that elitism is now absent from rural areas. As emphasized in Chapter 2, the predominant culture of the countryside may still be based on traditional perceptions of what is or should be rural and preserved (Cloke and Little, 1996). The irony of this is that such values may now be held by recent ex-urban incomers who may hold them not only more strongly than long-standing rural dwellers, but also at the latters' expense, as rural economies change and require flexible responses.

Impacts of Tourism and Recreation in Rural Areas

Although tourism continues to be viewed by some as a panacea for the economic and social ills of the countryside, it:

- is essentially an economic tool;
- needs to be part of a portfolio of strategies contributing to successful rural development; and
- is not appropriate in all rural areas, but opportunity costs and factors for its

comparative advantage will vary considerably from one type of rural area to another.

Economic factors reducing tourism's effectiveness as a rural development tool include income leakages, volatility, a declining multiplier, low pay, imported labour, the limited number of entrepreneurs in rural areas and the conservatism of investors. Ironically, one of the least favoured circumstances in which to promote tourism is when the rural economy is already weak, since tourism development is likely to create income and employment inequalities. Rather, rural tourism is better suited to act as a complement to an existing thriving and diverse rural economy (Butler and Clark, 1992: 175).

Although work by Archer (1973, 1982) and others on economic multipliers has been employed to explore the economic benefits of tourist expenditure in rural areas, few studies have embraced a sufficiently comprehensive economic analysis of positive impacts. Page and Getz (1997) suggest that one possible explanation for this may be related to the persistence of a 'farm tourism' focus in many rural tourism evaluations.

Table 1.2 provides a summary of the impacts of tourism and recreation in and on rural areas. Such a descriptive list masks a number of key questions:

- What are the trade-offs between the social and environmental (negative) impacts and economic benefits?
- How far, for example, do rural designations of special area status designed to protect environments actually act to attract and focus tourists in self-fulfilling honeypots?
- Can the benefits to one sector (e.g. species conservation) be realistically measured against the negative impacts felt in a related sector (e.g. disturbance to wildlife)?
- Most tourists in rural areas are urbanites, so who benefits and who loses from the development of tourism and recreation in rural areas? Certainly the debate over the mutual misunderstanding between town and country has seen increasing politicization of the perceived conflict between urban and rural values and aspirations (Chapter 2).
- How far are such benefits and losses set within wider social and economic processes of unequal access to resources and opportunities?

How has the relationship between tourism and recreation and other aspects of the rural economy, society and environment changed over time? The role of tourism in the context of rural restructuring is potentially crucial: how does it contribute to rural and regional development (Box 1.1)? The challenges of rural restructuring, the major potential threats to rural environments and the dynamic social composition of many rural areas, require an understanding and management of rural tourism which is firmly integrated into an appreciation of the (often urban-derived) dynamic social, economic, political, cultural, psychological and environmental processes shaping both reality and our perceptions of 'the rural', whether as recreational idyll or messy workplace.

Tourism and Recreation Issues in Rural Areas

In many parts of the world, rural areas have long provided the setting for recreation and tourism activities, which have not always been explicitly considered or branded as 'rural'. In recent decades, however, there has been a greater industry awareness of a requirement to segment and brand various aspects of tourism and recreation just at a time when the relationships between such activities and their rural contexts have been changing and becoming more complex. While the need to identify a rural 'niche' is perhaps one means whereby the tourism industry can escape from the perceived pejorative connotation of 'mass' tourism, complexity and change in rural sector relationships reflect:

- the dynamic and often uncertain economic and social environment in which rural development processes take place (Chapter 2); and
- the growing global importance and diversity of tourism and recreation activities, and the pressures and inter-linkages

Table 1.2. Summary of impacts of tourism and recreation in/on rural areas (sources: Mathieson and Wall, 1982; Grafton, 1984; White, 1985; Getz, 1986, 1993, 1994; Ciacco, 1990; King, 1991; McKercher, 1993; Hannigan, 1994; Hoggart *et al.*, 1995; Page and Getz, 1997; Sharpley and Sharpley, 1997; Butler *et al.*, 1998).

Socio-economic	Cultural	Physical: built and 'natural'
'*Positive*'		
Provide source of new, alternative or supplementary income and employment	Reinvigorate local culture	Contribution to conservation and protection
Help reduce gender and other social power imbalances	Instil sense of local pride, self-esteem and identity	Assist refurbishment and re-use of abandoned properties
Encourage collective community activity		
Provide opportunities for retaining population in areas that might otherwise experience depopulation		
Enable areas to be repopulated		
Overall multiplier effects, although in rural areas these tend to be lower		
'*Negative*'		
Economic leakages	Manufacture or distort local 'culture' for commodification and staged authenticity	Habitat destruction
Local price inflation	Destroy indigenous culture	Littering, emissions and other forms of pollution
Labour in-migration		Congestion
Distort local employment structure		New construction sprawl, perhaps grafted on to existing settlements
Distort local housing market		
Reinforce perception of women's employment as low paid and part-time and an extension of 'the domestic role'		
Self-contained complexes with tenuous links to the local economy		
Seasonal patterns of demand		

(global–local, urban–rural) which that brings (Chapters 4 and 5).

Most notably, recreation and tourism activities in a number of rural settings have been dramatically transformed from being relatively passive and minor elements in the landscape to becoming active and significant agents of environmental, economic and social change. Just within the past decade, such changes have attracted attention from local, regional, national and supranational policy-makers. However, this is not to suggest any consistent approach to, or agreement upon, the nature, development and significance of tourism and recreation in rural areas. Even among European Union (EU) members there may be significant differences in:

- definitions of both 'rural' and 'rural tourism'; and

Box 1.1. Potential rural development aspects of tourism (after Cavaco, 1995: 145; Lane, 1998: 3).

Playing an increasingly important and diversified role in local development, especially in revitalizing and reorganizing local economies, and improving the quality of life
Tourist flows can be generators of at least supplementary income in farming, craft and service sectors
Rendering the possibility to realize the economic value of specific, quality-based production of foodstuffs, as well as of unused and abandoned buildings, unique scenery, spaces and culture
Despite often being characterized by host–guest differences, rural tourism can open up the possibility of new social contacts, especially in breaking down the isolation of more remote areas and social groups
Opportunities to re-evaluate heritage and its symbols, the environment and the identity of rural places
Rural tourism development strategies should assist polices of environmental, economic and social sustainability

But tourism can be a relatively fragile element of rural development:

- inward investment, new firm creation and employment generation may be limited owing to the small scale and dispersed nature of the industry which tends to offer low returns on investment;
- it requires many skills to be successful;
- it often tends to be in the hands of those rural entrepreneurs, such as farmers, small town and village business and local officials, who often do not have specific training in tourism;
- it involves many micro-enterprises;
- capital is often in short supply;
- the timescale for success is usually short

- the priority given to, and the understanding of, the potential role of recreation and tourism in rural areas.

Tourism is widely seen as being of considerable economic and social benefit to rural areas through the income and infrastructural developments it may bring to marginal and less economically developed regions. Considerable attention has thus been given in the EU to the support and enhancement of rural tourism initiatives (Mormont, 1987; Bethemont, 1994; Hjalager, 1996; Priestly *et al.*, 1996), within the wider context of rural development (Chapter 4). But, national and supranational organizations, government views and industry perceptions may differ or even conflict. Industry vested interests may result in over-inflated expectations for rural tourism development such as the WTO's claim of 'Rural tourism to the rescue of Europe's countryside' (WTO, 1996; Butler *et al.*, 1998).

The intent of this book is to address, in an accessible way, issues facing rural change, the role and position of tourism and recreation within that dynamic context, and the resulting complex of relationships, opportunities and constraints within which the development of tourism and recreation may proceed in rural areas. Much of this discussion is set within the context of a rapidly changing European environment, but draws upon principles and practice from, and acknowledges its significance for, other developed and less developed rural areas around the world.

Global processes

This book is set within the context of a number of dynamic processes:

- The increasing importance and diversity of rural tourism and recreation as one of the fastest growing elements of tourism, itself one of the world's largest and fastest-growing industries (Lane, 1994b).
- Rural restructuring and the emergence of the post-productivist, post-industrial countryside (Box 1.2). Although the context and pressures for such restructuring may differ, the role of tourism as a potentially important element of the restructuring process requires a heightened awareness of the importance of, and provision of the appropriate tools for, the sustainability of tourism-related rural development.
- As an important and growing element of many national and regional economies, rural tourism is being employed as a key

component of national and regional image construction and projection, with or without the compliance of those living in the area.
- Tourism and recreation also play a pivotal role in debates concerning the extent to which rural areas should be developed or conserved (Sharpley and Sharpley, 1997).

Other texts

It is not intended to embark on a literature review, but to note that a number of English-language volumes on rural tourism were published in a relatively short time towards the end of the 1990s (Page and Getz, 1997; Sharpley and Sharpley, 1997; Butler *et al.*, 1998; Hall and O'Hanlon, 1998) following a dearth of such new texts over several years previously (a notable exception being Bouquet and Winter, 1987). Together with Butler's (1998) essay in a collection on the geography of rural change, they represented a much needed attempt to (re-)establish organizing frameworks for:

- the study of tourism and recreation in rural areas;
- the evaluation of its relationship with rural economies and economic restructuring processes;
- an embedding of tourism and recreation within social and political processes of change in the countryside;
- an understanding of its relationship with other areas of tourism and leisure; and
- an appreciation of its intrinsically dynamic and heterogeneous characteristics.

However, the level of attainment of these objectives was variable.

Further, in more recent years, tourism and recreation has tended to receive rather marginal attention in English-language analyses of rural development processes. In Hoggart *et al.*'s (1995: 177–181) important work on rural Europe, for example, there are less than half a dozen pages addressing questions of tourism and the rural economy.

Questions

- Does this relative neglect tell us something about the ambivalent way in which tourism is viewed in relation to rural development and restructuring?
- Is it significant that works on cognate aspects of rural society and rural development (e.g. Agg and Phillips, 1998) rarely acknowledge the (rural) tourism literature?

Box 1.2. Transition to a post-productivist countryside.

This represents a shift from production (for urban markets) to consumption (usually by those from urban areas)

Agriculture remains the principal land use in rural areas, but loses its dominant position in relation to:

- the rural economy; and
- local society and politics

Post-productivism is characterized by:

- diversification, pluriactivity;
- environmental sensitivity;
- divergence within farming; and
- dynamism

It creates a much more heterogeneous countryside, in terms of:

- land use;
- social composition;
- economic activity;
- modes of regulation; and
- place representation

Changing Analytical Emphasis

Certainly social scientific evaluation of rural change has itself undergone a reconfiguration in the past 10–15 years (Phillips, 1998):

- new theoretical perspectives have been applied to such issues as rural demographic change and urban-to-rural migration, rural resources and service provision in the countryside, and the nature of rural communities;
- there has been a rise in importance of themes relating to issues of social identity, social difference and the construction and reception of cultural images of the countryside.

Until well into the 1980s, many studies of rural life remained strongly empirical (Table 1.3). Studies of 'rural communities' were notable in this respect Harper (1989), and a number drew, albeit often implicitly, on the theoretical arguments of Ferdinand Tönnies and his distinction between *Gemeinschaft* and *Gesellschaft* relations (Tönnies, 1957). The former was attributed to community relations based on close human relationships developed through kinship, common habitat and cooperation, while the latter 'society' relations were seen to be created through impersonal ties and relationships based on formal exchange and contract. These terms mirrored closely Emile Durkheim's (Durkheim, 1933) respective notions of *organic* and *mechanical solidarity*.

Some later writers suggested that such a characterization of social relations could be linked to a spatial division between urban and rural. Rural areas were frequently described as places of community or *Gemeinschaft* while urban places were seen as contexts of impersonal society or *Gesellschaft*. But this was to ignore the clear organic solidarity expressed through spatial contiguity that, for example, the 'Bethnal Green' studies found in the East End of London in the 1950s and 1960s (e.g. Young and Wilmott, 1957). Yet many studies perpetuated what Williams (1985: 96) described as one of the most powerful of 'modern myths', in which social changes such as industrialization and urbanization are seen as representing a decline in the character of society.

From the later 1970s, a number of rural researchers began to argue for the adoption of a 'radical' or 'critical' approach to rural studies (Newby and Buttel, 1980; Hoggart and Buller, 1987). Among other attributes this acknowledged that instead of a singular view of the 'rural', people appeared to have multiple and apparently often contradictory feelings and perceptions about it, rendering the management of the rural environment potentially much harder.

An important feature of this analytical approach was to permit the study of rural population change, resource conflict and management, access to services and rural community change to effectively become the study of the outcome of relations, structures and agents of political economy. A shift from rural depopulation to counter-urbanization was interpreted as the result of an urban-to-rural shift in industry, itself seen as the result of reorganization of

Table 1.3. Empirical rural research trends (source: Phillips, 1998).

Themes	Selected key publications
Local success in the implementation of a development policy	Parker, 1984; Hill and Young, 1991
Local success in market competition	Drudy and Drudy, 1979; McCleery, 1991
The existence of people with resources and desire to live in the countryside	Joseph *et al.*, 1988, 1989; Bolton and Chalkley, 1990
Resource conflicts and their 'management'	Coppock and Duffield, 1975; Patmore, 1983; Cloke and Park, 1985
Access or lack of access to services	Moseley, 1979; Shucksmith, 1981; Clark, 1982; Phillips and Williams, 1982

a capitalist economy (e.g. Day *et al.*, 1989). Subsequently, a 'restructuring approach' emerged seeking to integrate the relations of property and occupation with those of consumption and commodification (Cloke, 1993a; Lowe *et al.*, 1993; Marsden *et al.*, 1993). It was recognized that rural areas had increasingly become spaces of consumption as opposed to spaces of production. Attention was drawn to the way particular social groups sought particular forms of rurality and how they acted, both individually and collectively, to achieve their own rural idylls (Murdoch and Marsden, 1994, 1995).

The work of Cloke and Thrift (Cloke and Thrift, 1987, 1990; Thrift, 1987) has suggested that contemporary rural change is linked to a shift from a manufacturing-centred economy to a more service-centred economy, in which capitalist–working class relations based on ownership of capital and labour are overlain by social relations based on skills and qualifications, consumption decisions and political power created through corporations and state bureaucracies. These new social relations are seen to lead to new sources of social power in addition to those produced from the capital–labour relation, and to the emergence of a new service class able to utilize these new sources of power. This new class has both the power and the desire to live in the countryside (it can therefore be seen as a major colonizer of the countryside) and once living there it changes, restructures or reconstitutes the countryside.

Early service-class migrants can influence later class colonization, either positively by expanding work, housing, communication and consumption in an area, or negatively by seeking to conserve the area from the impact of more colonization. Further, Cloke and Thrift (1987, 1990) criticized the notion that rural social conflict necessarily stems from middle-class incomers disrupting an established geographical community by displacing working-class locals, arguing that:

- many of those considered to be 'local' will be in the middle or higher social classes; classic examples are farmers, which Newby (1987) see as the archetypal petite bourgeoisie;
- in-migration in many areas has been going on for such a long time that one may well be witnessing middle-class replacement of middle-class population: a growing literature suggests that the middle class is far from uniform and potentially fractious (e.g. Bourdieu, 1984; Savage *et al.*, 1988); and
- not all contemporary rural colonists are middle class: Cloke *et al.* (1994) reported that several rural areas in England had received significant proportions of lower income in-migrants.

In challenging the theoretical validity of such an approach, Savage *et al.* (1992: 104) examined the differences in the way social groups consumed various products and activities on the basis of market research carried out by the British Market Research Bureau, and suggested that each of the middle classes they identified had its own particular set of consumption practices and cultural principles (Table 1.4). Others have further argued that the countryside may not only frequently be a middle-class territory, but also in many respects a racialized, nationalized, aged, sexualized and gendered space (Cloke *et al.*, 1995; Murdoch, 1995; Agg and Phillips, 1998).

The philosophies of postmodernism and post-structuralism entered rural studies in the early 1990s (Cloke, 1993b; Halfacree, 1993) and, for example, the study of difference and 'neglected others' emerged (e.g. Bell and Valentine, 1995; Kinsman, 1995; Halfacree, 1996; Milbourne, 1997). Studies have suggested that both 'New Age travellers' and the rural middle class show elements of what might be called *Gemeinschaft* in that they value emotional attachments to place and to an imagined socialized community; both groups also exhibit tribal characteristics such as an emphasis on the symbolic over the material, the ritualization of living and a clear differentiation in behaviour between members and outsiders (Hetherington, 1995; Urry, 1995b). Post-structuralists have led rural social research towards an engagement with the cultural analysis of 'landscapes' (Cosgrove and Daniels, 1988; Daniels, 1993), 'nature' (Bell, 1994; Lawrence, 1995)

Table 1.4. Social class consumption practices and cultural principles (source: Phillips, 1998; after Savage *et al.*, 1992).

Social group	Cultural principle or habitus	Consumption practices
Public sector welfare professional	Ascetic	Health and sport living High culture
Private sector professionals and service workers	Postmodern	Healthy and extravagant living Mix of high and low culture No overarching organizing principle
Managers and government bureaucrats	Inconspicuous consumption	Low participation in high culture Preference for a cleaned-up countryside

and 'communities' (Williams, 1985; Short, 1991).

Drawing on the ideas of Baudrillard (1983a,b), notions of rurality which may often bear little relation to actual rural conditions have been examined to evaluate the ways in which they influence how people act (Cloke, 1992). Murdoch and Pratt (1993) proposed that the notion of rurality should be replaced by the idea of post-rurality, which does not relate to any standard definition of what the rural is, but does encompass any phenomenon that people may take to be rural. The countryside therefore becomes a hyper-reality in which the representations of rurality, even those acknowledged as fictions, actively influence structuring of rural space and society (Phillips, 1998).

There has thus followed an increasing awareness of the fluidity and multidimensionality of people's social identity. Harrison (1991), Clarke *et al.* (1994) and Urry (1990, 1995b,c) have argued that people may temporarily adopt new identities when they participate in leisure pursuits and political protests, resulting in a breakdown of established lines of social differentiation (*detraditionalization*) and social interaction, leading to *new socializations*, which are like communities in that people share a common identity and goals but are different in that people become members from choice (rather than as a consequence of birth, occupation or place of residence) (see Chapter 7).

The theoretical re-positioning of tourism and recreation in rural areas (e.g. Urry, 1992, 1995a,c; Clarke *et al.*, 1994; McNaughton, 1995) continues.

Defining the 'Rural'

Later in this volume it is argued that tourism and recreation in rural areas is a more appropriate term than 'rural tourism and recreation', not least because some elements of leisure in rural areas, such as theme parks, may be of a scale and character which do not relate to the surrounding rural areas. If this is the case, it raises the question of attempting to clarify what is meant by 'rural'. However, 'rurality' has remained an elusive quality over which to seek definitional agreement. Robinson's (1990) evaluation of rural change argued that although 'rural' areas defined themselves with respect to the presence of particular types of problems, there existed common economic, social and political structures in both urban and rural areas.

Definitions of 'rural' vary both in scale and philosophy. They tend to express cultural differences between, and functional requirements within, regions and countries, the varying parameters of which supranational overviews have attempted to grapple (e.g. Box 1.3). While national governments use specific criteria to define 'rural', often based on the population density of settlements, there is no universal agreement on the critical population threshold which distinguishes between urban and rural populations, although some com-

Box 1.3. Supranational views of the rural (sources: OECD, 1994; Council of Europe, 1996: 3).

(a) OECD definition of a rural area

At local level, a population density of 150 persons per square kilometre is the preferred criterion. At the regional level, geographic units are grouped by the share of their population that is rural into the following three types: predominantly rural (50%), significantly rural (15–50%) and predominantly urbanised regions (15%).

(b) The Council of Europe's components of a rural area

For the purposes of its European Charter for Rural Areas, the Council of Europe (1996) employed the term 'rural area' to denote the following characteristics:

a stretch of inland or coastal countryside, including small towns and villages, where the main part of the area is used for:

a. agriculture, forestry, aquaculture and fisheries;
b. economic and cultural activities of country-dwellers (crafts, industry, services, etc.);
c. non-urban recreation and leisure areas (or natural reserves);
d. other purposes, such as for housing.

monality is emerging within Europe (Table 1.5).

Different types of rural areas

The diversity of economic situations in rural areas of Europe was recognized by the EU LEADER programme (*Liaisons Entre Actions pour la Développement des Economies Rurales*) (Farrell and Thirion, 2000), whose researchers evolved a ninefold classification of common types of rural economic situation to be found either in isolation or in combination (Table 1.6, Box 1.4). Owing to their definition and geographical coverage (Objective 1, 5b and 6 areas), LEADER programmes I and II were designed to create new economic opportunities in most of the areas concerned, with the exception of those with an 'outward-looking' economy, relatively prosperous agricultural areas, and areas situated in the immediate vicinity of towns. Some aspects of tourism in different rural areas are indicated in Box 1.4.

Lane (1994b) suggests that there are three main characteristics which clearly identify areas as rural:

1. Population density and size of settlement

As the OECD (1994), among others, has emphasized, however, although rural areas

Table 1.5. Examples of varying national criteria for defining 'rural' (sources: Randall, 1985; Robinson, 1990; Lane, 1994a,b; OECD, 1994; Hoggart *et al.*, 1995: 22; Sharpley and Sharpley, 1997: 13).

Country	Criterion
Austria	Places of fewer than 1000 people, with a population density of fewer than 400 per km^2
Denmark	Agglomerations of fewer than 200 inhabitants
England and Wales	No formal definition but the Countryside Agency excludes settlements with more than 10,000 inhabitants
Ireland	Distinction between aggregate urban areas and aggregate rural areas in Ireland is set at 100 inhabitants
Italy	Settlements of fewer than 10,000 people
Norway	Agglomerations of fewer than 200 inhabitants
Portugal	Parishes of fewer than 10,000 people
Scotland	Local authority areas of less than 100 persons per km^2
Spain	Settlements of fewer than 10,000 people
Switzerland	Parishes of fewer than 10,000 people

Table 1.6. LEADER typology of rural (socio-) economic 'situations' (source: Farrell and Thirion, 2000).

Type	Area characteristics
1	Agriculture employs a sizeable proportion of the working population and still forms the basis of the economy
2	Rich, not highly labour-intensive agriculture
3	Traditional large-scale landholdings continue to predominate (latifundia)
4	Natural or protected land plays a key role
5	Geared towards tourism, with small-scale facilities
6	A large proportion of second homes and/or residential homes (for the elderly, the disabled, etc.)
7	A large number of small businesses
8	In a peri-urban location
9	A predominantly elderly population and/or a high proportion of people are on welfare assistance

Box 1.4. Detailed characteristics of rural area type 5 (source: Farrell and Thirion, 2000).

Type 5 areas: geared towards tourist accommodation, based on small-scale facilities, are characterized by:

- small, family-run facilities;
- a highly consolidated identity and social structure;
- a large proportion of the working population involved in tourism, some on a part-time basis;
- close ties between the various local business sectors;
- a cottage industry and small- and medium-sized enterprises that have developed to supply local markets (including the tourist market);
- restrictions on building and demands for infrastructure, considerable community control over the environment and the use of resources and, in some cases, a deliberate policy to limit tourist numbers;
- intensive use of housing.

Examples: alpine areas of Austria and Italy, especially those populated by minorities or communities with a strong identity.

have low population densities and a built environment dominated by the natural and/or the farmed/forested environment, the average rural population density varies enormously between and within countries. Rural areas cannot necessarily be characterized by low population densities and relatively small settlements (as conditions in many less developed countries and notably in some parts of China and India testify).

However, as Sharpley and Sharpley (1997: 14) argue, crucially, in the context of tourism, it is not the figures themselves that are of importance, although they do indicate the difficulty in achieving internationally accepted criteria of rurality. Rather, it is the comparison between the tourist's (usually urban) home environment and the characteristics of the destination that mark it as rural (Harrison, 1991), and which in turn contribute to the social construction of the countryside and its idyllic dimensions (see also Sørensen and Nilsson, 1999). In other words, it is the relative contrast of experience that is significant rather than necessarily the absolute intrinsic character. Given the urban origins of the majority of recreationalists and tourists in rural areas, Sharpley and Sharpley suggest that the more sparsely populated an area is, the more attractive it is likely to be to tourists (Plate 1.1).

2. Land use and economy

Rural areas may be defined as those with economies based on traditional agrarian/ forestry industries, or at least the extraction

Plate 1.1. The 'empty' Scottish Highlands: attractive and attracting?

(but not usually the processing) of natural resources. However, the rural/urban dichotomy in terms of economic activity is becoming ever less distinct, particularly in the developed world. The continuing decline in the relative importance of the agricultural sector and the growth of the post industrial service sector has led to many new industries, including tourism, being developed in rural areas. Further, in many regions, both economically developed and less developed, small-scale, rural industrial activity has been a 'traditional' or ideologically inspired (e.g. Chinese communes) phenomenon, contributing to culturally (Chapter 2) and ideologically (Chapter 4) constructed rural idylls very different from those conceived in Western Europe, North America and Australasia (Plates 1.2 and 1.3).

The relevance of this to tourism is that it is not only the character of rural land use and economic activity, but also its intensity and

Plate 1.2. Depiction of the rural idyll of the Chinese Cultural Revolution in an example of the ideologically inspired 'peasant painting movement' of the 1970s.

Plate 1.3. Reinforcers of the idyll: a Chinese 'peasant painter' and an example of his work, 1977.

diversity that may influence an area's potential for rural tourism development. Thus, intensively farmed areas or prosperous and diverse rural economies will have less need to develop tourism and may be less attractive to tourists; and economically marginal areas which depend on traditional, small-scale agrarian industries will have a greater need for economic diversification and may be more attractive to tourists (Sharpley and Sharpley, 1997: 14). But the capacity of such areas to support tourism may be inherently severely limited, thereby raising the paradox of environmental fragility by its very nature attracting agents of potential destruction to experience the intrinsic qualities they may be unwittingly destroying in the process.

3. Traditional social structures

Of all the perceptions of rurality, perhaps the most widely held, particularly among urban residents, is that the countryside retains the traditional social structures and values that have been largely lost in modern, urban society:

- a sense of 'community' (Chapter 5);
- local rather than cosmopolitan cultures; and

- a way of life that is somehow slower, more 'natural' and in tune with nature, less materialistic and more complete than in urban societies.

The extent to which this is a romantic idyll and hideously distorted representation of rural life as opposed to an objective assessment of rural society remains a subject of both debate and research (Chapter 2). Rural societies possess a variety of characteristics which, collectively, may identify them as being more traditional than contemporary urban societies. But many rural areas are in a constant state of change, not least in relation to their absorption or rejection of urban social and spatial values, structures and characteristics. Certainly rural societies do not necessarily exhibit 'traditional' attributes.

Yet the apparently undiminished, idealized, 'traditional' perception of rural societies has several implications for tourism development (Chapter 2):

- tourists are motivated by the desire to see or experience different, traditional lifestyles as part of the ever-increasing interest in heritage;
- if carefully managed, tourism can contribute to the maintenance of these traditional social and cultural structures; and
- conversely, tourism can easily undermine social structures and threaten the stability of rural societies and cultures, contributing to the potential destruction of the very object that attracts tourists in the first place.

Thus, there is a clear need for careful planning and management of tourism to maintain the character and well-being of rural societies.

But as there is usually no sharp dividing line between urban and rural areas, there can be hypothesized a crude scale of rurality – a 'rural–urban continuum' (Lane, 1994b) – along which different situations can be positioned. However, functional and spatial continua may not necessarily be coterminous, further complicating identification of the 'rural'. In a critique of empirical rural analysis, Hoggart (1990) argued that:

- general classifications of urban and rural areas are of limited value; and
- the undifferentiated use of 'rural' in research had posed an obstacle to the further development of social theory, not least because such use cannot accommodate inter-rural differences and urban–rural similarities.

Further, many rural areas may be viewed as inextricably linked to national and international political economies, reflecting changes brought about by processes of:

- increased mobility of people, goods and information, eroding the autonomy of local communities;
- delocalization of economic activity rendering impossible the definition of homogeneous economic regions;
- new specialized uses of rural spaces (as tourist sites, parks and development zones), creating new specialized networks of relationships, many of which are no longer localized;
- people inhabiting a given rural area including a diversity of temporary visitors as well as residents; and
- rural spaces increasingly performing functions for non-rural users and existing independently of the action of rural populations (Mormont, 1990).

Consequently, rather than being part of an urban–rural continuum (or continua), Mormont (1987) conceptualized rural areas as a set of overlapping social spaces, each with their own logic, institutions and network of actors (e.g. users and administrators). From this position it has been argued that rural space needs to be defined in terms of how the occupants perceive it: as a social construct where the occupiers of rural spaces interact and participate in activities such as recreation and tourism (see Chapter 2).

Taking this a stage further, Sørensen and Nilsson (1999: 4) argue that the attraction of the countryside lies in what urban life cannot offer, and thereby a definition of the rural is predicated on a negative assumption: countryside life is what urban life is not. They further attempt to complement this by suggesting that the notion of 'rural tourism' shares the same origins as the notion of 'alternative tourism', thus again conceived by means of negation:

> non-urban, i.e. rural; non-coastal, i.e. non-hedonistic; non-mass i.e. small-scale; non-packaged i.e. individualistic ... this ... comes close to be(ing) perceived as an anti-tourism tourism... Thus, the attraction of the rural not only consist(s) of images and attractions of the rural, but also of images of modes of tourism.
>
> (Sørensen and Nilsson, 1999: 7)

Defining 'Rural Tourism'

A variety of terms are employed to describe tourism activity in rural areas: agritourism/agrotourism, farm tourism, rural tourism, soft tourism, alternative tourism, ecotourism and several others, which have different meanings from one country to another, and indeed from one user to another (e.g. Box 1.5). Further, the term 'rural tourism' has been adopted by the European Community (EC) to refer to all tourism activity in a rural area. This is doubly problematic in that while, helpfully, it draws away from the dominance of farm-related activity inherent in such terms as agri- and agrotourism, it: (i) ignores large-scale mass recreation complexes such as Center Parcs (and Finland's Santa Park), located in otherwise rural areas; and (ii) it begs the question of how rural tourism is defined.

Box 1.5. Terms describing forms of tourism in rural areas (adapted from Sharpley and Sharpley, 1997: 9).

Agri-/agrotourism: although often used to describe all tourism activities in rural areas (covering, for example, festivals, museums, craft shows and other cultural events and attractions), more frequently either term relates to tourism products which are 'directly connected with the agrarian environment, agrarian products or agrarian stays': staying on a farm, whether in rooms or camping, educational visits, meals, recreational activities, and the sale of farm produce or handicrafts (Jansen-Verbeke and Nijmegen, 1990).

Farm tourism: explicitly farm-related and most usually associated with tourism involving staying in farm accommodation and seeking experiences from farm operations and attractions (e.g. Gladstone and Morris, 1998, 1999).

Wilderness and forest tourism: may be implicitly included within notions of rural tourism, or they may be regarded as separate (e.g. Meier-Gresshoff, 1995; Asikainen, 1997). In a number of countries they will not be relevant, or their relevance will vary considerably. For example, while Finland has a domestic tradition of forestry recreation, the establishment of community forests in England only took place in the early 1990s, and although most community forest plans devote some space to recreation issues, economic and sustainability concerns underpin most of the proposals, although much potential exists (Bull, 1996, 1999).

Green tourism: although in some countries the term 'green tourism' refers specifically to tourism in the countryside ('green areas'), it is more commonly used to describe forms of tourism that are considered to be more environmentally friendly than traditional, mass tourism, or as a marketing ploy to suggest such eco-friendliness, even where it may not exist. Variously employed synonymously with 'alternative' (Butler, 1990; Wheeller, 1993), 'responsible' (Wood and House, 1991), 'soft' (Slee, 1998), or 'new' (Poon, 1993) tourism, green tourism is portrayed as an approach to tourism development which seeks to develop a symbiotic relationship (Budowski, 1976) with the physical and social environment on which it depends, and implicitly seeks to attain sustainability ideals. Such terminology has been particularly important in what some might view as little more than a make-over of the marketing of certain types of mass activity which might otherwise be characterized as entailing a parasitic rather than symbiotic relationship. Indeed, the 'green' of green tourism might be seen to apply to some tourists' unquestioning consumption of eco-related labelling (also below).

Ecotourism: a form of nature tourism (tourism to natural, unspoilt areas) which assumes active promotion of environmental conservation and direct benefits for local societies and cultures, together with the provision for tourists of a positive, educative experience. It has been viewed as offering opportunities for the integration of rural development, tourism, resource management and protected area management (Hvenegaard, 1994), and is regarded as a subset of rural tourism (see Chapters 7 and 8). However, specialist interest in aspects of the natural environment – such as birdwatching or geology – does not necessarily presuppose environmental awareness in a holistic sense, and the above reservation about eco-labelling particularly applies.

In an oft-quoted paper, Bernard Lane (1994b), has argued that key elements of rural tourism in its purest form can be identified (Box 1.6). In danger of slipping into a circular argument of ever-diminishing proportions, this view of course begs such key questions as:

- What is rural?
- What is traditional?
- How far are definitions and perceptions shared, both between local people themselves and between locals and visitors?
- How inclusive or exclusive may such constructions consequently be, regarding ethnicity, gender, age, ability, class, employment and geographical background of both those engaged in consuming those activities and those locally benefiting from such consumption behaviour?

Sharpley and Sharpley (1997: 20) therefore suggest that 'rural tourism' may be defined both conceptually, as a state of mind and technically, according to activities, destinations and other measurable, tangible characteristics.

Lane's (1994b: 9) earlier position elaborates on this and concludes that in the face of the diffusion and increased variety of rural tourism and recreation activities it is difficult to produce a complex definition of rural tourism which can apply in all contexts. He cites the problems as follows:

- Urban/resort-based tourism may spill out into adjacent rural areas.
- Rural areas are difficult to define, and the criteria used for such purposes vary between countries.
- Not all tourism which takes place in rural areas is strictly 'rural'; it can be 'urban' in form, and merely be located in a rural area. This is not simply the corollary of the first point: 'theme parks', time shares, or leisure hotel developments may be located in rural areas not contiguous to urban areas (Clarke *et al.*, 1994); most tourists live in urban areas, and tourism itself can be an urbanizing influence on rural areas, encouraging cultural and economic change through social transmission.
- Different types of rural tourism products have developed in different regions (e.g. Denman and Denman, 1993; OECD, 1993; Oppermann, 1995, 1996; Taguchi and Iwai, 1998) (see Chapters 7 and 8). Farm-based holidays are much rarer in rural USA and Canada than in Europe. Rural 'inns' are being developed in Japan, but rural bed and breakfast (B&B) is virtually unknown there (Iwai and Taguchi, 1998).
- The impact of global markets, communications and telecommunication continuously changes market conditions and orientations for traditional products.
- The rise of environmentalism has led to increasing control by 'outsiders' over land use and resource development.
- Although some rural areas still experience depopulation, others are experiencing an inflow of people for retirement or to develop new 'non-traditional' businesses.
- The once clear distinction between urban and rural is now blurred by suburbanization, long distance commuting and second-home development.

Box 1.6. Key elements of ('pure') rural tourism (sources: Lane, 1994b: 14; OECD, 1994).

Located in rural areas
Functionally rural: built upon the rural world's special features of small-scale enterprise, open space, contact with nature and the natural world, heritage, 'traditional' societies and 'traditional' practices
Permits participation in the activities, traditions and lifestyles of local people
Provides personalized contact
Rural in scale – both in terms of buildings and settlements – and, therefore, usually small-scale
Traditional in character, growing slowly and organically, and connected with local families. It will often be very largely controlled locally and developed for the long-term good of the area
Of many different kinds, representing the complex pattern of rural environment, economy, history and location
A high percentage of tourism revenue benefiting the rural community

So Why Distinguish and Separate 'Rural Tourism'?

Both conceptually and empirically there may be 'no sharp discontinuity between urban and rural resources for recreation but rather a complete continuum from local park to remote mountain park' (Patmore, 1983: 122). If this is the case, it makes classifying tourism and recreational environments and their uses for specific reasons and purposes rather meaningless if they are part of no more than a simple continuum of recreational and tourism resources; thereby denying attempts to understand the factors which influence users to seek and consume such resources in a cultural context, such as social access, and the politics of rural land ownership (Shaw and Williams, 1994: 224).

Further, the impact of tourism *on* rural areas is of course not restricted to the activities of tourism *in* rural areas. For example:

- Coastal mass tourism development in Spain, Yugoslavia and elsewhere, notably in the period 1950–1980, stimulated significant coastwards employment migration from rural hinterlands, often damaging the demographic and economic structures of those inland areas (e.g. Poulsen, 1977; Lever, 1987; Barke and France, 1996).
- Rural residents may themselves be the consumers of tourism and recreation in both rural and non-rural environments. Their experiences of, or exclusion from, domestic and international tourism will help to shape the way they view their rural environment and the nature and appropriateness of tourism development within it.

On the one hand there is a need to view rural tourism and recreation as part of both:

- overall processes of tourism and recreation activity; and
- a holistic view of the rural resource base as a multifaceted environment capable of accommodating a wide range of uses and values (Hall and Page, 1999: 178) which, none the less, compete with other uses and values (e.g. Table 1.7).

On the other hand, rural tourism and recreation activities are distinctive, they require resources and management which are essentially different in content and scale from other forms of tourism activity and reside within a particular set of environments which, while difficult to define, together represent a distinctive and recognizable 'sector', reinforced by popular images of rusticity and idyll.

Yet, few societies and governments have pursued explicit rural tourism policies or have even recognized 'rural tourism' as a distinct category for statistical data purposes. Further, there is no agreement among EU member countries on how to measure this phenomenon. The Finnish government's approach in adopting a national rural tourism policy supported by an explicit administrative structure is therefore important in this respect (see Chapter 4). Even here, however, there is a debate as to the wisdom of separating rural tourism as a distinct and explicit policy arena.

Table 1.7. Activities directly competing with tourism and recreation for limited rural resources (adapted from Patmore, 1983: 124).

Agriculture
Forestry
Some conservation activities
Water abstraction
Mineral extraction
Military training
Peri-urban and rural residential growth
Industrial parks
Large industrial plant (e.g. nuclear power stations)
New transport demands, e.g. bypasses, road widening, vehicle parks, new rail routes, airport development and extension (ironically, stimulated by global tourism growth)

Structure of the Book

What is, perhaps, striking about tourism development – and particularly 'rural' tourism, its study and analysis – is the suffusion of paradox and irony, the interweaving of such apparent binary oppositions as continuity and change, myth and reality, mass and niche, sustainability and unsustainability, (principles and practice?), even positive and negative, good and bad. The discourse and the practice is littered with propaganda terms which suggest or imply the existence of qualities which in reality may be more apparent than real: 'community', 'development', 'green', 'niche', 'industry', 'product', 'embedding', 'partnership'.

Through the potential obfuscation and confusion of the use and abuse of such often overly familiar terms, the authors of this book have determined that five key themes are sufficiently crucial in acting as binding agents for the work that their relative importance for each chapter requires highlighting. While these themes are semantically immersed in the qualities noted above, their employment as signifiers is meant to assist in the de-mystification of their intent. The themes are:

- change
- unsustainability
- integration
- transparency
- paradox

and as a means of easy reference, their relative significance is indicated at each chapter's opening.

Chapter 2, 'Social Construction?' takes up the social themes outlined in this chapter by: (i) examining the dynamic rural social and economic context within which increasing demands for recreation and tourism are taking place; (ii) evaluating the social and cultural impacts that such demands are imposing on rural areas; and (iii) assessing the changing nature of recreation and tourism in rural areas and the potential conflicts which exist between such activities. In so doing, the chapter aims to assist an understanding of the social construction, myth and commodification of the countryside as a series of recreational 'products'.

Chapter 3, 'The "S" Word', has three key objectives. These are to: (i) briefly trace the emergence of 'sustainability' as a key concept in the development debate; (ii) examine the interaction of the social, economic and environmental dimensions of recreation and tourism development in rural areas, and the need for a holistic approach to their management in the face of a perceived 'implementation gap' in sustainability ideals; and (iii) provide a critique of such sustainability ideals and the obfuscation surrounding notions of sustainability in relation to tourism development. A central argument in the chapter is that by placing so much emphasis on sustainability, tourism academics and practitioners have diverted attention away from arguably more pressing problems and more realistically attainable goals. Tensions between sustainability ideals and political reality are expressed in the question of tourism transport, and in particular use of the motor car.

In Chapter 4, 'Managing?', three key objectives are pursued. These are to: (i) briefly examine the different levels of policy influencing recreation and tourism development in rural areas, emphasizing the connectedness between local and global processes; (ii) emphasize the need to view recreation and tourism development in rural areas within the wider context of the management of rural resources; and (iii) evaluate the challenges posed for such management and the key issues for the development of recreation and tourism in rural areas arising from them. The chapter particularly focuses on public sector activity, highlighting the recognized inadequacies of strategic policy for tourism and recreation in rural areas. Discussing policy levels ranging from the supranational to the local, the chapter illustrates management issues and tensions through questions of access and land use conflicts, and highlights the important management role of interpretation.

Chapter 5, 'Embedding Rural Tourism Development?', concentrates on local level, largely private and non-governmental organization (NGO) development activity, and its interrelationships with rural 'communities' and other stakeholders. The chapter has four key objectives. These are to: (i) critically evaluate the notion, role and use of local 'community'; (ii) assess the concept of community-based tourism development within a rural context; (iii) examine the role of partnerships, collaboration and networks in embedding small- and/or medium-sized enterprise- (SME)-based tourism and recreation development within rural 'communities'; and (iv) evaluate the implications of such processes for rural development.

Chapter 6, 'A Sideways Look at Tourism Demand', focuses on changing patterns of tourism consumption, and its aim is to establish a means of identifying demand for tourism and recreation in rural areas. This is achieved by: (i) illustrating the limits of 'traditional' market segmentation for rural tourism and recreation consumption; (ii) analysing demand within the framework of Sharpley's (2000) consumption typology; and (iii) appraising the potential for identifying a segment or segments for rural tourism markets. The chapter illustrates the complexities of demand not *from* identified segments, but *for* particular experiences.

Chapter 7, 'The Nature of Supply or the Supply of Nature?', illustrates a range of products that constitute supply. Through its focus on farm tourism, ecotourism, cultural tourism, adventure tourism and activity tourism, it seeks to illustrate the ways in which products and services: (i) reinforce the countryside's role as a site of consumption rather than production; and (ii) further develop the process of rural commodification. Throughout the chapter, evidence emerges of the ways in which new forms of consumption may alter the nature of supply and, accordingly, the supply of nature.

Chapter 8, 'Where Demand Meets Supply: Markets for Tourism and Recreation in Rural Areas', focuses on the processes relating to the convergence of demand and supply. The chapter has two emphases: (i) the marketing of rural tourism and recreation; and (ii) market conditions in which businesses operate. The marketing orientation identifies the existence of two distinct markets – for rural tourism, and tourism in rural areas – distinguishing them according to the importance of the countryside for consumer satisfaction. It produces a model to analyse the likelihood of the existence of niches that are said to constitute rural tourism; a much-vaunted claim. The chapter goes on to explore the development context for small rural businesses working in the fields of tourism and recreation.

The final chapter (Chapter 9) summarizes the main points of the book and concludes by raising questions and issues for further debate.

Chapter Summary

This chapter has introduced the rest of the volume in three basic ways. It has done this by:

- examining in outline the issues relating to, dimensions of, and questions surrounding, recreation and tourism in rural areas;
- evaluating the nature of, and requirement for, definitions of key concepts and terms; and
- outlining the structure and purpose of the book and introducing key themes characterizing the interrelationships between rural development processes, recreation and tourism.

References

Agg, J. and Phillips, M. (1998) Neglected gender dimensions of rural social restructuring. In: Boyle, P. and Halfacree, K. (eds) *Migration into Rural Areas*. John Wiley & Sons, Chichester, pp. 252–279.

Archer, B. (1973) *The Impacts of Domestic Tourism*. University of Wales Press, Cardiff.

Archer, B. (1982) The value of multipliers and their policy implications. *Tourism Management* 3(2), 236–241.

Asikainen, T. (1997) *Maaseutumatkailun Kehittäminen*. Matkailun Osaamiskeskus, Savonlinna, Finland.

Barke, M. and France, L.A. (1996) The Costa del Sol. In: Barke, M., Towner, J. and Newton, M.T. (eds) *Tourism in Spain: Critical Issues*. CAB International, Wallingford, pp. 265–308.

Baudrillard, J. (1983a) *In the Shadow of the Silent Majorities*. Semiotext(e), New York.

Baudrillard, J. (1983b) *Simulations*. Semiotext(e), New York.

Bell, D. and Valentine, G. (1995) Queer country: rural lesbian and gay lives. *Journal of Rural Studies* 11(2), 113–122.

Bell, M. (1994) *Childerley: Nature and Morality in a Country Village*. Chicago University Press, Chicago.

Bethemont, J. (ed.) (1994) *L'Avenir des Paysages Ruraux Européens*. Laboratoire de Géographie Rhodanienne, Lyon.

Bolton, N. and Chalkley, B. (1990) The population turnaround: a case study of North Devon. *Journal of Rural Studies* 6(1), 29–43.

Bouquet, M. and Winter, M. (eds) (1987) *Who From Their Labours Rest: Conflict and Practice in Rural Tourism*. Gower, Aldershot.

Bourdieu, P. (1984) *Distinction: a Social Critique of the Judgement of Taste*. Routledge, London.

Budowski, G. (1976) Tourism and conservation: conflict, co-existence or symbiosis? *Environmental Conservation* 3(1), 27–31.

Bull, C. (1996) Access opportunities in Community Forests: public attitudes and access developments in the Marston Vale. In: Watkins, C. (ed.) *Rights of Way: Policy, Culture and Management*. Pinter, London, pp. 213–225.

Bull, C.J. (1999) The tourism potential of England's community forests. *International Journal of Tourism Research* 1(1), 33–48.

Butler, R.W. (1990) Alternative tourism: pious hope or Trojan horse? *Journal of Travel Research* 28, 40–45.

Butler, R. (1998) Rural recreation and tourism. In: Ilbery, B. (ed.) *The Geography of Rural Change*. Addison Wesley Longman, Harlow, pp. 211–232.

Butler, R. and Clark, G. (1992) Tourism in rural areas: Canada and United Kingdom. In: Bowler, I., Bryant, C. and Nellis, M. (eds) *Contemporary Rural Systems in Transition*. Vol. 2: *Economy and Society*. CAB International, Wallingford, pp. 166–186.

Butler, R.W., Hall, C.M. and Jenkins, J. (eds) (1998) *Tourism and Recreation in Rural Areas*. John Wiley & Sons, Chichester.

Cavaco, C. (1995) Rural tourism: the creation of new tourist spaces. In: Montanari, A. and Williams, A.M. (eds) *European Tourism: Regions, Spaces and Restructuring*. John Wiley & Sons, Chichester, pp. 127–149.

Cherry, G.E. (1993) Changing social attitudes towards leisure and the countryside, 1890–1900. In: Glyptis, S. (ed.) *Leisure and the Environment*. Belhaven, London, pp. 22–32.

Ciacco, C. (1990) L'urbanisation touristique des espace ruraux en Sicile. In: Korcelli, P. and Galczynska, B. (eds) *The Impact of Urbanization upon Rural Areas*. Institute of Geography, Polish Academy of Sciences, Warsaw.

Clark, G. (1982) *Housing and Planning in the Countryside*. John Wiley & Sons, Chichester.

Clarke, G., Darrall, J., Grove-White, R., Macnaghten, P. and Urry, J. (1994) *Leisure Landscapes – Leisure, Culture and the English Countryside: Challenges and Conflicts*. Council for the Protection of Rural England, London.

Cloke, P. (1992) The countryside: development, conservation and an increasingly marketable commodity. In: Cloke, P. (ed.) *Policy and Change in Thatcher's Britain*. Pergamon Press, Oxford, pp. 269–295.

Cloke, P. (1993a) The countryside as commodity: new spaces for rural leisure. In: Glyptis, S. (ed.) *Leisure and the Environment*. Belhaven, London, pp. 53–67.

Cloke, P. (1993b) On 'problems and solutions'. The reproduction of problems for rural communities in Britain during the 1980s. *Journal of Rural Studies* 9(2), 113–121.

Cloke, P. and Little, J. (eds) (1996) *Contested Countryside Cultures*. Routledge, London.

Cloke, P. and Park, C. (1985) *Rural Resource Management*. Croom Helm, London.

Cloke, P. and Thrift, N. (1987) Intra-class conflict in rural areas. *Journal of Rural Studies* 3, 321–334.

Cloke, P. and Thrift, N. (1990) Class change and conflict in rural areas. In: Marsden, T., Lowe, P. and Whatmore, S. (eds) *Rural Restructuring: Global Processes and their Responses*. David Fulton Publishers Ltd, London, pp. 165–181.

Cloke, P., Milbourne, P. and Thomas, C. (1994) *Lifestyles in Rural England*. Rural Development Commission, London.

Cloke, P., Phillips, M. and Thrift, N. (1995) The new middle classes and the social constructs of rural living. In: Butler, T. and Savage, M. (eds) *Social Change and the Middle Classes*. UCL Press, London, pp. 220–238.

Coppock, T. and Duffield, B. (1975) *Outdoor Recreation: a Spatial Analysis*. Macmillan, London.

Cosgrove, S. and Daniels, S. (1988) Introduction: iconography and landscape. In: Cosgrove, S. and Daniels, S. (eds) *Iconography and Landscape: Essays on Symbolic Representation, Design and Use of Past Landscapes*. Cambridge University Press, Cambridge, pp. 1–10.

Council of Europe (1996) *Recommendation 1296 (1996) on a European Charter for Rural Areas.* Council of Europe, Strasbourg. http://stars.coe.fr/ta/ta96/erec1296.htm

Daniels, S. (1993) *Fields of Vision: Landscape Imagery and National identity in England and the United States.* Polity Press, Cambridge.

Day, G., Rees, G. and Murdoch, J. (1989) Social change, rural localities and the state: the restructuring of rural Wales. *Journal of Rural Studies* 5, 227–244.

Denman, R. and Denman, J. (1993) *The Farm Tourism Market: a Market Study of Farm Tourism in England.* The Tourism Company, Hereford.

Drudy, P. and Drudy, S. (1979) Population mobility and labour supply in rural regions: North Norfolk and Galway Gaeltacht. *Regional Studies* 13, 91–99.

Durkheim, E. (1933) *The Division of Labour in Society. Free Press.* MacMillan, New York.

EuroBarometer (1998) *Facts and Figures on the Europeans' Holiday.* EuroBarometer for DG XXIII, European Commission, Brussels.

Farrell, G. and Thirion, S. (2000) *Economic Competitiveness: Creating a Territorial Development Strategy in the Light of the LEADER Experience.* 'Rural Innovation' dossier no. 6 part 4, LEADER European Observatory. European Commission, Brussels. http://www.rural-europe.aeidl.be/rural-en/biblio/com-ecostars.coe.fr/ta/ta96/erec1296.htm

Getz, D. (1986) Tourism and population change: long term impacts of tourism in the Badenoch-Strathspey District of the Scottish Highlands. *Scottish Geographical Magazine* 102(2), 113–126.

Getz, D. (1993) Tourist shopping villages: development and planning strategies. *Tourism Management* 14(1), 15–26.

Getz, D. (1994) Residents' attitudes toward tourism: a longitudinal study in Spey valley, Scotland. *Tourism Management* 15(5), 247–257.

Gladstone, J. and Morris, A. (1990) The role of farm tourism in the regeneration of rural Scotland. In: Hall, D. and O'Hanlon, L. (eds) *Rural Tourism Management: Sustainable Options.* The Scottish Agricultural College, Auchincruive, pp. 207–221.

Gladstone, J. and Morris, A. (1999) Farm accommodation and agricultural heritage in Orkney. In: Brown, F. and Hall, D. (eds) *Peripheral Area Tourism: Case Studies.* Research Centre of Bornholm, Bornholm, Denmark, pp. 111–120.

Grafton, D.J. (1984) Small scale growth centres in remote rural areas. *Applied Geography* 4, 29–46.

Halfacree, K. (1993) Locality and social representation: space, discourse and alternative definitions of the rural. *Journal of Rural Studies* 9, 23–37.

Halfacree, K. (1996) Out of place in the country: travellers and the rural idyll. *Antipode* 28(1), 42–72.

Hall, D. and O'Hanlon, L. (eds) (1998) *Rural Tourism Management: Sustainable Options.* The Scottish Agricultural College, Auchincruive.

Hall, C.M. and Page, S.J. (1999) *The Geography of Tourism and Recreation.* Routledge, London.

Hannigan, K. (1994) National policy, European structural funds and sustainable tourism; the case of Ireland. *Journal of Sustainable Tourism* 2, 179–192.

Harper, S. (1989) The British rural community: an overview of perspectives. *Journal of Rural Studies* 5(2), 161–184.

Harrison, C. (1991) *Countryside Recreation in a Changing Society.* TML Partnership, London.

Hetherington, K. (1995) *On the Homecoming of the Stranger: New Social Movements or New Socialisations?* Lancaster Regionalism Group working paper 39, University of Lancaster, Lancaster, UK.

Hill, N. and Young, N. (1991) Support policy for rural areas in England and Wales: its assessment and qualification. *Journal of Rural Studies* 7(3), 191–206.

Hjalager, A.-M. (1996) Agricultural diversification into tourism. *Tourism Management* 17(2), 103–111.

Hoggart, K. (1990) Let's do away with rural. *Journal of Rural Studies* 6, 245–257.

Hoggart, K. and Buller, H. (1987) *Rural Development: a Geographical Perspective.* Croom Helm, London.

Hoggart, K., Buller, H. and Black, R. (1995) *Rural Europe: Identity and Change.* Arnold, London.

Hvenegaard, G. (1994) Ecotourism: a status report and conceptual framework. *Journal of Tourism Studies* 5(2), 24–35.

Iwai, Y. and Taguchi, K. (1998) Rural tourism in Japan: a case study of Hokkaido farm-inns. In: Hall, D. and O'Hanlon, L. (eds) *Rural Tourism Management: Sustainable Options.* The Scottish Agricultural College, Auchincruive, pp. 277–286.

Jansen-Verbeke, M. and Nijmegen, K. (1990) The potentials of rural tourism and agritourism. *Problemy Turystyki* 13(1–2), 35–47.

Jenkins, J.M. and Prin, E. (1998) Rural landholder attitudes: the case of public recreational access to 'private' rural lands. In: Butler, R.W., Hall, C.M. and Jenkins, J. (eds) *Tourism and Recreation in Rural Areas.* John Wiley & Sons, Chichester, pp. 179–196.

Joseph, A., Keddie, P. and Smit, B. (1988) Unravelling the population turnaround in rural areas. *Canadian Geographer* 32, 17–39.

Joseph, A., Smit, B. and McIlravey, G. (1989) Consumer preferences for rural residences: a conjoint analysis in Ontario, Canada. *Environment and Planning* A 21, 47–64.

King, R.L. (1991) Italy: multi-faceted tourism. In: Williams, A.M. and Shaw, G. (eds) *Tourism and Economic Development: Western European Experiences*. Belhaven, London, pp. 61–83.

Kinsman, P. (1995) Landscape, race and national identity. *Area* 27(4), 300–310.

Lane, B. (1994a) Sustainable rural tourism strategies: a tool for development and conservation. *Journal of Sustainable Tourism* 2(1–2), 102–111.

Lane, B. (1994b) What is rural tourism? *Journal of Sustainable Tourism* 2(1–2), 7–21.

Lane, B. (1998) Rural tourism: global overviews. *Rural Tourism Management: Sustainable Options. Conference Programme*. The Scottish Agricultural College, Auchincruive, p. 3.

Lawrence, M. (1995) Rural homelessness: a geography without a geography. *Journal of Rural Studies* 11(3), 297–307.

Lever, A. (1987) Spanish tourism migrants: the case of Lloret de Mar. *Annals of Tourism Research* 14, 449–470.

Lowe, P., Murdoch, J., Marsden, T., Munton, R. and Flynn, A. (1993) Regulating the new rural spaces: the uneven development of land. *Journal of Rural Studies* 9(3), 205–222.

Marsden, T., Murdoch, J., Lowe, P., Munton, R. and Flynn, A. (1993) *Constructing the Countryside*. UCL Press, London.

Mathieson, A. and Wall, G. (1982) *Tourism: Economic, Physical and Social Impacts*. Longman, Harlow.

McCleery, A. (1991) Population and social conditions in remote areas: the changing character of the Scottish Highlands and islands. In: Champion, T. and Watkins, C. (eds) *People in the Countryside: Studies of Social Change in Britain*. Paul Chapman, London, pp. 144–159.

McKercher, B. (1993) Some fundamental truths about tourism: understanding tourism's social and environmental impacts. *Journal of Sustainable Tourism* 1(1), 6–16.

McNaughton, P. (1995) Public attitudes to countryside leisure: a case study of ambivalence. *Journal of Rural Studies* 11(2), 135–147.

Meier-Gresshoff, M. (1995) Qualitätstandards im Landtourismus – eine europäische Herausforderung. In: Haart, N., Steinecke, A. and Treinen, M. (eds) *Qualitätsmanagement im Landtourismus in Europa. Erfahrungen, Beispiele, Herausforderungen*. Europäisches Tourismus Institut GmbH an der Universität Trier, Trier, Germany, pp. 36–46.

Milbourne, P. (ed.) (1997) *Revealing Rural 'Others': Representation, Power and Identity in the British Countryside*. Pinter, London.

Mormont, M. (1987) Tourism and rural change. In: Bouquet, M. and Winter, M. (eds) *Who From Their Labours Rest? Conflict and Practice in Rural Tourism*. Avebury, Aldershot, pp. 35–44.

Mormont, M. (1990) Who is rural? Or, how to be rural: towards a sociology of the rural. In: Marsden, T., Lowe, P. and Whatmore, S. (eds) *Rural Restructuring: Global Processes and Their Responses*. David Fulton Publishers Ltd, London, pp. 21–44.

Moseley, M.J. (1979) *Accessibility: the Rural Challenge*. Methuen, London.

Murdoch, J. (1995) Middle class territory? Some remarks on the use of class analysis in rural studies. *Environment and Planning* A 27, 1213–1230.

Murdoch, J. and Marsden, T. (1994) *Reconstituting Rurality*. UCL Press, London.

Murdoch, J. and Marsden, T. (1995) The spatialization of politics: local and national actor spaces in environmental conflict. *Transactions of the Institute of British Geographers* 20(3), 368–381.

Murdoch, J. and Pratt, A. (1993) Rural studies: modernism, postmodernism and the 'post-rural'. *Journal of Rural Studies* 9, 411–427.

Newby, H. (1987) *Country Life: a Social History of Rural England*. Weidenfeld and Nicholson, London.

Newby, H. and Buttel, F. (1980) Towards a critical rural sociology. In: Buttel, F. and Newby, H. (eds) *The Rural Sociology of Advanced Societies: Critical Perspectives*. Croom Helm, London, pp.1–35.

OECD (1993) *What Future for our Countryside: a Rural Development Policy*. OECD, Paris.

OECD (1994) *Tourism Strategies and Rural Development*. OECD, Paris.

Oppermann, M. (1995) Holidays on the farm: a case study of German hosts and guests. *Journal of Travel Research* 34(1), 63–67.

Oppermann, M. (1996) Rural tourism in southern Germany. *Annals of Tourism Research* 23, 86–102.

Page, S.J. and Getz, D. (eds) (1997) *The Business of Rural Tourism: International Perspectives*. International Thomson Business Press, London.

Parker, K. (1984) *A Tale of Two Villages: the Story of the Integrated Rural Development Experiment in the Peak District, 1981–84*. Peak Park Joint Planning Board, Bakewell.

Patmore, J.A. (1983) *Recreation and Resources: Leisure Patterns and Leisure Places.* Blackwell, Oxford.

Phillips, D. and Williams, A. (1982) *Rural Housing and the Public Sector.* Gower, Aldershot.

Phillips, M. (1998) Social perspectives. In: Ilbery, B. (ed.) *The Geography of Rural Change.* Addison Wesley Longman, Harlow, pp. 31–54.

Poon, A. (1993) *Tourism, Technology and Competitive Strategies.* CAB International, Wallingford.

Poulsen, T.M. (1977) Migration on the Adriatic coast: some processes associated with the development of tourism. In: Kostanick, H.L. (ed.) *Population and Migration Trends in Eastern Europe.* Westview, Boulder, Colorado, pp. 197–215.

Priestly, G.K., Edwards, J.A. and Coccosis, H. (eds) (1996) *Sustainable Tourism? European Experiences.* CAB International, Wallingford.

Randall, J.N. (1985) Economic trends and support to economic activity in rural Scotland. *Scottish Economic Bulletin* 31. HMSO, Edinburgh, pp. 10–20.

Robinson, G.M. (1990) *Conflict and Change in the Countryside.* Belhaven Press, London.

Savage, M., Dickens, P. and Fielding, A.J. (1988) Some social and political implications of the contemporary fragmentation of the service class. *International Journal of Urban and Regional Research* 12, 455–476.

Savage, M., Barlow, J., Dickens, P. and Fielding, A.J. (1992) *Property, Bureaucracy and Culture: Middle Class Formation in Contemporary Britain.* Routledge, London.

Sharpley, R. (2000) The Consumption of tourism revisited. In: Robinson, M., Long, P., Evans, N., Sharpley, R. and Swarbrooke, J. (eds) *Reflections on International Tourism: Motivations, Behaviour and Tourist Types.* Business Education Publishers, Sunderland, pp. 381–391.

Sharpley, R. and Sharpley, J. (1997) *Rural Tourism. An Introduction.* International Thomson Business Press, London.

Shaw, G. and Williams, A.M. (1994) *Critical Issues in Tourism: Geographical Perspectives.* Blackwell, Oxford.

Short, J. (1991) *Imagined Country.* Routledge, London.

Shucksmith, M. (1981) *No Homes for Locals?* Gower, Farnborough.

Slee, B. (1998) Soft tourism: can the Western European model be transferred into Central and Eastern Europe? In: Hall, D. and O'Hanlon, L. (eds) *Rural Tourism Management: Sustainable Options.* The Scottish Agricultural College, Auchincruive, pp. 481–496.

Smith, R. (1983) *Britain's National Parks.* Cassell, London.

Sørensen, A. and Nilsson, P.Å. (1999) Virtual rurality versus rural reality in rural tourism – contemplating the attraction of the rural. *8th Nordic Symposium in Hospitality and Tourism Research, 18–21 November, Alta, Norway.*

Taguchi, K. and Iwai, Y. (1998) Agri-tourism in Austria and its implications for Japanese rural tourism. In: Hall, D. and O'Hanlon, L. (eds) *Rural Tourism Management: Sustainable Options.* The Scottish Agricultural College, Auchincruive, pp. 527–538.

Thibal, S. (1988) *Rural Tourism in Europe.* Council of Europe, Strasbourg.

Thrift, N. (1987) Manufacturing rural geography. *Journal of Rural Studies* 3, 77–81.

Tönnies, F. (1957) *Community and Association.* Routledge and Kegan Paul, London.

Towner, J. (1985) The Grand Tour: a key phase in the history of tourism. *Annals of Tourism Research* 12(3), 297–333.

Towner, J. (1996) *An Historical Geography of Recreation and Tourism in the Western World 1540–1940.* John Wiley & Sons, Chichester.

Urry, J. (1990) *The Tourist Gaze: Leisure and Travel in Contemporary Societies.* Sage, London.

Urry, J. (1992) The tourist gaze and the environment. *Theory, Culture and Society* 9(3), 1–26.

Urry, J. (1995a) A middle-class countryside? In: Butler, T. and Savage, M. (eds) *Social Change and the Middle Classes.* Routledge, London, pp. 205–219.

Urry, J. (1995b) *Consuming Places.* Routledge, London.

Urry, J. (1995c) Social identity, leisure and the countryside. In: Urry, J. (ed.) *Consuming Places.* Routledge, London, pp. 211–229.

Wheeller, B. (1993) Sustaining the ego. *Journal of Sustainable Tourism* 1(2), 121–129.

White, P.E. (1985) Modelling population change in the Cilento region of southern Italy. *Environment and Planning* A 17, 1401–1413.

Williams, R. (1985) *The Country and the City.* Hogarth, London.

Wood, K. and House, S. (1991) *The Good Tourist: a Worldwide Guide for the Green Traveller.* Mandarin, London.

WTO (World Tourism Organization) (1996) Rural tourism to the rescue of Europe's countryside. *WTO News* 3, 6–7.

Young, M. and Wilmott, P. (1957) *Family and Kinship in East London.* Routledge and Kegan Paul, London.

2

Social Construction?

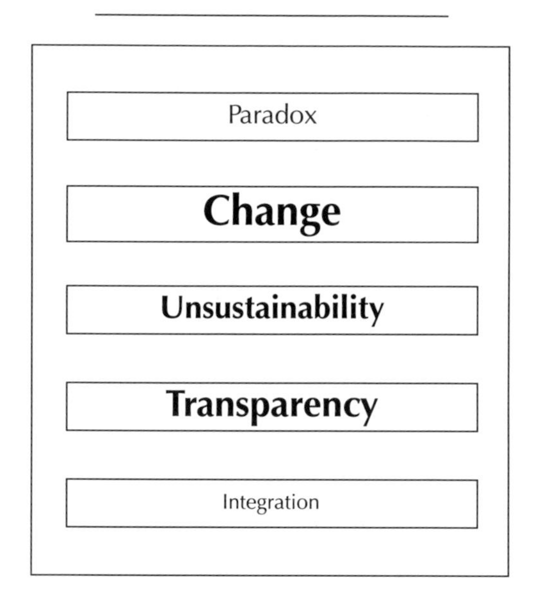

The pace of change in rural areas is accelerating and largely irrevocable.

(Middleton, 1982: 54)

The main themes which inform this chapter are the nature and consequences of *change*: economic (and political) restructuring placing new or renewed demands on the role of tourism and recreation; and social change brought about particularly by counter-urbanization. The latter result in tensions arising from incomers' and recreationalists' perceptions of, and lifestyles within, rural areas, which may also be experiencing social exclusion. Key issues of *transparency* would appear to follow from this and from the increasing extent and range of tourism and recreation activities pursued in rural areas which often appear to have mass appeal (and perhaps implicitly *unsustainable* outcomes). *Paradoxes* arise from the blurred dichotomies of 'local' and 'incomer', 'resident' and 'visitor', and from the role of incomers helping to perpetuate and intensify the myth of the rural idyll while implictly wishing to protect its tangible elements from the tourists for whom the myth may be equally impelling.

Building on the previous, introductory, chapter, this chapter has four basic objectives. These are to:

1. Examine the dynamic rural social and economic context within which increasing demands for recreation and tourism are taking place;
2. Evaluate the social and cultural impacts that such demands are imposing on rural areas;
3. Assess the changing nature of recreation and tourism in rural areas and the potential conflicts which exist between such activities; and
4. Assist the reader in understanding the social construction, myth and commodification of the countryside as a series of recreational 'products'.

Rural Change and Restructuring

Restructuring processes have been apparent across most industrialized countries since the 1970s, and rural areas have not been exempt from significant economic, social and political change. Prior to the Second World War, the rural systems of most developed countries retained a degree of homogeneity and distinctiveness, despite the growth of commercial agriculture. This is often no longer the case as the weakening of former structures has been brought about as the result of several dimensions of restructuring:

- delayed reform of inconsistent protectionist subsidy systems such as the EU's Common Agricultural Policy (CAP), which have distorted the structural and spatial dimensions of agricultural production (Jenkins *et al.*, 1998);
- the collapse of peripheral areas unable to shift to a more capital intensive economy;
- the selective process of industrialization of much of the remaining agricultural sector;
- the pressures of urban and ex-urban development (Butler and Hall, 1998a,b); and
- political and economic transformation in post-communist Central and Eastern Europe raising policy issues contrasting to, yet interrelated with, those of Western Europe, in the latter case in terms of both the adoption of Western 'advice' and models, and the aspiration for integration through EU accession (Hall and Danta, 2000).

From 1980 to 1996, employment in agriculture in the then 12 countries of the EU almost halved from 9.5% to 5% of the working population. The trend accelerated in the late 1980s and 1990s, with most EU states experiencing a 40–70% reduction in their agricultural workforce. In Central and Eastern Europe, the unemployment situation has been inverted to some extent: a collapse of urban-based manufacturing has resulted, in some cases, in a 50–60% increase in the agriculturally dependent rural population. In Romania, for example, 35–40% of the population is still dependent on agricultural employment (Edmunds, 1999).

Factors which have been responsible for profound changes in agriculture and for the people who depend on it have also contributed to the obverse change of rendering rural areas attractive and realistic places for many (ex-urbanites) to live and work. These forces have included:

- mechanization, which has drastically reduced agrarian labour requirements, stimulated continuing rural-to-urban or rural-to-rural migration, and has rendered both residential and non-residential properties available for new uses or for the same uses by different residents with often markedly different values and lifestyles; and
- the trend towards a greater centralization of governmental and commercial activities, which has contributed to a reduction or elimination of much service provision in rural settlements.

The combination of these two factors has seen many villages no longer able to function as conventional residential settlements as decreasing numbers of farms and diminishing agrarian populations reduce the labour force and weaken the local community's ability to sustain the previous range of goods and services. In many rural areas, notably where the extensive characteristics of agribusiness are not dominant, rural repopulation by non-farm populations is taking place (Stabler, 1993). This is being stimulated by an increase in demand for retirement, commuting and leisure properties, and has contributed to notable demographic and socio-economic change in many rural areas.

In Central and Eastern Europe, the post-communist societies are often referred to as being in 'transition': a term employed (not always consciously) to represent a prescriptive set of uni-linear conceptual attitudes which locate the shift away from central economic planning almost exclusively in terms of market-orientated reform. Strictly defined, 'transition' is concerned with moving between two known points, the final dimension of which in this case is the integration, or prospect of integration, of former communist states into the world economy, notably through EU accession. As an alternative framework concept, 'transformation', although embracing fundamental structural change, is less concerned with an end state, being open-ended and allowing for the substantial (converging and diverging) differences which exist between former communist countries. 'Transformation' implies flexible approaches which respect cultures, sovereignty and people's apprehensions, and which can be imbued with ideals of sustainability and equality which cannot easily be accommodated within 'transition'.

One attempt to understand and account for the complexities of post-communism created both by diversity and by the persistence of some communist-period institutions, practices and mentalities is by means of the path dependence approach (Linz and Stepan, 1996; Stark and Bruszt, 1998). This is based on the premise that each country has a distinctive and unique path of extrication from state socialism: that certain variables play a key role in facilitating some outcomes and constraining others.

For example, the way in which state power has been taken into private hands has been an important factor determining the nature of post-communist transformation in each country. Recent research (Riley, 2000) has suggested that the concept of embeddedness may provide a useful analytical tool for understanding such processes, setting overtly economic activity within a framework whereby it can be seen to be shaped by social and political processes. The post-communist privatization of power has often been pervaded by vertical and horizontal networks of reciprocity which have their roots in the communist period ('crony capitalism'), and which may support or impede restructuring processes (Grabher and Stark, 1997), such as the privatization of tourism assets and infrastructure (e.g. Koulov, 1996). Phillips (1996) recognized two groups of 'gatekeepers' in the structural transformation of tourism enterprise management practices in Russia:

- 'new' tourism managers who relied on old vertical structures and entrenched cultural expectations; and
- those entrepreneurs who, while apparently comfortable with new conditions, were likely to be 'reconstructed' communist *nomenklatura*, equally well connected with other 'reconstructed' entrepreneurs.

The extreme outcome of such groups' networking and 'partnership' approaches (Chapter 5), particularly where the institutions of civil society have not been firmly established (e.g. in Albania and in parts of the former Soviet Union), has been the privatization of power resulting in the development of mafia-type organizations (Anderson, 1995; Frisby, 1998).

'Landscape' change

In Western economies, an interrelated rise of agribusiness and decline of traditional family farming has brought striking changes to the nature and function of farms and of rural landscapes. The appearance of both large corporate and small individual ex-urban property owners has resulted in changes in attitudes towards both the control of and access to the countryside. In some rural contexts, therefore, just when demands are becoming more complex and varied and are increasing rapidly, the resources and opportunities to meet these demands are also changing but may actually be diminishing. These forces of rural change can be viewed as:

- endogenous, such as reduced protectionism, policies supporting multiculturalism; population loss, especially of younger skilled people; or gain, ageing populations, increased leisure time, changing family structures; and
- exogenous, relating to the operation of transnational corporations, technological innovation, global financial markets and economic restructuring. Certainly rural restructuring is enmeshed in the process and influences of globalization, and cannot be viewed in isolation from it.

The effects of rural change may be masked or overlain within many near-urban or fringe zones which remain 'rural' in administrative, and thus also in statistical, terms. For example, statistics for economic activity, unemployment and population decline in rural areas may be severely distorted in these and other particular areas by:

- the influx of retired newcomers;

- the inclusion of country dwellers who commute to work in urban areas; and
- the relatively large proportion of part-time and seasonal employment (Brown, 2000).

As noted in Chapter 1, in some rural areas reversing a trend of depopulation, a number of factors have been crucial in stimulating and sustaining this process of counter-urbanization, which has been particularly marked in the past 30 years (e.g. Champion and Watkins, 1991):

- the consumption aspiration of many people to seek rural lifestyles (e.g. Sinclair, 1990; Murdoch and Pratt, 1993);
- significant numbers of expanding businesses relocating into rural or peri-urban areas to take advantage of lower costs and ease of transport access via regional highways;
- state and supranational policies favouring investment in rural areas, attracting employment and residents into previously stagnating or declining regions;
- wider economic and technological changes resulting in industrial restructuring; and
- the overall 'natural' spatial expansion of dynamic urban areas, particularly encouraged in Europe in the 1980s under a number of free-market oriented governments (Bolton and Chalkley, 1990).

The first of these may well be the most important in many areas, and the level of social integration resulting from the process may be crucial for the health and self-perception (and thus the 'imaging') of rural areas. One view is that significant numbers of the new, ex-urban inhabitants of rural towns and villages bring with them 'a set of values said to emerge from rural communities of the past' (Cloke *et al.*, 1991: 39). In so doing they attempt to conserve a rural idyll while opposing any form of modern development that is likely to spoil their new-found rural lifestyle. Many villages are in danger of becoming fossilized and sterilized (Box 2.1): the gentrification of erstwhile agricultural areas may act to convert villages into little more than extensions of bourgeois suburbs with complementary luxury and fashion shops acting to force out more mundane activities. Apocryphal stories abound of ex-urban BMW or Volvo owners complaining about dirty farm animals.

In the context of rural tourism, the implications of this may seem contradictory:

- 'typical' rural villages are likely to attract visitors eager to experience the image of rurality, created, directly or indirectly, by counter-urbanization; yet
- tourists may not be welcomed by the rural newcomers (their erstwhile urban compatriots) who may have been instrumental in 'preserving' or reinforcing that tangible landscape of such images (Box 2.2).

Somewhat paradoxically, given the above view, rural incomers are helping to transform the social and physical fabric of the settlements they chose to live in, wittingly or otherwise. The intensity of such a process is variable across Europe, and indeed across individual countries, as it is dependent on a combination of local, regional and national factors. In their countryside idylls, socially and physically mobile incomers may enjoy the space and fresh air of rural living without

Box 2.1. The rural future? (source: Hart, 2000).

Once installed in Rose Cottage ... the townies ... are the most vociferous campaigners against any new, low-cost, and probably rather ugly housing in the village: squat, grey, pebble-dashed, and proudly boasting aluminium window-frames. Precisely the kind that low-waged locals need to buy or rent. And so the English village – that ancient, 1,000-year-old, living, breathing organism inhabited by those who work on the land – is going the same way as the bluebell woods...

And sometime in the near future – perhaps 10 years, 20 at the most ... there will be ... no 'real' local people left in our countryside... There will be no collapsing sheds with rusting, corrugated-iron roofs, no rotting muck-heaps covered in black plastic and old tractor tyres, no cow-shit in the lanes as the animals go for milking. All that messy business of farming and livestock husbandry – birth, copulation and death – will be safely hidden away behind the polite facades of factory farming. Villages will be pristine.

Box 2.2. Policy response? (source: Hetherington, 1999).

UK Cabinet Office report 1999: *Rural Economies*

- Warned that large parts of England risk becoming the near-exclusive preserve of the affluent unless strong measures are taken to provide affordable houses for local rural people.
- Advocated banning second home ownership in the most popular parts of the countryside in order to make way for local people on average incomes.
- Urged measures to lift stringent planning controls which protect the best farming land in an attempt to encourage tourist ventures and rural businesses as a response to agricultural decline.
- Suggested voluntary 'tourist taxes' and the consideration of road tolls in popular rural areas to raise finance for housing and other amenities.
- Suggested that councils should be given new planning powers to designate areas for 'social and affordable housing'. While this would not involve forcing second home owners to leave newly created zones, it could mean special legal agreements between planners, builders and buyers for new houses to underpin a 'homes for locals' rule. Such a policy was introduced on a small scale in the Peak District National Park, where restrictions have been placed on 250 new houses.

Key dimensions in England:

- estimated 203,000 second homes;
- a further 300,000 holiday homes, rented to others and occasionally used by owners;
- 62,000 new houses needed to meet indigenous rural demand: a third of all rural public sector rented housing, amounting to almost 100,000 homes, were sold off in the 1980s and 1990s.

having to forgo the economic, cultural and technological advantages of the city. Their numbers may be sufficient to help a local rural area retain or even revitalize services and facilities such as schools, post offices and convenience goods shops. The positive EU view is that such newcomers may bring new entrepreneurial skills (Box 2.3) and an invigoration of the local demographic profile.

But one adverse side-effect of this 'counterurbanization' is the inflation of rural house prices, compounding a longer-term trend for young people born in the countryside to migrate to urban areas for perceived better employment and lifestyle opportunities. In England alone 1700 new residents are moving into the countryside every week. Almost half of all rural dwellers were born in urban areas (Countryside Agency, 2000). Less clear is the extent to which 'traditional' rural dwellers are moving into nearby urban public housing estates, removed from their 'heartland' (Hart, 2000).

A wide range of public and private bodies has adopted tourism and recreation as sources

Box 2.3. Incoming entrepreneurs: southern Portugal (source: Anon, 2000: 18–22).

In the Serra de Monchique in southern Portugal, two kinds of foreign settlers are recognized: retired people, and 'entrepreneurs', who, in contrast to what is often the case in Wales or in Ireland, are not necessarily 'the fringe' who will do whatever it takes to flee the urban system, but are those 'who felt their country of origin was unsuitable to fulfill their project. Almost all are innovators. They are a wonderful resource for local development, a resource that is unfortunately often underutilised'.

In the municipality of Barão de São João, where the young families are almost all English, German, Dutch or Swiss, the primary school has 19 foreign children and 3 Portuguese children. 'The foreigners have helped us keep open the school, the post office, several cafés and five grocery shops, including one that sells a wider range of organic products than in Lisbon.'

Networks of neo-ruralites have formed, especially according to the language and sector of activity. Organic production, the ecology and alternative sources of energy weave powerful links: Amanda Twohig, for example, sells her organic jams in places like Vera Diesselbrede's natural food shop in Aljezur. Vera's companion, Franz Wagner had opened a restaurant in Algarve in 1979. But like all the other neo-ruralites who were moving there at the time, he was faced with the problem of no electricity. Forced to provide it himself, he discovered a passion for alternative sources of energy and created, with two fellow Germans, the Sistemas de Energias Alternativas Portugal Lda company, now a national leader in the assembly and installation of solar and wind power equipment.

of potential regeneration in the face of declining agrarian incomes and limited industrial employment opportunities (Hudson and Townsend, 1992) (e.g. Box 2.4). And while tourism represents just one of several potential diversification opportunities, it is viewed by some as possessing the added benefit of drawing upon existing 'natural' resources of landscape and the accessibility of open space (Bull, 1995), albeit at a price (see Chapter 4). Indeed, at least partly as a result of rural economic restructuring, a number of social issues have become apparent whose problems may be exacerbated by rural tourism and recreation development (see below).

'Real' Rural Dwellers: Marginalized and Politicized, as well as Mythologized?

'Traditional' rural dwellers may feel that they are losing their identity and/or are being marginalized in national decision-making processes which are perceived to be increasingly urban based and oriented, whether at a national or supranational level. This has been expressed, for example, in the UK with the formation of a 'Countryside Alliance' (Box 2.5) and its march on London in 1998, and in France with regular demonstrations by farmers. Paradoxes arise here due to:

- the extremes in wealth and lifestyles enjoyed by rural dwellers (not least among and between farmers);
- the roles of rural second home owners who may otherwise be urban based; and
- local and regional contrasts in the urban-to-rural migration component of demographic change.

'Social exclusion' tends to be employed as a short-hand label for what can happen when individuals or areas suffer from a combination of linked problems such as unemployment, poor skills, low income, poor housing, high crime environments, bad health and family

Box 2.4. The Council of Europe's European Charter for Rural Areas (source: Council of Europe, 1996: 15–16 (see also Chapters 7 and 8)).

Guidance on rural tourism: having advocated a diversification from agriculture into alternative forms of land use, in its 'guidance' the Council of Europe suggested the following:

1. Parties should take all necessary legal, fiscal and administrative measures to develop tourism in rural areas in general and agricultural tourism in particular, taking account of the carrying capacity of the areas concerned. In particular this can be done by encouraging the provision of rural hostels and by ensuring that farmers who offer tourist accommodation on their farm in addition to their agricultural activities are encouraged to do so.
2. In implementing this policy, parties should aim for a balance between the indispensable development of tourism, the protection of nature and the potential offered by existing infrastructures and services by maintaining the quality of the landscape and the environment and preserving traditional architecture and materials.

Guidance on SMEs, commerce industry and craft:

Parties should take measures for the purpose of:

a. Promoting small and medium-sized businesses of an industrial, commercial or craft nature: on the one hand, by improving the framework conditions through the simplification of administrative and fiscal procedures and through tax concessions for investment; and, on the other hand, by improving infrastructures and by granting reduced-interest loans to businesses and entrepreneurs. Finally, it could be useful and efficient to reduce taxes to encourage small traders to remain in business in rural communities;
b. Providing appropriate facilities for the integration and counselling of businesses;
c. Promoting the establishment of advanced, high-technology companies with high added value, as well as service companies using automatic data transmission and processing systems;
d. Fostering the improvement of the production, processing and marketing of regional products as well as assisting schemes in favour of high-quality craft activities.

Box 2.5. The UK Countryside Alliance manifesto (source: Countryside Alliance, 1998: 1–2).

'To champion the countryside, country sports and the rural way of life'

Preserve the freedoms of country people and their way of life
Lead campaigns for country sports, their related trades and activities, and the countryside
Cooperate closely with other organizations to promote and protect the rural way of life
Promote conservation and the viability of the countryside as part of the national heritage
Increase awareness and develop understanding of rural issues across the political spectrum
Undertake research and provide authoritative information to politicians, the media and the public
Develop education programmes for all ages, to promote a better understanding in town and country of the countryside and rural issues
Advance animal welfare and expose the dangers of the 'animal rights' agenda

breakdown. It has tended to be seen as an urban issue, affecting inner-city neighbourhoods and urban public housing estates, yet social exclusion also has a strong rural presence, although mythical images of a rural idyll held by some incomers and tourists act to mask this.

The characteristics of social exclusion in rural areas often have important differences compared with urban situations:

- Socially excluded households in rural areas tend to be geographically scattered. By contrast, social exclusion is often concentrated in urban areas, especially on housing estates.
- The manifestation of social exclusion differs; for example, rural housing problems may relate more to affordability than to quality and rural employment problems may relate more to low pay and seasonality than to unemployment (e.g. Box 2.6).
- Distance, isolation and poor access to jobs, services and other opportunities compound the problems for rural people.
- More traditional attitudes in rural areas about self-sufficiency can lead to social exclusion going undeclared or unheeded as rural communities may also be seen by others as more self-contained and mutually supportive, with less need of external support.

Policies which aim to tackle social exclusion need to reflect these differing circumstances. Ways of enhancing policy to confront and tackle social exclusion in rural areas include:

Box 2.6. Indicators of rural social exclusion in England and Wales (source: Brown, 2000; Countryside Agency, 2000).

3 million rural dwellers live below the official poverty line of half the average national income
1.4 million rural people of working age have no academic qualifications
Average farming income in 1999 was £9900 per head: its lowest level since entering the Common Agricultural Policy
70% of rural parishes had no general store in 1997
43% of rural parishes had no post office
83% had no GP based in the parish
49% had no school
75% had no daily bus service; 44% of rural parishes never had a bus before 9 a.m.; 77% never had a bus after 7 p.m.
The poorest 10% of households are twice as likely to own a car if they live in a rural area, than if they live in a metropolitan area. This is a substantial cost
More than 10,000 affordable homes per annum are required to meet the needs of low income households in rural areas
17,000 households in rural districts are priority homeless
The gulf in incomes and opportunities between the rural affluent and the rural deprived is accelerating

- establishing an explicit rural dimension in all social exclusion policy activity;
- developing indicators more sensitive to rural circumstances; for example, the index of multiple deprivation should give greater prominence to rural problems;
- supporting investment in building community capacity in rural areas; and
- adopting access standards to key services.

The extent to which recreation and tourism development can contribute to an amelioration of exclusion and deprivation will vary according to the particular circumstances of the rural area. Indeed, there may be no impact or possibly a negative one. In the following invited contribution, Andrew Copus and Marsaili MacLeod discuss and evaluate indicators of social well-being in rural areas as a means of identifying areas of need and informing policy responses to it (including the development of tourism and recreation).

Invited Viewpoint

Indicators of Rural Well-being

Andrew Copus and Marsaili MacLeod

Although 'well-being' (like the closely related terms 'poverty', 'disadvantage', 'quality of life', or 'social inclusion/exclusion') is an intrinsically subjective and flexible concept, appropriate indicators and the capacity to establish spatial patterns of 'well-being' are a fundamental prerequisite for effective rural development policy, since they:

- highlight issues which need to be addressed;
- identify target groups or areas; and
- facilitate monitoring of policy impacts.

Clearly, the role and significance of indicators is not unique to the rural policy context; indeed it mirrors developments in many other fields. There are, for example, close parallels with, and lessons to be learned from, regional economic development and environmental policy.

Content and underlying concepts

Although some recent work attempts to take a 'rounded' view of well-being (including social dimensions), most rural indicators and typologies focus primarily on economic characteristics such as employment, incomes and aspects of the cost of living. There are two interrelated reasons for this: availability of data and the predominantly economic objectives of rural policy.

Most rural well-being indicators and typologies are based on official, secondary data. Such sources are, for historical reasons, relatively rich in information relating to economic aspects of rural life, but yield very few variables indicative of social aspects, such as community cohesion or the personal value placed on 'rural life'. The latter are, of course, much more difficult to quantify, and although their importance is widely recognized both by rural dwellers and by rural sociologists, very little progress has been made to translate these into indicators.

Similarly, rural policy tends to be directed towards maintaining incomes in declining rural industries, promoting employment growth in new activities, or (less commonly) compensating rural dwellers for the higher costs of living in the countryside. Only recently, and perhaps primarily because of the perceived indirect economic benefits, have pilot programmes been introduced in the UK to address community/social aspects of rural well-being. However, the inclusion of these aspects of rural well-being is problematic, since social and economic patterns do not necessarily correspond. In the views of many rural dwellers the problems highlighted by official statistics are, to a greater or lesser extent, compensated for by social/community attributes. Thus, a study of rural disadvantage carried out in Scotland concluded that:

Continued overleaf

rural people's subjective assessment of their poverty or disadvantage is often at odds with objective definitions. The vast majority of respondents asserted that they were advantaged by their rural lifestyle rather than disadvantaged by it, and many households rejected the objective assessment of their position.

(Shucksmith and Philip, 2000: 9)

Data sources and related issues

The relative dependence on official data sources has restricted the choice of content and emphasis of rural well-being indicator and typology studies, and has also had implications for the scale of analysis and methodology. In the UK, for example, most studies have depended heavily on the decennial population census. Unemployment claimant and annual employment survey data have also been widely used. These sources have yielded key variables such as population density, population change, economic activity rates, unemployment rates and industrial structure indicators (dependence on primary industries, importance of services or 'knowledge-based' industries).

The use of valuable new variables such as the incorporation of benefit claimants data into the UK Department of the Environment, Transport and the Regions (DETR) 1999 index of deprivation (Noble *et al.*, 2000), reflects two trends: (i) government data processing is becoming increasingly computerized; and (ii) private sector companies are building up large databases facilitating local 'profiling'. The 1999 index of deprivation, and the parallel indicators of rural disadvantage produced by the Countryside Agency (Carruthers, 2000), represent the first of a new generation of indicators, benefiting from a broader and more appropriate range of raw variables, as a result of the current interest in enhancing official data collection procedures.

In consequence, there is increasing potential for direct measures of housing conditions, educational attainment, service accessibility and health conditions to accompany economic constituents as objective indicators of well-being. However, there continues to be limited data for measuring the increasingly important values people place on their surrounding physical and social environment which, in rural areas, contain important public and quasi-public goods such as a clean environment and 'safe' communities, which contribute to the quality of life.

Across Europe, household surveys are increasingly used as a means of estimating the more subjective perceived quality of life aspects in addition to objective living conditions. The European Commission Household Panel (ECHP) survey, for example, includes subjective and non-monetary indicators of households' economic situation. However, many national household surveys and other sources of official statistics have failed to distinguish between rural and urban areas and, furthermore, the disaggregation of sample surveys to small area geographies renders the results meaningless.

Scale of analysis

Patterns of rural well-being are, by definition, best carried out using small area data. However, in the UK, small area analysis presents a range of difficulties due to the proliferation of incompatible spatial units (electoral wards, postcode sectors, parishes) which are only now being addressed through geographical information system (GIS) apportionment procedures (see below). As a result, some UK work has used a rather crude spatial framework, such as local authority districts, after preliminary screening to exclude urban areas, either on the basis of a multivariate analysis of 'rurality', or on a simple population density criterion.

Small area analysis, while benefiting from the preliminary exclusion of 'urban' data, has to recognize the existence of a rural–urban (or perhaps more accurately a core–periphery) continuum, and the difficulties of comparing accessible commuter zones with remote sparsely populated areas. In some cases the heterogeneity of rural areas is incorporated through the inclusion of a 'peripherality' indicator, while in others it is left implicit, to be revealed by statistical associations in other variables. The use of small area data also raises methodological difficulties in sparsely populated areas, where numbers are small, and 'densities' or percentage indicators can fluctuate widely. Change indicators are particularly vulnerable to such problems. Some argue that the adoption of a signed chi-square methodology can overcome this difficulty (see below).

Another, largely ignored statistical issue associated with small area analysis is known as the modifiable statistical area problem (MAUP: see Openshaw, 1984; Martin, 1991). This simply relates to the fact that when random point data are converted to ratio data for a grid of spatial units, the resulting pattern depends to some extent on the configuration of the area boundaries. In practical terms all that one can hope to do is to minimize the effect by using relatively small spatial units which as far as possible separate areas known to have different characteristics (such as town and country).

Methodological choices and their implications

There are, broadly, two methodological options for generating a synthetic index, or a typology of rural well-being. The first, perhaps most popular in the 1970s and 1980s, is based on multivariate statistical methods, such as factor or cluster analysis. The second is some form of 'multi-criteria analysis'. The first of these has the attraction of allowing the individual weighting of raw variables to be determined by the statistical procedure itself (usually on the basis of strength of correlation between raw variables). However it must be recognized that the outcome is much influenced by the initial selection of variables, and by a number of decisions relating to procedural choices within the overall analysis.

Multi-criteria methods essentially depend on the operator setting criteria or thresholds for each raw variable (in the case of a typology), or applying weights to each variable on the basis of informed opinion (when creating a synthetic index). Prior to this the data may be transformed mathematically (often standardizing them through the calculation of Z scores), or variables may be grouped and composite indicators calculated for a set of 'themes' (an implicit form of weighting).

In recent years an interesting methodological evolution has taken place in the context of the DETR's index of local conditions (recently renamed as the index of deprivation). This had its origins in an urban 'multiple-deprivation' indicator developed from 1981 population census data (Noble *et al.*, 1999) which involved the identification of 'groups at risk' through eight standardized indicators with thresholds, deprived areas being assumed to be those where most of these groups were present. The 1991 index of local conditions moved away from an analysis of 'groups at risk' to a set of more direct indicators of deprivation, organized into a set of 'domains', and from Z scores to a signed chi-square statistic. The advantage of the latter is that it is not subject to the small number problem where percentages or rates are calculated for sparsely populated areas. It is in effect a 'volume' rather than an 'intensity' indicator of deprivation. It can also be used to estimate policy budget allocations. The 1999 revision of the index maintained the 'domains' concept, but rejected the signed chi-square methodology in favour of simple 'intensity' measures. In the absence of denominators for inter-censal years, small area population estimates have been derived from official estimates at the local authority area level.

Some examples of the patterns identified by well-being indicators

Two official reports on Scottish rural life (Scottish Office, 1992, 1996) identify the problems of parts of the Highlands and Islands (notably the Western Isles, Sutherland, Ross and Cromarty, Caithness and Lochaber), in terms of population change, unemployment and low incomes, but do not attempt to synthesize the different variables or map patterns of 'well-being'. The second of these reports does include a typology of districts but, disappointingly, this distinguishes between areas largely in terms of population density and settlement pattern.

A more comprehensive multivariate approach to small area indicators of economic fragility (Copus and Crabtree, 1992) highlighted Shetland, the Western Isles, Orkney, Sutherland and Skye and Lochalsh as the most problematic districts of rural Scotland. Analysis at the parish level suggested that the most fragile areas covered much of the Western Isles and Shetland, but that there were significant east–west contrasts within the Highland mainland. The nine indicator variables included in the analysis were selected to match Objective 5b designation criteria, and the authors were able to draw conclusions regarding the validity of the official designation.

More recent work by Tzamarias (1994), Copus and Petri (1999) and Hannell *et al.* (2000), although derived from different databases and using different methodologies, have generated very similar patterns of economic fragility. The first author used a combination of factor and cluster analysis, while the other researchers used similar approaches to that of the 1999 review of the index of local disadvantage: a hierarchical multi-criteria analysis comprising (in both cases but differing in detail) four 'dimensions'.

Continued overleaf

In England and Wales, as discussed above, two key indicators of well-being have been produced in recent years: the DETR's index of local deprivation (Noble *et al.*, 1999, 2000) and the Countryside Agency's (formerly Rural Development Commission) work on indicators of rural disadvantage, which was associated with the designation of 'rural priority areas' (Rural Development Commission, 1992).

Conclusions

Rural well-being is a subjective and flexible concept. UK attempts to quantify and map it have so far been thwarted by both policy expediency and inadequacies in published data, both of which have tended to result in an emphasis on economic aspects at the expense of social considerations. However, methodological advances have been made in recent years, and conceptual and policy horizons are expanding to accommodate broader, and often more positive, issues relating to social and human capital. Although it is probably true to say that existing indicators of rural well-being lag some way behind the conceptual basis which is becoming more generally accepted, it is realistic to assume that this will provide an incentive for improving published data, and that, assisted by continuing advances in data handling capabilities, much more sophisticated indicators will emerge in the coming years.

Andrew Copus and Marsaili MacLeod

Residents or Visitors? Second Homes

A phenomenon which can distort considerably the social and physical indicators of rural well-being is that of second homes. One of the major infrastructural changes resulting from recreational development in rural areas has been a growth in second home ownership, especially in more popular destination areas such as the English Lake District (Coppock, 1977). In this region some 16% of all properties are second or holiday homes, a figure rising to a third in some specific parts of the Lakes (Sharpley and Sharpley, 1997).

Such levels of second home ownership may often give rise to tourism and recreation being blamed for some rural housing-related problems. This perception has been expressed in its most extreme form in the damage or destruction of such homes perpetrated by extreme 'local' groups, notably in the 1980s, protesting at both the presence of second homes and their ownership by 'foreigners' (mainland French in the case of Corsica, and English in Mid- and North Wales). Such reactions are a rare occurrence, and while leisure development may indeed contribute to local housing problems, it may be just one of a matrix of factors, and in many rural areas may play no part at all. Planning policies, restraints on housing development, changes in market trends for and availability of rented property, as well as patterns of demographic and economic change, may all be more significant than the impact of recreation-related factors.

None the less, the 'absentee' ownership and only temporary use of holiday or second homes does present a range of potential impacts for rural societies:

Positively:

- Old or redundant buildings may be given a renewed lease of life through renovation or conversion into accommodation and thereby improve the visual amenity and physical fabric of an area.
- Local people may be provided with temporary or permanent employment as the result of second home development.
- Additional spending in local shops and on other facilities and services is likely to be generated within the local economy.

Negatively:

- New development can have an adverse effect on the visual and environmental amenity of an area, degrading the landscape and/or causing the destruction of vegetation and other 'natural' features.
- Significant levels of second home ownership in any rural area will reduce the availability of housing for local people, a

situation exacerbated where planning policies restrict new housing developments.

- Demand for second homes raises the costs of housing and such local inflation may prevent local people who cannot afford to buy houses at such prices from entering the housing market or may force them out of it.
- In such circumstances younger people in particular may find they are unable to afford to live locally, and move away to urban areas, causing ruptures in the rural social structure (exacerbated by the characteristics of the 'incomers'). Such migratory activity is of course also stimulated by lifestyle, employment and mobility aspirations, all of which may be more important than the impact of second homes.
- An influx of more affluent 'outsiders' can provoke local resentment and negative behaviour responses. However, there exist a number of studies which portray examples where second home owners have attempted to socially integrate with the local community, such as British home owners in France (Buller and Hoggart, 1994).

In the wider context of rural social exclusion and the dynamic and place-specific processes of depopulation and counter-urbanization, a major policy challenge is establishing an equilibrium between demand pressures from higher income urban residents for the purchase of rural residences for recreation or permanent settlement, and the often pressing housing and associated needs of 'traditional' rural residents. This might involve the need for total exclusion of further second home ownership in a particular location (Box 2.2). There may be an uneasy tension as a result of different socially constructed village qualities held between the residents of 'rustic' cottages, whose prices have been inflated through incomer demand, and 'local' residents in unattractive yet relatively low-cost housing schemes developed to enable them to purchase new homes at realistic rates.

Changing Recreational Demand

The growth of second home ownership in rural areas is perhaps just the tangible tip of a leisure-related iceberg. It has become something of a conventional widsom (Butler, 1998; Butler *et al.*, 1998), that up to a quarter of a century ago most leisure activities in rural areas were related closely to the character of the setting, and were clearly different from those activities engaged in in urban areas (Chapter 1). These 'traditional' pursuits have been characterized as relaxing, relatively passive, perhaps nostalgia-related, with forms of activity such as walking, picnicking, fishing and landscape photography. Most, if not all of these articulated a need to escape from day-to-day urban life into an environment of contrasting pace and setting where the physical and human elements were thought to blend in harmony. While such 'traditional' recreational practices are still widely pursued in rural areas, during the last quarter of a century many other activities have emerged which have been characterized as different: more active, competitive, prestige- or fashion-related; perhaps technological, modern, individual, and fast, ranging from off-road motor vehicle driving, survival games and hang-gliding, to gentrification of properties, 'eco-tourism' and fashionable shopping (Butler *et al.*, 1998) (see also Chapter 7; Plate 2.1).

In short, while 'traditional' rural recreational pursuits are essentially an escape from

Plate 2.1. Traditional? Recreational cyclists at the Carnac prehistoric stone site, Brittany.

urban industrial lifestyles relating directly to the environment in which they are set, 'new' activities represent the transfer and imposition of urban values on rural areas, to the extent that the specific context of location is far less important and in some cases almost irrelevant (Tables 2.1 and 2.2). In some cases this requires the penetration of remote areas by motorized transport. In others there is the need for the establishment of specific facilities and resorts to cater for the greater and more sophisticated demands placed on rural resources, increasing the likelihood of new forms of impact and conflict.

Within this context of change several factors have contributed to a shift in both the nature and importance of rural leisure (Butler, 1998):

- a substantial increase in the level of participation;
- major changes in agriculture;
- images created in the mass media;
- skilful marketing and the creation of demand;
- significant shifts in public tastes and fashion;
- the effects of a variety of technological changes and innovation which have produced lower priced and more user-friendly equipment; and
- improved mobility and access, although in the latter case the conflicts of incompatible uses have led to increasingly acrimonious debates on access rights.

Several trends have complemented this growth:

- almost all activities which have traditionally taken place in rural areas have recorded significant rates of growth;

Table 2.1. Rural leisure activities (source: Butler, 1998: 214).

Traditional activities	New activities
Driving	Snow skiing
Walking	Snowmobiling
Visiting historic sites	Mountain biking
Picnicking	All terrain/off-road vehicle
Nature study	Orienteering
Photography	Survival
Sightseeing	Windsurfing
Fishing	Endurance sports
Visiting rural operations	Paragliding

Table 2.2. Characteristics of rural leisure activities (after Butler, 1998: 216).

Traditional activities	New activities
Relaxing	Challenging
Family/group oriented	Individualistic
Non-competitive	Competitive, prestigious
Passive	Active
Non-mechanized	Mechanized
Rural landscape complementary	Rural landscape irrelevant
Rural land uses complementary	Rural land uses competitive
Low cost	High cost
Low per capita impact	Relatively high per capita impact
Low technology	High technology
Non-urban	Urban related
Minimum skill or training required	Skill demanding

- policy changes have increased the supply of opportunities; for example use of reservoirs for sailing, waterskiing, windsurfing and fishing;
- changes have taken place in informal recreational use of facilities designed for other purposes; for example, forest access roads are used by walkers and latterly mountain bikers, although this presents land use conflicts;
- widespread public interest in the environment and the growth of both passive and active environmentally aware groups; and
- a significant rise in popularity and demand for participation in activities not exclusively rural in nature but located in rural areas; for example, golf, sports facilities, leisure centres, amusement and holiday parks (see also Chapter 8).

In this characterization of a shift from the traditional to the new, from the passive to the active, there appear to be two related paradoxes. First, while 'traditional' recreational activities in rural areas certainly have been more in sympathy with the natural environment and less related to the harnessing of technology, it is difficult to characterize them as essentially relaxing. Rambling, hillwalking and mountain climbing groups emerged in the 19th and early 20th centuries across Europe; indeed there were notably large numbers of (cross-border) hillwalking and mountaineering groups in central Europe prior to the Second World War (Hall, 1991). As Mirja Nylander indicates in Chapter 4, cycling groups also became popular across the continent in the early to mid-20th century, and their traditions survive in most countries, as Les Lumsdon shows in Chapter 7. Mass youth groups, whether altruistically motivated (such as the Scout movement) or ideologically prescribed (Hitler Youth, Communist Young Pioneers), carried a tradition of active and purposeful rural recreation through much of the 20th century.

Second, the above point reflects a wider paradox, that of a broader societal change from an 'active' tradition of people entertaining themselves, in pre-television, pre-mass motoring days – whether in the home gathered around the piano, or in the 'wild' gathered around the camp fire – to a culture of passivity, with people expecting to be entertained with minimal effort, or at least in a sedentary manner, through television and video, fast food and Internet surfing (see also Chapter 9).

Such a characterization of societal change from active (production?) to passive (consumption) superficially would appear to contradict, or at least provide a conceptual counterpoint to, the recognition by Butler (1998) and others of two major constructions of the countryside for tourism and recreation: (i) a 'traditional' (passive) context of recreation seeking the contrasting (to urban) qualities of rurality, peace, tranquillity, open space; and, (ii) a 'contemporary' (active) pattern of consumption, whereby the rural environment is merely the context for activities which articulate urban-imposed reflexive values of fashion, status and body-awareness.

Social construction of rurality

Certainly, the pattern of rural recreation characterized as 'contemporary' or 'new' is a vibrant and growing sector, benefiting from diversification as people seek more adventure and independent forms of travel (see Chapter 7). It has reinvigorated the appeal of rural destinations (albeit in potentially conflicting ways) and opens new avenues for commercial opportunities. But such opportunities depend a great deal on understanding the nature and processes of the social construction of rural areas, and the tensions they may induce.

The attraction of rurality for leisure and for incoming residential purposes, may transcend its tangible characteristics and qualities, such as open space, fresh air and tranquillity by also representing something special to visitors. This abstract concept, a social construction 'used by people in everyday talk' (Halfacree, 1993), represents the way in which many visitors' and incomers' meaning of 'rural' is 'constructed, negotiated and experienced' (Cloke, 1992: 55; Squire, 1994).

Although the symbolic significance of the countryside is often considered to have arisen relatively recently in reaction to industrialization and urbanization, pastoral images of the countryside originated in ancient times (Short, 1991: 29). But as modern (urban) life has become faster, more stressful and less 'authentic', so the 'rural' has taken on a more utopian, mythical status as being a simpler, slower, more natural, more meaningful and thus 'superior' state compared with the urban. This 'rural idyll' becomes, 'a peculiar blending of nostalgia, wholesomeness, heritage, nature and culture, combining the romantic combination of man and nature working in harmony, captured on calendars and Christmas cards throughout the developed world' (Butler *et al.*, 1998: 14; Plate 2.2).

Such construction, however, may not only vary from individual to individual, but collectively may represent cultural differences between regions and countries. For example, in England, recreationalists and policy-makers may be guided by a rural 'aesthetic' (Harrison, 1991) which springs from some 'romantic, pre-industrial idyll, a "chocolate box" countryside of meadows, villages and country lanes' (Sharpley and Sharpley, 1997: 16). By contrast, in North America, for recreational purposes rurality is conceived often as preserved 'wilderness' typified by the western US national parks. Much of Europe, including Scotland, may fall somewhere between these polar models.

The social construction of rural areas and cultures has a further significant international dimension, which to some extent parallels that of the domestic rural/urban construction. The attraction of many international destinations may rely on the cultural significance which tourists attribute to them. Often, Western tourists view less developed countries as more traditional than their own, albeit exhibiting more stark cultural differences than the rural areas of their home countries. As a consequence, many countries and regions are sold to tourists through the reinforcement of popularly held images based on an 'authentic' rurality (MacCannell, 1976; Cohen, 1988; Silver, 1993) which is perceived (usually by tourism industry decision makers) to meet the social constructions of visitors rather than the actual reality of the destination.

Plate 2.2. Idyllic? Horse fair, Wallachia, Romania.

Such consumption and commodification of the countryside can thus lead to rural production being based on establishing new commodities or in re-imaging and rediscovering places for recreation and tourism. Although economic, political and social restructuring processes across Europe have provided vehicles for transformation, the critical factors stimulating demand for the consumption of rural products stem from changes in taste – transformed social constructions – following the emergence of a service economy (Urry, 1988) in the post-productivist countryside (Chapter 1, Box 1.2). These tastes have influenced social groups who have adopted similar values in the consumption of rural areas.

Certainly, a perceived 'post-Fordist' shift has been identified empirically by such researchers as Hummelbrunner and Miglbauer (1994) and Boissevain (1996), suggesting that the balance of demand for tourist services is moving from a pattern of mass consumption 'to more individual patterns, with greater differentiation and volatility of consumer preferences and a heightened need for producers to be consumer-driven and to segment markets more systematically' (Urry, 1991: 52). Yet, as post-communist processes in East–Central Europe have reflected most explicitly (e.g. Hall, 1998), there has also been a resurgence and continued global growth of mass tourism markets. Indeed, both by the very numbers involved in tourism and recreation activities in rural areas and by the way in which the 'special interests' noted above have been embedded within an overall growth of tourists and recreationalists in rural areas, conditions in the market would appear to question the validity of a perceived shift away from the mass (see Chapters 8 and 9).

What is also significant, although for how long remains to be seen, is that from a supply perspective, the emergence of a 'new rural tourism' has manifested itself in terms of 'an increasing interest in rural tourism among a better-off clientele, and also among some holidaymakers as a growing environmental awareness and a desire to be integrated with the residents in the areas they visit' (Bramwell, 1994: 3). This raises the questions of:

- how rural areas are being used to provide tourism and recreational experiences;
- how businesses are pursuing market-orientated approaches within the context of such apparent trends in cultural and environmental interest (if not environmental 'awareness', in the sense of 'enlightened' behaviour); and
- how such rural areas will respond and cope if such specialist interest is merely the precursor of, or 'complement' to, mass demand.

Alongside significant structural changes, rural areas have been subject to a much greater range of uses, which have inevitably raised conflicts both between recreation and tourist uses and other forms of land use, and between the various forms of recreation and tourism (see also Chapter 4). For example:

- between motorized and non-motorized recreational users; for example, cross-country skiers and snow-mobilers, walkers, horse-riders and off-road vehicle drivers; and
- between non-mechanized users of the same facilities; for example, pony trekkers and mountain bike riders, canoeists and anglers, and hikers and hunters (Butler *et al.*, 1998: 13).

Such conflicts are likely to increase as both the overall demand from recreational and tourist uses and the breadth of those uses increase. In some areas, this situation is resulting in, and is being exacerbated by, restrictions on access to open countryside, raising significant policy and management challenges (Chapter 4).

Spirit of Rural Place: Lost and Found? Image and Commodification

> As you get to know Europe slowly, tasting the wines, cheeses and characters of the different countries you begin to realize that the important determinant of any culture is after all – the spirit of place.
>
> (Durrell, 1969: 156)

The loss of the 'rustic' in some rural areas has only intensified the search for and emphasis on it in others. While *sense* of place – through the marketing and image promotion of culture and heritage in particular localities – may have been reasserted, a loss of *spirit* of place may have been brought about as a result of a rapidly changing and diminishing base of 'traditional' rural activities and people, as the holistic *raison d'être* of some rural places has been all but lost.

Kotler *et al.* (1993: 100) consider place in terms of four components: character, fixed environment, service provision, and entertainment and recreation. Yet transcending all of these is purpose: the basis for the development of that place within its particular environmental context and with its specific demographic and cultural characteristics. Perhaps here is one of the paradoxes of the search for the idyll: the *spirit* of place, an introspective, functioning, perhaps utilitarian set of purposes for a working 'community' and its environment, is irrevocably dispelled when either the original purpose for that community is lost or changed, or when 'outsiders', either through residence or regular visits, begin to generate demonstration effects and reflexive attitudes.

As Oscar Wilde might have put it (albeit much better), each tourist seeking the rural idyll kills the thing he or she loves, but may also help to manufacture something much more 'appealing' in the process. This suggests that if *spirit* of place is the authentic, warts-and-all sense of original purpose of a locality which is almost inevitably eroded by time and progress, then the commodified *sense* of place, resulting from the re-imaging and possibly repopulating of a cultural landscape which has outlived its original purpose, is likely to appeal to a wider audience than the previous authenticity. Much, however, may be lost along the way, which is then an issue of regional and national development policy concern.

In relation to the rural tourist's paradoxical search for the idyll, however, Sørensen and Nilsson (1999) argue that, contrary to previous somewhat condescending analyses, tourists in rural areas (at least those surveyed in Denmark) are well aware of the discrepancy between rural authenticity and the idyll which they seek (see also Chapter 9). Indeed, they claim it is the tension between these two which renders the experience the more rewarding.

Certainly, the importance of image for rural areas has only relatively recently been appreciated. For the not necessarily complementary reasons of tourism and residential property promotion and attraction of inward investment for economic development, major efforts have been made in a variety of settings to consciously 'improve', establish or change the sense of place of rural areas through the creation and re-creation of specific images. Given the diverse purposes of such images, much more research is required into their selection processes and the balance of interests represented within them (see also Chapter 5).

Butler and Hall (1998a: 117) suggest four major characteristics of rural imaging processes, any or all of which may be present:

1. The development of a critical mass of visitor attractions and facilities;
2. The hosting of events and festivals;
3. The development of rural tourism strategies and policies often associated with new or renewed regional tourism organizations and the related development of regional marketing and promotion campaigns; and
4. The development of leisure and cultural services and projects to support the regional marketing and tourism effort.

Images may not be authentic or 'correct' (Dewailly, 1998), but the overall image of rural areas appears highly 'positive' in most of the developed world, because of, or perhaps despite, the images promoted. 'Strategic place marketing' (Kotler *et al.*, 1993: 18) is seen to be necessary to meet the perceived needs of a locality's stakeholders in order to 'improve livability, investibility and visitability' (Kotler *et al.*, 1993: 99). Place marketing thus involves the construction or selective tailoring of particular images which become 'enmeshed with the dynamics of the global economy' (Sadler, 1993: 175).

That rural 'communities' can become objects of tourism consumption has encouraged some localities to reproduce themselves specifically for tourists: to identify themselves with the way in which they are 'named' and 'framed' as tourist attractions. Tourism industry demands for 'authentic' local cultures which may be associated with a specific location create 'back-stage' and 'front-stage' areas; the tourist gaze is restricted to the 'staged' authenticity of the 'front-stage' regions. However, in the process, local community relations themselves may become commodified (Richards and Hall, 2000).

Yet local residents may resent the images they are supposed to represent, particularly if used for (political) propagandist (Hall, 1981) or commercial promotion (Morgan and Pritchard, 1998) purposes, or as reflections of negative media images (e.g. Howie, 2000). Local 'community' life and its integration with the landscape is often an essential part of the marketing image and branding of the (rural) tourism product. It is clearly crucial to avoid damaging or compromising the way of life around which the local attraction is based (Edwards *et al.*, 2000). Yet the power and demand for the realization of traditional, 'idyllic' images of timeless sustainability and its commodification, may well act to stifle the articulation of real, local identity.

Anthropological research in more developed countries (e.g. Kohn, 1997) has pointed to the increasingly blurred nature of the boundary between the identities and roles of hosts and guests, particularly where there is little or no cultural difference. Guests may stop visiting and become hosts; hosts may be longer-term visitors themselves, such as seasonal migrants. Residents' attitudes to tourism and tourists may change over time, either positively or negatively. As a result, sense of place and of 'community' may become blurred.

Drawing on the work of Fees (1996) in his analysis of conflicts between the 'local born and bred' and the 'incomers', Sørensen and Nilsson (1999) produced a typology to demonstrate the complexity of motivations and to suggest that rather than a host/guest dichotomy, there can be recognized a continuum of residential and visiting positions in rural areas which can be separated into a number of types between the two poles (Box 2.7).

Friends and relatives visiting and visited further extend the range and interplay of rural identities. Although increasing attention is being paid to the range of impacts and activities surrounding recreational visits to relatives and friends (e.g. Pearce, 1995; Seaton and Palmer, 1997), the complexity of relationships between hosts and guests and between different categories of guests in this context is only beginning to be understood. The following invited viewpoint from Steven Boyne, which is part of a research project funded by the Scottish Executive Rural Affairs Department (SERAD), begins to shed some light on the significance of some of these 'visiting friends and relatives' (VFR) relationships in rural areas.

Box 2.7. A rural residents–visitors continuum (source: Sørensen and Nilsson, 1999: 8–9).

Holiday-tourists: holiday tourists staying in the area; for example, in a cottage, an inn or at a farm
Transit-tourists: holiday tourists who consume the experiences and recreational values of the area, but are accommodated outside of the area
Day-visitors: visitors having their permanent residence within day trip distance, using the area for recreation
Staying with friends and relatives: visitors with socially defined connections to the area
Weekend-visitors: regular users of rural residences who 'go rural' at weekends
Permanent tourists: two-home residents who reside in the countryside on a part-time basis. Alternation between urban and rural residence is beyond a work/holiday distinction
Resident tourists: persons who have moved to the countryside for reasons rooted in aesthetics and ideology. The countryside is perceived as a more authentic, real and aesthetically attractive place for life and family
Other incoming permanent residents: persons whose residence is based on tangible matters (e.g. employment). Aesthetic or recreational qualities of the area are less important
Local born and raised residents: persons born and raised in the area. Not necessarily residing there always, their stays outside the area have a temporary character

Invited Viewpoint

Hosts, Friends and Relatives in Rural Scotland: VFR Tourism Market Relationships Explored

Steven Boyne

Although VFR tourism enjoyed increased attention from academics and marketing organizations during the latter years of the 20th century, its role and impacts in rural areas remain poorly understood in comparison with 'normal' holiday tourism. This short contribution highlights the significance of guests' geographical origin in relation to patterns of VFR activity in rural Scotland. An examination of the relationship between guests' geographical origin and the proportion of their trip spent staying with friends or relatives, suggests that friendship and kinship networks have a significant role in attracting international tourists to rural areas of Scotland.

During the summer of 1999 a postal questionnaire which targeted hosts of VFR tourists was administered to just over 1000 households in four rural and semi-rural case study areas of Scotland. The response rate of 34.2% yielded data from 364 households, some 75% of which had hosted VFR guests in the 12 months prior to the study. Based on data relating to each respondent household's last VFR hosting experience, the research found that the majority of VFR trips were undertaken by residents of Scotland who stayed with friends and relatives typically for one, two or three nights, before returning home again, indicating that, excepting mode of accommodation, most VFR tourism trips may be very similar to short-break tourism. Additionally, a significant proportion of the respondents' VFR guests had

Continued overleaf

travelled from the rest of the UK (England, Wales and Northern Ireland) and overseas, and it was found that when the data are disaggregated on the basis of visitors' geographical origin, significant differences in spending and visitor patterns are revealed.

Of the four variables analysed – status of visitor (i.e. friend or relative), purpose of visit, migratory status of host and guest's geographical origin – only the geographical origin of guests was consistently found to be a statistically significant factor in relation to the selected individual data. These data dealt with VFR trips, nights, hosts' incremental expenditure, activities, trip purpose, 'residual' nights and other types of accommodation used by respondents' VFR guests. The nature of these relationships is described below.

Trip numbers, duration and hosts' expenditure

For the case study areas, Scotland and the rest of the UK are the most important VFR markets in terms of trips, nights and residents' incremental spending incurred as a direct result of their VFR hosting activities. However, on a spend per trip basis, greater levels of spending tend to be incurred by hosts of guests from Europe and further afield. This is due to the increased number of nights these guests spend on average with their hosts. But the relationship between guests' origin and hosts' spending is not unilinear: on a spend per night basis, the greatest levels of spending are by hosts of guests staying for three nights or less (typically guests travelling within Scotland) at approximately £30 per night (€42). When guests stay for longer periods of time, although total spending increases, on a per night basis, spending decreases significantly to, on average, approximately £13.50 per night (€22).

Economic impact data were collected by asking respondents to detail their incremental expenditure broken down into several categories. From these disaggregated data, the greatest economic impact from hosts' spending was clearly to be seen in the retail sector (suppliers of groceries and provisions) (52%), followed by the catering and entertainment sector (27%).

Although, proportionately, hosts' spending on activities and day visits is small, estimates calculated from the sample data suggest that this may be worth between £7.6 and £16 million to Scotland's rural economy when these figures are factored upward to represent spending by all households in rural Scotland. As these data are calculated using median and trimmed mean values for both number of VFR hosting experiences per household per year and number of nights per VFR visit, the results represent upper and lower estimates. The actual value for hosts' incremental spending will, most likely, lie somewhere between these boundaries.

The following section goes on to describe the nature of activities undertaken by the survey respondents and their VFR guests, who are, once again, segmented by their geographical origin. In this way, a broad indication is given of how different VFR markets are influencing different rural tourism industry sectors.

Activities undertaken during VFR trips

Some 30% of all respondents reported that their guests undertook no activities during their VFR visit. Of the remaining trips, guests' origin was also found to be a significant factor in relation to the type of activities undertaken during the VFR visit. The activities undertaken by the remaining VFR guests were disaggregated into the following three categories: (i) recreational and sporting activities; (ii) events and visiting other friends and relatives; and (iii) retail and service-centred activities (including eating out, pubs and clubs, shopping and touring, sightseeing and visitor attractions). Analysis shows that overseas VFR visitors are the least likely to participate in recreational and sporting activities with only 33.3% of this group partaking. Conversely, for the retail and service-centred activities this group has, proportionately, the greatest level of participation (74.1%) while 'domestic' Scottish VFR guests demonstrate the lowest levels of participation (39.6%) in this activity category. Statistical significance for these findings was established at the 1% level using chi-square analysis.

Trip purpose, 'residual' nights and supplementary accommodation

Analysis of the responses relating to trip purpose reveals that guests' origin had a statistically significant association with their trip purpose. Specifically, VFR guests travelling from outside Scotland were more likely to stay with friends or relatives 'for a holiday' than those guests travelling within Scotland; the majority of whose visits to friends or relatives (65%) were primarily to visit their hosts. Related data suggest that these differences may be due to the fact that 'more distant' guests include a visit to friends or relatives as an element of their holiday itinerary rather than as the sole purpose of their visit: travellers whom we may describe as 'partial VFRs'. 'Residual nights' were thus identified as nights spent by guests away from home, but not staying with their friends and relatives.

Visitors from further afield tend on average to stay longer with friends and relatives and to undertake a greater number of residual nights. Indeed, only 20% of VFR guests travelling within Scotland undertake *any* residual nights, compared with 56% for UK visitors and 77% for overseas visitors. Regarding the type of accommodation used by partial VFRs during the non-VFR component of their trip, fully 81% of residual nights were spent in commercial accommodation. Overseas visitors, however, show the greatest propensity to stay with other friends or relatives (38% of all respondents' overseas guests did so), presumably as they attempt to visit as many of their friends and family as possible while visiting their destination. This suggests that VFR may be an important dimension of international tourism in rural Scotland and elsewhere.

Steven Boyne

Re-imaging in and of the Global Village

There follow two evaluations of rural imaging/re-imaging: (i) the role of popular culture – particularly film and television – in contributing to the imagery and promotion of rural areas; and (ii) processes of re-imaging in post-communist Central and Eastern Europe. Both represent in their very different ways some of the effects of major global processes which significantly impinged upon rural areas in the last decades of the 20th century.

In the case of popular culture, the enormous consumption phenomenon of television and video and the invasive role of television 'soaps' have conspired both to influence the image and re-imaging of rural areas and to promote particular locations for media-related consumption. In the case of Central and Eastern Europe, political and economic restructuring has had the effect of both impoverishing and liberating rural areas: the former, through the collapse of guaranteed food markets, the uncertainty of land markets and exposure to global competition, and the latter through the removal of constraints on migration and private enterprise and a resurgence of the expression of national culture and (implicitly non-communist) heritage.

Re-imaging Rurality through Popular Culture

> Herefordshire is a county of red earth, green meadows, quiet woods and pretty black and white villages, with traditional farming land, largely untouched by time. In the south are the spectacular gorges of the River Wye and the lovely woodland trails of the Forest of Dean; westward lies the tranquil Golden Valley leading into Offa's Dyke. To the east, Elgar country rises to the Malvern Hills with the finest ridge walk in England, whilst to the north of the county lie the unspoilt farmlands of the Teme and Lugg valleys with a host of beautiful villages.
>
> (Farm Holiday Bureau, 1996: 2)

In a number of countries, tourism promoters have for some time employed cultural motifs with which to project the image of particular places or regions (e.g. Herbert, 1996), with regions and localities competing for cultural associations (e.g. Lister, 2000). Thus, in the UK, 'Constable country' promotes an area of south-eastern England (south Suffolk–north Essex) of far from dramatic topography but with the pastoral tranquillity and (questionable) cloud effects associated with the 19th century landscape painting of John Constable. 'Hardy country' promotes Dorset in south-west England, with the more dramatic landscapes of the 'Wessex' of Thomas Hardy's 19th century regional novels. 'Summer Wine country', however, is firmly, if somewhat infirmly, rooted in contemporary popular culture: a popular television comedy series (*Last of the Summer Wine*) involving three old men doing silly things in the rolling topography of rural West Yorkshire in northern England (Burgess, 1992).

Reflecting the way in which television, film and video have overtaken the role of the written word as key vehicles for reaching mass audiences with place images, the promoters of tourism, residential property and economic development have sought to exploit geographical associations with popular media iconography.

Certainly, film and television studios have long encouraged the popularity of visits to the locations where films and television programmes are made: for example, Universal Studios in Orlando, Granada Television in Manchester (site of the longest-running British soap *Coronation Street*). But only relatively recently have tourism authorities and promoters taken advantage of the popularity of particular locations because of their inclusion in a film or television 'soap' (Butler, 1990; Riley and van Doren, 1992; Riley, 1994; Pym, 1995). Before this, film companies were encouraged to locate films in particular areas because of the economic benefits which would be gained from increased demand for goods and services (including local residents as film 'extras') from the local area during the filming, not from visitors coming to see where the film was made. This has changed in the last two decades.

According to Riley *et al.* (1998), if some part of a film is extraordinary or captivating, it acts as an icon which viewers – consumers – attach to a location shown in the film. Such an icon can be the film's symbolic content, a single event, a favourite performer, a location's physical features, or a theme, which represents the most popular and familiar elements of the movie. Such icons become the focal point for visits to the location; for example, Australian Bush culture in *Crocodile Dundee* (located in Kakadu National Park) and Native American culture and natural scenery in *Dances with Wolves* (South Dakota plains) (Riley *et al.*, 1998: 924). Building on such appeal, therefore, the basis of film-induced tourism is that films can enhance awareness of, and a sense of association with, locations that can be marketed as places of tourist consumption. The mass medium creates an exotic world that does not exist in reality but can be recreated through a visit to the location(s) where it was filmed. Such a mythic quality may be superimposed upon a rural location which may already be socially constructed as 'idyllic'. Locational attractions can be prolonged with very successful films, which may be screened for several months in cinemas, and then made available on video, DVD and later shown on television and cable networks. Tooke and Baker (1996) found that for four UK film locations visits increased in the first year by 30–90%, while Riley *et al.* (1998) identified that the effect of movies on locations in the USA could last for at least 4 years and increase visits by 40–50%.

In the case of Scotland, impacts have been identified at a number of levels. Nationally, the tourism interest generated by *Braveheart* was claimed to be worth £14 million, although such figures should be treated with caution. In relation to the film, the town of Stirling received media publicity estimated to be worth £3 million (STB, 1995). Tourism has also followed in the wake of contemporary popular media depiction and representation of specific localities in Scotland. For example, in the village of Pennan on the Moray Firth in the north-east of Scotland, where the 1983 film *Local Hero* was filmed, a much visited icon from the film is the village's public telephone box, even if it was moved from its real location for the purposes of the film. The small west coast village of Plockton, regularly visited for its locational association with the popular television series *Hamish Macbeth*, also experiences short periods of heightened interest because the waterside location of its cottages featured in the now cult film of 1974, *The Wicker Man*, starring Christopher Lee and Britt Ekland (Bruce, 1996). The extent to which subsequent tourist activity at such locations reinforces media images or helps to generate new identities is not well researched, and quantification of visitation resulting from media exposure is poor.

However, the place-specific nature of popular media-led tourism is a potentially powerful tool if harnessed for policy purposes. Such harnessing is currently being pursued in at least two ways:

- Publicizing and promoting the locations featured in film and television. For this reason, in 1999 the British Tourist Authority (BTA) – the arm of UK tourism promotion and marketing aimed at foreign visitors – set up a 'movie map' website providing details, on a cross-referencing basis, of films and soaps shot in the UK, and their locations (BTA, 1999; Buncombe, 1999).
- Inducing film makers to employ particular locations or regions for shooting on the assumption that a successful film will assist image projection and the attraction of tourists and/or inward investment (e.g. see McCubbin, 1999).

Many attractions visited as a result of film-induced tourism may not have been attractions before and, superficially, may appear to be far from appealing; for example, the industrial streets of Sheffield in *The Full Monty*. Certainly, Bradford Metropolitan Council has used media imagery to good effect in assisting the regeneration of this post-industrial textile city. The city's promotion was placed within a wider regional framework encompassing the North Yorkshire Moors, Brontë country (Haworth village, home of the Brontë sisters), a preserved steam railway line (Keighley and Worth Valley) passing across the moors to Howarth, and the village of Esholt, to the north of Bradford, which for several years was the location for the long-running and widely popular rural television soap opera *Emmerdale* (Hayward, 1997; Hayward and Brabbs, 1998). This is set in and around the southern fringes of the Yorkshire Dales National Park:

> where the golden-green valley of Wharfedale and the wild expanses of Ilkley moor give way to the rugged Pennine hills ... Over the years, the magnificent landscape of the Yorkshire Dales has cast its spell upon many thousands of visitors: a captivating blend of wilderness and softness, of dark gritstone crags and white limestone, with subterranean cave systems as big as cathedrals. Lush pastures criss-crossed with dry-stone walls sweep up to heather moorland and the high Pennine fells, whilst down below, meandering rivers suddenly rush headlong over spectacular waterfalls, only to lose their haste once more as they chatter on at a more respectable pace.
>
> (Anon, nd: 4)

In the last full year of filming there, Esholt was host to over 750,000 visitors (Davidson and Maitland, 1997). Indeed, with *Emmerdale* as possibly the most popular rural television soap across Europe (Sands, 2000), images of Esholt have become absorbed into numerous websites, chat rooms and discussion groups (e.g. *Hem*, 1999; MTV3, 1999).

But Esholt has shared with many other popular media-induced mass tourism attractions a number of location problems resulting from such tourism:

- congestion and carrying capacity problems (e.g. Herbert, 2000);
- excessive merchandising, including the production of cheap, poor quality souvenirs;
- local price inflation;
- demand for natural or man-made elements of the film icon (e.g. Watson-Smyth and Garner, 1999) to the point of theft and vandalism;
- imitative behaviour (even attempted and successful suicide has been identified: Riley *et al.*, 1998; Willan, 2000); and
- the development of multiple websites which can depict confusing and possibly contradictory images of a rural location.

Perceived invasion of privacy, disruption to normal life and the projection of a local image to which they do not subscribe, may be just some of the factors generating opposition to, or at least disaffection with, such development from local residents. Yet the interrelationship of media popularity and place promotion is likely to increase because:

- the visual medium appears to be more influential on current and doubtless future generations;
- various levels of government are pursuing film production companies with increasing vigour in order to have films located within their territory; and
- demand for rural areas which have

retained their traditional images are likely to increase rather than lessen (Butler, 1998: 221).

The challenge for policy-makers and resource managers is perhaps threefold, in that such locations need to develop additional attractions and strategies to: (i) extend the stay of visitors; (ii) enhance the spending potential of visitors; and (iii) compensate for the eventual decline of media-related attractions (although this may not apply to those soaps which continue indefinitely).

Rural Tourism and Heritage: the Re-imaging of Central and Eastern Europe

The societies of Central and Eastern Europe (CEE) contain many and diverse rural cultures which present myriad opportunities for small-scale, high income, locally controlled tourism generation. The negative impacts of political and economic change have often been significant in the region's rural areas. But with a spatially and structurally dynamic mix of mass and specialist markets to target, there are increasing opportunities for rural attractions to act as a basic resource for tourism organized and sustained through locally owned small enterprises.

The re-imaging of CEE's rural areas, arising out of a commodification of the countryside and restructuring processes (Gannon, 1994), has witnessed in the past decade rural and nature tourism receiving substantial promotion, with professional marketing undertaken by local and central government, NGOs and private sectors. For example, Poland moved to promoting itself as a 'natural' destination; tourism literature became notably special interest-oriented (e.g. Witak and Lewandowska, 1996) and emphasized a spatially redistributive dimension. Croatia, while still dependent on the role of its long coastline (Croatia National Tourist Board, 1998), has been looking to its interior to promote nature- and culture-based tourism (Meler and Ruzic, 1999). Slovenia explicitly reconfigured its tourism emphasis with 'The green piece of Europe' branding in 1996, and subsequently adopted an explicit fivefold product segmentation policy (Hall, 1999). In 1995 the Romanian Ministry of Tourism identified rural tourism as a major growth area (Light and Andone, 1996).

In a region with a diversity of cultures and histories, 'heritage' tourism can generate income and employment for both rural and urban areas. Of course, the irony, if not paradox, of employing the past as an element of restructuring for the future, particularly for newly independent states drawing on their pre-communist semi-colonial heritage, has been long debated (e.g. Hewison, 1987). 'Heritage' is clearly far from being a value-free concept: economic power and politics influence what is preserved and how it is interpreted (Chance, 1994; Lowenthal, 1997). Promotion of rural and urban heritage as an integral element of cultural history, was characteristic of the communist period (and earlier). Under the communists, however, such heritage promotion as the development of open-air 'village museums' (e.g. Focşa, 1970) tended not to be primarily for international tourism purposes but was meant to inculcate a sense of identity and pride among each country's own citizens. In contrast, places of pilgrimage, such as the Roman Catholic shrine to the Black Madonna at Częstochówa in southern Poland and the Hercegovinian village of Medjugorje, site of the now somewhat discredited recurrent apparition of the Virgin (Vukonić, 1992), were often irritants to the communist authorities and not endorsed as visitor attractions.

Almost conversely, the legacy of communism itself has become an aspect of heritage and has attracted international tourism interest. However, as Light (2000a,b) argues, this is a heritage which is defined and constructed largely outside of CEE. Within the respective countries, he argues, there is often little desire to remember the period of communism. Indeed, the legacy of this period is seen to be strongly dissonant with post-communist aspirations. This is expressed in the apparent lack of interest to intepret the legacy of communism for tourists, and in attempts to deny or remove the period from each country's past and to create a new imagery which is consistent with post-communist identity.

The resurgence of nationalist expression alongside a (re-)creation of new states systems has encouraged some countries to employ the heritage industry as a means of reinforcing national or particular ethnic identity (Burns, 1998; Hall, 1999). The relationship between heritage, tourism and identity has been crucial for a number of particularly newly independent post-communist states in their pursuit of national image building. For some governments of the region the post-communist reinvigoration of a sense of historical perspective and a heightened awareness of nationality has encouraged a manipulation of the rapidly growing heritage industry to reinforce an exclusive national or particular ethnic identity.

For example, in the tourism promotion brochure *Serbia: Landscape Painted from the Heart* (Popesku and Milojević, 1996), the cultural 'landscape' portrayed reveals an exclusive concentration on Serbian/Orthodox tradition. The role of Western assistance is not insignificant, however, as the UK public relations firm Saatchi and Saatchi was instrumental in producing this brochure. Although one-third of the total population of Serbia is (or at least was in 1996) not Serbian, there is no representation of minority ethnic Hungarian or Albanian (or Romanian, Slovak, Croat or Turkish), Catholic or Muslim heritage. By erasing significant minority groups from this particular cultural landscape, the Serbian authorities were implicitly compromising and ideologically challenging the tourist, resurrecting an arena of ethical conflict which was formerly encountered by tourists to much of the communist world (although, ironically, usually not in Yugoslavia), and indeed to other totalitarian regimes. Put simply, international tourism was being employed as an explicit propaganda tool (Hall, 1981) to reinforce the Serbian authorities' ethnocentric conception of national identity. Certainly, the 'otherness' of race, gender, sexuality, age and ableism and their role as determinants of tourism power dimensions (Morgan and Pritchard, 1998; Pritchard and Morgan, 2000) has barely been addressed in the region (although see Hall, 2001).

Indeed, the re-imaging of rural areas in CEE for tourism and economic development purposes raises an array of issues which are now becoming intertwined with national objectives associated with EU accession (Hall and Danta, 2000). The pre-accession requirement for further economic restructuring in rural areas is also generating additional pressures on rural and regional diversification and re-imaging processes.

Chapter Conclusions and Summary

Because the pace of change in rural areas is accelerating, its impacts are felt more strongly. The restructuring processes common to most industrialized countries have wrought significant economic, social and political change in rural areas, of which tourism and recreation development have been both agent and subject.

The shift from rural depopulation to counter-urbanization has been identified together with an associated research focus on the integration of the relations of property and occupation with those of consumption and commodification. The reversal in the trend of rural to urban migration results from a number of influences, perhaps most notably the aspirations of many people to adopt a rural lifestyle. Where this involves the expression of values representative of past rather than present rural milieux, it can result in opposition by newcomers to any form of development that will mar the rural idyll they have achieved for themselves. The receptivity of old and new rural residents to tourism development and, in turn, such communities' attractiveness to tourists in rural areas, adds a further dimension to issues of tourism's social sustainability.

Questions of social exclusion are exacerbated where development reinforces prevailing power relations. Attempts to quantify and map rural well-being are constrained by the concept's relative subjectivity. Rural residents' perceptions of their well-being may be at odds with a generally held view, and further research may establish new indicators with which to measure qualities of rural life.

Subjective, emotional attachments to imagined place and/or community may bear no relation to objective reality yet may influence the ways in which people behave. Representations of rurality, even those known to be false, may actively structure rural spaces. The demand for pretty villages or the construction and commodification of cultural associations act to shape the appearance of rural settlements in order to satisfy the needs of visitors. Awareness of such processes needs to be raised as part of development processes.

This chapter has viewed the rural context for recreational and tourism experiences in largely social, cultural and economic terms. It has attempted to provide:

- an examination of the dynamic rural social and economic context within which increasing demands for recreation and tourism are taking place;
- an evaluation of the social and cultural impacts that such demands are imposing on rural areas;
- an assessment of the changing nature of recreation and tourism in rural areas and the potential conflicts which may exist between these activities; and
- an understanding of the social construction, myth and commodification that rural areas are subject to as part of the tourism and recreation development process.

Chapter 3 embeds these social, cultural and economic issues within a wider environmental and global context in addressing the concept, appropriateness and implications of sustainability for recreation and tourism processes in rural areas.

References

Anderson, A. (1995) Organised crime, mafia and governments. In: Fiorentini, G. and Peltzman, S. (eds) *The Economics of Organised Crime.* Cambridge University Press, Cambridge, pp. 33–60.

Anon (2000) Neo-ruralites bring relief. *LEADER Magazine* 22, 18–22. http://www.rural-europe.aeidl.be/rural-en/biblio/pop/contents.htm

Anon (nd) *Inside Emmerdale.* Yorkshire Television, Leeds.

Boissevain, J. (ed.) (1996) *Coping with Tourists.* Berghahn, Oxford.

Bolton, N. and Chalkley, B. (1990) The population turnaround: a case study of North Devon. *Journal of Rural Studies* 6(1), 29–43.

Bramwell, B. (1994) Rural tourism and sustainable rural tourism. *Journal of Sustainable Tourism* 2(1–2), 1–6.

Brown, D. (2000) Not so Merrie England. *The Guardian* 15 June. http://www.guardianunlimited.co.uk/country/article/0,2763,332466,00.html

Bruce, D. (1996) *Scotland the Movie.* Polygon, Edinburgh.

BTA (British Tourist Authority) (1999) *Movie Map.* BTA, London. http://www.visitbritain.com/moviemap/moviemap.htm

Bull, A. (1995) *The Economics of Travel and Tourism.* Longman, Melbourne.

Buller, H. and Hoggart, K. (1994) The social integration of British home owners into French rural communities. *Journal of Rural Studies* 10(2), 197–210.

Buncombe, A. (1999) TV locations to star in UK tourism push. *The Independent* 27 February.

Burgess, C. (ed.) (1992) *Welcome to Summer Wine Country.* Huddersfield District Newspapers, Holmfirth.

Burns, P.M. (1998) Tourism in Russia. *Tourism Management* 19(6), 555–565.

Butler, R. (1990) The influence of the media in shaping international tourist patterns. *Tourism Recreation Research* 15(2), 46–55.

Butler, R. (1998) Rural recreation and tourism. In: Ilbery, B. (ed.) *The Geography of Rural Change.* Addison Wesley Longman, Harlow, pp. 211–232.

Butler, R.W. and Hall, C.M. (1998a) Image and reimaging of rural areas. In: Butler, R., Hall, C.M. and Jenkins, J. (eds) *Tourism and Recreation in Rural Areas.* John Wiley & Sons, Chichester, pp. 115–122.

Butler, R.W. and Hall, C.M. (1998b) Tourism and recreation in rural areas: myth and reality. In: Hall, D. and O'Hanlon, L. (eds) *Rural Tourism Management: Sustainable Options.* The Scottish Agricultural College, Auchincruive, pp. 97–108.

Butler, R., Hall, C.M. and Jenkins, J. (1998) Introduction. In: Butler, R., Hall, C.M. and Jenkins, J. (eds) *Tourism and Recreation in Rural Areas.* John Wiley & Sons, Chichester, pp. 3–16.

Carruthers, P. (2000) *Indicators of Rural Disadvantage.* The Countryside Agency, Cheltenham.

Champion, T. and Watkins, C. (eds) (1991) *People in the Countryside: Studies of Social Change in Rural Britain.* Paul Chapman, London.

Chance, S. (1994) The politics of restoration: the tension between conservation and tourism in Samarkand and Bukhara. *Architectural Review* 196(1172), 80–83.

Cloke, P. (1992) The countryside: development, conservation and an increasingly marketable commodity. In: Cloke, P. (ed.) *Policy and Change in Thatcher's Britain.* Pergamon Press, Oxford, pp. 269–295.

Cloke, P., Phillips, M. and Rankin, D. (1991) Middle-class housing choice: channels of entry into Gower, South Wales. In: Champion, T. and Watkins, C. (eds) *People in the Countryside: Studies of Social Change in Rural Britain.* Paul Chapman, London, pp. 38–52.

Cohen, E. (1988) Authenticity and commoditisation in tourism. *Annals of Tourism Research* 15(3), 371–386.

Coppock, J. (1977) *Second Homes: Curse or Blessing?* Pergamon Press, Oxford.

Copus, A.K. and Crabtree, J.R. (1992) Mapping economic fragility: an assessment of the Objective 5b boundaries in Scotland. *Journal of Rural Studies* 8(3), 309–322.

Copus, A.K. and Petri, S. (1999) Pre-school education in rural Scotland. Working paper, University of Aberdeen/Scottish Agricultural College, Aberdeen.

Council of Europe (1996) *Recommendation 1296 (1996) on a European Charter for Rural Areas.* Council of Europe, Strasbourg. http://stars.coe.fr/ta/ta96/erec1296.htm

The Countryside Agency (2000) *Social Exclusion.* The Countryside Agency, Cheltenham, UK. http://www.countryside.gov.uk/activities/rural/socialexclusion

Countryside Alliance (1998) *The Alliance: Manifesto.* Countryside Alliance. http://www.countryside-alliance.org/alliance/brochure.htm

Croatia National Tourist Board (1998) *Come to Croatia the Coast is Clear.* Croatia National Tourist Board, Zagreb. http://www.htz.hr/eng/home/info1.htm

Davidson, R. and Maitland, R. (1997) *Tourist Destinations.* Hodder and Stoughton, London.

Dewailly, J.-M. (1998) Images of heritage in rural regions. In: Butler, R., Hall, C.M. and Jenkins, J. (eds) *Tourism and Recreation in Rural Areas.* John Wiley & Sons, Chichester, pp. 123–137.

Durrell, L. (1969) Landscape and character. In: Thomas, A.G. (ed.) *Spirit of Place: Letters and Essays on Travel: Lawrence Durrell.* Faber and Faber, London, pp. 156–163.

Edmunds, M. (1999) Rural tourism in Europe. *Travel and Tourism Analyst* 6, 37–50.

Edwards, J., Fernandes, C., Fox, J. and Vaughan, R. (2000) Tourism brand attributes of the Alto Minho, Portugal. In: Richards, G. and Hall, D. (eds) *Tourism and Sustainable Community Development.* Routledge, London, pp. 285–296.

Farm Holiday Bureau (FHB) (1996) *Stay on a Farm in Herefordshire.* FHB, Hereford.

Fees, C. (1996) Tourism and the politics of authenticity in a North Cotswold town. In: Selwyn, T. (ed.) *The Tourist Image: Myth and Myth Making in Tourism.* John Wiley & Sons, Chichester, pp. 121–146.

Focşa, G. (1970) *Muzeul Satului din Bucureşti.* Meridiane, Bucharest.

Frisby, T. (1998) The rise of organised crime in Russia: its roots and social significance. *Europe-Asia Studies* 50(1), 27–49.

Gannon, A. (1994) Rural tourism as a factor in rural community economic development for economies in transition. *Journal of Sustainable Tourism* 2(1–2), 51–60.

Grabher, G. and Stark, D. (eds) (1997) *Restructuring Networks in Post-Socialism: Legacies, Linkages and Localities.* Oxford University Press, Oxford.

Halfacree, K. (1993) Locality and social representation: space, discourse and alternative definitions of the rural. *Journal of Rural Studies* 9, 23–37.

Hall, D.R. (1981) A geographical approach to propaganda. In: Burnett, A.D. and Taylor, P.J. (eds) *Political Studies from Spatial Perspectives.* John Wiley & Sons, Chichester, pp. 313–330.

Hall, D.R. (ed.) (1991) *Tourism and Economic Development in Eastern Europe and the Soviet Union.* Belhaven, London.

Hall, D.R. (1998) Central and Eastern Europe. In: Williams, A.M. and Shaw, G. (eds) *Tourism and Economic Development in Europe.* John Wiley & Sons, Chichester, pp. 345–373.

Hall, D.R. (1999) Destination branding, niche marketing and national image projection in Central and Eastern Europe. *Journal of Vacation Marketing* 5(3), 227–237.

Hall, D.R. (2001) Central and Eastern Europe. In: Apostopoulos, Y., Sonmez, S.F. and Timothy, D. (eds) *Women as Producers and Consumers of Tourism in Developing Regions.* Greenwood, Westport, Connecticut.

Hall, D. and Danta, D. (eds) (2000) *Europe Goes East: EU Enlargement, Diversity and Uncertainty*. The Stationery Office, London.

Hannell, T., Petri, S. and Copus, A.K. (2000) Mapping patterns of economic vitality in the northern periphery area. Working paper of MILIEUX Northern Periphery Programme Project, Aberdeen. http://www.nordregio.se/stats/milieux/stat_map_report.PDF

Harrison, C. (1991) *Countryside Recreation in a Changing Society*. TML Partnership, London.

Hart, C. (2000) All farmed out. *The Guardian* 12 August. http://www.guardianunlimited.co.uk/country/article/0,2763,353398,00.html

Hayward, A. (1997) *The Emmerdale Companion*. Yorkshire Television, Leeds.

Hayward, A. and Brabbs, D. (1998) *Emmerdale: Behind the Scenes*. Yorkshire Television, Leeds.

Hem till Gården Emmerdale (1999) Stockholm. http://hem.passagen.se/emerdale(sic)/

Herbert, D. (1996) Artistic and literary places in France as tourist attractions. *Tourism Management* 17(2), 77–86.

Herbert, I. (2000) Villagers in a lather over the invasion of TV soaps. *The Independent* 25 November.

Hetherington, P. (1999) Second homes ban urged in popular country areas. *The Guardian* 11 December. http://www.guardianunlimited.co.uk/country/article/0,2763,191437,00.html

Hewison, R. (1987) *The Heritage Industry: Britain in a Climate of Decline*. Methuen, London.

Howie, F. (2000) Establishing the common ground: tourism, ordinary places, grey areas and environmental quality in Edinburgh, Scotland. In: Richards, G. and Hall, D. (eds) *Tourism and Sustainable Community Development*. Routledge, London, pp. 101–118.

Hudson, R. and Townsend, A. (1992) Tourism employment and policy choices for local government. In: Johnson, P. and Thomas, B. (eds) *Perspectives on Tourism Policy*. Mansell, London, pp. 49–68.

Hummelbrunner, R. and Miglbauer, E. (1994) Tourism promotion and potential in peripheral areas: the Austrian case. *Journal of Sustainable Tourism* 2(1–2), 41–50.

Jenkins, J., Hall, C.M. and Troughton, M. (1998) The restructuring of rural economies: rural tourism and recreation as a government response. In: Butler, R., Hall, C.M. and Jenkins, J. (eds) *Tourism and Recreation in Rural Areas*. John Wiley & Sons, Chichester, pp. 43–67.

Kohn, T. (1997) Island involvement and the evolving tourist. In: Abrams, S., Waldren, J. and Macleod, D.V.L. (eds) *Tourists and Tourism: Identifying with People and Places*. Berg, Oxford, pp. 13–28.

Kotler, P., Haider, D.H. and Rein, I. (1993) *Marketing Places: Attracting Investment, Industry and Tourism to Cities, States and Nations*. The Free Press, New York.

Koulov, B. (1996) Market reforms and environmental protection in the Bulgarian tourism industry. In: Hall, D. and Danta, D. (eds) *Reconstructing the Balkans*. John Wiley & Sons, Chichester, pp. 187–196.

Light, D. (2000a) An unwanted past: contemporary tourism and the heritage of communism in Romania. *International Journal of Heritage Studies* 6(2), 145–160.

Light, D. (2000b) Gazing on communism: heritage tourism and post-communist identities in Germany, Hungary and Romania. *Tourism Geographies* 2(2), 157–176.

Light, D. and Andone, D. (1996) The changing geography of Romanian tourism. *Geography* 81(3), 193–203.

Linz, J. and Stepan, A. (1996) *Problems of Democratic Transition and Consolidation*. Johns Hopkins University Press, Baltimore, Maryland.

Lister, D. (2000) Villages vie to be real home of 'Under Milk Wood'. *The Independent* 8 January.

Lowenthal, D. (1997) *The Heritage Crusade*. Viking, London.

MacCannell, D. (1976) *The Tourist: a New Theory of the Leisure Class*. Macmillan, London.

McCubbin, S. (1999) Scotland the movie playing to full houses in the film industry. *Scotland on Sunday* 1 August.

Martin, D. (1991) *Geographic Information Systems and their Socioeconomic Applications*. Routledge, London.

Meler, M. and Ruzic, D. (1999) Marketing identity of the tourist product of the Republic of Croatia. *Tourism Management* 20, 635–643.

Middleton, V.T.C. (1982) Tourism in rural areas. *Tourism Management* 3(10), 85–99.

Morgan, N. and Pritchard, A. (1998) *Tourism, Promotion and Power: Creating Images, Creating Identities*. John Wiley & Sons, Chichester.

MTV3 (1999) *MTV3 Internet – Emmerdale*. MTV3, Helsinki. http://scully.mtv3.fi/msc/page-emmerdale/

Murdoch, J. and Pratt, A. (1993) Rural studies: modernism, postmodernism and the 'post-rural'. *Journal of Rural Studies* 9, 411–427.

Noble, M., Penhale, B., Smith, G., Wright, G. and Owen, P. (1999) Measuring multiple deprivation at the local level. Index99 project working paper, Oxford University, Oxford. http:/index99.apsoc.ox.ac.uk

Noble, M., Penhale, B., Smith, G., Wright, G. and Owen, P. (2000) Index of deprivation 1999 review, final consultation, report for formal consultation, stage 1: domains and indicators. Index99 project working paper, Oxford University, Oxford. http:/index99.apsoc.ox.ac.uk

Openshaw, S. (1984) Ecological fallacies and the analysis of areal census data. *Environment and Planning* A 16, 17–31.

Pearce, P.L. (ed.) (1995) The visiting friends and relatives market. *Journal of Tourism Studies* 6 (special edition).

Phillips, R. (1996) Communism strikes back: cultural blockages on the road to reform in the post-Soviet tourism sector. In: Robinson, M., Evans, N. and Callaghan, P. (eds) *Tourism and Culture: Image, Identity and Marketing*. Business Education Publishers, Sunderland, pp. 147–164.

Popesku, J. and Milojević, L. (1996) *Serbia: Landscape Painted from the Heart*. National Tourism Organization of Serbia, Belgrade.

Pritchard, A. and Morgan, N. (2000) Constructing tourism landscapes – gender, sexuality and space. *Tourism Geographies* 2(2), 115–139.

Pym, J. (1995) *Merchant Ivory's English Landscape: Rooms, Views and Anglo-Saxon Attitudes*. Abrams, New York.

Richards, G. and Hall, D. (2000) The community: a sustainable concept in tourism development? In: Richards, G. and Hall, D. (eds) *Tourism and Sustainable Community Development*. Routledge, London, pp. 1–14.

Riley, R. (1994) Movie induced tourism. In: Seaton, A.V. (ed.) *Tourism: State of the Art*. John Wiley & Sons, Chichester, pp. 453–458.

Riley, R. and van Doren, C. (1992) Movies as tourism promotion: a push factor in a pull location. *Tourism Management* 13(3), 267–274.

Riley, R., Baker, D. and Van Doren, C.S. (1998) Movie induced tourism. *Annals of Tourism Research* 23(4), 919–935.

Riley, R.C. (2000) Embeddedness and the tourism industry in the Polish Southern Uplands: social processes as an explanatory framework. *European Urban and Regional Studies* 7(3), 195–210.

Rural Development Commission (1992) *Review of Rural Development Commission's Priority Areas*. Rural Deelopment Commission, London.

Sadler, D. (1993) Place-marketing, competitive places and the construction of hegemony in Britain in the 1980s. In: Kearns, G. and Philo, C. (eds) *Selling Places: the City as Cultural Capital, Past and Present*. Pergamon, Oxford, pp. 175–192.

Sands, B. (2000) *Emmerdale Net*. http://www.emmerdale.clara.net/visit.htm

Scottish Office (1992) *Scottish Rural Life*. HMSO, Edinburgh.

Scottish Office (1996) *Scottish Rural Life Update*. HMSO, Edinburgh.

Seaton, A.V. and Palmer, C. (1997) Understanding VFR tourism behaviour: the first five years of the United Kingdom Tourism Survey. *Tourism Management* 18(6), 345–355.

Sharpley, R. and Sharpley, J. (1997) *Rural Tourism. An Introduction*. International Thomson Business Press, London.

Short, J. (1991) *Imagined Country*. Routledge, London.

Shucksmith, M. and Philip, L. (2000) *Social Exclusion in Rural Areas: a Literature Review and Conceptual Framework*. Scottish Executive Central Research Unit, Edinburgh.

Silver, I. (1993) Marketing authenticity in Third World countries. *Annals of Tourism Research* 20(2), 303–318.

Sinclair, D. (1990) *Shades of Green: Myth and Muddle in the Countryside*. Paladin, London.

Sørensen, A. and Nilsson, P.Å. (1999) Virtual rurality versus rural reality in rural tourism – contemplating the attraction of the rural. *8th Nordic Symposium in Hospitality and Tourism Research, 18–21 November, Alta, Norway*.

Squire, S.J. (1994) Accounting for cultural meanings: the interface between geography and tourism studies revisited. *Progress in Human Geography* 18, 1–16.

Stabler, J. (1993) Rural community rationalization. In: *Towards a Whole Rural Policy for Canada*. ARRG Working Paper 7, Rural Development Institute, Brandon, Manitoba.

Stark, D. and Bruszt, L. (1998) *Postsocialist Pathways*. Cambridge University Press, Cambridge.

STB (Scottish Tourist Board) (1995) *'Braveheart' and 'Rob Roy' Film Impact Analysis*. Scottish Tourist Board, Edinburgh.

Tooke, N. and Baker, M. (1996) Seeing is believing. The effect of film on visitor numbers in screened locations. *Tourism Management* 17(2), 87–94.

Tzamarias, N. (1994) Microtypology of rural desertification in Scotland. Working Paper 17 of EU AIR3 – CT94 – 1545 (The Impact of Public Institutions on Lagging Rural and Coastal Areas), The Scottish Agricultural College, Aberdeen.

Urry, J. (1988) Cultural change and contemporary holidaymaking. *Theory, Culture and Society* 5, 35–55.

Urry, J. (1991) The sociology of tourism. In: Cooper, C.P. (ed.) *Progress in Tourism, Recreation and Hospitality Management*, Volume 3. Belhaven, London, pp. 48–57.

Vukonić, B. (1992) Medjugorje's religion and tourism connection. *Annals of Tourism Research* 19(1), 79–91.

Watson-Smyth, K. and Garner, C. (1999) Location groupies force sale of the UK's second most famous front door. *The Independent* 17 November.

Willan, P. (2000) Death in Venice is big tourist attraction. *The Guardian* 20 November. http://www.guardianunlimited.co.uk/Archiv/Article/0,4273,4093385,00.html

Witak, A. and Lewandowska, U. (eds) (1996) *Poland: the Natural Choice*. Sport i Turystyka, Warsaw.

3

The 'S' Word

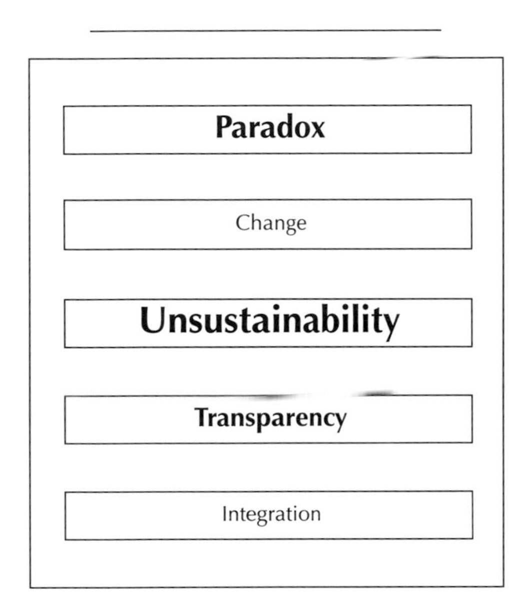

> The modern forms of mass travel and tourism can be among the most powerful forces our industrialised society has developed – capable of enriching our lives, yet at the same time of degrading and deforming them.
>
> (Neale, 1998: xviii)

The central theme of this chapter is *unsustainability*, not least of the notion of sustainable tourism itself. It is directly addressed through an examination of the nature and impacts of tourism transport in rural areas, and laterally through a critique of the concept of sustainability for rural tourism. *Paradox* is thus manifested: implicitly, through the unsustainability of the sustainability concept, and its promotion within tourism development to help sustain unsustainable rural economies; and explicitly by highlighting the employment of environmentally degrading transport forms by 'green' and 'ecotourists'. Also, paradoxically, while it is clear that there is a pressing need for *transparency* in the employment of sustainability terminology, the use and misapplication of such concepts remains obfuscatory.

Building on the previous chapter's evaluation of the social, cultural and economic dimensions of tourism and recreation in rural areas, this chapter has four key objectives. These are to:

1. Trace the emergence of 'sustainability' as a key concept in the development debate;
2. Briefly examine the interaction of the social, economic and environmental dimensions of recreation and tourism development in rural areas, and the need for a holistic approach to their management in the face of a perceived 'implementation gap' in sustainability ideals;
3. Provide a critique of such sustainability ideals and of the obfuscation surrounding notions of sustainability in relation to tourism development; and
4. Examine some of the paradoxes of sustainability debates by focusing on the problem of tourism transport in rural areas.

The Concept of Sustainability

As a much-debated global policy issue, the essence of sustainable development, drawing upon holistic ecological concepts, is that economic development is dependent on the sustained well-being of the physical and social environment on which it is based (Barbier, 1987; Redclift, 1987; Butler, 1991). Three key publications have been crucial in the promotion of the concept of sustainability in development processes. First, the World Conservation Strategy (WCS) (Box 3.1), launched in March 1980 (IUCN, 1980), promoted the adoption of sustainability measures in the face of a wide range of pressing global environmental problems. The concept of sustainable development was enshrined in this strategy for the conservation of the Earth's living resources, and it highlighted the crucial relationship between economic development and the conservation and sustenance of those resources. Although not an international treaty, government agencies from over 100 countries participated in its preparation.

Second, the report of the World Commission on Environment and Development (WCED) (1987) (chaired by the Norwegian Prime Minister Gro Harlem Brundtland and usually referred to as the Brundtland Report), firmly established the concept and practice of sustainable development in the policy arena in order to 'make development sustainable to ensure that it meets the needs of the present without compromising the ability of future generations to meet their own needs' (WCED, 1987: 43). Five key principles of sustainability were identified (Box 3.2).

Third, the World Conservation Union's *Caring for the Earth* carried the sustainability debate forward and slightly shifted the emphasis of sustainable development to 'Improving the quality of life while living within the carrying capacity of supporting ecosystems' (IUCN, 1991: 10).

None the less, the focus of sustainable development remains centred around:

- concern for the long-term health and integrity of the global environment in its widest, holistic sense;
- meeting present and future needs; and
- improving the quality of life for current and future generations.

Its ethos should be the fulcrum around which policies for economic, social, cultural and ecological development interact and synergize, to ensure that economic development at all levels is contained within socio-cultural and ecological limits.

Box 3.1. World Conservation Strategy objectives (sources: IUCN, 1980; Butler and Hall, 1998).

To maintain essential ecological processes and life-support systems (such as soil regeneration and protection, the recycling of nutrients and the cleansing of waters), on which human survival and development depend

To preserve genetic diversity (the range of genetic material found in the world's organisms), on which depend the breeding programmes necessary for the protection and improvement of cultivated plants and domesticated animals, as well as much scientific advance, technical innovation and the security of the many industries that use living resources

To ensure the sustainable use of species and ecosystems (notably fish and other wildlife, forest and grazing lands), which support millions of rural communities as well as major industries

Box 3.2. World Commission on Environment and Development basic principles (sources: WCED, 1987; Bramwell and Lane, 1993; Butler and Hall, 1998).

Holistic planning and strategy-making
Preservation of essential ecological processes
Protection of both human heritage and biodiversity
Development embracing productivity which can be sustained over the long term for future generations
Achievement of a better balance of fairness and opportunity between nations

Sustainability and the Rural Dimension

Notions of sustainable development influence a range of policy actions, not least rural policy (e.g. Murdoch, 1993). Unfortunately, the holistic ethos of sustainability has often been lost sight of as applications of sustainability have tended to be focused on either: individual components of rurality, such as the sustainability of agriculture; or relating development to considerations of the 'natural' environment in relative isolation; rather than taking an integrated approach to the interdependence of socio-cultural, economic and ecological elements of rurality. Yet sustainability, as indicated above, must, by definition, be approached in a holistic manner.

In the case of rural change through the growth of monocultural agribusiness, for example, an evaluation of sustainability cannot simply restrict itself to an evaluation of the loss of wildlife variety and habitat or the diminution of access in rural areas through the removal of long-established footpaths. It also needs to embrace an evaluation of the impact on local employment through the introduction of scale 'efficiencies' and technology application, and with that likely employment reduction and analysis of the consequent loss of local income and of the local services it might otherwise sustain.

Key Issues for Tourism and Recreation and Rural Sustainability

As rural communities are seen to be increasingly incapable of being sustainable without a diverse economic base, so tourism and recreation have been viewed, and adopted, as an integral component in the diversification of that base. Yet, the sustainability of tourism for rural areas appears to have been rarely considered until relatively recently. This, at least partly, reflects the assumption made by policy-makers, planners and academics that the apparently contradictory aims of economic, social and ecological development can be easily reconciled (Curry, 1992); that rural tourism is compatible with sustainable development principles; this assumption has tended to underscore the way in which many policy-makers have encouraged tourism development for rural and 'natural' areas. Yet several commentators have identified a significant 'implementation gap' (Wheeller, 1993; Butler and Hall, 1998) between the policy ideal and its application. This often reflects the fact that policy-makers may regard tourism development in isolation from the other components providing the social, economic and ecological contexts for rural development processes.

For example, in areas experiencing counter-urbanization (Chapter 2), incomers are more likely to have conservation and environmental concerns and will be less attuned to the changing physical needs of either the local agrarian economy or mass recreation. Yet conventional wisdom (e.g. Pretty, 1995; Joppe, 1996; Pearce *et al.*, 1996) tells us that it is essential for local populations' interests to be taken into consideration when tourism development takes place, and for members of the host 'community' to have a participative role in the decisions leading to that development (see also Chapter 5).

In the case of heritage trails, for example (e.g. Bartis, 1998; see also Chapter 7), it would appear to be important that local people have a vested interest in the sustainability of developments in order that future generations may benefit from that heritage consumption. Yet this raises questions about contested heritage, how it is defined and 'constructed'. Further, the potential conflicts between 'new' and 'traditional' forms of tourism and recreation competing for the same recreational space and environmental attributes but in functionally different ways – for example landscape viewing and rally motorcycling – may be considerable.

It is thus necessary for tourism to be appropriately embedded within the particular set of linkages and relationships which make up the components of rurality (see Chapter 7) and contribute to rural development. As a holistic discipline, sustainable rural development must embrace tourism and recreation as but one component of the policy mix for development; while tourism and recreation in turn must complement the multiplicity of other rural components' uses, needs and demands in order for it to be regarded as appropriate and a potential contributor to sustainability.

A number of preconditions are required to help this to be achieved (Butler and Hall, 1998):

- Analysis of rural areas prior to the introduction or expansion of tourism entailing careful consideration of the economic, social and ecological 'fit' of tourism with existing linkages and relationships in order to ensure that the full range of development objectives can be met.
- A detailed consideration of such factors as opportunity cost and cumulative effects.
- Implementation of a comprehensive monitoring programme employing sustainability indicators.
- The maintenance of an economically viable rural population which is engaged in 'rural' activities, sustaining rural culture and identity. Care is needed in avoiding the 'freezing' of employment opportunities and rural living standards, otherwise out-migration, especially of the young, is likely to result.
- Policy formulation needs to recognize and take into account that tourism both affects and is affected by contemporary rurality.
- The visual complexity of the rural landscape, and the subsequent visual fulfilment of rural images and myths, generates amenity values for locals and visitors alike. An integrated approach to development of this rural resource is therefore essential.
- All actors need to be convinced that a sustainable approach is in their economic interests.
- Understanding the social and political constructions of the rural must therefore become an integral part of sustainable rural tourism. A major contradiction of rural tourism is that much of its popularity appears to be based on images of an unchanging, simpler and problem-free countryside when the reality has been one of variable and often rapid change.

Unsustaining Tourism?

Although sustainability of tourism activity is a much discussed concept (e.g. Tourism Concern and WWF, 1992; Wheeller, 1993; Bramwell, 1994; Cater and Lowman, 1994; Lane, 1994; Murphy, 1994; Coccossis and Nijkamp, 1995; Bramwell *et al.*, 1996; Coccossis, 1996; France, 1997; Mowforth and Munt, 1998; Swarbrooke, 1999), the paradoxes inherent in notions of 'sustainable tourism', not least for rural areas, and in its relationship with sustainable development, clearly require further critical reflection. In the management of rural development, if sustainability is to be meaningful, policy concerns for tourism and recreation should embrace ethical and welfare considerations (Hall and Brown, 1996). Continually, questions such as the following should be posed:

- Should rural tourism be encouraged if it leads to increased social and economic inequality in rural communities?
- How appropriate is it to propagate rural tourism initiatives if the majority of the benefit is received by urban communities?
- How much adverse landscape and environmental change as a result of rural tourism is acceptable?

(Unwin, 1998)

The following short critique by Richard Sharpley provides a succinct comment on the contradictions of 'sustainable tourism', yet also emphasizes the positive opportunities tourism can bring to rural development.

Transport, Tourism and Unsustainability

Chapters 6–8 of this book follow Sharpley's advice in recognizing and evaluating the value and importance of different tourist markets. None the less, different tastes and forms of consumption, particularly in economically developed societies, are facilitated by an increasing tendency for tourists and recreationalists to adopt apparently unsustainable practices in their travel behaviour to (and possibly in) rural areas: the use of the motor car (and aircraft).

Overall, transport within rural areas represents at least two dimensions of unsustainability.

Invited Viewpoint

Sustainable Rural Tourism Development: Ideal or Idyll?

Richard Sharpley

Since the early 1990s, the concept of sustainable tourism development has achieved almost universal acceptance as a desirable and (politically) appropriate approach to, and goal of, tourism development. At the global, national and local levels, innumerable organizations representing destinations and industry sectors have published sustainable tourism development plans and sets of principles, while tourists themselves have been increasingly exhorted to behave responsibly; to become 'good' tourists. In the rural context in particular, sustainability has evolved as the guiding principle of tourism development. Indeed, the terms 'rural tourism' and 'sustainable tourism' have become virtually synonymous, reflecting the intimate and mutually dependent relationship between tourism and the rural environments and cultures within which it occurs (Bramwell and Lane, 1993).

However, despite the widespread support for the principles and objectives of sustainable tourism development, it remains a contested concept. Not only is it variously interpreted (Hunter, 1995), but also its validity as a means and objective of tourism development is being increasingly questioned in many quarters. In a general sense this is not surprising, given the fact that sustainable tourism's 'parental' paradigm, sustainable development, is itself inherently contradictory and the subject of intense debate (Redclift, 1987). More specifically, it is logical to assume that sustainable tourism should conform with the basic principles and objectives of sustainable development. However, until recently there has been a consistent failure to 'fit' tourism, as a particular socio-economic activity and widely utilized development vehicle, on to the sustainable development template. To do so reveals a number of significant distinctions between the two, suggesting that 'true' sustainable tourism development – that is, the achievement of sustainable development through tourism – is not a viable proposition.

A complete consideration of the issues is not possible here (see Sharpley, 2000). Essentially, however, the concept of sustainable development embraces certain principles and requirements which cannot be fulfilled through tourism. In particular:

- The adoption of a holistic approach which integrates tourism's developmental and environmental consequences within a global socio-economic and ecological context is impossible given the fragmented, multi-sectoral, private-sector dominated and profit-motivated tourism production system.
- Sustainable development focuses on long-term fair and equal access to resources and opportunities based on self-reliance and endogenous development. However, such inter- and intra-generational equity is unlikely to be achieved through tourism given the structure, ownership and control of the tourism industry which more closely resembles the dependency model of development theory.
- Research has indicated that, in a tourism context, the adoption of a new social paradigm relevant to sustainable living, a fundamental requirement for sustainable development (IUCN, 1991), is unlikely to occur. In other words, the emergence of the 'green' tourist, frequently cited as the justification for promoting sustainable forms of tourism, cannot be taken for granted. For example, the promotion of specific sustainable rural tourism projects in the UK elicited a low level of interest on the part of visitors (Countryside Commission, 1995).

It is for these and other reasons that a dichotomy exists between the general principles and objectives of sustainable development and their application to the specific context of tourism. Whereas sustainable development is concerned with the longer-term equitable and endogenous development of societies based on minimal non-renewable resource depletion (a process to which sustainable tourism development should, in theory, contribute), the principal approach manifested in sustainable tourism policy documents and in practice has, with few exceptions, become 'overly tourism-centric and parochial' (Hunter, 1995). That is, the prime objective of sustainable tourism has become the environmentally sustainable development of tourism itself; the aim has become to preserve the natural, built and socio-cultural resource base on which tourism depends in a specific time and place in order to permit the long-term survival of tourism.

This is, of course, sound business sense; all businesses or industries strive to maintain their resource base for long-term survival and profit. However, the important point here is that the inherent weakness of the sustainable tourism development concept and the consequential focus on sustaining tourism itself has

Continued overleaf

resulted in a value-laden, product-centred approach to tourism development. This is manifested primarily in small-scale, environmentally appropriate projects which seek to provide meaningful and rewarding two-way experiences for tourists and local communities. In other words, the concept of sustainable tourism represents a highly prescriptive approach to the development of tourism which requires specific forms of production and consumption which, as suggested above, are largely in opposition to the structure and characteristics of the tourism industry and the demands of tourists themselves.

In short, although tourism development remains wrapped in the politically attractive clothing of sustainable development, its inevitable inward, product-centred focus has, to a great extent, removed the 'development' element of the process. That is, attention is primarily paid to the environmental credentials of tourism development projects. In itself, this cannot be criticized, yet the focus on sustainable tourism development has had a number of important and interrelated implications for the development of tourism in general and rural tourism in particular.

First, there is a need to detach tourism from the concept of sustainable development. That is, the vogue for sustainable tourism development has diverted attention away from the fact that other forms of tourism development have made, and continue to make, a significant contribution to socio-economic development in destination areas. That contribution is primarily made through the creation of income and employment opportunities, with subsequent linkages to other sectors of the economy, such as construction, transport services and food production. In other words, in development theory terms, tourism development most closely reflects the traditional economic growth-based modernization process, with tourism acting as a 'growth-pole' from which economic and developmental benefits diffuse outwards. This is most certainly the case in many well-known 'mass' tourism destinations (for example, Spain and Cyprus), while tourism's development potential in rural areas is primarily manifested in its contribution to economic growth and diversification; the creation of new jobs/businesses or farm diversification and pluriactivity. Indeed, rural tourism development has been driven by the need for economic growth and diversification and it is important, therefore, that tourism's potential contribution to rural economic growth is not diluted by the over-specificity of the principles of sustainable tourism.

Second, an inherent paradox of sustainable (tourism) development is that, although one of its fundamental principles is local community involvement and control, the nature of development is highly prescribed. In particular, the product-centric focus of sustainable rural tourism and guided sets of principles, such as the early *Principles for Tourism in the Countryside* in the UK (Countryside Commission/ETB, 1989), do not, in effect, permit local communities to decide what form of tourism development is suitable for them. Different rural areas and communities have different social and economic needs, and different resources and attractions. There is a need, therefore, to recognize the appropriateness to local needs of different forms of tourism or tourism development (albeit within environmental parameters). For example, locally owned, small-scale projects may be suited to some rural communities, but for others, particularly with high levels of unemployment, larger-scale, non-traditional developments such as inland resorts or time-share developments may make a greater contribution to the local economy.

Third and finally, the primarily product-centred focus of sustainable tourism has also diverted attention from the fact that tourism is, essentially, a business. Its customers are tourists who, even within the specific context of rural tourism, seek an enormous variety of experiences. Some may participate in 'traditional' rural recreational pursuits; for others, the countryside may be an appropriate setting for particular sporting activities; while yet others may seek experiences according to their family or other characteristics. To put it another way, sustainable tourism limits the potential for development by attempting to adapt the market to a relatively specific product. However, for the contribution of tourism to rural areas to be optimized (again, to the extent that the rural environment is not degraded), the implicitly elitist perspective of sustainable tourism must be replaced by one which recognizes the value and importance of different tourist markets.

Inevitably, addressing the specific issue of sustainable tourism development not only oversimplifies the complexities of effectively managing the multipurpose rural resource, but it also sidesteps relevant contextual debates, such as the extent to which the countryside should be developed or protected. Nevertheless, the central thrust of the argument here is that tourism is playing an increasingly important role in rural development. Quite evidently, tourism development should be, as far as possible, environmentally benign yet, at the same time, there is a need to move beyond the constricting principles of sustainable tourism development. Not only do such principles detract attention from developing tourism according to local needs and opportunities and from the need for effective marketing, but they also limit tourism's fundamental role, its contribution to rural development.

Richard Sharpley

With serious social exclusion implications (Chapter 2), the widespread decline of public transport provision in rural areas reflects a changing rural population, a rapid growth in car ownership levels, a decline in rural retailing and other services, which requires rural dwellers to travel further, changed attitudes over the appropriate role of government in transport provision, and the changed economics of that provision and its implications for passenger convenience:

> The country bus ... had one great attraction. It was there when you wanted it. When the shopping was done you could make your way to the bus – not too far away – and settle into your seat for a gossip until it was time for it to go. Just as the car began to be an alternative, the buses were moved on, and the larger firms, seeking more miles from each bus, tended to reschedule services so that they no longer waited on the stand. Instead the passengers waited, come rain or shine, till it suited the bus to come and pick them up.
>
> (Hibbs, 1986: 144)

Thus was generated the widely held perception that cars are more necessary in rural areas than in cities. A resultant growth in car use in rural areas and its impacts (Box 3.3), clearly contradict idyllic images of tranquillity, open space and fresh air. This is exacerbated by the increasing commuting use of rural areas by urban workers, who may purchase goods and services outside of the resident community, thereby threatening the viability of existing retail and service outlets in such communities (Butler and Hall, 1998).

Secondly, the transport factor alone has the power to demolish tourism's claims of, or aspirations towards, sustainability (e.g. see Box 3.4). At a local level, while only 11% of the UK population lives outside urban areas, at present rates, rural traffic might treble in volume by 2025 (Countryside Commission, 1992). Such growth reflects the transport implications of new forms of rural – particularly activity – tourism:

- the penetration of traffic to more remote rural locations, which are more likely to be isolated from public transport routes;
- the additional greater reliance on private motor transport because of the need to convey such intrinsically bulky items as golf or ski equipment, surfboards, dinghies and hang-gliders (Charlton, 1998); and
- the likelihood of increased congestion, particularly at peak holiday periods, causing greater inconvenience for both rural dwellers and visitors, further exacerbating the problems associated with car use in rural areas.

On a global scale, the increase in air travel for tourism is contributing significantly to climate change and ozone depletion. Yet such is the mode of travel to less developed countries employed by significant numbers of 'green' and 'ecotourists' (Plate 3.1).

Box 3.3. Problems arising from increased car use in rural areas (source: after Sharpley and Sharpley, 1997: 138).

1. A decline in public transport services areas, reducing:
the mobility of rural residents who do not own, or do not wish to use, a car;
the accessibility of the countryside for potential tourists who do not have the use of a car
2. Longer-term negative impacts on flora and fauna from vehicle emissions
3. Visual, aural and atmospheric pollution from congestion and major traffic flows
4. Construction of new roads, or improvement and widening of existing roads, leading to:
loss of natural habitats;
the compromising, damaging or destruction of sites of natural and heritage importance;
the diminution of rural open space
5. Road building generates the development of ancillary infrastructure, such as car parks, lay-bys, roadside restaurants, filling stations and other facilities designed to serve the car-bound traveller
6. Demands for cheaper fuel

These can lead to impacts such as the influence of car park location on concentrating visitors at particular sites, thereby contributing to greater erosion on nearby footpaths, vegetation trampling and littering.

Box 3.4. Car-borne sustainable tourists? (source: Caffyn, 2000).

Following proposals in the report *Tourism and the Scottish Environment: a Sustainable Partnership* (STCG, 1991), a Tourism and Environment Task Force (TETF) was established in Scotland. It published *Going Green* (TETF, 1993), a guide for tourism businesses, and developed a number of Scotland-wide initiatives on issues such as footpaths and caravan sites. A more targeted approach was also developed by establishing a series of area-based tourism management programmes (TMPs). The work of TETF – to promote sustainable use of Scotland's natural and built environment for tourism – was embraced in an updated Scottish Tourism Strategic Plan (STB, 1994; further updated in 2000), which aimed to:

- promote awareness and understanding of the interactions between tourism and the natural and built environment;
- develop a planned approach to tourism development which integrates tourism and environment issues;
- market Scotland as a tourism destination based on the sustainable use of the natural and built environment; and
- promote the adoption of environmentally sensitive practices.

(TETF, 1996: 2)

Although the TMPs have tried to encourage ecologically sound practices among individual businesses, a major weakness has been the lack of an attempt to define sustainability and demonstrate its application (TETF, 1996: 12). As a consequence, apart from a few exceptions, most tourism businesses involved with TMPs have not perceived benefits, and are unlikely to do so until the market for environmentally aware tourism in Scotland is more significant. This perhaps reflects the relatively poor level of environmental awareness and education within the domestic market. Further, greater efforts are required to encourage sustainable activities and forms of transport such as cycling at destination areas.

The fact that 87% of visitors to the Trossachs TMP, for example, arrive by car, and 80% continue to use their cars to travel around the area, undermines the basis of such projects' sustainability ideals.

Plate 3.1. Arrivals at one of South America's most popular nature tourism destinations: the Iguaçu/Iguassu Falls on the border between Brazil and Argentina, both of which have developed international airports nearby to assist access for 'green' tourists.

The motor car: maker and breaker of recreation in rural areas?

Clearly, not all rural areas are subject to the same variety or level of impacts. Much depends on such variables as the physical characteristics and fragility of different areas, the level of recreational use, population densities, the accessibility of rural areas. Nevertheless, the contradiction of the motor car literally providing the vehicle for more and different rural recreation and tourism activities while causing considerable, probably irrevocable, local and global damage in the process, represents paradoxes in that:

- road transport and specifically the motor car is the least suitable form of transport in terms of its impact on the environment and society; it represents one of the greatest threats to the physical and socio-cultural well-being of rural areas, particularly in the more popular rural tourism destinations;
- for the individual traveller the car is one of the cheapest and most convenient and flexible forms of motorized transport;
- for many governments 'provision of adequate road capacity for forecast levels of traffic was seen as the most efficient means of ensuring maximum mobility in the economy' (Docherty, 1999: 18);
- the motor car's external costs to society in terms of energy use, pollution, land use, mortality and health care are virtually incalculable: some 92% of EU external costs of transport derive from road transport, with motor cars accounting for

around 60% (Pearce, 1993; Rothengatter and Mauch, 1994); and

- alternative and more sustainable forms of transport are being sought by rural tourism planners and managers.

There are several management approaches which can be taken to combat problems of motor car use in rural areas (e.g. Mitchell, 1991), the first two of which at least are not sustainable.

Do nothing

First, allowing congestion to act as its own deterrent is the simplest and most negative approach. Yet: congestion is often localized and seasonal; many car drivers may have become conditioned to traffic jams, through generational habituation; and, of course, the wider environmental implications of such an approach are considerable

'Predict and provide'

A second approach is to improve the road network and car park provision. But while building new roads, upgrading existing ones and providing more parking may improve accessibility in the short term, such acts will simply generate even more traffic in a self-perpetuating spiral. Therefore, in many rural areas, such as national parks, the policy is now to implement traffic management schemes that match the level of traffic to the existing road network rather than adapting roads to accommodate greater volumes of traffic.

Indeed, a number of policy instruments are potentially available to restrain motor transport use: restrictive policies, economic incentives/disincentives, policies to influence attitudinal change, integrated land use planning, priority for public transport, support for benign modes, and application of technological innovation (Hall, 1998).

Restrictive policies

The debate on traffic access to, and congestion problems at, rural honeypots such as national parks has a long history (Mulligan, 1979; Eaton and Holding, 1996; Countryside Commission, 1997). In the UK, over half of road traffic growth in rural areas in the 1990s has been leisure-related (Barrett, 1995; Cullinane and Stokes, 1998), with over 90% of visitors to national parks in England and Wales arriving by car (Countryside Commission, 1996b).

Certainly, UK national parks have been active in pursuing traffic management policies (e.g. DoE, 1995; Fewings, 1996; Coleman, 1997), most of which have been of the 'carrot' variety (Cullinane and Cullinane, 1999); although, for example, in experimental schemes in the Derwent Valley of the Peak District National Park, roads have been closed to motorized traffic, and visitors have been encouraged to explore the region on bicycles. Otherwise, relatively little influence appears to have been exerted on modal choice (Eaton and Holding, 1996). The (English) Countryside Agency's concepts of 'greenways' and 'quiet roads' in rural areas (Box 3.5) giving priority to walkers, cyclists and horse-riders (Countryside Commission, 1996a; Countryside Agency, 2000b) seems unlikely to alter this balance. Recognition of, and planning for, sustainable carrying capacities would appear to be an essential element of rural-based strategies (e.g. Ashworth and Larkham, 1994).

Box 3.5. 'Greenways' and 'Quiet roads' (source: Countryside Agency 2000b).

These are two initiatives in England which aim to give better mobility and access for people on foot, bicycle or horseback or for people with disabilities. Since June 1998 there have been eight *Greenways* demonstration areas and two *Quiet roads* demonstration areas.

Greenways: designed for shared use and largely exclude motorized vehicles. They are in and around towns, cities and the countryside

Quiet roads: minor rural roads, already lightly trafficked where extra traffic measures aim to improve their attractiveness for non-motorized users

In the USA, for example, the use of private cars is now banned in Yosemite National Park and visitors are required to use the provided transport system. But generally, such schemes are only viable in managed areas where access may be restricted, and often appear to be unpopular with sufficient proportions of electorates to inhibit support from politicians.

Economic incentives/disincentives

The imposition of taxation and/or economic disincentive measures aims to increase the relative costs of motor travel to represent its true external cost to society, and to encourage changes in land use policy. The advocacy of ecological tax and fiscal impositions has been well argued for some time (e.g. Whitelegg, 1993), but implementation has been limited, for example a carbon-related tax was introduced in Sweden in 1990 and revised upwards in 1994 (Sterner, 1994; Maddison *et al.*, 1996).

In theory, open access to road networks could be rationed through area licensing systems or by employing electronic distance charging. Using roadside monitors, differential rates could be charged according to the time of day and congestion conditions. Precedents exist with differential charging employed on public transport in an attempt to dissuade discretionary travel during peak periods. Much tourist road transport, for example, could potentially be charged out of peak traffic times, given the usually discretionary nature of leisure travel (Hall, 1999), although this is less helpful in addressing honeypot peak periods. Charges for road damage could be related to the distance a vehicle travels, its weight and number of axles; this could apply equally to tourist coaches as to heavy goods vehicles (e.g. see Langmyhr, 1997). From Norwegian experience, it has been argued that as people become conditioned to them, toll systems become easier to deploy both to restrain traffic and to stimulate congestion pricing (Larsen, 1995; Odeck and Brathen, 1997).

Attitudinal and behavioural change

Policies to reduce the negative externalities of transport use need to be aimed at changing attitudes at a number of levels of both public and political awareness. Educational campaigns (Peake, 1994), through targeted information, publicity and community programmes (e.g. INPHORMM, 1998; Pilling and Turner, 1999) need to emphasize the full external effects of travel behaviour. These should encourage acceptance and understanding of the need for change, and to change attitudes towards the use of non-car modes – public transport, cycling and walking – by promoting their positive aspects. This embraces common cause with that dimension of the pursuit of sustainable tourism which argues that tourists need to be ecologically and culturally aware and sensitive in their travel behaviour, and for tourism companies and the global travel industry to adopt philosophies and practices embracing sustainability ideals, as expressed, for example, through codes of conduct (Mason and Mowforth, 1996; Orams, 1997). However, implicit in both but rarely explicitly expressed, and never by the tourism industry, is the environmentally beneficial effect that less travel would bring. Quite clearly, (leisure) travel exerts substantial externality effects at a global level, as witnessed by increasing concern over the growth and impact of international air travel. But in the UK alone, motor vehicle emissions account for over 17% of carbon dioxide, 45% of nitrogen oxides and 85% of carbon monoxide (Transport 2000, 1987). As carbon dioxide emissions represent about half of the greenhouse gases claimed to be influencing climate change, the global environmental impact of road transport therefore appears significant, and is likely to become more so. Yet thus far just 8% of the world's population owns a car; the potential growth in ownership and in the consequential environmental impacts is enormous (Sharpley and Sharpley, 1997: 137). In an era of increasing leisure time and longer-distance travel, when freedom to travel is equated with democracy and human rights, restrictions on travel are politically difficult even to contemplate. Yet ever-increasing mobility may require some future global imposition on 'unnecessary' travel, involving rationing and mandatory alternatives to spatial mobility, such as virtual reality travel and tourism (Brown, 1998: 123–124).

Supporting public transport

The development and promotion of an efficient, cheap and integrated public transport system is considered by many to be the only realistic means of overcoming the problems of transport to and within the countryside. Indeed, cycling and walking notwithstanding (see below), public transport is often seen as the only sustainable form of transport with social and environmental benefits associated with it. For example, an effective public transport system:

- improves the accessibility of rural areas;
- significantly reduces the environmental impacts that result from widespread car usage, particularly when travel by rail is compared with road travel;
- is more healthy when linked to local forms of sustainable transport such as cycling and walking; and
- has potential to improve the rural tourism experience by allowing people to relax without the responsibility of driving (Sharpley and Sharpley, 1997).

However, the successful implementation of public transport policies for rural areas faces a number of hurdles:

- public transport, particularly in rural areas where demand may be related to the tourism seasons, tends to be unprofitable and, therefore, operators require a significant level of financial subsidy which, certainly in most Western economies, is no longer forthcoming;
- services must also be integrated at both the local and national level in order to make public transport easy to use; information and timetables need to be easily and widely available;
- it must be effectively promoted; and
- as noted above, the apparently entrenched attitude of most car owners, mutually reinforced by development policies for housing, recreation and shopping, which are based around private car ownership and usage. Education, significant inducements and a change of attitude are required to encourage people to leave their cars at home.

Tourism is, of course, synonymous with transport (Page, 1994, 1998, 1999) and, to participate in rural tourism, visitors must be able to travel to and around the countryside. Moreover, a major attraction of rural tourism is the opportunity to do so spontaneously and freely. However, the car, as a symbol of that freedom and spontaneity, paradoxically also poses a major threat to the attraction of rural areas and, therefore, what is perhaps required is a combination of:

- greater investment in public transport;
- restrictions on car access;
- taxation and pricing policies;
- a shift in national transport policies and effective marketing; and
- public awareness programmes.

Sustainable Recreational Transport: Walking for Health

While cycling (Chapter 7) and walking are the least unsustainable methods of transport currently available to us, alone they are usually insufficient to provide recreational transport to and in rural areas. Following the observations on the increasing involvement of technology for the 'new' forms of recreational pursuits in rural areas (Chapter 2), and the unsustainability which follows from that (as indicated above), there are clear sustainability arguments for reversing this process in both structural and spatial terms. There is now much research to provide evidence of important health gains for those who take regular exercise (Box 3.6), and leisure walking may have one of the most favourable benefit-to-risk ratios of all recreational activities.

All leisure pursuits carry some form of risk. Such activities as mountaineering, motor sport and hang-gliding carry the highest fatality risk, which must, irrespective of other considerations, reduce their notional sustainability factor. By contrast, leisure walking carries the least risk of most recreational activities. If this factor is coupled with the intensity of effort which is considered necessary to produce a health benefit – that which demands about 50% of an individual's maximal oxygen intake (Shepherd, 1997) – conducted with modest vigour and sustained for 1 h about 3–5 days per week, walking for leisure would appear to

Box 3.6. Benefits of recreational walking (source: Ball, 1998).

Reduction in the risk of:

- coronary heart disease; reduced by as much as one-third to one-quarter among men expending a comparatively modest 2000 or more kcal per week compared with those who are sedentary;
- stroke;
- osteoporosis (particularly important for women);
- hip fracture;
- diabetes mellitus; and
- colon and other cancers.

Appropriate physical activity is also reported as enhancing creativity and having an overwhelming positive impact on the psychological well-being of the elderly, in addition to a plethora of physical benefits.

combine both low risk and high benefit. The main advantages of an exercise programme based on walking are therefore that it is:

- a practical form of recreation relevant to everyday activities;
- free and readily accessible; and
- a safe way of improving cardio-vascular fitness.

However, walking appears to decline in society with economic development. A complex of societal changes contribute to this trend:

- the growth of private motorized transport, its apparent convenience and speed of movement;
- a consequent constraint on walking and cycling because of fear of injury and air pollution;
- the condition and perceived safety of parks, woodlands and open spaces; and
- questions of access to natural recreational areas.

For these reasons many health authorities and governments have been instrumental in promoting the benefits of walking. Practical demonstrations of how walking can be encouraged and sustained within local areas have tended to take place in urban communities with access to parks or situated on the fringes of built-up areas.

The Health Walks project

The Health Walks project (Boxes 3.7 and 3.8), inspired by a local general practitioner (Dr Bird) in Oxfordshire, in the English south Midlands, encourages walking as part of a fitness or treatment programme for people of all ages. It is a holistic approach to health care which aims to stimulate an awareness of the local countryside and provide a focus for the local community. The project is based on the belief that the community and local environment have a major impact on individuals' well-being.

Many of the doctor's patients had health problems linked to weight and lack of exercise. Dr Bird realized that walking improved his own mood and health but few of his patients were actually walking in his locality. In 1994 he drew up a series of walking routes between 1 and 4 miles long, graded them according to difficulty and worked out the ideal walking times for people according to their age and current fitness. The routes were promoted by a pack of walking cards, and proved popular. Later he introduced a programme of led walks for people who would not walk on their own. Local volunteers lead these with support from a fitness instructor. Over 16,000 walks took place in the first 5 years.

Standard approaches to health promotion focus largely on eradicating disease. If people live in a place with poor community spirit and few recreational opportunities, even in the absence of disease, many will remain in what Dr Bird describes as a 'neutral' state. By actively involving the community the Health Walks approach attempts to take the individual into a positive state of well-being. In this respect, 'Health Walks' offer the transition from health promotion to promoting holistic well-being, an area which most health ser-

Box 3.7. Health Walks: the practice (source: Fairbanks, 1997).

The project is divided into four main parts; each part is integrated with the other.

Circular routes are carefully selected, mapped out and colour-coded according to their difficulty. Walks are further divided into 'soft-top' (i.e. un-surfaced footpaths) and 'hardtop' (e.g. pavements). These walks are signed with 'Health Walk' waymarkers.

Health Walk Guides are published to accompany each walk. These are designed for people who are not regular walkers. Local history details, a three-dimensional illustrative map and drawings are added to raise awareness of the local environment and to engender a sense of pride and ownership of the scheme. On the back of each leaflet is an innovative medical table indicating the calories used and a MET value (a measure of the energy used by exercising compared with resting) for each walk.

Daily organized walks are programmed in order to motivate individuals to continue exercising and because many individuals, particularly women, feel vulnerable walking alone. Each walk is led by two volunteers who have been trained to provide appropriate exercises before the walk. The front leader sets the pace while the back marker remains with the slowest member. The walking groups are graded according to the fitness of the members. Grade A is for fast walkers, Grade B for the moderately fit and Grade C for the unfit.

Annual fitness assessment is the goal for people to aim for and is open to everyone in the community. People's fitness levels are calculated and converted to a fitness index using 100 as the ideal average fitness. This allows individuals to follow the progress of their fitness year on year.

Box 3.8. Walking the Way to Health Initiative: key features (source: Countryside Agency, 2000a).

Grants to set up a 'walking for health' scheme for community, health and leisure organizations concerned with improving people's health; but not individuals or commercial companies
Training for every volunteer and health, leisure and community professional involved in local schemes
Insurance to cover liability
Accreditation and evaluation of schemes to help them grow and improve

vices cannot usually afford to address. People's increasing awareness of their local environment is thus seen to improve the well-being of their community and to open up new opportunities for a range of physical recreational exercises. In this respect urban and peri-urban open spaces are seen as a 'Green Gym', conceptually positioned towards the centre of the urban–rural continuum.

Such an approach is clearly pursuing sustainability principles in:

- advancing people's physical and mental health;
- most notably encouraging those living in urban areas to undertake healthy recreational activity who otherwise may be excluded from access to the countryside or to formal recreational activities;
- helping (urban) residents view their local environment from perhaps a new and more holistic perspective; and
- apparently reducing the need for travel to the countryside for recreational activity.

The importance of this for rural areas lies in the argument that pressures of recreational demand can be reduced. Conceptually it would appear rather neat to suggest that rural values can be sustainably adopted within urban areas and can reverse the trend of the imposition of largely unsustainable urban recreational values on the countryside. There is, of course, a flaw if not paradox in this argument not least since, rather like the arguments surrounding virtual reality travel, a taste for healthy recreational walking in urban or peri-urban green space may actually stimulate increased demand for travelling to rural areas to pursue the activity further on a more extensive basis (for example on the UK's core paths network) and in more 'natural' surroundings.

Although initiated in a relatively affluent area where obesity and lack of exercise were likely to reflect chosen lifestyle rather than poverty or poor diet, the demonstration effect of the initial idea stimulated a UK government sponsored initiative. The Walking the Way to Health Initiative (WHI) aims to encourage around 1.5 million inactive people to reduce their risk of heart disease and enjoy their local environment simply by walking. WHI is promoted by the Countryside Agency and the British Heart Foundation to encourage regular and brisk local community walks for people who take little exercise or live in areas of poor health. The initiative is supporting 200 local 'walking for health' schemes over 5 years and began in October 2000.

This last example of recreational activity and the evolution of a government policy dimension embracing it, helps to illustrate:

- the underlying interdependence between the rural and the urban in most developed societies, and the potential significance of bringing 'rural' values to the urban (Box 3.9); and
- some of the welfare dimensions of sustainability which, while often implicit in recreational activity and management have tended not to be in the forefront of debates on tourism and sustainability (e.g. Hall and Brown, 1996).

Chapter Conclusion and Summary

Sustainable development, with its demands for the holistic and equitable, and its long-term focus, may limit the potential for economic development which often takes a short-term and rather more sectoral approach. Local needs, and the stimuli for economic growth, are often incompatible with the aims of sustainable development. Tourism and recreation development needs to be part of a region's rural development. But the planning and coordination required to achieve this are unlikely to arise from grassroots initiatives and thus an unsustainable element of tourism development must be accepted. Regions marketing themselves as destinations should promote a prior understanding of the limits to change they will accept, and develop a means of measuring the quality of environments that are placed at risk by intended tourism development processes.

This chapter has attempted to place the development of tourism and recreation in rural areas within debates concerning the sustainability of rural development and the role of sustainability in tourism and recreation development in rural areas. It has done this by:

Box 3.9. Rural in the urban: horticultural recreation.

Although perhaps more notable in the UK than in several other European countries, the pursuit of gardening, whether within the home (e.g. Groening and Schneider, 1999; Bhatti and Church, 2000) or on a nearby allotment (e.g. Crouch and Ward, 1997; Crouch, 1999), has a long tradition. Although previously thought of as a leisure activity for older males, gardening has been rejuvenated through media popularity and notably with the projection of younger females as icons of this recreational activity. Visiting the formal and informal gardens of stately homes and other cultural and heritage attractions has more recently been complemented by the attraction of gardens in their own right. Garden open days, attendance at garden shows and exhibitions and the popularity of shopping at garden centres and nurseries, involve substantial levels of participation from hosts as well as visitors. This is perhaps an explicit contemporary example of rural values being imported into urban areas: being at one with the soil and in harmony with the seasons, attracting wildlife and growing food for consumption. Of course this is not new: landscape gardeners and more recently urban planners and the discourse of urban living ('garden suburb', 'urban village') have long attempted to bring a sense of the rural to the urban, more usually for those better placed to be able to afford it.

While gardening is perhaps one example of sustaining rural values for recreation in urban areas, leisure walking is potentially more important.

- tracing the emergence of 'sustainability' as a key concept in development debates;
- briefly examining the interaction of the social, economic and environmental dimensions of recreation and tourism development in rural areas, and the need for a holistic approach to their management in the face of a perceived 'implementation gap' in sustainability ideals;
- providing a critique of such sustainability ideals and of the obfuscation surrounding notions of sustainability in relation to tourism development; and
- examining some of the paradoxes of sustainability debates by focusing on the problem of tourism transport in rural areas.

The following chapter places the foregoing discussion concerning the interaction of social, economic and environmental dimensions of recreation and tourism development in rural areas, and the sustainability implementation gap, within policy and management contexts.

References

Ashworth, G. and Larkham, P.J. (1994) *Building a New Heritage: Tourism, Culture and Identity in the New Europe.* Routledge, London.

Ball, D. (1998) Leisure walking and health. *Countryside Recreation News* 6(2). http://www.cf.ac.uk/cm/news/62/art1.html

Barbier, E.B. (1987) The concept of sustainable economic development. *Environmental Conservation* 14(2), 101–110.

Barrett, G. (1995) Transport emissions and travel behaviour: a critical review of recent European Union and UK policy initiatives. *Transportation* 22, 295–323.

Bartis, H.H. (1998) A National Black Heritage Trail in the Eastern Cape Province, South Africa: is it an option? In: Hall, D. and O'Hanlon, L. (eds) *Rural Tourism Management: Sustainable Options.* The Scottish Agricultural College, Auchincruive, pp. 17–28.

Bhatti, M. and Church, A. (2000) 'I never promised you a rose garden': gender, leisure and home-making. *Leisure Studies* 19, 183–197.

Bramwell, B. (1994) Rural tourism and sustainable rural tourism. *Journal of Sustainable Tourism* 2(1–2), 1–6.

Bramwell, B. and Lane, B. (1993) Sustainable tourism: an evolving global approach. *Journal of Sustainable Tourism* 1(1), 6–16.

Bramwell, B., Henry, I., Jackson, G., Goytia Prat, A., Richards, G. and van der Straaten, J. (eds) (1996) *Sustainable Tourism Management: Principles and Practice.* Tilburg University Press, Tilburg, The Netherlands.

Brown, F. (1998) *Tourism Reconsidered: Blight or Blessing?* Butterworth-Heinemann, Oxford.

Butler, R.W. (1991) Tourism, environment and sustainable development. *Environmental Conservation* 18(3), 201–209.

Butler, R.W. and Hall, C.M. (1998) Conclusion: the sustainability of tourism and recreation in rural areas. In: Butler, R.W., Hall, C.M. and Jenkins, J. (eds) *Tourism and Recreation in Rural Areas.* John Wiley & Sons, Chichester, pp. 249–258.

Caffyn, A. (2000) Developing sustainable tourism in the Trossachs, Scotland. In: Richards, G. and Hall, D. (eds) *Tourism and Sustainable Community Development.* Routledge, London, pp. 83–100.

Cater, E. and Lowman, G. (eds) (1994) *Ecotourism: a Sustainable Option?* John Wiley & Sons, Chichester.

Charlton, C. (1998) Public transport and sustainable tourism: the case of the Devon and Cornwall rail partnership. In: Hall, C.M. and Lew, A.A. (eds) *Sustainable Tourism: a Geographical Perspective.* Longman, Harlow, pp. 132–145.

Coccossis, H. (1996): Tourism and sustainability: perspectives and implications. In: Priestley, G.K., Edwards, J.A. and Coccossis, H. (eds) *Sustainable Tourism? European Experiences.* CAB International, Wallingford, pp. 1–21.

Coccossis, H. and Nijkamp, P. (eds) (1995) *Sustainable Tourism Development.* Avebury, Aldershot.

Coleman, C. (1997) Tourist traffic in English national parks – an innovative approach to management. *Journal of Tourism Studies* 8, 2–15.

Countryside Agency (2000a) *£11.6m initiative launched to get the nation on its feet.* Countryside Agency, Cheltenham. http://www.countryside.gov.uk/news/article.asp?NewsItemID=86

Countryside Agency (2000b) *Quiet Roads/Greenways.* Countryside Agency, Cheltenham. http://www.quiet-roads.gov.uk/

Countryside Commission (1992) *Road Traffic and the Countryside.* Countryside Commission, Cheltenham.

Countryside Commission (1995) *Sustainable Rural Tourism: Opportunities for Local Action.* Countryside Commission, Cheltenham.

Countryside Commission (1996a) *A Living Countryside: Our Strategy for the Next Ten Years.* Countryside Commission, Cheltenham.

Countryside Commission (1996b) *Peace in the Parks – But Too Many Cars, Survey Reveals.* Press release, Countryside Commission, Cheltenham. http://www.coi.gov.uk/depts/GCM/coi4029c.ok

Countryside Commission (1997) *Rural Traffic: Getting It Right.* Countryside Commission, Northampton.

Countryside Commission/ETB (English Tourist Board) (1989) *Principles for Tourism in the Countryside.* Countryside Commission/ETB, Cheltenham.

Crouch, D. (1999) The intimacy and expansion of space. In: Crouch, D. (ed.) *Leisure/Tourism Geographies: Practices and Geographical Knowledge.* Routledge, London, pp. 257–276.

Crouch, D. and Ward, C. (1997) *The Allotment: its Landscape and Culture.* Faber and Faber, London.

Cullinane, S. and Cullinane, E. (1999) Attitudes towards traffic problems and public transport in the Dartmoor and Lake District National Parks. *Journal of Transport Geography* 7(1), 79–87.

Cullinane, S. and Stokes, G. (1998) *Rural Transport Policy.* Pergamon, Oxford.

Curry, N. (1992) Recreation, access, amenity and conservation in the United Kingdom: the failure of integration. In: Bowler, I.R., Bryant, C.R. and Nellis, M.D. (eds) *Contemporary Rural Systems in Transition,* Vol. 2. CAB International, Wallingford, pp. 141–154.

Docherty, I. (1999) *Making Tracks: the Politics of Local Rail Transport.* Ashgate, Aldershot.

DoE (Department of the Environment) (1995) *Rural England: a Nation Committed to a Living Countryside.* HMSO, London.

Eaton, B. and Holding, D. (1996) The evaluation of public transport alternatives to the car in British National Parks. *Journal of Transport Geography* 4(1), 55–65.

Fairbanks, R. (1997) 'Health Walks'. *Countryside Recreation News* 5(2). http://www.cf.ac.uk/cm/news/5/art5.html

Fewings, J. (1996) A rural transport package for Dartmoor. *Town and Country Planning* 56(6), 180–182.

France, L. (ed.) (1997) *The Earthscan Reader in Sustainable Tourism.* Earthscan, London.

Groening, G. and Schneider, U. (1999) In: Crouch, D. (ed.) *Leisure/Tourism Geographies: Practices and Geographical Knowledge.* Routledge, London, pp. 149–163.

Hall, D.R. (1998) Urban transport, environmental pressures and policy options. In: Pinder, D.A. (ed.) *The New Europe: Society and Environment.* John Wiley & Sons, Chichester, pp. 435–454.

Hall, D.R. (1999) Conceptualising tourism transport: inequality and externality issues. *Journal of Transport Geography* 7, 181–188.

Hall, D. and Brown, F. (1996) Towards a welfare focus for tourism. *Progress in Tourism and Hospitality Research* 2(1), 41–57.

Hibbs, J. (1986) *The Country Bus.* David and Charles, Newton Abbott.

Hunter, C. (1995) On the need to re-conceptualise sustainable tourism development. *Journal of Sustainable Tourism* 3(3), 155–165.

INPHORMM (1998) *Using Transport Information, Publicity Campaigns and Community Programmes to Reduce Car Use and Encourage Alternative Modes of Travel. A Review of Current Practice in Europe.* Transport Studies Group, University of Westminster, London.

IUCN (World Conservation Union) (1980) *World Conservation Strategy.* IUCN, Morges, Switzerland.

IUCN (World Conservation Union) (1991) *Caring for the Earth: a Strategy for Sustainable Living.* IUCN, Gland, Switzerland.

Joppe, M. (1996) Sustainable community tourism development revisited. *Tourism Management* 17(7), 475–479.

Lane, B. (1994) Sustainable rural tourism strategies: a tool for development and conservation. *Journal of Sustainable Tourism* 2(1–2), 102–111.

Langmyhr, T. (1997) Managing equity – the case of road pricing. *Transport Policy* 4(1) 25–39.

Larsen, O.I. (1995) The toll cordons in Norway. *Journal of Transport Geography* 3(3), 187–197.

Maddison, D., Pearce, D., Johansson, O., Calthrop, E., Litman, T. and Verhoef, E. (1996) *Blueprint 5: the True Costs of Road Transport.* Earthscan, London.

Mason, P. and Mowforth, M. (1996) Codes of conduct in tourism. *Progress in Tourism and Hospitality Research* 2, 151–167.

Mitchell, J. (1991) Tourism and public transport in national parks. MSc thesis, University of Strathclyde, Glasgow.

Mowforth, M. and Munt, I. (1998) *Tourism and Sustainability. New Tourism in the Third World.* Routledge, London.

Mulligan, C. (1979) The Snowdon Sherpa: public transport and national park management experiment. In: Halsall, D. and Turton, B.J. (eds) *Rural Transport Problems in Britain.* Institute of British Geographers Transport Geography Study Group, Keele, pp. 45–55.

Murdoch, J. (1993) Sustainable rural development: towards a research agenda. *Geoforum* 24(3), 225–241.

Murphy, P.E. (1994) Tourism and sustainable development. In: Theobald, W.F. (ed.) *Global Tourism: the Next Decade.* Butterworth-Heinemann, Oxford, pp. 274–290.

Neale, G. (1998) *The Green Travel Guide.* Earthscan, London.

Odeck, J. and Brathen, S. (1997) On public attitudes towards implementation of toll roads – the case of Oslo Toll-Ring. *Transport Policy* 4(2), 77–83.

Orams, M.B. (1997) The effectiveness of environmental education: can we turn tourists into 'greenies'? *Progress in Tourism and Hospitality Research* 3, 295–306.

Page, S.J. (1994) *Transport for Tourism.* Routledge, London.

Page, S.J. (1998) Transport for recreation and tourism. In: Hoyle, B.S. and Knowles, R.D. (eds) *Modern Transport Geography*, 2nd edn. John Wiley & Sons, Chichester, pp. 217–240.

Page, S.J. (1999) *Transport and Tourism.* Longman, Harlow.

Peake, S. (1994) *Transport in Transition.* Earthscan, London.

Pearce, D. (1993) *Blueprint 3.* Earthscan, London.

Pearce, P., Moscardo, G. and Ross, G. (1996) *Tourism Community Relationships.* Pergamon, Oxford.

Pilling, A. and Turner, J. (1999) Is targeting the way forward for travel awareness campaigns of the future? Paper, RGS-IBG Annual Conference, University of Leicester, Leicester.

Pretty, J. (1995) The many interpretations of participation. *In Focus* 16, 4–5.

Redclift, M. (1987) *Sustainable Development: Exploring the Contradictions.* Methuen, London.

Rothengatter, W. and Mauch, S. (1994) *External Effects of Transport.* Union Internationale des Chemin de Fers, Paris.

Sharpley, R. (2000) Tourism and sustainable development: exploring the theoretical divide. *Journal of Sustainable Tourism* 8(1), 1–19.

Sharpley, R. and Sharpley, J. (1997) *Rural Tourism. An Introduction.* International Thomson Business Press, London.

Shepherd, R.J. (1997) What is the optimal type of physical activity to enhance health? *British Journal of Sports Medicine* 31, 277–284.

STB (Scottish Tourist Board) (1994) *Scottish Tourism Strategic Plan.* STB, Edinburgh.

STCG (Scottish Tourism Coordinating Group) (1991) *Tourism and the Scottish Environment – a Sustainable Partnership.* STB, Edinburgh.

Sterner, T. (1994) Environmental tax reform: the Swedish experience. *European Environment* 4(6), 20–25.

Swarbrooke, J. (1999) *Sustainable Tourism Management.* CAB International, Wallingford.

TETF (Tourism and Environment Task Force) (1993) *Going Green – a Practical Guide for Tourism Businesses Wishing to develop an Environmentally friendly Approach.* TETF, Edinburgh.

TETF (Tourism and Environment Task Force) (1996) *Action Plan 1996–9.* TETF, Edinburgh.

Tourism Concern and WWF (1992) *Beyond the Green Horizon. A Discussion Paper on Principles for Sustainable Tourism.* WWF UK, Godalming.

Transport 2000 (1987) *No Through Road.* Transport 2000, London.

Unwin, T. (1998) Ethical dimensions of rural tourism in Estonia. *Ethics in Tourism Virtual Conference.* http://www.mcb.co.uk/services/conferen/jan98/eit/3_unwin.html

WCED (World Commission on Environment and Development) (1987) *Our Common Future.* Oxford University Press, Oxford.

Wheeller, B. (1993) Sustaining the ego. *Journal of Sustainable Tourism* 1(2), 121–129.

Whitelegg, J. (1993) *Transport for a Sustainable Future: the Case for Europe.* Belhaven Press, London.

4

Managing?

Paradox

Change

Unsustainability

Transparency

Integration

Senior civil servants and ministers are to be given rural awareness training as part of a package of measures to help farmers and boost the countryside's profile within Government. Ministers and Whitehall mandarins are to be trained in 'rural policy skills and awareness', and civil servants will be sent on secondment to 'rural bodies' to learn how the countryside works.

(Woolf, 2000)

The key themes of this chapter certainly revolve around the oft-cited *paradox* of the need for effective management and planning of tourism and recreation in rural areas but the often absence or poorly developed nature of policy strategy. *Integration* is crucial here, both vertical and horizontal, between the various stakeholders and strategic bodies with an active interest and role in policy formulation. *Integration* is also a critical dimension for the way in which tourism and recreation are managed within processes of rural development. If planning and management are undertaken in response to perceived niche rather than mass activity, the lack of *transparency* in the industry's relationships with those planners and managers can only result in explicit *unsustainability*. *Change* is everywhere evident.

Much has been written on the basic principles – explicitly sustainable or otherwise – of tourism and recreation policy and planning (e.g. Inskeep, 1991; Dowling, 1993; Gunn, 1994; WTO, 1994), and it is not the purpose of this chapter to reiterate those texts. Rather, building on the previous chapter's critique of 'sustainability', this chapter aims to pursue three key objectives. These are to:

1. Briefly examine the different levels of policy influencing recreation and tourism development in rural areas, emphasizing the connectedness between local and global processes;
2. Emphasize the need to view recreation and tourism development in rural areas within the wider context of the management of rural resources; and

3. Evaluate challenges posed for such management and key issues for the development of recreation and tourism in rural areas arising from these challenges.

Policy Issues

It is often suggested that significant differences exist in public policy objectives between tourism and recreation in rural areas. Recreation is often seen as a social service, with policies aimed at securing access to resources and providing opportunities for locals and visitors; while, by contrast tourism is usually viewed as an agent for stimulating economic development or redevelopment, rather than comprising an element of public sector provision (Butler *et al.*, 1998: 4). But several commentators have noted that such distinctions are becoming blurred as the leisure use of rural areas becomes more ubiquitous and varied, as noted in Chapter 2.

Although a rapidly growing area of activity, the rural leisure 'industry' is highly fragmented, in terms of its operational structures, patterns of activities, markets and operating environments (Pearce, 1989). The significance of this is that it renders any analysis of the policy arena problematic, but in particular it has tended to exacerbate situations where need has run ahead of availability of proactive policies for development and management. Further, in the past, major tourism organizations have tended to concentrate on resorts and urban centres, often marginalizing rural areas, perhaps unwittingly, as somewhat secondary, 'sightseeing territory', rather than as a complex of tourism and recreation resources. This has had the effect of industry strategy for rural areas lagging behind developments on the ground, further exacerbating the fragmentary and unmanaged nature of much supply-side linkage and provision. Unsurprisingly, therefore, opinions on the appropriateness of certain policies for particular places may differ substantially (Bramwell, 1994).

In some ways complementing horizontal industry fragmentation is the vertical multiplicity of levels at which rural policy implementation may take place. National, regional, local and individual entrepreneurial levels of endeavour can be identified. But the roles of and relationships between these levels of operation, and between them and other relevant bodies, may:

- be unclear, overlap and duplicate, or leave unnoticed gaps in strategic provision;
- differ significantly from one culture to another; and
- exacerbate problems of identifying the appropriate level for policy decisions and the nature of the policy interventions (e.g. whether spatially or sectorally applied).

A number of authors have pointed to an almost universal lack of policy and support strategies for rural tourism at higher levels of administration (Page and Getz, 1997). Is this because of the perceived low capital and employment generation characteristics of the sector? Does it reflect basic problems of poor statistical bases? Or is it the fact that rural tourism in many countries is predominantly domestic and therefore considered able to be left to look after itself?

For whatever reason, policy for the planning, management and development of tourism and recreation in rural areas often appears woefully inadequate to cope with a rapidly growing element of a dynamic, mass global activity. This, in turn, has offered tourism academics one of their more frequently employed clichés: the 'policy implementation gap' (e.g. Pigram, 1993; Butler and Hall, 1998: 254). Virtually every textbook with a policy chapter therefore argues the need for: better planning and management, and more effective integration with rural development policies, thereby producing comprehensive and integrated approaches which are necessary to optimize the benefits of tourism and recreation development for rural areas, their residents and workers, as well as for tourists and recreationalists (e.g. Sharpley and Sharpley, 1997: 112, 114).

The characteristics, roles and objectives of such policy approaches are variously described (e.g. Dernoi, 1991; Fagence, 1991; Pigram, 1993; OECD, 1994; Page and Getz, 1997; Sharpley and Sharpley, 1997; Hall and Jenkins, 1998), but in essence amount to the following:

- Regeneration: the need to revitalize rural areas – generating employment and inward investment – and reallocate rural resources particularly in relation to the relative and/or absolute decline of agriculture in economic, societal and land use terms.
- Integration: (i) 'horizontal', recreation and tourism being embedded within rural development strategies, encouraging local economic linkages and dynamic growth; and (ii) 'vertical', viewed within the broader perspective of regional and national tourism and leisure strategy.
- Interdependence: balancing the various components that contribute to the fragmented reality of tourism and recreation activity in rural areas.
- Stewardship: overseeing, caring for, protecting (where necessary) and monitoring the fragile physical and human resources which constitute the 'rural environment'. Other authors may refer to this as 'sustainability'.
- Mediation: explicitly intervening in land use and other spatial and social conflicts, for example, applying development controls to prevent second home ownership from dominating villages and other rural areas to the detriment of the local community.
- Catalysm: aiding infrastructural, service and welfare provision and other benefits through the process of recreation and tourism development.
- Spatiality: awareness and employment of local and regional specialization, locational and initial advantage, intra- and inter-regional complementarities (including those of the rural–urban spatial and societal interface and continua).
- Opportunism: exploring the combinations of compatible types of activities with particular places (Hudson and Townsend, 1992).
- Realism: appreciating that not all areas will benefit from tourism and recreation development, and that where it does take place, such development will not necessarily benefit the local 'community' (see Chapter 5).
- Quality: responding appropriately under suitable conditions to the increasing high quality demands of tourists in rural areas.

In Chapter 5 issues of community-level and community-driven development are addressed, and the current conventional wisdom advocating networks and partnerships in tourism development is evaluated, with an implicit emphasis on private and NGO sector (supply-side) activities. This chapter largely focuses on public sector involvement in decisions affecting the development of tourism and recreation in rural areas. At whatever level, public sector intervention may represent a response to:

- market failure, such as environmental degradation or lack of infrastructure provision;
- market imperfection, such as the potential for social exclusion (Chapter 2); and
- public concerns about market outcomes, which refer to either or both of the above.

(Hall and Jenkins, 1998: 21–22)

Although the 1980s saw a significant shift away from central planning and public ownership in Western Europe in the 1980s and in CEE in the late 1980s and early 1990s, public sector involvement in tourism policy, or at least policies impinging on tourism development, is still widespread, from the ideological overtness of China, Cuba and North Korea, to the quango-ized and hesitant intervention of Western social democracies. In the latter at least, tourism is not immune from shifts in political philosophy (Hall and Jenkins, 1998: 20) but retains an electoral importance for political parties by virtue of its perceived employment and income generation roles.

The Role of the Supranational

While the WTO and its predecessor the International Union of Official Travel Organizations (IUOTO) have tended to be strong advocates of government direction in tourism, within Western Europe it has been somewhat ironic that at supranational level financial support (and credible policy) for rural tourism from the EU has been derived from areas other than those concerned with tourism. This is because the erstwhile DGXXIII has had no specific budget for tourism activities and has been unable to fund individual projects. Yet the European Commission (EC) has been increasingly involved in tourism since the early 1980s, in cooperation with the Council of Europe, the European Parliament, the Economic and Social Committee and the Committee of the Regions (Edmunds, 1999). The Tourism Advisory Committee, set up in 1986 to exchange information and facilitate consultation and cooperation on tourism, comprises representatives from the 18 European Economic Area (EEA) countries who provide information on the measures taken at national level in the area of tourism. This committee meets about three times a year (see also Davidson and Maitland, 1997; Hall and Jenkins, 1998: 20).

Tourism initiatives receive support from a range of EU programmes. The major funds for promoting regional, economic and social development in the EU are the so-called Structural Funds, which provide support for economic development and are targeted at regional and national programmes managed by the member states and jointly funded by the EC. These are the single largest source of EU funding for tourism, particularly in the less advanced regions. The Structural Funds include the European Regional Development Fund (ERDF), the European Social Fund (ESF) and the European Agriculture Guidance and Guarantee Fund (EAGGF). Tourism is recognized in Europe as making a valuable contribution to regional development and job creation and, in the period 1994–1999, the EU Structural Funds contributed €7.3 billion to tourism projects.

Many regional activities also receive funding from other EC programmes in diverse fields such as research and technology development, environmental protection, improving the competitiveness of SMEs and preservation of cultural heritage. These often require cooperative efforts between organizations in two or more member states. The necessary restructuring of EU programmes as a precursor to eastern and Mediterranean enlargement of the EU will significantly influence policy impacts on tourism and recreation in rural areas (Hall and Danta, 2000).

As an explicit recognition of the need for rural development both from a bottom-up perspective and from a wider perspective than just agricultural support, the 1996 European Conference on Rural Development, and its Cork Declaration (Box 4.1) acted as an important forerunner of the LEADER rural development programmes. These have proved an important catalyst in stimulating local tourism projects integrated within rural development processes.

The Cork Declaration was in part a response to the perceived requirement for both a higher priority for, and a bottom-up approach to, the restructuring needs of Europe's rural areas. Arguing that rural development must address all socio-economic sectors in the countryside, the Declaration saw the strategic need to promote local capacity building for sustainable development in rural areas and, in particular, to encourage private and community-based initiatives which are well integrated into global markets. It explicitly drew tourism and recreation into the context of integrated rural development processes, an approach taken up in subsequent LEADER programmes.

LEADER is one of the most proactive EU programme areas, operating under the umbrella of Agricultural Policy and Rural Development for the advancement of disadvantaged rural areas of the EU. Its 'bottom-up' approach to development has experienced three sequential phases: LEADER, LEADER II and LEADER+ programmes.

Basic characteristics of, and differences between, the last two programmes are indicated in Table 4.1. Notably, LEADER+ embodies a shift in policy emphasis from need to potential economic vitality. For example, project plans need to state explicitly how feasible products can become viable. The LEADER+ programme promotes integrated schemes conceived and implemented by active partnerships operating at the local level. The objectives are to encourage and support rural actors in thinking about the longer-term potential of their area and encourage the implementation of integrated, high-quality, original strategies for sustainable development which experiment with new ways of:

- enhancing the natural and cultural heritage;
- reinforcing the economic environment in order to contribute to job creation; and
- improving the organizational abilities of their community.

It would appear that LEADER+ does not

Box 4.1. The Cork Declaration: edited text of the European Conference on Rural Development, November 1996 (source: European Commission, 1997).

Ten point rural development programme for the EU

1. *Rural preference*: Sustainable rural development must be put at the top of the agenda of the EU, and become the fundamental principle which underpins all rural policy in the immediate future and after enlargement. This aims at reversing rural out-migration, combating poverty, stimulating employment and equality of opportunity, and responding to growing requests for more quality, health, safety, personal development and leisure, and improving rural well-being. The need to preserve and improve the quality of the rural environment must be integrated into all Community policies that relate to rural development. There must be a fairer balance of public spending, infrastructure investments and educational, health and communications services between rural and urban areas. A growing share of available resources should be used for promoting rural development and securing environmental objectives.

2. *Integrated approach*: Rural development policy must be multidisciplinary in concept, and multisectoral in application, with a clear territorial dimension. It must apply to all rural areas in the Union, respecting the concentration principle through the differentiation of co-financing for those areas which are more in need. It must be based on an integrated approach, encompassing within the same legal and policy framework: agricultural adjustment and development, economic diversification – notably small and medium scale industries and rural services – the management of natural resources, the enhancement of environmental functions, and the promotion of culture, tourism and recreation.

3. *Diversification*: Support for diversification of economic and social activity must focus on providing the framework for self-sustaining private and community-based initiatives: investment, technical assistance, business services, adequate infrastructure, education, training, integrating advances in information technology, strengthening the role of small towns as integral parts of rural areas and key development factors, and promoting the development of viable rural communities and renewal of villages.

4. *Sustainability*: Policies should promote rural development which sustains the quality and amenity of Europe's rural landscapes (natural resources, biodiversity and cultural identity), so that their use by today's generation does not prejudice the options for future generations. In our local actions, we must be aware of our global responsibilities.

5. *Subsidiarity*: Given the diversity of the Union's rural areas, rural development policy must follow the principle of subsidiarity. It must be as decentralized as possible and based on partnership and cooperation between all levels concerned (local, regional, national and European). The emphasis must be on participation and a 'bottom up' approach, which harnesses the creativity and solidarity of rural communities. Rural development must be local and community-driven within a coherent European framework.

6. *Simplification*: Rural development policy, notably in its agricultural component, needs to undergo radical simplification in legislation. While there should be no re-nationalization of the CAP, there should be more subsidiarity in decisions, decentralization of policy implementation and more flexibility overall.

7. *Programming*: The application of rural development programmes must be based on coherent and transparent procedures, and integrated into one single programme for rural development for each region, and a single mechanism for sustainable and rural development.

8. *Finance*: The use of local financial resources must be encouraged to promote local rural development projects. Greater participation by the banking sector (public and private) and other fiscal intermediaries must be encouraged.

9. *Management*: The administrative capacity and effectiveness of regional and local governments and community-based groups must be enhanced, where necessary, through the provision of technical assistance, training, better communications, partnership and the sharing of research, information and exchange of experience through networking between regions and between rural communities throughout Europe.

10. *Evaluation and research*: Monitoring, evaluation and beneficiary assessment will need to be reinforced in order to ensure transparency of procedures, guarantee the careful use of public money, stimulate research and innovation, and enable an informed public debate. Stakeholders must not only be consulted in the design and implementation, but involved in monitoring and evaluation.

Box 4.1. *Continued*

Conclusion

We urge Europe's policy-makers:

- to raise public awareness about the importance of making a new start in rural development policy;
- to make rural areas more attractive to people to live and work in, and become centres of a more meaningful life for a growing diversity of people of all ages;
- to support this ten-point programme and cooperate as partners in the fulfilment of each and every one of the goals, which are embodied in this declaration; and
- to play an active role in promoting sustainable rural development in an international context.

intend to target unsuccessful areas. The implication of this is the probable reinforcement of the gulf between those areas with and without 'success factors' (see Chapter 8).

Representing some of the better EU examples of bottom-up development activity, LEADER has faced a number of constraints in its operations:

- relationships between programme activists and pre-existing tourist boards and planning authorities (municipality, region, province, national park, national government) may vary and express tensions in the competition for power and influence; and
- conflicting attitudes towards necessary levels of support for tourism have been evident: while tourism initiatives in rural areas have received varying degrees of support from regional, national and community sources, these have been relatively small and rarely have they been the outcome of a clearly stated rationale or policy. For example, over the period 1989–1994, 12.3% of the rural development funding and just 0.6% of the total Structural Fund was devoted to supporting tourism initiatives (Edmunds, 1999: 43).

LEADER+ is structured around three actions: (i) support for integrated territorial rural development strategies of a pilot nature based on the bottom-up approach and horizontal partnerships; (ii) support for inter-territorial and transnational cooperation; and (iii) the networking of all rural areas in the EU (European Commission, 2000a). But there is a structural paradox here: can strategies based on a bottom-up philosophy provide the necessary regional structures required to realize the regional potential implicit in the goals of integrated territorial development and of inter-territorial and transnational cooperation?

Rural Tourism Policy, Regional and National Development

Despite the rhetoric of, on the one hand, European integration and transnational strategy cooperation, and on the other the 'hollowing out' of the state and need for 'community'-driven sustainable policy (Chapters 3 and 5), national level policy and strategy setting is often still paramount. In the following invited contribution from the Secretary General of Finland's Rural Tourism Working Group, the crucial factor of attempting to integrate tourism within a wider rural development strategy is well exemplified.

This contribution is important in raising a number of issues within a national context which are rarely represented in English language texts. Yet as one of the few European countries to pursue a specific rural tourism policy, the experience of Finland may be instructive. Not only does this contribution provide a useful insight into the organizational framework and administrative structure of rural tourism in Finland, but it interrogates tourism's role in rural restructuring processes along economic, environmental and cultural dimensions. Key issues of training provision, networking and quality product development are addressed. The social construction and re-imaging of the Finnish countryside is an important theme, and is set within the Nordic tradition of 'everyman's right' of recreational access (see later in this chapter).

While a wide range of domestically driven factors encourage government intervention in rural tourism and recreation, many of the problems and opportunities associated with its development have an international and

Table 4.1. Comparison of LEADER II and LEADER+ programmes (edited from European Commission, 2000b).

LEADER II	LEADER+
Objectives	
Promote innovative, demonstrative actions (multisectorial and integrated) and disseminate them throughout the European Union (transferable)	Maintain the experimental nature of the area-based development strategies but place more emphasis on: quality projects sustainable effects strategies developed on the basis of a unifying theme, that complement the mainstream and are transferable actions that encourage job creation
The areas	
Objective 1, 6 and 5b areas (10% of funding for bordering areas) The seven outermost regions use REGIS II funds Areas whose population is less than 100,000	All the areas of the EU and the outermost regions Areas whose population is between 10,000 and 100,000 (with some exceptions) Areas whose critical mass in human and financial resources is sufficient The Member States can extend LEADER+'s application to any rural area
The beneficiaries	
Public and private partnerships; local area groups (LAGs) Public or private partnerships (other collective bodies)	Public and private partnerships (LAGs) Socio-economic partners and associations
The measures	
Four main measures: Acquisition of skills Rural innovation programmes Transnational cooperation Networking Differs from Structural Programmes Sub-measures: Technical assistance Vocational training Rural tourism Small businesses, crafts and services Development and marketing of local products Environmental protection and quality of life	Three priority actions: Rural development strategies (area-based, integrated, pilot, transferable and complementary) Inter-territorial and transnational cooperation Networking (+ Skills acquisition measure for new areas) Complements the structural programmes Specific themes: New technologies and know-how for the competitiveness of products and areas Quality of life in rural areas Adding value to local products Making the best use of natural and cultural resources Priority groups: Young people Women
Cooperation between rural areas	
Transnational cooperation between LEADER II groups from at least two EU countries	Inter-territorial cooperation (in the Member State) and transnational cooperation between rural areas (including non-LEADER beneficiaries and non-LEADER areas) to: Reach a critical mass Find complementarities

probably multicultural dimension (Hall and Jenkins, 1998: 25), and require new policy approaches. This is certainly evident in the tensions expressed in the following piece which probably typify the situation in a number of countries: a largely unprofessionalized, almost hobbyist approach taken by many entrepreneurs because of the hitherto relatively secure domestic market, being confronted by new and strengthening demands for variety and quality from a range of international markets.

Facing up to the problems and opportunities brought about by the collapse of neighbouring USSR, Finland joined the EU in 1995 and has produced subsequently one of the more distinctive contributions to European rural and regional policy debate.

Invited Viewpoint

National Policy for 'Rural Tourism': the Case of Finland

Mirja Nylander

Rural tourism policy context

According to OECD definitions, Finland is the most rural country in the EU, with only about a fifth of the population living in urban areas. Further, many of those urban dwellers own rural land and/or have part-time rural pursuits. Attachment to the countryside – finding tranquillity by a lake, in a forest – is a deep-seated component of Finnish culture. The Rural Tourism Working Group of the Finnish Government has defined rural tourism as: customer-oriented tourism in rural areas. It is based on rural areas' natural facilities and resources – culture, nature, landscapes – and on family and small-scale entrepreneurship. Rural tourism is a term used specifically in connection with rural policy (Maaseutumatkailun Teemaryhmä, 2000b), and for policy purposes a threefold categorization of rural areas is used:

1. Sparsely populated rural areas including archipelagos;
2. Rural core areas; and
3. Rural areas near towns.

The first two categories are those rural areas with the greatest problems such as unemployment and depopulation (Maaseutupolitiikan Yhteistyöryhmä, 1996: 20–22).

In Finland, the year 2000 saw the production of a new rural policy programme and national tourism strategy, and a new rural tourism strategy and development programme for the 'Agenda 2000' period. Finland has a relatively small population of about 5 million, and has to look towards neighbouring overseas markets such as Sweden, Germany and Russia to generate significant tourist numbers.

Rural tourism statistical data collection began in Finland in 1996 as the first step towards producing a rural tourism strategy and development programme. Data are now available covering type and amount of accommodation, and of other services and programmes, for 2080 rural tourism entrepreneurs across Finland. The research which has generated this information will continue until at least 2003 (KTM Toimiala-Infomedia, 1999).

Tourism employs about 3% of the total workforce in Finland. In 1995 the Tourism Development Centre of Finland estimated that tourism provided work equivalent to 75,000 person-years, of which rural tourism represented 2000 person-years. The figures have not changed much since then, but regional development has been uneven. The capital, Helsinki, and nearby communities, provide almost half of the country's tourism employment (Suomen Matkailun Kehitys Oy, 1997).

The prerequisites for rural tourism were created by the process of urbanization which triggered a romantic return to nature to enjoy its comforting pleasures. This led to the rise of a summerhouse culture among the upper middle class of the late-19th century. 'Mass' rural tourism was first conducted by boarding house and spa businesses in the 1910s and 1920s: here was fresh air to breathe, healthy meals to eat, various cures and medically controlled bathing (Tarasti, 1997). Rural camping and cycling gained popularity in the 1930s and had their heyday in the 1950s. Hiking also gained in popularity in the

Continued overleaf

1950s, on skis as well as on foot. Lapland was 'discovered' at this time, and increasingly employed for this purpose (Tarasti, 1997). But that decade also saw the growth of urban, car-owning families taking an interest in farm holidays.

In the 1960s farmers began to build cottages for rent, and since the mid-1970s this has been the central form of rural tourism accommodation and service in Finland. The product consists of separate, fully equipped lake- or seaside cottages with saunas and rowing boats at visitors' disposal. In many places fishing permits are included. Finnish cottage holidays experienced a massive influx of foreign tourists as a result of the devaluation of the currency (the Finnish mark: FIM) in the late 1960s and early 1970s. Germans, in particular, subsequently returned annually to the same locations. In the 1990s Russians and Spaniards discovered this form of tourism in Finland. Indeed, international tourism receipts almost doubled during the 1990s, from about FIM 4.6 billion in 1990 to FIM 8 billion (€1.5 billion) in 1997 (KTM, 1997: 9). The most important overseas markets for rural tourism in Finland are Russia, Germany and Switzerland. Domestic tourists still dominate numerically, however, representing over 80% of rural tourists and over 75% of total visitors.

Charter trips, especially Mediterranean packages and longer-haul destinations, compete for the domestic market. For Finns, Baltic shopping 'cruises' to Tallinn, Estonia (2.5 million round-trips annually), and Stockholm (4.5 million) are a strong attraction. The short break market is increasing: in 1999, Finland hosted 3.6 million overnight stays from overseas tourists and 11.8 million from domestic tourists (KTM, 1997).

Product development and diversification and quality improvements are now critical. A grading system has been put into place for cottages, and is being piloted for other sectors (Tarasti, 1997; Maaseutumatkailun Teemaryhmä, 1999). The Finnish concept of rural tourism has been extended to encompass a wide range of services available for tourists in the countryside. Of 2080 rural tourism entrepreneurs surveyed, about 90% provide accommodation (amounting to 43,800 beds), 40% catering (B&B is increasing and over 480 entrepreneurs deal with this kind of business), and 60% have activity programmes including nature-based pursuits, the most important of which are fishing (70%), rowing and/or canoeing (55%), hiking and cross-country skiing (50%) (Maaseutumatkailun Teemaryhmä, 1999).

Particularly in northern countries, seasonality can have serious socially disruptive effects; some communities are overwhelmed by visitors for short periods of the year and empty for much of the rest of the time. Seasonality is arguably the biggest challenge for rural tourism development and sustainability in Finland. The 2 months of the short summer season provide insufficient income to allow businesses to operate profitably. The next 7 years of product development will see a concentration on activities particularly aimed at shoulder periods: culture-based programmes, local cuisine and handicrafts, and designated routes, all aimed at introducing rural life to the visitor over an extended season. Real product and market segmentation is only beginning to take place, a situation which has been rightly criticized as long overdue (Kivi, 1998; Maaseutumatkailun Teemaryhmä, 2000b).

Organizational framework for tourism policy

A summary framework of the Finnish policy structure is illustrated in Table 4.2. The Ministry of Trade and Industry is responsible for tourism as a part of economic life and entrepreneurship, and a main recent task has been to assemble a new strategy for tourism in Finland to supersede that for 1996–2000 (Tarkastusmuistio, 2000: 30).

The function, goals and organization of the Finnish Tourist Board (MEK) have been the subject of lively debate since its establishment in 1971. MEK is a state-owned agency which receives financial support from government and, for marketing operations, from the tourism industry. A redefinition of the organization's tasks and strategic policy is seeing MEK concentrating on overseas marketing and product development work (Tarkastusmuistio, 2000: 32–33). Other ministries with their local agencies are also involved in tourism as indicated in Table 4.2. A major challenge for tourism policy in Finland is to better coordinate these agencies and to identify clear areas of responsibility.

A key body administering rural tourism policy in Finland is the Rural Policy Committee, whose members, representing ministries and NGOs, are appointed by government. The committee's main tasks are to coordinate rural development measures and to promote effective use of resources channelled into rural areas. To help promote the comprehensive development of rural tourism, the Committee established the Rural Tourism Working Group in 1995, with a term of office extending until the end of 2002. It has formulated a 3-year rural tourism action programme to guide national rural tourism policy as part of the government's Rural Areas Programme.

Table 4.2. Summary of functions of major national tourism-related bodies in Finland (source: Tarkastusmuistio, 2000: 30, 32–33).

Ministry of Trade and Industry	Finnish Tourist Board (MEK)	Ministry of Forestry and Agriculture	Ministry of Environment	Ministry of Education
Economic development and entrepreneurship	Overseas promotion and marketing initiatives	Oversees involvement of farmers and landowners	Oversees nature-based strategies	Oversees culture-based strategies
Policy coordination and strategy formulation	Product development			
International cooperation	Cooperation with the Ministry of Trade and Industry			
Promotion				

Since 1997 about FIM 100 million have been spent annually on rural tourism development. Money for development work and investments has come from EU programmes 5b and 6, INTERREG, LEADER and PESCA initiatives, and from government sources (KTM Toimiala-Infomedia, 1999: 19). There has been much discussion about the efficiency of these projects (totalling 960, mainly for product development and marketing), and the Ministries of Trade and Industry and Interior have been evaluating all such projects.

The greater Regional Organizations (RO) of Lapland, The Lakeland, Finn West, Kings Road (see Box 4.2) and Åland are particularly important for overseas marketing; they receive financial support from regional councils and territorial tourism organizations. There are currently about 40 territorial marketing organizations which get their support from municipalities and counties. In all these organizations rural tourism entrepreneurs and their products tend to be overshadowed by larger-scale activities such as hotels and spas. Small entrepreneurs often have insufficient funds for large marketing efforts, and tend to be insufficiently responsive to either market demand or the changing nature of supply services. Although this organizational structure is dynamic, the entrepreneurs have not developed a strong presence, and most of them do not have travel agency rights; they cannot sell travel packages. Although the Finnish Rural Tourist Entrepreneurs Association, established in 1995, is a national association, it has only 260 members. Its main tasks are to look after the professional, social and general economic interests of rural tourism entrepreneurs and to develop rural tourism.

Box 4.2. The King's Road (sources: Anon, 2000; Finnish Tourist Board, 2000).

Travel the same road that kings and czars have travelled since the 13th century

(Anon, 2000)

The King's Road is an ancient highway of great cultural significance which follows an important medieval mail coach route. It links the Nordic capitals of Oslo and Stockholm with Turku and Helsinki in Finland and eastwards to St Petersburg in Russia. Originally, the King's Road served as an important connection between the powerful kingdoms of Sweden and Russia.

It presents a good example of the marketing of cultural routes across Europe, to assist, through transit tourism, in the regeneration of rural and peripheral regions through which it passes.

Tourism and rural restructuring

Rural tourism's contribution to the economic restructuring of rural areas

The Finnish Ministry of Forestry and Agriculture began efforts to diversify agriculture in the mid-1980s. After 2 years of pilot schemes the financing structure and methods were ready to support farmers who

Continued overleaf

wanted to diversify into tourism – mostly to build accommodation such as cottages – and other activities. The results of this policy are clearly seen in the structure of rural tourism: around 1985 about 1000 rural tourism entrepreneurs set up their businesses and over 1000 more have been established since then. About 70% of the companies have a farm, and tourism is the main income for 16% of the companies. Total accommodation capacity is 43,800 beds and some 700,000 tourists visit rural tourism places. The capacity utilization rate is just 30%, and only in July is it over 70%. On this basis, rural tourism business is not profitable, posing major policy challenges (Maaseutumatkailun Teemaryhmä, 1999).

One objective of the Rural Tourism Strategy and Development Programme is to achieve a 50% utilization rate by 2007 (Maaseutumatkailun Teemaryhmä, 2000b). Over 100 marketing organizations are marketing rural tourism products, and more than half of the entrepreneurs are marketing themselves. The large number of organizations, and thus both duplication of effort and lack of clarity of message, is seen as one reason for relatively poor marketing results (Maaseutumatkailun Teemaryhmä, 1999).

Total income from tourism is estimated at FIM 40 billion, of which the contribution from rural tourism is only 2%. Most of the money goes to large carriers and retailers. In 1998 agriculture, fishing and hunting accounted for 1.3% of Finnish gross domestic product (GDP); forestry for 2.6%. The total labour force in agriculture and forestry was 144,000, of which 83% were employed in the food sector. In 1997 the number of farms was about 139,000, with only about 2000 deriving some income from tourism (Finfood, 1999). It is estimated that by 2005 the number of farms will have fallen to 70,000: 52,000 will be traditional farms. Increasing the capacity utilization rate and diversifying the range of products and services will boost rural tourism's annual turnover to FIM 2 billion by 2007, to provide 6000 person-years of employment, a threefold increase over the current level. Rural tourism in Finland is seen as an essential part of the rural economy together with wood and food processing, but alone it can never be the saviour of the countryside (Maaseutupolitiikan Yhteistyöryhmä, 1996; Maaseutumatkailun Teemaryhmä, 2000b).

Rural tourism's contribution to the cultural restructuring of rural areas

Culture is an essential element of rural tourism, its infrastructure and products. In Finland, from the early 1980s the Association of Rural Advisory Centres was training rural women for rural festivities, food and tradition (Maaja Kotitalousnaisten Keskus, 1986). Since 1998 there has been the national project, 'Culture as strength for rural tourism'; a model inventory to be used for a culture survey in rural areas and with companies is ready. This survey entails an inventory and analysis of traditional landscapes, built environment, buildings and interiors, history, rural tourism services, food and domestic architecture, furniture and textile use. A culture development programme is being formulated on the basis of this analysis. This kind of survey is seen as a useful tool to help improve and maintain rural culture and develop products which enable visitors to appreciate that Finns respect their own culture (Maaseutumatkailun Teemaryhmä, 2000a).

Food has been heavily researched in Finland for tourism purposes, and was the first theme to be promoted for the German market, in 1996, by MEK and by the Rural Tourism Working Group. Programmes in Finland such as: (i) 'Taste of Counties', (ii) 'Best of Counties', and (iii) 'Counties à la Carte' (Lappi, Pohjois-Karjala, etc.), aim to raise awareness among both domestic and international visitors of the quality and variety of Finnish cuisine, and to provide a strong element of local and regional identity, emphasizing the rural context and culture of such food and drink production. A problem identified, however, is the need to encourage cooperation and coordination between project managers and entrepreneurs in product development and promotion. This is esential if value-added benefits are to be gained from rural economic back-linkages.

Rural tourism, environmental restructuring and sustainability of rural areas

The Declaration of Cork which followed the European conference on rural development in 1996 emphasized that sustainable rural development should become the fundamental principle to underpinning rural policy, and this ethos has been adopted in Finland. The rural tourism policy programme defines sustainable rural tourism as any form of tourist development or activity which respects the environment, ensures long-term conservation of natural and cultural recources, and is socially and economically acceptable and equitable. To develop rural tourism in a sustainable way is one of the key elements in rural tourism strategy (Tarasti, 1997; Maaseutumatkailun Teemaryhmä, 2000b).

Discussion concerning sustainable tourism began in Finland after the Brundtland report (WCED, 1987) and was further stimulated by the United Nations Conference on the Environment and Development (UNCED) in Rio de Janeiro in 1992 (Borg, 1997). The MEK produced its first national guidelines for sustainability in 1993: *Sustainable Tourism – 90's Challenge to Tourism.* Subsequently, MEK identified 30 regional projects dealing with sustainable rural tourism (MEK, 1994). At the same time the Ministry for Environment together with MEK financed national projects to identify best practice, processes and guidelines for tourism entrepreneurs in hotels and restaurants (Parviainen and Pöysti, 1995). In 1998 a guidebook of environmently friendly tourism for rural tourism entrepreneurs was prepared alongside the development of an education programme. Some 200 tourism entrepreneurs now have their own environmental strategies (Maaseutumatkailun Teemaryhmä, 2000a).

The last 10 years in Finland have seen a period of lively activity with the development of nature trails, footpaths, motor sledge routes, horse-riding trails, canoeing, cycling and skiing routes. Development of nature trails, footpaths and skiing routes is based on the plan for Finnish hiking routes made in the 1970s. Thousands of kilometres are ready or under construction. These trails and routes could be economically very important for environmentally friendly rural tourism entrepreneurs if they linked one tourism place with another. However, from their inception they were designed to pass through isolated areas, and therefore are not located close to tourism services.

Rural tourism's contribution to the image restructuring of rural areas

In addition to culture and rural people, water bodies, forests, landscapes and four distinct seasons are the main elements of the image of rural tourism in Finland. The rural tourism policy programme suggests that image restructuring should employ the threefold classification of rural areas. The products of these areas can be grouped into eight nationwide themes: pure gifts of nature, traditional celebrations and work, tasty traditional dishes, hot summer activities, idyllic farms, snow-crunching winter activities, cottages rich in atmosphere and enchanting countryside tours with B&B (Maaseutumatkailun Teemaryhmä, 2000b). A major aim of rural policy is to transform the traditional image of the countryside from that of a place for natural resource exploitation and poor quality service into one of economically sound and improving entrepreneurs with strong networks offering high quality products (Maaseutupolitiikan Yhteistyöryhmä, 1996). One constraint on image restructuring is the ethos of 'Everyman's right', Finnish common law giving every citizen the basic right to freely enjoy the countryside; a consequence of which is that Finns are not accustomed to paying for nature-based recreation.

Issues for debate

While Finland explicitly recognizes 'rural tourism' as an area of activity for policy focus, no such functional-geographical distinction is recognized for policy purposes in most other European countries. 'The rural' is (still) deeply rooted within Finnish culture and expressed in rural land ownership patterns, while in other countries processes of urbanization and patterns of rural land ownership have divorced many (Western) Europeans from their rural roots. Yet, while Finland's rural tourism is strongly rooted in its people, greater cooperation and coordination and a sense of professionalism are required at all levels if Finland's rural tourism products are to become internationally competitive.

In Finland, rural tourism has only been recognized as a separate entity for policy purposes since 1995, and a rural tourism policy was completed in late 2000, as part of wider rural policy. A number of questions are raised by this approach:

- Is it appropriate for Finland to pursue a separate rural tourism (as opposed to other forms of tourism) policy?
- Does the Finnish experience provide a model for other European or less developed countries, or is it uniquely appropriate for Finland?
- If tourism needs to be viewed in its wider developmental context and never in isolation, is it realistic to try to isolate rural dimensions from their wider tourism context through an explicitly rural tourism policy?

Mirja Nylander

Policy and Governance

The balance between representing and embedding bottom-up values and the need for bringing to bear top-down resources, is a delicate one (Chapter 5). Publicly declared strategic actions therefore need to be framed with care and sensitivity, to embrace and represent host communities, business interests and environmental considerations. This ideal may be less realistic for developing countries, where a top-down approach may be perceived as necessary to kick-start or give an impetus to rural tourism development and to better integrate it into national tourism and development policy, as in the case of India (e.g. Box 4.3).

As the 'hollowing out' of the state places more emphasis at both supranational and local/regional levels, there is increasing emphasis within approaches to economic development and regional strategy on the importance of partnerships, networks and cooperation between institutions (see also Chapter 5). At the local level, a wide range of governmental, parastatal and non-governmental stakeholders have a direct interest in the development of tourism and recreation as an element of integrated rural and regional devel-

Box 4.3. High profile for rural tourism in Indian policy (source: Government of India, 1997; Sood, 1998).

Direct employment in the tourism sector during 1995/96 was about 8.5 million or 2.4% of the total labour force. The development of rural tourism in India has formed part of an action plan drawn up to identify new tourism destinations and to develop infrastructure in existing tourist regions for implementation during the Ninth National Plan period (1997–2002).
Six tourism sectors were prioritized for the plan period:

- indigenous and natural health tourism;
- rural and village tourism;
- pilgrim tourism;
- adventure tourism;
- heritage tourism; and
- youth and senior citizens' packages.

Rural tourism was targeted as a sector having substantial growth potential particularly in the North-eastern region, Sikkim, and Jammu and Kashmir.

Key elements of policy:

- to dovetail rural tourism into district level plans;
- to remove inter-state barriers to allow free movement of tourists between states;
- to involve the private sector in upgrading and expanding existing airports at Guwahati, Bagdogra, Srinagar and Dehradun as gateways to enable easier international access to rural areas; and
- to encourage people's participation in tourism development, including Panchayati Raj institutions (village councils), local bodies, NGOs and enterprising local youth (sic), in order to create public awareness and to achieve a wider spread of tourist facilities.

Inter-ministerial group proposals:

- Identification of 50 destinations where tourism infrastructure needed improvement.
- The civil aviation ministry should assist in the formation of a regional airline and helicopter service covering Himachal Pradesh, Jammu and Kashmir, Punjab, Uttar Pradesh, and the Eastern and North-eastern region. (Negotiations were undertaken with local airlines which have light aircraft able to land and take off in hilly areas. It was anticipated that air-linking of these remote tourist spots would increase flow of traffic and spur their development.)
- The Tourism Finance Corporation of India (TFCI) and the India Tourism Development Corporation (ITDC) should play an important role in setting up hotel management and food craft institutes and identify new hotel projects in the North-eastern region.
- Environment, coastal zone and forest regulation to be enforced in a pragmatic manner for tourism projects and powers for approval to be delegated to the states.
- The promotion of Buddhist pilgrimage should be assisted, including the upgrading of air, rail and road services for Bodh Gaya (a 'Buddhist rail circuit' is being developed).

opment. South-west England has long been a popular holiday destination region for visitors from across the UK. As coastal resorts experience relative decline from tourism, and as agricultural hinterlands face economic reorientation, local agencies have sought a range of strategies for economic regeneration and restructuring (e.g. Meethan, 1998). Thus, in the case of South Somerset local authority (Box 4.4), notions of sustainability, SME support, equal opportunities, community involvement and partnership working are invoked almost as the mantras of post-industrial economic (re-)development strategy. As indicated in Chapters 3 and 5, however, most of these concepts and their operationalization are far from unproblematic.

Access, Land Ownership and Land Use Issues

> Achieving the right balance between accessibility and isolation is a major planning challenge in rural tourism.
>
> (Page and Getz, 1997: 200)

Access, land ownership and land use issues articulate several contemporary debates and tensions surrounding recreation and tourism in rural areas, ranging from issues of personal freedom, cultural tradition, the protection of fragile ecosystems, social construction and values to shortcomings in rural policy implementation, unclear management strategies and changing legislative contexts.

In a number of European contexts, public access to rural land is actually diminishing as a result of the following:

- Changing patterns of ownership and an increasing reluctance of many landowners to accept traditional access to their property for general recreation. Questions of insurance liability, damage to property and loss of privacy are significant factors in this trend.
- As increasing numbers of urbanites acquire leisure or retirement properties in rural areas, they regard and treat those properties as private preserves, just as the landed elite jealously guarded their own leisure estates centuries before.
- Agribusinesses, adopting a corporate outlook,

Box 4.4. South Somerset Council's Economic Development and Tourism Strategy for 1998/99 (source: South Somerset District Council, 1999).

Context

The Local Government & Housing Act 1989 requires all local authorities in England and Wales undertaking economic development activity to prepare an annual economic development strategy which includes tourism.

Aims and objectives

To achieve economic growth:

- in a sustainable environment;
- through well-paid, secure jobs;
- through successful existing businesses;
- with a commitment to the principles of equal opportunities and community involvement; and
- through partnership working and joint funding.

An economic regeneration focus designed to:

- help businesses to set up and grow;
- target the need to reduce social exclusion; and
- involve local communities in developing and implementing actions for their areas.

This explicit shift from a solely economic development programme necessarily incorporates social, cultural and environmental objectives to comprise an action plan compatible with and complementary to the principles of Local Agenda 21.

Box 4.4. *Continued*

Tourism, promotion and development objectives

Sustainable tourism

Key actions:

- Develop sustainable concepts and ideas that support local tourism and are enjoyed by local people.
- Walks: for example (i) publish walk guides in an area based format; (ii) help produce, on behalf of the Bristol to Weymouth Rail Partnership, a 'trails by rail' guide detailing walks from stations on the route.
- Cycling: (i) look to republish and improve 100-mile cycle route by including shorter sections and incorporating other routes within it; (ii) help establish Langport as a centre for cycling and walking through development of the Langport and River Parrett visitor centre.
- Disabled visitor information: produce a guide aimed at helping disabled visitors and residents.

Visitor services

Key actions:

- Bristol to Weymouth Rail Partnership: produce a 'trails by rail' publication/market line to residents along its length.
- Manage visitor information centres at Yeovil and Podimore to provide a new quality service to tourists and locals.
- Support, provide advice/training and day-to-day assistance to community tourism initiatives including six local information centres.
- Quality grading: move towards an inspected-only accommodation guide in 2000; hold trade liaison meetings.

Partnerships

Key actions:

- Support, influence and initiate partnerships with other bodies/organizations which can help achieve objectives, such as: local chambers of trade and town councils; West Country Tourist Board; West of England Tourism Group; EU; South West Film Commission; Blackdown Hills Project.
- Pays de la Loire: continue to develop this partnership in this region. Expected outputs to include Hotels du Patrimoine brochure, exchanges between chateaux and historic houses and gardens, and learning surrounding green tourism on sensitive sites.

are also less likely to accept informal and unpaid access to their lands by the public for recreation than was the traditional farming landowner, who probably had to deal with far fewer, and less impacting visitors. In addition, the landscapes produced by many agribusinesses may be neither aesthetically nor functionally appropriate for leisure activities.

Access to the countryside is an obvious prerequisite for rural recreation and tourism, and growing demand suggests a greater need for access. Yet the recreational desirability of access needs to be balanced with both other land use demands and the longer-term needs of protection or conservation. With an increase in such potentially conflicting demands on rural resources, difficult management decisions have to be taken. The Scandinavian/Nordic countries have had a strong tradition of free access coupled with clear obligations. Yet even in Sweden it has been suggested that *Allemansträtt,* the traditional free right of access to the countryside (Box 4.5), should be limited to Swedish citizens as a result of concern over the misuse of these rights by overseas tourists (Sandell, 1995).

In the UK, Scotland has a slightly different system to that of England and Wales, and in both legislative change is currently being pursued. The natural environment has long been important for the image of Scotland, yet the Scottish countryside is a contested space:

Box 4.5. Summary of access in Sweden, Norway, Germany and Denmark (sources: Anon, 1998; Oloffson, 1998).

In all countries there is a close link between rights and responsibilities; Scandinavian freedom of access principles entail balancing strong responsibilities on the visitor

There is a high degree of consensus working between all the parties, with a general commitment to make the arrangements work

There is a general acceptance by all the parties of the strong right to access, and this common understanding provides strength to joint working

There is a quite simple approach to the basic legislation: the emphasis is less on the law and more on management, education and establishing a strong culture of responsibility in recreation

Within this framework of consensus-working there are clear roles for all the main parties: (i) national agencies are responsible for oversight and support to the others; (ii) local authorities lead in management and mediation; and (iii) land-owning and recreation bodies work to improve management and the promotion of responsible behaviour

Motorized recreation is strongly controlled; foot access has the greatest level of freedom, but good provision is made for cycling and riding on surfaced tracks and paths

All have either extensive or at least some rights of access over uncultivated land, for example, in woodland or at the coast

Denmark and Germany have for their enclosed farmlands an arrangement of general access to existing paths and tracks – in Germany known as the *Betretungsrecht* – based on tradition and local custom which are now enshrined in law, although the arrangements in any one part of Germany are founded on local management and legislation at the *Land* level

In Denmark, access to paths and tracks was opened up in 1992 and, although opposed by landowners initially, it has come to work reasonably well

In each of these countries, there is a historical and traditional underpinning to the present access arrangements:

- Norway has converted its traditional rights into legislation, in particular the Open-Air Recreation Act of 1957;
- Swedish customary rights are embedded in the constitution.

Inevitably, the detailed differences between the countries reflect differences in patterns of land tenure, densities of population and recreational pressures: in all four countries, visitors take access at their own risk.

access rights have been an arena of conflict and the ownership structure of land in Scotland has had a major effect on the landscape and the recreational uses that take place on it (Cramb, 1996; Wightman, 1996). In the 20th century there were arguments about the roles of various land using activities, a long-running debate about freedom to roam in open country (SNH, 1992), and an unresolved debate about protection and enhancement of the highest quality environments (Scottish Office, 1996). In the UK, as across the EU, farmers and other rural land owners, as 'stewards' of the rural landscape, may receive a number of inducements to care for the 'natural' environment for both conservation and recreational purposes (Box 4.6), a potential tension which is not always easily resolved. Many land managers see tourists and recreationalists as imposing a cost (Crabtree *et al.*, 1992) rather than providing an opportunity. This reflects both the reality of the burden that rural recreation can place on sporting and productive enterprises (such as disturbing game, or road accidents with lambs) and the negative approach of some conservative land managers towards tourism (Slee, 1998: 94).

In the following invited piece by Fiona Simpson, the question of access and land management in relation to recreation and tourism in rural areas is examined in further detail, placing the dynamic Scottish situation within a wider European context.

Box 4.6. Rural stakeholders: stewards of the landscape (source: Rilla, 2000: 20–22, 38–40).

Less favoured areas (LFAs), established in the UK in 1975, cover 52% of the country. Within these areas farmers receive grants to maintain breeding cows and sheep and grants higher than the basic rate for improvements and conservation work on the farm. The highest payments are received in the most severely disadvantaged hill farm areas.

The Farm and Conservation Scheme was set up in 1989 providing grants for:

- land improvement and energy saving: 25% in LFAs and 15% elsewhere;
- waste handling facilities: 50%; and
- environmental and countryside work: 35–50%.

The Wildlife and Countryside Act of 1981 allows national park authorities to make voluntary management agreements with farmers and landowners to encourage conservation aims. Farmers receive compensatory payments to offset practices not put into place that would be profitable but potentially economically harmful.

Environmentally sensitive areas (ESAs) were introduced in 1986 to help protect some of the most beautiful parts of the countryside. Guidelines encourage farmers and landowners to manage their land in ways which conserve and enhance the landscape, wildlife and historic features. A 10-year agreement is linked to annual payments. Examples include exclusionary fencing near eroded areas and hedgerow improvement and maintenance for wildlife habitat and animal fencing.

Invited Viewpoint

Access and Land Management

Fiona Simpson

Cultural acceptance of the synergies between man and nature are central to any debate on access to the countryside. Such relationships form an ingrained part of society in countries like Sweden and Norway, where a universal right of access is a tradition, and embedded within national constitutional frameworks. In these countries, the close links between rights and responsibilities have been a fundamental influence on the closer relationship which exists between town and country. As a result, access to the countryside is based on the concept of consensus, which in turn is grounded in a common acceptance that the 'right to roam' is a legitimate part of society.

However, the different attitudes to access to the countryside are likely to be influenced by a range of factors, including population density, the extent of pressure for recreational activities, social history and environmental conditions. In the UK, such a tradition of urban and rural interdependence is less widely accepted; many urban dwellers now have little or no connection to, or understanding of, the countryside. Social trends not only show that people are becoming increasingly interested in outdoor recreation, but also that pressure for such activities, coupled with commercially oriented agricultural practice, are resulting in increasing pressure on the natural environment. Perhaps as a result, access, and in particular its implications for land managers, has been subject to growing scrutiny over recent years in the UK. In England and Wales, the Countryside Agency has been involved in developing new rights of access to open countryside, which do not apply to agricultural land, except for extensive areas of grazing.

In Scotland, recent legislation on land reform focuses on new rights associated with access provision to the countryside. As a result the government quango Scottish Natural Heritage (SNH) has been focusing on the preparation of a new Scottish Code of Outdoor Access to replace the long-standing Countryside Code. Through promoting responsible behaviour, the new Code aims to ensure that land management, conservation and other aspects of countryside management are not prejudiced by an increase in public access.

The new legislation is likely to have a direct impact on relationships between land managers, recreational users of the countryside, and more generally local communities, particularly on the urban fringe. This is perhaps the most interesting, but also potentially the most divisive, aspect of the proposed changes. As consultation has progressed, land manager organizations such as the National Farmers Union (NFU), landowner organizations, and other interest groups, acting as custodians of the rural landscape, have highlighted their concerns about the potential increase in people gaining access to the countryside. At the same time, a plethora of user groups such as the Ramblers' Association, Cyclists' Touring Club and environmental campaigners, have used the prospective changes to reinforce their lobbying for a universal right of access.

This debate has been well publicized, with the views of proponents remaining largely polarized. However, there has also been increasing recognition that the issues are not necessarily representative of relationships as they are evolving at the local level. Research carried out on behalf of SNH, which tests the impact of the proposed legislation in Scotland (Land Use Consultants, unpublished), shows that while bodies like the NFU have played a key role in the debate, a significant proportion of their members are neither aware of, nor concerned about, the changes proposed by the new legislation. Similarly, national user groups could be viewed as representing only a small, relatively well informed, and often economically privileged part of society. Indeed, the people who might benefit most from access, who may be socially excluded or suffer from poor health as a result of inactivity, are perhaps those who are least likely to be affiliated with traditional access user groups (e.g. see Chapter 3).

Land managers do share a number of common concerns about access, which will require further attention if the new legislation is not to further polarize the contemporary debate on society and the countryside. Farmers in urban fringe areas feel particularly vulnerable to irresponsible access (resulting in vandalism, theft and damage to crops and livestock). If not carefully managed, public access can affect farm quality assurance schemes or may prejudice specialist breeding programmes. Sporting interests and game conservation can also be adversely affected by ill-informed access choices. Furthermore, many farmers who may be willing to play a more positive role in access provision, remain concerned about the liability implications of a member of the public being injured on their land. These issues require attention, and will form an important component of the Outdoor Access Code. The legislation should also provide scope for enhanced support structures and advice for land managers, moving away from the emphasis on the conflict-based approach, embodied by the traditional rights of way system.

The new legislation provides an opportunity to extend our understanding of access, and to ensure that broader 'communities of interest' become involved in managing resources. The proposed changes include a requirement for each local authority to establish at least one access forum to oversee the planning and management of access at the local level and, potentially, mediate between individuals and their wider community as a whole where problems arise. Membership of access forums is likely to comprise a range of stakeholders, including key agencies, land managers and user groups. However 'wider' communities, comprising people who might not normally be included in the access debate will also be encouraged to participate, testing the extent to which access can become synonymous with inclusion.

Bringing together land managers with members of the community who have not been 'filtered' by factors like car ownership and pre-existing knowledge of the countryside to ensure that they behave responsibly (Whitby, 1997), could prove a significant step forward in overcoming the long entrenched 'town and country' debate. While land managers in the urban fringe have particular problems compared with those in more peripheral locations, the boundaries between those who do and do not understand the ways of the countryside are becoming more blurred, and are less commonly defined by whether someone's home is in an urban or rural area. Indeed, many more peripheral rural areas now contain residents who are barely connected to the farming community, as a result of the growing numbers of people 'retreating' to the countryside from the city, and maintaining a commuter lifestyle.

It is critical that 'communities' that are identified for membership of local access forums are recognized as being more inclusive than traditional user groups. Defined in this way, not only does the term 'community' extend beyond the traditionally enthusiastic proponents of access, it also includes land managers themselves. At the same time, land manager representation on local access forums should extend beyond a perfunctory acceptance that national bodies are representative of their interests. In areas with mixed farming, it is critical that the different needs of livestock and arable farmers, and those involved in sporting and game conservation are each represented to ensure their different problems and needs are fully accounted for.

Continued overleaf

Although understanding and anticipating potential problems will be important, it is also likely that a more inclusive approach to countryside access will only emerge when the full range of potential benefits that it can result in, are better understood. The new legislation provides an opportunity to move beyond traditional debates, limited by perceptions based on stereotypes, towards a more consensus-based approach to access management. The extent to which this will be achievable, given that the 'right to roam' has not formed an integral part of society in Scotland, as has been the case in Scandinavia and other Northern European countries, will only be understood in the longer term. However, it is a goal worth pursuing. Access can be beneficial not only for communities, but also for land managers. It has the potential to support a growing role for land managers as countryside stewards, as agriculture continues to shift away from an emphasis on operational efficiency towards a more sustainable approach to environmental stewardship. This in turn will help to reinforce the legitimacy of agriculture within a society that is neither fully aware of, nor universally sympathetic to, rural decline.

Fiona Simpson

Management Challenges: Equity, Protection, Proscription, Payment

A major challenge for the management of recreation and tourism in rural areas is therefore the need to balance: (i) demand for more and different types of access, as more people want to visit the countryside and pursue a growing range of recreational activities; and (ii) the need for conservation and protection of the rural natural and cultural environment.

One increasingly favoured management policy to access questions is to impose a charge for consuming the countryside, and this is discussed at some length by Sharpley and Sharpley (1997: 133–137). As concern for the environmental impacts of recreation and tourism has grown, increasing attention has been focused on the potential role of access fees as a means of reducing such impacts in rural areas. As the carrying capacity of many popular destination areas has been exceeded, resulting in unsustainable levels of recreational use and, in some cases, serious damage to the physical fabric of the countryside, it has been argued that putting a price on rural recreation can be an effective means of alleviating some of these problems. As ability to pay and willingness to pay have been seen as significant factors affecting demand for recreation and tourism in rural areas (Bovaird *et al.*, 1984), by implication, pricing can be used to manipulate, or ration that demand.

Employment of charging, as a visitor management tool, is predicated on the assumption that if the cost of a visit to the countryside increases, only those people who place a higher value on the experience will continue to visit, assuming the expected benefits outweigh the visit's costs. Precedent for the imposition of entry fees to specific rural areas was established in the USA when federal car-entry permits were introduced at Mount Rainier National Park in 1908 (Harris and Driver, 1987). Within a few years Yosemite and Yellowstone National Parks were also charging fees (Walsh, 1986). Most US national parks now impose an entry charge, as do many other parks, recreational sites, nature reserves and other designated areas around the world. A key element in most of these situations is that the fees collected from visitors can be seen to contribute towards their own pleasure by helping to pay for: the management cost of the park or attraction and the costs of providing visitor services and facilities. Further, if pricing is promoted as contributing to conservation, there is greater likelihood of gaining support in its implementation (Leuschner *et al.*, 1987).

The logic of environmental economics argues that, for any economic activity, including tourism and recreation, to be sustainable in the long term, and for scarce resources to be allocated and used rationally, the full cost of that activity must be 'internalized' by the producer and, inevitably, passed on to the consumer (Sharpley and Sharpley, 1997: 136). Both the rural tourism industry and rural recreationalists should therefore be held responsible for the environmental costs resulting from recreational activity. Counter arguments to imposing charges are usually based on grounds of ethics or precedent:

- On health grounds at least, rural recreation is widely considered to be beneficial both for the individual and for society and should be promoted as such (as indicated in the previous chapter).
- Free access to the countryside is a moral right: imposing any form of charge is therefore an infringement of personal freedom.
- Most domestic recreationalists already pay for access, albeit indirectly, through tax and other payments.
- The process of charging acts to ration demand according to an ability to pay and is therefore discriminatory, against just those segments of society who might benefit most from being encouraged to visit the countryside.
- Charging can be used as a means of extracting profits from a site or attraction on the pretext of altruistic conservation motives (e.g. Fyall and Garrod, 1998).

Indeed, the last argument reveals a sustainability paradox implicit in environmental economics, wherein charging promotes exclusion, yet sustainability implies inclusiveness and equity. Yet, clearly, the global trend is towards access charging as increasing numbers of recreationalists wish to pursue an ever-widening and more impacting range of activities, thereby placing unsustainable demands on finite rural resources. So, paradoxically 'it is recognised that all forms of tourism, including rural tourism, to be sustainable ... will, in the future, have to pay their way' (Sharpley and Sharpley, 1997: 137). But if, because of increasing pressures, rationing in some form is inevitable, does it have to be based on ability to pay? The issues of ameliorating impacts, funding conservation and recreation, and providing equitable access seem to have become somewhat entangled here. In the case of 'wild places'/wilderness areas, there is a requirement for particular recreation management approaches. The 1964 US Wilderness Act – the outcome of a protracted debate concerning the need to protect diminishing wildland environments – provided the stimulus for wilderness protection in many other places.

In crowded Europe, wild places are modified to some extent and the imprint of past human use may often be visible. But their inherent qualities are no less at risk from land use change and development, including the growth of recreational use. Wild places may be perceived by economic sector management as functionally empty and thereby available for development activities which may be difficult to locate or pursue elsewhere, such as afforestation, hydroelectric power development, and improved regional road access.

Wildness, which may or may not be perceived as a different quality to wilderness, is both an aesthetic and an experiential concept; naturalness, solitude, and a sense of challenge and hazard are key components in its definition, although the threshold at which people perceive wildness may vary according to individual sensitivity and past experience (Mackay, 1997). This emphasizes the fact that in small, crowded European countries where wildness is a rare commodity, there is a need to raise awareness and understanding of the issue of its protection and sustainable approaches to its use so that wildness can be more clearly identified as an important quality of land which needs better protection.

The establishment of national parks and other protected areas in Europe has gone some way in achieving this, although the nature and status of such parks varies considerably across the continent and their very designation may induce a honeypot effect for recreationalists (FNNP, 1993), placing them under even greater management pressures.

Managing Land Use Conflicts

Conflicts of interest between the different users of any piece of land are inherent in any dynamic society. The requirements of environmental protection, recreation (which may or may not be environmentally friendly) and other land use demands are perhaps most severely expressed in national parks and other areas of similar designation, where apparently paradoxical functions of conservation, leisure and indigenous economic activity are supported: 'helping visitors to enjoy, appreciate and understand the park's unique character, whilst working with local people to conserve their livelihoods and the landscape, wildlife and cultural heritage' (NNPA, 1999). The potential and actual land use conflicts arising from this management responsibility may be considerable (Box 4.7), and although management responses will vary, an increasingly important role can be played by interpretation in attempting to mitigate the impacts of such conflicts (e.g. Box 4.8). Other conflicts, as exemplified in the Northumberland National Park (NNP) in north-east England (Box 4.9) may require more substantive responses.

Management through Interpretation

Interpretation is increasingly being adopted as a major and important tool for recreation management particularly in protected or sensitive areas, and may be employed in conjunction with codes of conduct (e.g. UNEP/IE, 1995; Mason and Mowforth, 1996). Although often associated with landscape, interpretation is far more elaborate and has far wider implications for the management of recreation and tourism in rural areas. Barrow (1994), for example, has argued that interpretation is based on three types of planning (Fennell, 1999: 197):

1. Town and country: where appropriate land use philosophies and techniques are employed for largely protective purposes.
2. Marketing: dealing with how best to understand various user groups and their particular needs and aspirations.
3. Education: employing educational theory in management strategy to understand how people learn and what to 'teach' them (e.g. Veverka, 1994).

The third element raises several questions surrounding the problem of contested interpretations. Who interprets? What values lie behind that interpretation? What are the consequences for those consuming the interpetation? What are the impacts on the objects being consumed through such interpretation?

Box 4.7. Land use conflicts related to recreation and tourism in national parks (source: NNPA, 1999).

Litter:

- can be life threatening to grazing stock and wildlife; and
- can damage farm machinery.

Disturbance and intrusion:

- visitors deviating from rights of way can lead to disturbance of stock and the daily life of people living and working in the countryside;
- noise and the presence of people and dogs can disturb nesting birds and frighten other animals from the area;
- walkers and cyclists break up the soil every time their boot or tyre touches the ground, allowing it to be more easily washed or blown away;
- trampling of vegetation can damage sensitive plant communities and consequently their dependent wildlife; and
- visitors may be tempted to pick wild flowers.

Uncontrolled dogs:

- sheep may be scared away from where they are feeding or sheltering;
- if they are stressed at lambing time the ewe may abort, giving birth to a dead lamb; and
- in severe cases sheep have been killed by dogs.

Damage to walls and fences:

- visitors can cause damage to walls and fences by climbing over them, especially to the unmortared dry-stone walls which are characteristic of much of northern England; and
- broken walls and fences allow stock to roam, leading to crop damage, road fatalities and the mixing of livestock belonging to different farms.

Box 4.8. Northumberland National Park management response to visitor pressures: informing and educating visitors (source: NNPA, 1999).

The national park information centres distribute educational leaflets and copies of *The Curlew Country Code*
Centres show slide and video presentations
Trained, well informed information assistants are available to talk to visitors
Voluntary wardens enhance ranger service patrols by providing on-site, up-to-date, one-to-one information for visitors at honeypot locations (usually car parks near popular attractions) at peak visitor times
Information panels are located at important sites and car parks, providing specific details about a site and advice on access
Total signing of all public footpaths and bridleways in the park is planned, although this in itself raises issues of aesthetic quality. The park authorities construct ladder stiles over walls and step stiles through fences where rights of way cross these boundaries
Specific notices are posted during lambing and haymaking to make visitors aware of the need to be especially considerate of farmers' needs at these times

Box 4.9. Northumberland National Park: land use conflicts exemplified (source: NNPA, 1999).

Footpath erosion: the Pennine Way at Hadrian's Wall

Conflict: increasing numbers of feet walking on popular sections of footpath cause ground vegetation to die and the soil to be exposed and then eroded. This problem is particularly bad along the visually stunning section of Hadrian's Wall between Steel Rigg and Housesteads where the Pennine Way follows the Wall.

Management response: historically, the right of way, the legal footpath, here actually ran along the top of Hadrian's Wall. This was clearly damaging the fabric and archaeological quality of the monument. The right of way was therefore successfully moved by the national park authority to run on the ground, alongside the Wall away from other important archaeology buried under the soil. This path has eroded, and in partnership with the land owners and the National Trust, the Northumberland National Park Authority (NNPA) has resurfaced the footpath in the most sympathetic way available: on level sections stone chippings have been used and on slopes stone pitching (similar to cobbles, but using larger irregular-shaped stones) has been employed to create a hard, sustainable surface able to resist erosion. The blocks and chippings used are of the locally occurring whinstone, taken from the ridge along which Hadrian's Wall runs. Over time the soil around these new surfaces revegetates, blending the new path into the landscape. Because Hadrian's Wall is in both the National Park and the World Heritage Site, special care has been required over the aesthetic appearance as well as the functionality of the work.

Military use: Otterburn training area (OTA)

Conflict: the purpose of UK national parks authorities is to 'conserve and enhance' and to 'promote the understanding and enjoyment' of the national park. In NNP it is clear that the movement of troops and artillery and the firing of live weapons by the military is in conflict with the national park's purpose. However, military forces have been a presence in the English–Scottish borders since Roman times, and the UK Ministry of Defence (MoD) has owned training grounds in Redesdale since 1911, 45 years before the NNP came into existence in 1956.

Management response: the MoD has allowed a low-input, low-output system of farming to continue by generous financial arrangements with its tenant farmers. This is valuable for wildlife conservation and has added benefits for archaeological conservation, especially with the excellent photographic records and consolidation work the military have undertaken. In addition there have been extensive tree planting schemes within OTA and support for conservation work continues. None the less, this situation serves to highlight the conflicting priorities of two government bodies protecting two diverse national concerns.

The following invited collaborative piece by Lesley Roberts and Gunnar Rognvaldsson indicates the potential value of interpretation – as education, entertainment, ethics – its ability to increase carrying capacities and also to assist prescription as a management tool. The authors evaluate the issue of different types of recreationalists and tourists potentially requiring interpretation in different quantities, qualities and distribution patterns. They conclude that interpretative materials can act as an important management tool, but that more research on their utility and impact is required.

Invited Collaboration

The Roles of Interpretation in Facilitating Access to and in the Countryside

Lesley Roberts and Gunnar Rognvaldsson

Substantial increases in participation in rural recreation and tourism have the potential to exacerbate existing and to create additional environmental impacts. In many countries across Europe where people's rights to access are well established, there exist concerns about such potential. In the UK, where rights of access are only now being enshrined in legislation, increases in rural visiting appear to have given rise to an expectation that they will result in inevitable environmental damage. Many landowners and managers are anxious about, and even hostile to, the principles of increased countryside access. Many public agencies, in contraposition, have the remit to support rural access and recreation within limits designed to safeguard land management and conservation activities.

The patchy evidence that exists, however, seems to indicate that the fear of damage may be greater than its reality. In her account of the iniquities of modern farming methods, Shoard (1980: 235) has pointed to a form of visitor conservatism in the countryside which, reinforced by an uncertainty about where people can and cannot go, 'inclines people to stick with the familiar'. She believes that 'trespassers will be prosecuted' and similar admonitions have sunk deep into the urban psyche so that visitors are afraid of the countryside rather than a threat to it. In the absence of robust research into spatial patterns of rural visiting at local levels, considerable evidence exists to support Shoard's claims. Primarily for fear of getting lost, most townspeople tend to use and stay on well-recognized paths and routes they have walked before. Their acknowledged lack of understanding of rural life has created in them an instinctive hesitation that easily discourages use of the countryside for recreation (Shoard, 1999: 10). More recent research into behaviour in the Scottish countryside (Costley, 2000) has shown that 89% of countryside visitors surveyed stressed the importance of 'responsible' behaviour. This suggests that countryside visitors seem to be aware that the rural environment demands a different kind of attention from urban surroundings, and to know that their behaviour should be adjusted accordingly. The lack of reported widespread damage suggests that most visitors to the countryside comply with what they see to be the requirements of nature. Of those who fail to demonstrate 'appropriate' behaviour, it may not be unreasonable to assume that they act out of ignorance rather than disregard or malice. If this is the case, then the problems can be tackled with educational and interpretative programmes. This contribution recognizes the potential for ignorance and misunderstanding to give rise to conflicts, in rural tourism and recreation as in other contexts, and argues a role for interpretative materials in the amelioration of such situations.

A growing recognition of the need for 'education' in tourism in general has resulted in the transmission of information in attempts to offset potential conflicts, often via the production of codes of conduct, many of which have had limited effects (Mason and Mowforth, 1996). Yet there are other contexts in which means of persuasive communication are very well developed: in the health education field, for example, and more generally in advertising where a great deal of research underpins attempts to influence consumer behaviour.

What is meant by 'interpretation'?

Classically defined, interpretation is 'an educational activity that aims to reveal meanings and relationships through the use of original objects, by first-hand experience, and by illustrative media, rather than simply to communicate factual information' (Tilden, 1957: 8). Good use of interpretation is illustrated by skilful communication of themes, perspectives and linkages. According to Ham (1992: 3), interpretation involves translating the technical, or the otherwise unknown, into terms and ideas that lay people can readily understand; and it involves doing so in a way that is both entertaining and interesting. Interpretation is the process by which information can be imbued with meaning, provoking thought, creating links and communicating to people a sense of understanding and appreciation.

Within rural tourism, the roles of interpretation are similar to those of environmental interpretation. Interpretation can enhance enjoyment (Ham, 1992), it may develop an appreciation of sense of place (Stewart *et al.*, 1998), and it can educate, challenge and provide insight (Tilden, 1957). It may facilitate attitudinal or behavioural change (Moscardo, 1996; Prentice, 1996), and it can relieve crowding and congestion (Moscardo, 1996). The potential for interpretative materials to make places and experiences accessible to tourists is well documented (Tilden, 1957; Uzzell, 1989; Ham, 1992; Moscardo, 1996).

Despite a recent recognition of the potential to influence rural tourism processes and practices in the interests of sustainability and conflict resolution, interpretation in the general tourism context has developed quite a different role from that of environmental interpretation. Primarily, the role of interpretation as a communication process designed to create interest in a product, process or place by stimulating enquiry, provoking thought and relating to experience, has been harnessed, not for the purposes of education, but for entertainment. Interpretative materials and experiences now form the core of the tourism product, and are evident in a range of visitor experiences in heritage centres, visitor centres, and at historic sites and countryside centres that provide a visitor experience. In this sense, interpretation may be perceived as a product rather than a process, and one that helps rural visitors to interpret and otherwise understand rural issues such as stock rearing or the contributions of genetic modification to agricultural production. New leisure forms that have appeared offer learning experiences staged as themes to provide entertainment by interpreting reproductions of the past, complexities of the present and concepts of the future (Rojek, 1993: 146). The subject of product development in this manner will be returned to in Chapter 7.

With the ability to appeal to emotions as well as intellects, however, interpretation can be an effective form of communication. It is interesting that while such a powerful way of connecting with people has become a core element of the tourism product, it is so little recognized as an effective means of addressing potential conflicts, and the resulting requirement for visitors and hosts alike to adjust attitudes and behaviours in the conflict resolution process.

Evidence of the use of persuasive communication in tourism to effect behaviour change can be found in the growing popularity of codes of conduct, presented as leaflets, stickers and videos. They have appeared in response to widespread inequalities in resort development within what are often peripheral areas of the world without the resources to maximize benefits of development equitably. Although there have been attempts to create codes of conduct for visitors and hosts alike, most address the former, aiming to raise tourist awareness and educate visitors as part of a wider tourism management strategy.

Theories of behaviour change

Behaviour does not change without a preceding change in attitude (Fishbein and Manfredo, 1992). In their turn, attitudes can be influenced by access to new information, appeals to emotion, and/or pressure from others resulting in new subjective norms and subsequent behaviour modification (Engel *et al.*, 1995: 387). In theory, therefore, it should be possible to influence hosts' and tourists' attitudes and behaviours to reduce problems and tensions at a local level by applying the principles of effective interpretation to visitor management processes.

Research undertaken into the potential of interpretation relates almost exclusively to tourism and the natural environment. A number of studies have been conducted, some in response to environmental concerns (Moscardo, 1996; Orams, 1996, 1997; Stewart *et al.*, 1998) and others out of a recognition of

Continued overleaf

the importance of interpretation techniques in responding to the needs of eco- and nature-based tourists (Travelweek Australia in Orams, 1996). The idea is approached by Stewart *et al.* (1998) in relation to *sense of place*; their question is 'does interpretation have the capacity to take visitors one step beyond wherever they happen to be when they arrive at a site so that empathy or "care" is developed towards the conservation of that place and sequentially to other places throughout the world?' The authors argue that well-conceived and managed interpretation can make a difference and indeed may have a cumulative effect encouraging the desired result of empathy with surroundings. They conclude, however, that further empirical research is required to uncover the intricacies of the relationships between people, place and interpretation. This development of a *sense of place* should underpin tourism management processes at destination level. For Dagnall and Atkinson (unpublished) this means that recreational use of land and water should be founded on care so that those who enjoy the outdoors are encouraged to respect its beauty, its wildlife, its operational needs and the privacy of those who live or earn their living there. Although Dagnall and Atkinson (unpublished) recommend the establishment of voluntary codes of conduct for site management, the use of interpretative methods is implicit in the process. Moscardo (1996) also claims that effective interpretation can alter behaviour, either directly through information, or indirectly through fostering visitor appreciation of a site. She reports on interpretation and built heritage management and believes that interpretation induces a *state of mindfulness* (Langer *et al.*, 1989), which is essential to learning.

> Mindful visitors will understand the consequences of their actions and be able to behave in ways that lessen their impacts on a site. Mindful visitors will also have a greater appreciation and understanding of a site, and such understanding can provide both support for changing their behaviours on site and for the conservation of the site.
>
> (Moscardo, 1996: 393)

There is a positive link between visitor enjoyment and visitor learning (defined as mindfulness) (Moscardo and Pearce, 1986). Importantly, the state of mindfulness can, Moscardo (1996) claims, be induced by effective interpretation.

A further study of interpretative material by Roggenbuck and Passineau (1986), evaluated the effectiveness of interpretation in determining positive attitudes and behavioural intentions, reductions in depreciative behaviour and stimulation of increased interest in resources. It showed varying results across groups but a generally positive role for interpretative materials in increasing knowledge gain, and developing positive attitudes and behavioural intentions. More recently, research in the field of interpretation and behaviour change has emphasized the importance of understanding visitors' needs and motivations, and prior knowledge, attitudes and beliefs in relation to a site before attempting interpretative design (Ballantyne, 1998).

In other words, interpretative materials must contain communication strategies that create links between visitor and theme, and enable people to establish personally meaningful connections within the interpretative experience. This requires that material be targeted at different types of visitor. In any case, it would be simplistic to assume that all tourists can be similarly influenced. Tourists are not a homogeneous, single-minded group; the tourist condition is not one single state (Mason and Mowforth, 1996). Routes to persuasion must take account of social settings and levels of attention that can be achieved (Carter, 2000).

Interpretative material as persuasive communication

Persuasive communication involves the use of verbal and visual messages to influence attitudes and behaviour and, as with interpretative techniques, the message may be designed to influence both affective and cognitive domains, appealing to emotions and intellect. It is perhaps one of the most complex communication processes and its effects are influenced by a number of factors:

- message content;
- message context;
- extent of involvement; and
- values and prevailing subjective norms.

Message content

Many traditional attempts at communication in order to influence tourists' behaviour have been seen to have had limited effects. Perhaps in order to be understood by all, many codes of conduct favour a direct style with informative content presented as instructions to visitors (Mason and Mowforth, 1996). Often prohibitive, they may be counter-productive if appearing prescriptive or patronizing, and such approaches are unlikely to have a favourable impact in a leisure context. Empirical research into the effectiveness of such directives is limited. Roggenbuck and Berrier (1982) reported that a number of empirical research programmes in North America found that the provision of such information achieved only mixed success in attempts to disperse wilderness campers.

Despite the earlier claim that interpretation has been largely overlooked as a means of site management, more recently, organizations such as the English national park authorities have tried to influence visitor behaviour in the countryside to address specific site problems by using interpretative material to varying degrees. For example, the Yorkshire Dales National Park Authority produces its educational handbook *Dales Care – Be a Green Tourist* in a less prescriptive manner than traditional codes (see Box 4.10).

Box 4.10. Yorkshire Dales National Park Visitor Code (source: Yorkshire Dales National Park, cited in Cooper *et al.*, 1998: 297).

Enjoy the countryside, by respecting its lifestyles, work and customs
Support local skills, services and produce
Wherever you go keep to public routes
Use gates and stiles to cross dry-stone walls, fences and hedges
Leave all gates as you find them, open or closed
Avoid trampling meadow grass by staying in single file through meadows in summer
Protect wild animals, trees and other plants. In particular, leave wild flowers for others to enjoy, and avoid disturbing birds and other animals
Keep your dog under close control, preferably on a lead
Leave livestock and farm machinery alone. Be aware of farmyard dangers
Take your litter home
Guard against risk of fire
Help to keep rivers, streams and lakes clean
Whenever possible use public transport
Take special care on narrow roads
Park thoughtfully. Where available use car parks
Respect other people's peace and quiet
Show consideration for those who use the countryside in other legitimate ways

Message context

Tourism presents models of communication aimed at behaviour change (or control) with an added challenge. Motivations to holiday, seek recreation and leisure are framed within the pursuit of pleasure. Successful interpretative design and delivery must address a range of issues in its accommodation of the complexity of tourists' consumption preferences. While Crompton (1979) found that the satisfaction of holiday motivations did not necessarily require a change in lifestyle, more recent research (Ryan, 1991: 27) recognizes the potential for the holiday to provide an opportunity for freedom from the normal constraints of home. Goffman (cited in Rojek, 1993) puts forward the notion of 'action places' where individuals engage in 'licensed revelry'. Many current leisure forms that present interpretations of realities fit Goffman's descriptions of such places where 'the rules of everyday life are relaxed and the boundaries of social behaviour are rolled back offer[ing] the experience of momentary escape from the encumbrances and pressures of everyday life' (Goffman in Rojek, 1993: 165).

Urry (1995: 188) believes that tourism is a conscious state in which conventional calculations of safety and risk are disrupted. Each of these 'states' offers potential for resistance to attempts to restrict personal choice and action within spaces for inner direction. Released from the responsibilities of everyday life, therefore, whether seeking rest and renewal, excitement, pleasure or socializing, tourists may

Continued overleaf

be reluctant to conform to the requirements of behavioural codes that are redolent more of the constraints of everyday regulated existence than of purchased holiday freedoms. The limits of interpretative material will be rigorously tested given this as an influencing factor.

In order to broaden the education process, however, codes of conduct need to reach the mass tourism sector as well as the niche markets for which they are currently prepared (Mason and Mowforth, 1996). If they are to do so, clearly they must learn to communicate by means other than basic exhortation.

Extent of involvement

In consumer behaviour generally, involvement is seen as an 'unobservable state of motivation, arousal or interest' (Dimanche *et al.*, 1991). Measured in relation to leisure and tourism contexts, it can be seen that importance and enjoyment are essential prerequisites to sustained involvement (Dimanche *et al.*, 1991). One purpose of effective interpretation should be to provide interactive modes of delivery of relevant and provoking material that have been found to attract and engage visitors and thus increase learning (Moscardo, 1996); thus contributing to a mindful visitor state and potentially, therefore, an enhanced sense of place.

The assumption is that the greater the extent of involvement in the process of tourism and the experience in relation to location, the more likely a tourist will be open to attitude and behaviour change when exposed to new information about it. This may be done by means of guided walks, game playing and other activities (Dagnall and Atkinson, unpublished). In the UK, Dartmoor National Park Authority's 'Moor Care' programme promotes increased involvement in the work of the park through 'letter-boxing', an activity encouraging active park visiting in a manner that tries to develop a sense of place (see Chapter 2).

Involvement does, however, require voluntary participation. In this regard, the work of Stewart *et al.* (1998) identified four main categories of interpretation users (as illustrated in Table 4.3). The study identified different visitor groups that approached and used interpretative materials in different ways. Clearly, where visitors shun interpretative materials, alternative means of influencing inappropriate behaviour must be sought.

Table 4.3. A typology of interpretation users (source: Stewart *et al.*, 1998).

Seekers	Visitors who actively seek out sources of information and interpretation
Stumblers	Those who come across interpretative material by accident
Shadowers	Those chaperoned by others through the interpretation that is offered (either formally or informally)
Shunners	Visitors who either show no interest in interpretation or deliberately avoid it

Values and prevailing subjective norms

According to the theory of reasoned action (Ajzen and Fishbein in Fishbein and Manfredo, 1992), many behaviours are under volitional control and therefore determined by intention. The theory assumes that people are capable of processing information systematically, and it has three main hypotheses:

1. That behaviour is linked to intentions;
2. That intentions result from varying degrees of attitude and subjective norms; and
3. That attitude and subjective norms create behavioural and normative beliefs.

The more a person believes that a certain type of behaviour will lead to positive outcomes (or prevent negative ones), the more likely he or she will be to develop a strong personal belief that will influence his or her behaviour. As a theoretical example, if a person believes strongly that by taking litter home, the environments he or she likes to visit will remain aesthetically pleasing, that person will do so despite the fact that others may not.

Subjective norm is a function of the influence of others on a person's attitudes and behaviour, and the individual's motivation to comply. A less strongly held personal belief in the importance of correct litter disposal, therefore, may make a decision more susceptible to influence from the subjective norm; the fact that littering is commonplace and public services are provided for its collection may indicate that it is not unacceptable. Where perceived volitional control is low and people feel their sole contribution cannot make a difference, they may change attitude but not necessarily behaviour: that is, they may believe that littering is wrong but do it anyway because everyone else seems to do so.

Following this theory, therefore, one is more likely to be successful in effecting a change in a given intention (and possibly behaviour) if one first alters the attitudes and/or subjective norms that correspond to it (Fishbein and Manfredo, 1992: 35). By example, in order to reduce littering at a site, interpretative material might deliver two messages: one to influence personal attitude (the way an individual feels about being personally responsible for creating litter); and one to i nfluence normative issues (the way an individual feels about the existence of litter generally).

The number and complexity of processes involved in the development of interpretative materials for site management may explain why their use is still relatively rare. An understanding of the social and psychological processes involved is not widespread within the professions charged with management. Furthermore, the failure to include interpretative programmes in many tourism development plans may be explained by the future-orientation and intangibility of outcomes that render them difficult to measure and therefore impossible to justify in economic terms.

However, the need to find ways of sustaining the growing demand for rural recreation and leisure should direct attention more closely to the potential of interpretative materials as a valuable site management tool. At the same time, pressure should be placed on academic institutions and public agencies to undertake further research in support of this nascent discipline.

Lesley Roberts and Gunnar Rognvaldsson

Chapter Conclusions and Summary

While the value judgements attached to many countryside access policy decisions may be contested, they may become increasingly recognized as being based on the premise that the countryside, as both a finite resource and a contested space, will be unable to support the capacity required of the projected growth of tourism and recreation. Some areas will support some activities. Fragile areas may be unsuitable for most recreational forms. Many types of tourism and recreation may be better managed in dedicated resorts and spaces.

Notions of selection, restriction and exclusion in rural tourism and recreation clearly conflict with the principles of social inclusion (Chapter 2). The European countryside has an existence value as well as a use value, and some means of permitting use without threatening viability must be found. There is little doubt, therefore, that increasing restrictions will be placed on access to areas such as national parks in the future due to the negative impacts of large numbers of visitors. Selection, restriction and exclusion may be the future tools of rural tourism management in coming decades, where the resource base is threatened. Later in this volume (Chapter 8) *the importance of the countryside* model is developed, which explicitly adds further dimension to processes by which such tools may be implemented. At a policy level, the model is useful in helping to focus attention on the ways in which the activities of rural visitors may provide insight into the importance they place on the countryside for consumer satisfaction.

Principles of social inclusion require access to potentially fragile resources by those who may have little experience in such settings. The extent to which the development and use of interpretative materials can assist in the management of rural tourism and tourism in rural areas is yet to be fully explored. Is there scope for re-evaluation of consumer values through tourism provision in rural areas or is the countryside merely another resource for consumption? What is the role of interpretation? Does it help people to understand and therefore benefit more from a countryside visit? Or, in 'putting it on a plate' does interpretation prevent people from exploring and interpreting the countryside for themselves, removing the challenge of discovery? And is this sacrifice less than that which accompanies habitat and landscape damage, and lifestyle acculturation?

This chapter has attempted to place the development of tourism and recreation in rural areas within policy and management contexts. It has done this by:

- examining different levels of policy which influence recreation and tourism development in rural areas, emphasizing the connectedness between local and global processes;
- emphasizing the need to view recreation and tourism development in rural areas within the wider context of the management of rural resources; and
- evaluating challenges posed for such management and key issues for the development of recreation and tourism in rural areas which arise from them.

The following chapter focuses on the 'community' level of rural development and management, evaluating the very concept of 'community' within the dynamic rural environment, and exploring the roles of networking and partnership for successful tourism and recreation development.

References

Anon (1998) Access in Europe. *Countryside Recreation* 6(3/4). http://www.cf.ac.uk/cm/news/art4

Anon (2000) *Guide to Baltic Capitals and King's Road.* EU Phare/Tacis and Interreg IIA.

Ballantyne, R. (1998) Interpreting 'visions': addressing environmental education goals through interpretation. In: Uzzell, D. and Ballantyne, R. (eds) *Contemporary Issues in Heritage and Environmental Interpretation.* The Stationery Office, London, pp. 98–111.

Barrow, G. (1994) Interpretative planning: more to it than meets the eye. *Environmental Interpretation* 9(2), 5–7.

Borg, P. (1997) *Kestävä Matkailu, Kestävän Matkailun Julkaisuja 1, Kestävä Kehitys – Kestävyys Matkailussa.* Matkailun Osaamiskeskus & Matkailun Verkostoyliopisto, Mynämäki, Finland, pp. 34–60.

Bovaird, A., Tricker, M. and Stoakes, R. (1984) *Recreation Management and Pricing.* Gower, Aldershot.

Bramwell, B. (1994) Rural tourism and sustainable rural tourism. *Journal of Sustainable Tourism* 2(1–2), 1–6.

Butler, R. and Hall, C.M. (1998) Conclusion: the sustainability of tourism and recreation in rural areas. In: Butler, R., Hall, C.M. and Jenkins, J. (eds) *Tourism and Recreation in Rural Areas.* John Wiley & Sons, Chichester, pp. 249–258.

Butler, R., Hall, C.M. and Jenkins, J. (1998) Introduction. In: Butler, R., Hall, C.M. and Jenkins, J. (eds) *Tourism and Recreation in Rural Areas.* John Wiley & Sons, Chichester, pp. 3–16.

Carter, J. (2000) Changing recreational behaviour. Paper, SNH Conference: Enjoyment and Understanding of the Natural Heritage – Finding the New Balance Between Rights and Responsibilities. Glasgow, 13–14 September.

Cooper, C., Fletcher, J., Gilbert, D., Wanhill, S. and Shepherd, R. (1998) *Tourism: Principles and Practice.* 2nd edn. Longman, Harlow.

Costley, W. (2000) Behaviour associated with access. Paper, SNH Conference: Enjoyment and Understanding of the Natural Heritage – Finding the New Balance Between Rights and Responsibilities. Glasgow, 13–14 September.

Crabtree, J.R., Appleton, Z., Thomson, K.J., Slee, R.W., Chalmers, N. and Copus, A. (1992) *The Economics of Countryside Access in Scotland.* The Scottish Agricultural College, Aberdeen.

Cramb, A. (1996) *Who Owns Scotland Now? The Use and Abuse of Private Land.* Mainstream Publishing, Edinburgh.

Crompton, J.L. (1979) Motivations for pleasure vacation. *Annals of Tourism Research* 6, 408–424.

Davidson, R. and Maitland, R. (1997) *Tourist Destinations.* Hodder and Stoughton, London.

Dernoi, L. (1991) About rural and farm tourism. *Tourism Recreation Research* 16(1), 3–6.

Dimanche, F., Havitz, M.E. and Howard, D.R. (1991) Testing the involvement profile (IP) scale in the context of selected recreational and touristic activities. *Journal of Leisure Research* 23(1), 51–66.

Dowling, R. (1993) An environmentally-based planning model for regional tourism development. *Journal of Sustainable Tourism* 1(1), 17–37.

Edmunds, M. (1999) Rural tourism in Europe. *Travel and Tourism Analyst* 6, 37–50.

Engel, J., Blackwell, R. and Miniard, P. (1995) *Consumer Behaviour.* 8th edn. Dryden Press, Fort Worth, Texas.

European Commission (1997) *The Cork Declaration.* European Commission, Brussels. http://www.rural-europe.aeidl.be/forum/forum2/corde-en.htm

European Commission (2000a) *Agricultural Policy and Rural Development. LEADER+: the Community Initiative for Rural Development (2000–2006).* European Commission, Brussels. http://www.rural-europe.aeidl.be/rural-en/euro/p.10.html

European Commission (2000b) *LEADER+: Commission Notice to Member States Laying Down Guidelines for the Community Initiative for Rural Development (LEADER+).* European Commission, Brussels. http://www.rural-europe.aeidl.be/rural-en/plus.htm

Fagence, M. (1991) Rural tourism and the small country town. *Tourism Recreation Research* 16(1), 34–48.

Fennell, D.A. (1999) *Ecotourism: an Introduction.* Routledge, London.

Finfood (1999) *Agrifacts.* Finfood News and Information Agency, Vantaa, Finland.

Finnish Tourist Board (2000) *The King's Road.* Finnish Tourist Board, Helsinki. http://www.thekingsroad.com

Fishbein, M. and Manfredo, M.L. (1992) A theory of behaviour change. In: Manfredo, M.L. (ed.) *Influencing Human Behaviour: Theory and Applications in Recreation, Tourism and Natural Resources Management.* Sagamore Publishing, Champaign, Illinois, pp. 29–48.

FNNPE (Federation of Nature and National Parks of Europe) (1993) *Loving Them to Death? Sustainable Tourism in Europe's Nature and National Parks.* FNNP, Grafenau, Austria.

Fyall, A. and Garrod, B. (1998) Sustainability and rural heritage: a question of price? In: Hall, D. and O'Hanlon, L. (eds) *Rural Tourism Management: Sustainable Options.* The Scottish Agricultural College, Auchincruive, pp. 153–168.

Government of India (1997) *Ninth Five Year Plan (1997–2002).* Government of India, New Delhi, 2 vols. http://www.nic.in/ninthplan/

Gunn, C. (1994) *Tourism Planning: Basics, Concepts, Cases,* 3rd edn. Taylor and Francis, London.

Hall, D. and Danta, D. (eds) (2000) *Europe Goes East: EU Enlargement, Diversity and Uncertainty.* The Stationery Office, London

Hall, C.M. and Jenkins, J.M. (1998) The policy dimensions of rural tourism and recreation. In: Butler, R., Hall, C.M. and Jenkins, J.M. (eds) *Tourism and Recreation in Rural Areas.* John Wiley & Sons, Chichester, pp. 19–42.

Ham, S.H. (1992) *Environmental Interpretation.* North American Press, Denver, Colorado.

Harris, C. and Driver, B. (1987) Recreation user fees – pros and cons. *Journal of Forestry* 85(5), 25–29.

Hudson, R. and Townsend, A. (1992) Tourism employment and policy choices for local government. In: Johnson, P. and Thomas, B. (eds) *Perspectives on Tourism Policy.* Mansell, London, pp. 49–68.

Inskeep, E. (1991) *Tourism Planning: an Integrated and Sustainable Development Approach.* Van Nostrand Reinhold, New York.

Kivi, E. (1998) Developing new experiences – rural tourism strategy in Finland. In: Hall, D. and O'Hanlon, L. (eds) *Rural Tourism Management: Sustainable Options. Supplement.* The Scottish Agricultural College, Auchincruive, pp. 39–51.

KTM (1997) *Toimialaraportti, Matkailun Ohjelmapalvelut.* KTM, Helsinki.

KTM Toimiala-Infomedia (1999) *Toimialaraportti – Maaseutumatkailu.* KTM, Helsinki.

Land Use Consultants (2000) Feasibility study: local authority pilot project. Unpublished report.

Langer, E.M., Hatem, J., Joss, J. and Howell, M. (1989) Conditional teaching and mindful learning: the role of uncertainty in education. *Creativity Research Journal* 2, 139–150.

Leuschner, W., Cook, D., Roggenbuck, J. and Oderwald, R. (1987) A comparative analysis for wilderness user fee policy. *Journal of Leisure Research* 19(2), 102–115.

Maaja Kotitalousnaisten Keskus (1986) *Syötä Vierasta Sanoilla Kunnes Keitto Kerkiävi.* Maaja Kotitalousnaisten Keskus, Helsinki.

Maaseutumatkailun Teemaryhmä (1999) *Tilastointihanke.* Maaseutumatkailun Teemaryhmä, Helsinki.

Maaseutumatkailun Teemaryhmä (2000a) *Maaseutumatkailu–lehti.* Maaseutumatkailun Teemaryhmä, Helsinki.

Maaseutumatkailun Teemaryhmä (2000b) *Maaseutumatkailu Strategia ja Kehittämisohjelma Vuoteen 2007.* Maaseutumatkailun Teemaryhmä, Helsinki.

Maaseutupolitiikan Yhteistyöryhmä (1996) *Toimiva Maaseutu, Maaseutuohjelma.* Maaseutupolitiikan Yhteistyöryhmä, Helsinki.

Mackay, J. (1997) Caring for wild places. *Countryside Recreation* 5(3). http://www.cf.ac.uk/cm/news/53/art3.html

Mason, P. and Mowforth, M. (1996) Codes of conduct in tourism. In: Cooper, C. (ed.) *Progress in Tourism and Hospitality Research,* Vol. 2. Belhaven Press, London, pp. 151–167.

Meethan, K. (1998) New tourism for old? Policy developments in Cornwall and Devon. *Tourism Management* 19(6), 583–593.

MEK (1994) *Ympäristöä Säästävän Maaseutumatkailun Edistämis-ja Kehittämishankkeita Suomessa 1990-luvulla.* YSMEK/MASE, Helsinki.

Moscardo, G. (1996) Mindful visitors, heritage and tourism. *Annals of Tourism Research* 23(2), 376–397.
Moscardo, G. and Pearce, P.L. (1986) Visitor centres and environmental interpretation: an exploration of the relationships among visitor enjoyment, understanding and mindfulness. *Journal of Environmental Psychology* 6, 89–108.
NNPA (Northumberland National Park Authority) (1999) *Conflicts of Land Use*. NNPA, Hexham. http://www.nnpa.org.uk/edinfo12.html
OECD (1994) *Tourism Policy and International Tourism in OECD Countries, 1991–1992*. OECD, Paris.
Oloffson, J. (1998) *The 'Allemansret': the General Rights to Public Access of the Wilderness* http://www.lysator.liu.se/nordic/scn/allemans.html
Orams, M.B. (1996) Using interpretation to manage nature-based tourism. *Journal of Sustainable Tourism* 4(2), 81–94.
Orams, M.B. (1997) The effectiveness of environmental education: can we turn tourists into greenies? In: Cooper, C. (ed.) *Progress in Tourism and Hospitality Research*, Vol. 3. Belhaven Press, London, pp. 295–306.
Page, S.J. and Getz, D. (eds) (1997) *The Business of Rural Tourism: International Perspetives*. International Thomson Business Press, London.
Parviainen and Pöysti (1995) *Suomi Ympäristöä Säästäväksi Matkailumaaksi. Ympäristökatselmuskokeilun Tulokset Kymmenessä Matkailuyrityksessä ja Ehdotukset Jatkotoimiksi*. MEK, Helsinki.
Pearce, D.G. (1989) *Tourist Development*. 2nd. edn. Longman, Harlow.
Pigram, J. (1993) Planning for tourism in rural areas: bridging the policy implementation gap. In: Pearce, D. and Butler, R. (eds) *Tourism Research: Critiques and Challenges*. Routledge, London, pp. 156–174.
Prentice, R. (1996) *Tourism and Heritage Attractions*. Routledge, London.
Rilla, E. (2000) *Unique Niches: Agritourism in Britain and New England*. Small Farm Center, University of California at Davis, Davis, California. http://www.sfc.ucdavis.edu/agritourism/printer.html
Roggenbuck, J.W. and Berrier, D.L. (1982) A comparison of the effectiveness of two communication strategies in dispersing wilderness campers. *Journal of Leisure Research* 14(1), 77–89.
Roggenbuck, J.W. and Passineau, J. (1986) Use of the field experiment to assess the effectiveness of interpretation. In: *Proceedings of the South Eastern Recreation Research Conference, Athens*, pp. 65–86.
Rojek, C. (1993) *Ways of Escape: Modern Transformations in Leisure and Travel*. Macmillan Press, London.
Ryan, C. (1991) *Recreational Tourism: a Social Science Perspective*. Routledge, London.
Sandell, K. (1995) Access to the North – but to what and for whom? Public access in the Swedish countryside and the case of a proposed national park in the Kiruna mountains. In: Hall, C.M. and Johnston, M. (eds) *Polar Tourism – Tourism in the Arctic and Antarctic Regions*. John Wiley & Sons, Chichester, pp. 131–145.
Scottish Office (1996) *National Heritage Designations Review*. Scottish Office, Edinburgh.
Sharpley, R. and Sharpley, J. (1997) *Rural Tourism: an Introduction*. International Thomson Business Press, London.
Shoard, M. (1980) *The Theft of the Countryside*. Temple Smith, London.
Shoard, M. (1999) *A Right to Roam*. Oxford University Press, Oxford.
Slee, B. (1998) Tourism and rural development in Scotland. In: McClellan, R. and Smith, R. (eds) *Tourism in Scotland*. International Thomson Business Press, London, pp. 93–111.
SNH (Scottish Natural Heritage) (1992) *Enjoying the Outdoors: a Consultation Paper on Access to the Countryside for Recreation and Understanding*. SNH, Edinburgh.
Sood, R. (1998) Rural tourism to be put on the fast track. *Indian Express* 14 August.
South Somerset District Council (1999) *Economic Development and Tourism Strategy*. South Somerset District Council, Yeovil. http://www.southsomerset.gov.uk/general/business/policy.htm
Stewart, E.J., Hayward, B.M. and Devlin, P.J. (1998) The 'place' of interpretation: a new approach to the evaluation of interpretation. *Tourism Management* 19(3), 257–266.
Suomen Matkailun Kehitys Oy (SMAK) (1997) *Matkailun Tulo – ja Työllisyysvaikutukset Suomessa 1995*. SMAK, Helsinki.
Tarasti, K. (1997) *Rural Tourism in Finland*. Council of Europe, Strasbourg.
Tarkastusmuistio (2000) *Matkailun Kehittäminen*. Tarkastusmuistio, Helsinki.
Tilden, F. (1957) *Interpreting Our Heritage*, 3rd edn. University of North Carolina Press, Chapel Hill, North Carolina.
UNEP/IE (United Nations Environment Programme, Industry and Environment) (1995) *Environmental Codes of Conduct for Tourism*. UNEP, Paris.
Urry, J. (1995) *Consuming Places*. Routledge, London.

Uzzell, D. (1989) The visitor experience. In: Uzzell, D. (ed.) *Heritage Interpretation*, Vol. 2. Belhaven Press, London, pp. 1–15.

Veverka, J.A. (1994) Interpretation as a management tool. *Environmental Interpretation* 9(2), 18–19.

Walsh, R. (1986) *Recreation Economic Decisions*. Venture Publishing, State College, Pennsylvania.

WCED (World Commission on Environment and Development) (1987) *Our Common Future*. Oxford University Press, Oxford.

Whitby, M. (1997) Countryside access: a traditional asset but growing fast. *Countryside Recreation* 5(4).

Wightman, A. (1996) *Who Owns Scotland*. Canongate, Edinburgh.

Woolf, M. (2000) Ministers get lessons on life in the country. *The Independent* 4 November. http://www.independent.co.uk/news/UK/Politics/2000–11/rural041100.shtml

WTO (World Tourism Organization) (1994) *National and Regional Tourism Planning: Methodologies and Case Studies*. Routledge/WTO, London.

5

Embedding Rural Tourism Development?

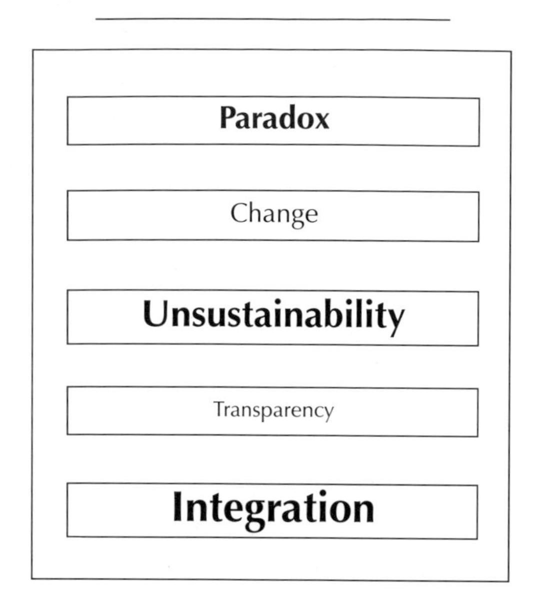

This chapter emphasizes the theme of *integration*: at a global level through the employment and growth of information technologies able to link and promote rural areas; and at a local and regional level through an emphasis on the need for establishing collaboration, networks and partnerships in tourism and recreation development. *Unsustainability* is reflected in the *paradox* of the use of the term 'community' implying small-scale, consensus and homogeneity, when any local area pursuing 'community'-led tourism is likely to contain diverse views and aspirations and tensions in the distribution of power.

Building on the Chapter 4 evaluation of policy and management at a number of levels, and the key site management role identified for interpretation, this chapter has four key objectives. These are to:

1. Critically evaluate the notion, role and use of local 'community'.
2. Assess the concept of community-based tourism development within a rural context.
3. Examine the role of partnerships, collaboration and networks in embedding SME-based tourism and recreation development within rural 'communities'.
4. Evaluate the implications of such processes for rural development.

If tourism in rural areas is essentially a tool of economic development, its lack of efficacy springs partly from its spatial dispersion. Following the ethos that Lane (1994) and others have promoted, the essence of 'rural tourism' is its small scale and 'rustic' characteristics. Hence, such relatively large-scale, 'mass' recreational developments of the Center Parcs variety, while being located in rural areas, are not 'rural tourism' but are an element of tourism in rural areas. Thus we are faced with a contradiction: 'rural tourism' being viewed as a tool of economic development, yet by its very nature and quality being too small and dispersed to be economically effective at a regional level. Hence it is perhaps understandable that for so long 'rural tourism' has tended to be associated with, and somewhat constrained by, the ethos of family-scale, very local impact, farm/agri/agro-tourism, much to the clear chagrin of Page and Getz (1997) and others.

Consideration of an alternative approach to the role of tourism in rural development might perhaps be sought through the concept of the rural growth pole. Notions of core and periphery within the periphery are not new: Andre Gunder Frank's (1967) dependent development notions (of centres in developing regions being the exploitative surrogates of the distant metropoles of global cores) and the reverse core–periphery concept of the Chinese countryside as its revolutionary core, were instructive and influential for several decades. Yet relatively few (developed) societies have sought rural development through growth pole policies, and even fewer have embraced tourism as an element of such integrated development. Israel, while manifesting particularly distinctive – and certainly ideologically and ethically contested – settlement policies, has developed an important tourism industry (e.g. Fleischer and Pizam, 1997) which is emphasizing the country's rural component through a neo-growth pole strategy highlighting 'community-based' development (Box 5.1).

Community, Participation, Sustainability and Rural Tourism

As often repeated in this volume, a holistic approach to sustainability requires that continuing/improved social, cultural and economic well-being of human communities is an integral component of environmental well-being. 'Community sustainability', 'community participation' and 'community rootedness' seem to have become prerequisites of sustainable tourism (although see Richard Sharpley's contribution in Chapter 3). Like 'sustainability', however, the concept of community is far from unproblematic (Box 5.2). In the context of tourism and recreation in rural areas its entanglement with notions of the rural idyll renders 'community' even more elusive.

As a term ripe with allusion and implication, 'community' has long been interpreted in a number of ways. Half a century ago, 94 definitions of 'community' could be compiled (Hillery, 1955). Forty years on, and within a tourism context, Urry (1995), building on the work of Bell and Newby (1976), could cite four different uses of the term:

1. Belonging to a specific topographical location.

Box 5.1. Tourism in a rural growth pole (source: Cohen and Lipman, 1998).

In the Upper Galilee region of Israel 95% of guest rooms are used for domestic tourism, mainly family holidays. In this essentially rural area a number of settlements have oriented their plans for economic development around tourism. One example is Rosh Pina, which, although founded in 1882, was until recently considered to be remote and of no tourist interest. In the 1990s the local council's master plan placed an emphasis on encouraging and investing in tourism. Policies for creating a supportive environment for 'community'-based tourism included designating land areas for tourism development, providing infrastructure, and clarifying the procedures required for approval in establishing tourism businesses. Some of the newly restored, original public buildings were offered for rent at subsidized rates to encourage new business start-ups.

The appearance of the town was improved with restoration of old stone buildings and attractive signposting was developed. The essentially domestic appeal of such settlements is emphasized by the fact that a centrepiece attraction is an audio-visual presentation illustrating the history of the settlement, and the town is described in Israeli tourism marketing as a pilgrimage centre. Of the 530 households in Rosh Pina about 70 are involved in tourism: small businesses to have developed include art galleries and craft shops, restaurants and coffee houses. The town is now an important stopping point for travellers en route to the Upper Galilee, the Golan Heights or the Mount Hermon ski slopes, and its success has served as both encouragement and support for rural tourism in the surrounding agricultural settlements. Rural activities available include horse-riding, canoeing down the Jordan River, demonstrations of bee-keeping, honey making and fruit picking.

Box 5.2. 'Community' problematics (adapted from Richards and Hall, 2000b: 1–2).

Does 'community' exist?
How defined: in spatial/social/economic terms?
Where should one place the spatial or temporal boundaries of the 'local' community?
Whose community?
Who are the 'locals' in the local community?
Who in the community should benefit from tourism?
How should the community be presented to the tourist?
The nature of community is dynamic, influenced by both globalization and localization
The emergence of a 'global community' also problematizes the concept of a local community
Aspatial communities, linked by bonds of common interest not place, exist within and across spatial communities

2. Defining a particular local social system.
3. A feeling of *communitas* or togetherness.
4. An ideology, often hiding the power relations which inevitably underpin communities.

In part inspired by the sustainable development debate (Chapter 3) and by the Cork Declaration and the EU LEADER programme (Chapter 4), the popularity of 'community' approaches to tourism development has led not only to 'community' becoming almost a shibboleth (Howie, 2000) – an idealized, inherently 'good thing' – but has encouraged an often vague and inconsistent use of the concept in social and/or spatial terms. Indeed, just like 'green', 'sustainable', 'niche' and other terms and concepts employed in relation to tourism in rural areas, use of 'community' can be viewed as having strong propagandist and certainly significant marketing dimensions.

If one accepts the existence of 'community', a wide range of types of 'communities' and groups within 'communities' can be identified, all of whom can respond differently to tourism development in their areas (Richards and Hall, 2000a). While several authors have argued that the community cannot be isolated from its locality or geographic context (e.g. Kappert, 2000), the aspatial 'community of interest' is often overlooked in the tourism literature, despite its relevance. This diversity of real and imagined communities suggests that to successfully implement community-based strategies for tourism development, more varied concepts and models are required.

For example, although it may be received wisdom that community participation is an essential prerequisite for the sustainability of a tourism project (Simmons, 1994; Joppe, 1996), encouragement of community involvement and ownership of development schemes in CEE has been constrained by three factors:

1. The legacy of almost half a century of centralized, top-down civil administration, affording local people little real opportunity to experience bottom-up development or for genuine opportunities to participate in meaningful local decision making.
2. The often pejorative equating of any form of collective action with the collectivized organization of communist days.
3. The well-recognized ambivalence of 'community' as a concept, embracing notions of spatial contiguity, social cohesion and interaction, reflexivity, overlain with often misplaced assumptions of shared aspirations and values.

Somewhat paradoxically, however, any ecologically inspired restriction of personal freedom, such as exclusion from environmentally sensitive areas or the banning of such pursuits as hunting, may be viewed locally as echoing the half-century of post-war communist imposition, and thereby meet resistance. The establishment of biosphere reserves and other protected areas including national parks (IUCN-EEP, 1990; Beynon, 2000) has required a considerable effort to involve local populations in the pursuit of sustainable tourism and ecological planning (e.g. Hall, 1993) (Plate 5.1).

The promoters of 'sustainable' tourism schemes may point to an impoverished local

Plate 5.1. Both local and international NGOs have been instrumental in promoting 'ecotourism' in the Danube Delta.

Plate 5.2. The rural 'community' may be rarely consensual.

infrastructure as representing a pristine, non-commercialized environment attractive to Western tourists in search of the European rural idyll of 'unspoilt' tranquillity. In contrast, local residents may well support such projects on the assumption that tourism will be the vehicle specifically to bring change and improvement to their local infrastructures and services (Hall, 1998, 2000c). Under such circumstances, the values of local 'community' are not shared by tourism promoters, and the discordance between tourist expectations and host aspirations is likely to be irreconcilable. Thus the paradoxes of 'sustainable' tourism being neither sustainable nor appropriate in the longer term are compounded by any marketing pretence of community-led tourism in a situation where local values may be far from consensual.

Indeed, it can be argued that here is a propaganda dimension of 'community' in its employment to imply a presumption of (within a spatially defined setting) the sharing of a set of common social characteristics and goals held by a local residential population. This use conveys the impression both of consensuality and relative homogeneity, and acts to mask the potential conflicts of interest and unequal power relations which exist even within the smallest human groups. Residents of a particular area may take only a limited interest in that area because the main focus of their activities – work or recreation – lies elsewhere (Hall, 1982) or perhaps because there are negative elements of their local environment which cause disaffection. This situation has been referred to as the 'community of limited liability' (Janowitz, 1951). Both internal and external perceptions of 'community', the articulation of local social and economic cohesion or disruption, are crucial factors in the support given to and likely success of local (tourism) development (Plate 5.2).

Indeed, research into social exclusion has re-emphasized the inequalities within and between self-recognized groups (e.g. Edwards, 1991; Keane, 1992; Cloke and Little, 1997; Milbourne, 1997) (Chapter 2). Yet the 'otherness' of race, gender, sexuality, age and ableism and their role as determinants of (tourism) power dimensions is only beginning to be addressed in this context (e.g. Kinnaird and Hall, 1996, 2000; Morgan and Pritchard, 1998).

The structural position of women in relation to rural tourism remains ambivalent. While providing perhaps one of the few opportunities for achieving managerial roles, because of its perceived part-time, low paid and 'domestic extension' nature, engagement in tourism employment can also contribute to women's marginal status in the rural workforce (Redclift and Sinclair, 1991). Rural tourism in CEE, for example, may be instrumental in shifting the balance of economic power within farm households and help to open up rural employment provision for women (Petrin, 1996; Siiskonen, 1996; Hall, 2001).

There may exist sensitive issues relating to indigenous peoples and traditional cultures, including land and resource rights, and cultural groups' roles as performers and entrepreneurs. Such people may experience particular business problems because of their perceived status, such as obtaining finance for projects, training, and access to decision-making roles within the wider community.

At its simplest, both the extent to which local residents benefit from, and their attitudes towards, tourism development, may vary considerably, resulting in tensions and disagreement within the 'community'. In other cases there may be an 'altruistic surplus' effect, whereby the potentially disadvantaged members of the 'community' may acknowledge a wider common benefit to be gained from tourism, and may consequently withdraw or constrain their opposition to or criticism of local tourism development or aspects of it (Faulkner, 1998). In extreme cases, local 'communities' may actively pursue and encourage the local development of tourism in the face of opposition from outside interests such as altruistic environmental groups (e.g. Ioannides, 1995) or less altruistic developers who have sought unsuccessfully for development rights.

It has become conventional wisdom to argue that 'communities' have important roles in terms of:

- providing the essential social 'glue' (e.g. Yarwood, 1996) between locality and inhabitants;
- linking between the local and the global: as the receivers and transmitters of the forces of globalization (Sassen, 1991); but also, almost paradoxically; and
- a potential seat of resistance against the homogenization which globalization threatens (Richards and Hall, 2000a).

The first of these roles may exist in some metaphysical way, although it comes close to falling within the embrace of the idealized rural idyll; the third is discussed later in this chapter. The second suggested role is far from being clear. For example, it has been argued that through the ubiquity of information technology, more remote regions and islands on the periphery of the global economy are able to (re-)assert their cultural identity and explore their socio-economic potential (Ray, 1998). Yet in the following invited contribution Seamus Grimes counsels caution in respect of the notion of peripheries being able to benefit significantly from exploiting such technology.

Invited Viewpoint

Extending the Information Society beyond Urban Locations: Prospects and Reality

Seamus Grimes

From the early 1980s, commentators have been suggesting that information society technologies (IST) would bring about a reversal of the urbanization process and open up opportunities for peripheral regions. The Irish experience to date provides some convincing evidence that peripheral regions can benefit significantly from exploiting these technologies, although the likelihood of dispersing opportunities to non-urban locations is less convincing based on the experience to date. In many respects Irish economy and society, with its firm agricultural base and its strongly rural character has been significantly transformed with its entry into the information society. An impressive economic turnaround has been achieved in the past decade based on the development of dynamic information society sectors such as software and international services. Despite its peripheral location within Europe, Ireland has succeeded in attracting significant inward investment, which in turn has helped to generate considerable indigenous activity. The challenge of extending these developments, however, to the less urbanized parts of the state remains.

Continued urban dominance

Despite the significant potential which IST present for extending economic and other forms of activity beyond urban locations, the reality to date is that the most recent period of economic restructuring, while witnessing both processes of centralization and decentralization, has seen a continuation in the dominant role of urban centres in the space economy. With the increasing industrialization of agriculture, the economy of rural areas has also undergone significant restructuring; the rural environment is redefined increasingly in terms of the needs of urban consumers rather than solely according to those of rural dwellers. Despite the basic inertia in the overall spatial pattern of economic activity and the entrenched position of urban locations, some shifts are beginning to occur on a small scale, associated with the new technologies, which present both threats and opportunities for rural areas.

Partly because of the continued attraction of urban locations for a wide range of activities associated with the information society, many urban areas have begun to suffer from the effects of over-development, such as congestion, shortages of highly skilled professionals and pressure on the housing market. With the rapid pace of development in the Irish economy in the past decade, Dublin city is a good example of this phenomenon. A significant proportion of the inward investment associated with the IST sector has located in Dublin, so that more than 80% of subsectors such as software and internationally traded financial services are concentrated in Dublin. While smaller provincial urban centres such as Galway and Limerick have also benefited from this development, many rural areas, particularly in the north-west and border regions, have failed to attract significant employment-creating investment. While the larger urban centres have benefited most from recent economic growth, it should not be forgotten that these areas, rather than rural areas, also contain significant concentrations of excluded and marginalized communities. In addition to not bringing about a more even spread of economic development spatially throughout the country, the information society has contributed to increased social polarization particularly within cities.

Among the many factors which continue to make large urban areas highly attractive as investment locations, are the larger pool of highly skilled personnel, the superior quality of information society infrastructure and the higher frequency of airline connections. Government policy can also have a significant impact on location decisions such as the case of international financial services in Dublin, which has been concentrated largely in one centre in order to create sufficient critical mass to make an impact internationally. It is also true to say that in an Irish context, the primary policy concern was to attract a sufficient level of inward investment to what was a relatively peripheral location anyway, and, secondly, to pay more attention to the regional development aspects of this investment.

Regional development prospects

Now that the Irish economy has been showing impressive positive results for a number of years, including significant employment expansion, and because of greatly reduced pressure on the need for further employment creation, owing to a reduction in the growth of the labour force, greater attention is now being given to regional development issues. It is opportune that this is happening at a time when other important shifts in policy are also occurring. At the European level, the eastern and most urbanized part of the country will no longer benefit from the higher level of structural funds associated with Objective 1 status, which will be reserved for the more poorly developed western and north-western regions.

While having sophisticated IST infrastructure is no guarantee that a region will prosper within the information society, it has become clear that an inferior provision of this infrastructure has been a barrier towards attracting IST investment to Ireland's less developed and more rural regions. The scale of the infrastructural inferiority outside Dublin has become apparent in recent times with the Border, Midlands and Western regions being poorly connected. It is no surprise, therefore, that these regions have benefited little from IST-related inward investment. Recent policy decisions were made to ensure that the north-western region's IST infrastructure would be sufficiently improved to benefit from the potential which the information society offers. Significant investment decisions based on a mixture of EU structural funds and private involvement have been announced to extend broadband infrastructure around the state, linking 120 different towns and cities in 21 counties. These links will help to pave the way for a new generation of businesses based on e-commerce and assist the attraction of investment to these regions. These developments dovetail with the two central goals of the state set recently for the Industrial Development Authority, to spread development to the regions relatively untouched by recent growth, and to move Irish industry up the value chain, creating more high-skill, high-earning jobs. It has been

Continued overleaf

suggested that ISTs can contribute towards the development of rural regions in two ways: firstly, in terms of how they contribute towards reducing the friction of distance from the market and, secondly, by how they facilitate remote regions to improve their knowledge base as 'learning regions' (Grimes, 2000).

Initially, some of the theorizing about the potential impact of ISTs on rural areas was overly optimistic, suggesting that they would have a major impact in reducing the effects of distance and inaccessibility of peripheral areas. More recent assessments in a Nordic context have been much less optimistic than the scenarios presented by writers such as Alvin Toffler at the beginnings of the 1980s (Hetland, 1998). Storgaard (1998), argues that, contrary to the common belief that high-tech activity is closely related to urban areas, highly advanced users of telecommunications are also found in rural locations. The main difference, however, is the number of such users, which can be insufficient to create the demand necessary for establishing the advanced infrastructure to serve rural users.

Whatever the varying fortunes of different regions in the information society, there is little doubt about the growing pervasiveness of the impact of ISTs on economies and regions. With the globalization of economic activity there has been an increasing separation of the different functions of large corporations, allowing such companies the flexibility of locating less-skilled operations in a wider variety of regions. This locational separation of functions is a consequence of the separation of production and consumption which characterizes this latest phase of economic activity. With the increasing industrialization of the services sector, activities such as telemarketing and data processing have become more mobile internationally. Corporate reorganization has become a significant factor in the redistribution of service employments across space. The concentration of corporate functions into specialized offices from core regions is providing opportunities for rural and peripheral regions. These developments have presented Ireland with significant opportunities in attracting inward investment, and while some dispersal of these activities to non-urban locations has been achieved, there has been a strong bias towards urban locations. It must not be forgotten that the changing geography of economic activity associated with ISTs is a direct result of the search for greater productivity and profitability.

Information society in Ireland

Within this increasingly globalized economy, dominated by corporate restructuring, one of Europe's most peripheral regions has succeeded in exploiting the decentralization of economic activity to an impressive degree. Irish economic performance in recent years has been most impressive with export growth between 1996 and 1999 almost double the growth of Ireland's export markets, leaving the country at the top of the OECD league. Employment growth during the same period was seven times the EU average and unemployment has been halved to 7%. In 1997 there were a quarter of a million more people in the workforce than in 1990, and this jobs boom has been largely fuelled by an influx of IST companies together with the development of indigenous companies reflecting software, computing and communication skills.

In Ireland the services sector has been the main source of employment increase during the 1990s, accounting for 40% of the growth between 1989 and 1999. In 1997, the international services sector accounted for more than two-thirds of net employment growth with rapid expansion in software, financial services, telemarketing and shared services. Employment in these sectors more than doubled between 1994 and 1998. Since 1998, the software industry shifted from third to second place as the biggest internationally traded sector in Ireland after food. This change reflects as well as any other the significant change in Ireland's economy and society, from being heavily based on agriculture and being strongly rural in character to one which is firmly based on the exploitation of information society skills in predominantly urban locations.

The spatial concentration of information society activities in urban locations is clearly reflected in the geography of the software sector, which already employs 20,000 and in which employment growth between 1995 and 1997 was 60%. Half the employment is in multinational companies, which are mainly involved in localization of products for the European market. In 1997, the value of software exports from indigenous companies was £400 million, while the value of total software exports was £4 billion. In 1998, 83% of all software employment and 76% of software companies were located in the greater Dublin area, and there was considerable resistance on the part of software companies to move outside the capital. As a result of the significant migration of software professionals into the city both from other countries and from other parts of Ireland, Dublin has already attained a critical mass of software activity. While there is some indication of software activity developing in other smaller urban centres such as Cork, Limerick and Galway, the proportion of total software employment in these centres is still quite modest.

International services is another information society sector which has contributed significantly to employment growth in Ireland in recent years. Almost 16,000 new jobs have been created in this sector in the past 3 years. Since 1980, Ireland, with only 1% of Europe's population, has attracted 45% of US investment in Europe in teleservices. Initially this investment was mainly traditional back offices involved in insurance-related data processing. Later, it took the form of call centres involved in technical backup for computer hardware and software companies, and more recently it has been shared services, many of which are involved in centralized finance, administration and transaction processing support.

Most of the earlier back offices were US-owned and were well dispersed throughout the country, even in small town locations. By 1990, nine such firms employing 1000 people were established. During the 1990s there was an influx of call centres, mainly through US companies seeking a cost-effective entry to European markets. Ireland moved aggressively to get in early on this growth sector, and by the end of 1993 there were nine such centres. To date there are 60 pan-European call centres in Ireland, accounting for about one-third of such centres in Europe. Their activities range from sophisticated technical services for computer software and hardware to European reservation centres for travel, airlines and car hire. While some level of dispersal has been achieved in recent years, much of the teleservice activity is concentrated in Dublin and some of the larger urban centres. The indigenous internationally traded services sector is even more concentrated, with 80% of companies and 77% of employment located in Dublin and the Mid-East region.

Telematics

The approach in Ireland towards exploiting ISTs has been strongly focused on reaping economic benefits through attracting inward investment and creating employment. The EU approach, as reflected in the considerable investment in the IST elements of the Framework Programme, has become more focused on broader social issues such as new forms of work, improving the competitiveness of public service activities and improving the quality of life of citizens. Ireland has also benefited significantly from a high level of participation in IST programmes such as the Telematics Applications Programme. The array of telematic projects arising from these programmes throughout Europe is impressive ranging from improving transport services and health services to helping small- and medium-sized enterprises (SMEs) become more involved in e-commerce. While much of this activity is experimental in nature, it is contributing significantly towards making the information society a reality.

While many EU-funded telematics projects are city-based, many of the developments arising from them present considerable potential for rural and peripheral regions. One of the important motivations for telematics projects is the provision for the 'urban needs' of rural residents, through, for example, creating high technology employment in less developed regions. The development of regional airport information systems is an example of how telematics can be applied to enhance the quality of life of rural residents. Another important motivating force behind such projects is the provision of public services such as health services in a cost-efficient manner. The introduction of such innovative systems in rural areas, however, would require very significant investment during the next 10–15 years. It is envisaged that a plurality of infrastructural and technical solutions will be provided to suit the requirements of regions with low population densities and thus low levels of demand.

While one of the major concerns of experimentation with telematics projects is to discover opportunities for peripheral areas, it is to be expected that much of the innovation will begin in urban core regions, where the demand for solutions to problems such as traffic congestion is very urgent. To some extent the problems of urban regions are presenting new opportunities for peripheral regions, by providing them with new sources of comparative advantage. It is essential that policy-makers realize that access to frequent air services must accompany improvements in telecommunications infrastructure in non-urban regions. Part of the challenge facing weaker regions includes the need to improve the competitiveness of SMEs, particularly in traditional weak sectors. In the area of health telematics, projects that develop the ability to monitor patients from a distance help to reduce the travel requirements of both patients and medical personnel, thus provide a better service.

Continued overleaf

Conclusion

On the basis of the Irish experience to date, I would be reasonably optimistic about the prospects for peripheral areas exploiting the benefits offered by IST. It is true to say that much of the IST activity in Ireland has been driven by foreign investment, but this in turn has helped to generate a small, though dynamic indigenous component in sectors like software and internationally traded services. Ireland has shown that its peripheral location in Europe has not been a major handicap in attracting inward investment. In terms of regional development, however, progress has been quite modest, with some provincial centres beginning to benefit from the dispersal of IST investment, and with some small clusters of university campus high technology companies emerging. Experimentation with telematics projects through the EU's Framework Programme, while being heavily subsidized, has developed some highly applicable innovations for the improvement of public services such as health and transport in peripheral areas. It is still too early to predict the extent to which exploiting ISTs can help to reverse the process of urbanization: it would be folly on the part of policy-makers, however, to underestimate the regional development potential of the new technologies.

Seamus Grimes

The Local and the Global

Information technologies in harness with the hollowing-out of the state (Chapter 4) through political devolution or post-communist transformation, have facilitated the resurgence (or reconstruction) of local identities, helping to create the potential for new forms of locally constructed tourism development, such as the presentation of Celtic heritage in Scotland (MacDonald, 1997) and Ireland (Stocks, 2000), or village-based tourism in Albania (Holland, 2001) and Romania (Roberts, 1996) (see Chapter 7).

The effectiveness of these strategies for local communities may depend on the way in which access to, and control of, the Internet and related tools develops (not least in the 'ownership' of local identities as web addresses). Further, local areas represented on multiple websites, run the risk of being represented by conflicting and potentially confusing images.

The popularity of a 'community' focus has generated a growing literature on community-based tourism and community development in tourism (e.g. Richards and Hall, 2000c). Peter Murphy's (1983, 1985, 1988) seminal examination of community tourism emphasized the importance for community-based tourism development to be related to local needs. Subsequent studies have broadened the scope of the term to embrace ecological and ethical factors and local participation and democracy isses, thereby contributing to a more holistic if no less paradoxical concept of local tourism sustainability. A number of studies have reflected on the perceived requirement to involve local communities in processes of sustainable tourism management and development (e.g. Taylor, 1995; Bramwell *et al.*, 1996). The corollary is that any truly sustainable approach to the 'natural' environment needs to be grounded in the communities and societies which draw upon the resources of that environment and contribute to its cultural construction (Richards, 1999).

Certainly, local communities have a key role in taking action to preserve their own immediate environment, as well as helping to form wider alliances with NGOs and pressure groups. Such external relationships of any community, as well as its internal power structures, are important for its own sustainability. The creation of a 'Europe of the regions' is assisting the development of new alliances and relationships between local areas across national boundaries of, for example, farmers, or based on town twinning arrangements, or on NGO initiatives.

In post-communist CEE, for example, locally based nature tourism has taken on a significance whereby local authorities and NGOs are providing an important counterbalance to the essentially urban-led tourism growth experienced in the more economically advanced countries of the region. Thus far, however, there has been relatively little published on the role of NGOs in relation to tourism and local development processes in

CEE; and there is a general gap in the literature on the relationship between tourism and environment in the region (Hall, 2000b).

Notably, there has tended to be less concern in the region regarding tourism's impacts on the environment than about the reality and image of environmental degradation constraining tourism development (an interpretation of sustainable tourism pointed to by Richard Sharpley in Chapter 3). Certainly, heavy concentrations of atmospheric emissions, water pollution and acid rain damage to forests (Carter and Turnock, 1993; Klarer and Moldan, 1997), have been acute in several of the region's existing and potential tourism areas. Yet nature reserves and national parks often date back to the inter-war years (IUCN-EEP, 1990). National environment programmes were drawn up in the 1980s, and several gained Western funding support in the 1990s. However, the region's environmental NGOs such as the Polish Ecology Club and Bulgaria's *Ecoglasnost,* which largely emerged towards the end of the communist era, until recently tended to express little interest in tourism. This is partly because much tourism before 1989 was domestically and regionally generated, while 'Western' international tourists actually presented welcome contact with the outside world. In the waning years of communism, the target of such NGOs tended to be the environmental consequences of state giganticism in industrial policy. Reflecting most CEE governments' attitudes at the time, service industries were regarded by NGOs as of secondary significance and largely lacking natural resource implications.

The impact of tourism on the region's environmental diversity and fragility therefore still requires substantially greater attention, planning and monitoring (Lukashina *et al.*, 1996). While the elimination of many international boundary constraints and tensions has opened up opportunities for local and national-level cross-border cooperation in recreational development and environmental protection (Karpowicz, 1993; Hall and Kinnaird, 1994), it has also exposed ecological 'havens' which, located in former border exclusion zones, were largely devoid of human impact for half a century. The reality of post-communist change in such areas is that much local cross-border 'tourism' generated by easier access and changing local economic fortunes has been of the petty trading variety (Konstantinov, 1996; Iglicka, 1998; Hall, 2000a), seeking to exploit supply and demand differentials – including those of natural resources – across frontiers. However, some local cross-border environmental groups have emerged to encourage awareness in tourists and recreationalists. Sakertour Greenscape (1998), for example, is a joint venture of Hungarian and Slovakian ornithologists which encourages cross-border environmental awareness through selective 'ecotourism' activities.

The World Travel and Tourism Council (WTTC, 1999) has evaluated a number of CEE countries' institutional capacity to pursue sustainability policies. While it identified the presence or development of a number of national level sustainable development coordination bodies and policy frameworks, explicit institutional response to the needs of Local Regional Agenda 21 and other aspects of local and 'community' sustainability appeared relatively poor (Table 5.1).

In an attempt to counterbalance such shortcomings, the number of NGOs in the region has increased greatly in recent years. In some cases national NGOs have used new participation mechanisms and opportunities to support and influence environmental policy development. But with emphasis in post-communist CEE on economic reform, issues of local social and cultural sustainability have received relatively little attention. Only small proportions of aid budgets have been allocated for the promotion of civil society, often linked to support for NGO development (Roberts and Simpson, 1999a,b).

In some cases, international NGOs such as WWF have provided financial support, training and other assistance for groups. Generally, however, most NGOs in the region have been small, locally organized and with limited resources. To be effective in lobbying for more sustainable policies, they need to build stronger networks and a better base of public support. They are often concentrated in major urban centres and may have poor representation in outlying regions, as a result of which villagers may look upon them with caution, if not suspicion, as was well articulated by

Table 5.1. Decision-making structures which address sustainability (adapted from WTTC, 1999).

Country	National sustainable development coordination body	National sustainable development policy	National Agenda 21 framework	Local Regional Agenda 21 frameworks	Environmental impact assessment law
Bulgaria	**	**	**	V	V
Czech Republic	V	V	V	V	V
Hungary	V	V	V	V	V
Poland	V	V	V	*	V
Romania	V	V	?	X	V
Slovenia	V	X	V	X	V
Yugoslavia	X	X	V	X	V

**, being developed; V, present; X, absent; *, few.

Holland (2001) in the case of southern Albania. This is understandable if NGOs are seen as parastatal entities, or suffused with corruption, or both (e.g. Roberts, 1996), and negative perceptions may be reinforced if local communities remain deprived of knowledge and balanced information regarding the nature of development and the role of such agents of change.

Yet tourism has often flourished in post-communist CEE despite rather than because of government action. With the post-communist reduction of the role of the state, most governments have shown an unwillingness or inability to invest in the tourism industry or to secure significant international funding for it. However, the relative flexibility and proactive stance of a number of parastatal bodies, sometimes in partnership, has stimulated initiatives in relation to the development of particular tourism products and value-added services. Rural and nature tourism, for example, has received promotion from local government (e.g. Bognar, 1996) and NGOs (e.g. Ruukel, 1996) as well as from private sectors and international agencies. None the less, the relationship between such market developments responding to evolving 'Western' tastes and the ever-growing domestic and post-communist regional demand for mass tourism needs careful planning and management, suggesting the need to combine the role of central government at a strategic level with local and regionally based partnership schemes.

Tourism has the potential to exacerbate uneven regional development through the differentiated integration of particular territories into changing domestic and global markets and networks of international capital. This has tended to result in a reinforcement of the economic dominance of metropolitan regions, and differentiation among poorer regions: urban-industrial rust belts, peripheral and certain rural areas. Spatial and structural distortions in post-communist economies have tended to focus activity on major urban areas in favoured regions, not least in tourism. Urban tourism – notably in Prague and Budapest – has become a mass activity, exacerbating congestion and infrastructural problems as well as distorting territorial development. Such spatial distortion is likely to intensify as CEE cities attempt to position themselves as major European cultural destinations (e.g. Goluza, 1996; Blonski, 1998).

Local power and enablement

Growth of the 'third sector' (after the public and private) of NGOs has sought to 'empower' communities in terms of the generative view of power, which assumes that everyone has skills and capabilities which can be combined in collective action for the common good. This contrasts with the distributive nature of most existing power structures which presuppose a scarcity of resources requiring allocation decisions and the need for actors in the system to compete with each other (Richards and Hall, 2000b: 7). For example, the substantial power that metropolitan cores are able to exercise over the rural periphery (van der Straaten, 2000), as expressed in the EU LEADER programme (Chapter 4), results in a provision of resources, which, while benefiting one community may create problems for another. Somewhat paradoxically for an avowedly holistic philosophy, most existing models of sustainable tourism appear implicitly to reinforce a distributive form of empowerment from above, rather than generative empowerment from within 'communities'.

The perceived interdependence between local communities, their environment and the tourists who visit them seems to underpin most models of sustainable tourism. But the positive and/or negative roles which tourism entrepreneurs and the tourism industry may play in any given location is often underestimated. Their objectives and aspirations may be rooted in local community values but equally may have been superimposed upon them through exogenous and not necessarily sympathetic forces.

Unequal distribution of power and uneven flows of information can disenfranchise members of the community when decisions are taken about tourism development (e.g. Dahles, 2000). In the most extreme cases, as in developing countries such as Indonesia, state power may be used to further the interests of developers to the detriment of small, local entrepreneurs, stifling grassroots approaches to development. This is likely to be coupled to policies of developing 'quality' tourism which may privilege external over local interests.

There may therefore be a credibility gap for disadvantaged (elements of) local communities who find themselves unable to identify with forms of tourism development which they may view as an imposition with its benefits accruing to outsiders (tourists and the probably exogenous tourism industry). This can result in at best indifference, but possibly opposition or resistance to such development. Local Agenda 21 (LA21) should offer potential for marginalized groups to be involved in tourism development, but in practice this can be frustrated by a lack of awareness, poor communication or an inhibiting division of responsibilities within local government and other authorities (Jackson and Morpeth, 2000) (see also Chapter 4).

Enabling local residents and employees to make informed decisions about the nature of tourism development clearly requires a free flow of appropriate intelligible and usable information within that community. Any bottom-up model of (tourism) development presupposes that all sections of the community are adequately informed which, of course, is rarely, if ever, the case. Not merely the quantity but the quality and interpretation value of information is vital: it needs to be in a form that local people can understand, relate to and act upon. For example, policies for environmental sustainability may be based on technocratically derived 'scientific' criteria which can exclude and disenfranchise those who are not, or who perceive themselves not to be, equipped to evaluate or counter the 'scientific' arguments of technocratic elites (Goodall and Stabler, 2000).

Further, in post-communist Europe and Asia, and notably in south-eastern Europe, political and economic instability may undermine participative models (Holland, 2001). Yet, such conditions, perhaps because of the breakdown of the formal structures of civil society, may also open opportunities for community (self-help) involvement which may not be present or apparent under more stable conditions.

In summary, Page and Getz, (1997) point to common patterns detected in residents' attitudes towards local tourism development, thereby alluding to the preconditions for successful embedding of tourism in local development processes:

- There is a need for residents to feel tangible benefits from tourism, and preferably some degree of control over its development and promotion. In the absence of perceived benefits, it is likely that local opposition will increase.
- If tourism is perceived to be the only development option, support is likely to increase: in communities with low economic activity and low tourism development there will be high hopes and expectations of tourism (Johnson *et al.*, 1994) but possibly less likelihood of success than in already economically robust rural areas.

- Some evidence suggests that long-term residents of rural areas are more likely to support growth and change than newcomers, usually because newcomers have moved for amenities which they do not want changed (Getz, 1994).
- The previous point may be confounded in those areas where incoming entrepreneurs form a new dynamic element of the 'community' (see Chapter 2).
- However, as tourism is rarely the sole rural economic activity of an area, its (potential) impacts and attitudes to it may be difficult to disentangle from those relating to other local production and consumption processes.

Sustaining the entrepreneur in 'the community'

As suggested in Chapter 7, the role of the tourism entrepreneur can be vital for the development of tourism and recreation in rural areas. Tourism comprises mostly SMEs and is dependent on innovation for the development of new products. Entrepreneurs can contribute to the economic and social glue of local communities. They represent, both practically and symbolically, an important counterweight to the growing power of transnational companies. Small-scale tourism enterprises have the catalytic potential to provide a vital force in 'communities' in helping to transform local resources into tourist products and services.

Yet, for example, relatively new 'community-based' entrepreneurs within CEE's indigenous tourism industry may be confronted by competition from large 'Western' multinational groups which, while perhaps important in helping to integrate the region into the global economy, pose potential threats to economic, cultural and political integrity and sovereignty at a time when governments may be seeking to reduce their responsibilities. In order for such small, local entrepreneurs to survive in the face of growing global competition and state regulation, they need to be supported in a number of ways (Richards and Hall, 2000a):

- The construction and maintenance of local networks; for example, local enterprise systems in less developed regions may depend on the activities of particular types of entrepreneurs: 'patrons', who provide the capital and resources necessary for tourism development, and 'brokers', who represent an essential interface between patrons and tourists, anticipating, translating and satisfying tourist needs through innovation and ingenuity (Dahles, 2000).
- The sustaining of direct links between local producer networks and consumer organizations. The sale of 'community friendly' tourism products can be supported by appropriate branding and consumer information.
- Network linkages to internal and external actors are also important for providing mutual support and for the dissemination of innovation and good practice. Effective networks can provide the conditions necessary for entrepreneurialism to flourish, and can be assisted by regional, national and supranational (e.g. EU) policies and frameworks. For example, in Friesland, The Netherlands, the public sector has played a key role in developing and supporting network development, providing financial subsidies for community initiatives and integrating different policy levels (Caalders, 2000). The ability of the public sector to support entrepreneurial development is also dependent on reliable information about the birth and death of tourism enterprises in the community (Koh, 2000).

The importance of economic back-linkages

Any local- or 'community'-based tourism development needs to establish or be rooted in strong back-linkages with the local economy if it is to sustain itself and its environment. The following invited opinion emphasizes the importance of economic back-linkages for embedding tourism development within the cultural and economic milieux of rural life. This is related specifically to the rapidly growing food and drink sector of rural tourism enterprise.

As competition between tourism destinations increases, aspects of local culture become an increasingly important part of the link between meeting tourists' and recreationalists' expectations of the 'rural' and helping to sustain the local economy, through reinforcing and buttressing 'traditional' activities and/or by providing markets for a restructured economic profile. Gastronomy would appear to play a particularly significant role in this, not only because cuisine is central to the tourist experience but also because gastronomy has become an important source of identity formation in most post-industrial societies (Richards, 2001). It has become a fashion accessory for the tourist and a badge of quality for food producing regions and localities (Plate 5.3).

As an important linkage between tourism and the agrarian rural economy, the role of cuisine for tourism, to be an appropriate and successful rural development tool, needs to be closely integrated with other aspects of rural development through such complementary activities as (Boyne *et al.*, 2001):

- encouraging innovative back-linkages with, and complementing a restructuring of, the local agrarian economy (such as stimulating niche specialist food – including non-standardized and organic – production and promotion) (e.g. Bowen *et al.*, 1991);
- stimulating locally rooted food-related SME growth and cooperation (e.g. Henderson, 2000);
- generating locally retained value-added benefits from production, processing and retailing (e.g. Sylvander, 1993);
- raising food quality and generating an awareness of the need to improve and maintain quality, at both the production and consumption ends of the gastronomic tourism chain (e.g. Gilg and Battershill, 1998; Ilbery and Kneafsey, 1998, 2000a,b) (see also Fiona Williams' contribution in Chapter 8); and
- strengthening local image and regional identity through the development and promotion of place-specific food brands, thereby helping to promote, albeit also commodifying, aspects of local culture and heritage (e.g. Bessière, 1998) through, for example, food and wine trails.

Plate 5.3. Cuisine can be an important element in the tourism experience and a tangible symbol of local identity and quality produce.

In the following invited viewpoint, Jacinthe Bessière brings a French perspective to this pan-European development.

Invited Viewpoint

The Role of Rural Gastronomy in Tourism

Jacinthe Bessière

In a context of changing rural land use and agricultural diversification, a part of tourism demand now focuses on rural areas. A new form of rural tourism in rural areas has emerged, sometimes called inland tourism, domestic tourism or green tourism. Responsible in France for 370 million tourism days in 1994, or 27% of global tourism trips and 20% of French national tourism (INSEE, 1996), this new sector of activity marks the move from a *campagne-repoussoir* to a *countryside of desire*, thereby invoking a new rural imagination. Today the pull of nature, the search for an *original communitas* (Amirou, 1995), the obsession with restoring the past to favour, all seem to be structuring the collective imagination of city dwellers. If we consider the tourist quest as a symbolic search for identity, then the countryside plays a compensatory and idealized role in the collective consciousness. Society's demand for the *local* reveals

Continued overleaf

an ideologically based demand in which return to the countryside means the re-invoking of a rustic peasant background in a world where an uncertain future is becoming less than desirable. Also – and above all – it is a demand grounded in a logic of gazing at and appropriating the countryside, desirous of living in enhanced surroundings where recognition, participation and proximity are comfortably united.

As a traditional element of cultural heritage, gastronomy is a major ingredient of tourist activities: eating contributes fully to the quality of a holiday and rural tourism can be a part of the re-appropriation of our gastronomic history. Established as a recognized national norm, French gastronomy is perceived as a common foundation, a collective marker. 'Eating well' is a sort of national code which qualifies, unites and identifies us. By inviting the diner to a new realm of identity, we start from the hypothesis that rural gastronomy is a response to expectations sparked by unease at the industrialization of contemporary eating habits.

> The tourist is not just a spectator at the movement ... he communicates personally with the region visited, by a few simple words and ceremonial greetings exchanged with the locals... Through the purchase of symbolic objects called souvenirs ... he magically appropriates Spain or Italy. Finally, he consumes the physical being of the country visited in a gastronomic meal, an increasingly widespread rite of cosmophagy.
>
> (Morin, 1962: 82–83)

At a time when travel and moving around have increasingly become social constants, democratized and undertaken by all, food and tourism remain intimately linked.

Birth of the rural tourism/local gastronomy pairing

In his historical analysis of the emergence of French regional cuisines, Csergo characterizes gastronomy as a type of cultural consumption of a local area and describes the way the culinary element has, since the end of the 19th century, become one of various affirmations of local identity along with postcards, place-based novels and geographic itineraries (Csergo, 1996).

It was not until the 1920s and the advent of motor tourism – which favoured the discovery of local regions – that 'gastronomic journeys' were born and developed and that the 'gastronomads', to use a term coined by Curnonski,[1] appeared. In 1921, with Marcel Rouff, Curnonski began publication of an eating guide symbolising 'the holy alliance of tourism and gastronomy'.[2] In the manner of an initiation trip the two journalists proceeded to undertake a 'Gastronomic Tour de France' which allowed them to make an inventory of the culinary riches of rural France. 'Monumental buildings, natural curiosities, the countryside and local pride are simply truffles, *fois gras*, capons or fattened pullets' (Csergo, 1996: 836). The *Michelin Guide*, born in 1901 of the encounter between the automobile industry and the new practice of leisure, reserved initially for drivers and presented as a dictionary of different places, lists Michelin sales points and garages but also curiosities, itineraries and restaurants. The famous red guide book became the bible of French gastronomy, gradually awarding stars to the best culinary halts. From the 1920s onwards the *Guides Bleus* also supplied gastronomic information.

From then on, treatises, guide books and itineraries on regional French cuisine acquired a powerful notoriety by conferring a new legitimacy on the local through the medium of tourism. Finally, thanks to the actions of hoteliers, restaurateurs, gastronomic associations (the Association of Regional Gastronomers was created in 1923) and regionalist movements, local gastronomy and its role within tourism gradually became the expressions of a new national model. Thus, through the incorporation and assimilation of products originating from a soil, a land and an expertise both local and rural, the 'culinary tourist', whom we shall attempt to analyse below, finds in the gastronomic element a place of attachment outside his or her everyday eating experience which is both physiological and symbolic.

The cultural appropriation of the 'culinary tourist'

Gastronomy holds a favoured place within the tourist quest. An ingredient of the holiday, it provides part of the sense of place. The meal and its elements reinforce the process of identification during the holiday. It can be that whereby, or wherefore, we favour or reject a particular place. Pavageau (1997: 599) well describes the place of the culinary in the journey: the imagined food world shares, he writes, 'in the complex alchemy which mobilises the individual to undertake a particular trip, punctuates the stages of the future journey with strong images, becomes involved in the very organization of the trip and is an integrative part of tourist activities'. Imagined, consumed, incorporated and, in some cases, brought back, the gastronomic product is a cultural and identifying marker of the region visited.

Being a tourist takes place outside a standardized day-to-day order, and the consumption of local cuisine forms part of this break with everyday reality by inviting the tourist into a new culinary universe: it places the tourist outside ordinary life by making him/her aware, if only ephemerally, of his/her culinary history. Holidays are privileged times for forgetting everyday eating habits sometimes marked by dieting or restraint. Furthermore, the culinary tourist or consumer acts as if by becoming closer to the product he or she has greater control and knowledge of it. In the act of buying from peasant markets or roadside stalls, or of eating food in its place of origin, the diner has the impression of escaping the laws of the market, or of short-circuiting the commercial chain.

Besides, one of the first acts of integration generally performed when one is elsewhere, outside one's habitual framework, is eating. Consuming the food of another group, borrowing its culinary practices; is this not a way of making contact with and appropriating another culture? Eating the foods and gastronomic specialities of the region visited, as well as adopting its table manners, provides a step to understanding, apprehending and integrating the cultural practices of elsewhere.

The meal and the table customs which accompany it integrate the tourist into the culture of the other by making him or her physiologically and psychologically absorb its cultural codes. If the tourist's experience comprises consumption of multiple symbols and representations, eating is also a symbolic act filled with cultural meaning. Thus 'eating local' produces a social integration of the tourist within the host group. On the other hand, refusing the food of the other can appear as a path of rejection and exclusion.

Consuming regional specialities *where they come from*, eating 'elsewhere' and 'differently' is an act of complicity with the place, a way of becoming part of the intimacy of that place and of the other, a symbolic consumption of a land, a region, a province, its climate, its history, its scenery. 'How better to appreciate a place, to establish a greater bond of complicity with it than to eat of its fruits, thereby embodying it in a real sense' (de la Soudière, 1995: 157). Thus food can be read as an intercultural encounter constitutive of individual and collective identities.

The 'canonization' of certain tourist sites, often called 'shrines', may be gastronomic in nature and give rise to 'must-see' sites: emblematic 'culinary spaces' which reveal the identity and culture of a given territory. Thus the recent labelling by the Conseil National des Arts Culinaires of 100 *Sites Remarquables du Gout* (Sites of Special Culinary Interest) provides an authentication of their richness and corroborates this sanctifying dimension of gastronomy. In order to feature, these sites must show proof of having both tourist and gastronomic attractions and they provide collective rallying points, common references and a sort of place of pilgrimage for a culinary tourist in search of alimentary reconciliation. Such gastronomic shrines complete the ritual of the journey as they punctuate the tourists' trips.

Another dimension which forms part of the tourism ritual is that of the purchase of souvenirs to bring back from one's journey. The souvenir embodies the link between the here and the elsewhere. It is the proof, the guarantee of an experience lived differently, as it broadcasts scents, images and flavours at one's or others' home at the end of the holidays. 'His home becomes a new elsewhere (from which he has returned) and this elsewhere ... has changed him ... He seeks to reduce the distance between this latter journey (and the next) by magic' (Urbain, 1993: 256). The food or gastronomic souvenir remains very much part of the tourism experience. Buying and bringing home local produce (wine, farm-produced foods) at the end of the trip, for example, prolongs and reinforces the journey. These products form part of the tourist's psychological return: recreating a recipe at home, eating 'the elsewhere' in one's everyday milieu, reactivates our holiday sensations, calling them to mind and commemorating them. The scent, savour and taste of the product all help to reintroduce a memory of elsewhere and the holiday and everyday worlds become interwoven thanks to the culinary souvenir. Like a venerated, sanctified object, the gastronomic souvenir shared and eaten among friends can also prolong the act of social distinction and differentiation.

The culinary imagination and the tourist imagination thus remain intimately linked. The current way of imagining the country summons up the tourism experience in the same way as the gastronomic experience. Indeed, the myth of the natural, the cult of the past and the search for belonging send us back just as much to the image of present-day rural life as to its gastronomy. Local cuisine could therefore

Continued overleaf

play the role of a unifying component of rural tourism on which would converge and rest a collection of aspirations and images. In this way the purifying and therapeutic images associated with the countryside are found in the consumption of and search for 'pure', 'natural' products which are likened to corporal and spiritual forms of therapy (physiological and psychological incorporation). The success of meals shared on farm accommodation or around the host's table seems to be the expression of a desire to communicate around food, a return to a sort of nostalgia for communal meals.

Ultimately, it is the erosion and standardization of traditional culinary practices that allows us to understand the resurgence of rural gastronomy, linked to local territorial production, and therefore to envisage the issue of the response of rural territories. In a context of changing urban culinary practices, to which the response has been a consecration of rural values, rural areas still seem guarantors of a stable and notably gastronomic identity linked with methods and cycles of production. Rural areas are thus seeing themselves becoming spaces of reconciliation, welcome and affirmation of culinary heritages.

1 Maurice Edmond Sailland, known as Curnonski (1872–1956), 'elected prince of the gastronomes'. He was a well-known culinary chronicler and author.
2 According to Simon Arbellot of the Académie des Gastronomes.

[Translated from French with the author's approval by Frances Brown]

Jacinthe Bessière

Partnerships, Collaboration and Networking Strategies

While back-linkages are important for local embedding, partnership and collaboration now represent the conventional wisdom for establishing and sustaining necessary vertical and horizontal linkages across and between localities and development sectors. The growing emphasis on partnership arrangements in tourism development is closely related to recent management and policy theory as well as to changes in the nature of the state. For example, government tourism organizations, local governments and economic development agencies are encouraged to engage in a greater range of partnerships, networks and collaborative relationships with stakeholders, including each other. This is part of the 'hollowing out of the state' (Milward, 1996) in which the state's role has been transformed from hierarchical control to dispersed governance among a number of separate, non-government entities, leading to evaluations of policy and governance employing an 'institutional thickness' framework (Box 5.3).

Strategic planning now places substantial emphasis on relations with stakeholders (Chapter 4) while the emergence of theories of collaboration (e.g. Gray, 1985, 1989; Wood and Gray, 1991) and network development (e.g. Powell, 1990; Freeman, 1991; Cooke and Morgan, 1993) highlights the importance of the links to be made between stakeholders in processes of mediation, promotion and regional development (Hall, 1999). For example, network development is an important common element in many EU regional development programmes such as LEADER (e.g. Zarza, 1996) (Chapter 4).

The need for tourism development to create links with stakeholders was recognized in the community tourism approach of Murphy (1983, 1985, 1988). In reality, the term 'stakeholder' often means industry and community-based groups in a destination context rather than wider public participation mechanisms. The difficulty in implementing 'community-based' tourism strategies reflects wider problems of effective destination management and tourism planning (Davidson and Maitland, 1997), and notably the diffuse nature of tourism activity within economic and social structures and the problems this creates for coordination and management.

Notions of collaboration, coordination and partnership are separate, though closely related, ideas within the emerging network paradigm. Networks refer to the development of linkages between actors (organizations and individuals) where linkages become more formalized towards maintaining mutual interests. The nature of such linkages exists on a continuum ranging from 'loose' linkages to coalitions and more lasting structural arrangements and relationships:

Box 5.3. The 'institutional thickness' framework and scales of governance.

Any discussion of tourism policy leads to a focus on the importance of institutions, key actors within them, policy discourses – the nature and content of discussions (Latour, 1997), policy communities, arenas for policy discussions, and the formal and informal networks that exist between the institutions/key actors involved (Rhodes and Marsh, 1992).

Of several 'institutional' approaches to analysis, Amin and Thrift's (1994, 1995) 'institutional thickness' framework has been employed to examine changes in economic governance, but can also be useful when analysing the governance of tourism and recreation. It problematizes the processes behind, and roles of, the actual institutions and actors which are involved, as well as the significance of the scales at which state activity is being constituted and re-constituted (Jessop, 1998).

A 'hollowing out' in, and of, national strategy and policy delivery (Painter and Goodwin, 1995; Jessop, 1998) has witnessed an emphasis on international and regional/local levels of governance. As a response to this, the 'institutional thickness' approach advocates that an appropriate way of addressing the problems of the governance of regions and/or localities can be through developing an institutionally based set of local networks and alliances (Raco, 1998) which allows a range of interests to be represented, and through which wider national and global economic forces can be integrated at a more localized scale. Four elements of 'thickness' can be highlighted:

1. *Institutional presence,* which refers to the range of institutions within a specified area organizing a variety of practices;
2. *Networking and interaction between institutions,* which includes the form and regularity of contacts;
3. *Structures of power, domination and control,* which help to ensure coalition building and collective representation; and
4. *A common agenda to develop upon,* in order to establish effective networks.

Such headings can be used to highlight whether regions have an appropriate 'institutional thickness' conducive to the effective governance of tourism and recreation. There are a number of criticisms of the approach, however:

- A focus on 'the local' underplays the powerful role national institutions and central-state policies may have locally, as well as often leading to an ignorance of the wider contexts in which regions operate (Peck and Tickell, 1994).
- The nature of local politics can often be contested while there is always the problematic possibility of the exclusion of marginal groups when constructing a local 'common agenda' (MacLeod, 1998). However, in this respect the concept does focus attention on the lack of 'leverage' of the various interest groups that have failed to develop an institutional form, structure or presence.
- An emphasis on institutions *per se* as a key driver for local and regional innovation may lead to an overly one-dimensional focus; processes behind institutionalization are equally, if not more, important.
- There can also be problems in 'measuring' the social capital which exists within institutions (MacLeod,1998).

- linkages or interactive contacts between two or more actors;
- intermittent coordination or mutual adjustment of the policies and procedures of two or more actors to accomplish some objective;
- *ad hoc* or temporary task force activity to accomplish a specific purpose or purposes;
- permanent and/or regular coordination between two or more actors through a formal arrangement to engage in limited activity to achieve a purpose or purposes;
- a coalition where interdependent and strategic actions are taken, but where purposes are narrow in scope and all actions occur within the participant actors themselves or involve the mutually sequential or simultaneous activity of the participant actors; and
- a collective or network structure where there is a broad mission and joint strategically interdependent action; such structural arrangements take on broad tasks that reach beyond the simultaneous actions of independently operating actors (Mandell, 1999).

Networks are a distinct, hybrid mode of coordinating economic activity that are alternatives to organization by markets or within firms (hierarchical transactions). They:

- involve firms of all sizes in various combinations;
- can be locally or internationally based;
- can occur at all stages of the value chain; and
- range from highly informal relationships through to contractual obligations (Hall, 1999).

Network development has received much attention in both academic and government circles in recent years. Networking has long been a hallmark of innovation organizations, and refers to a wide range of cooperative behaviour between otherwise competing organizations linked through economic and social relationships and transactions. Networked SMEs appear to be an important component of successful regional economies (e.g. Cooke and Morgan, 1993), and may offer considerable potential to assist in cushioning the effects of economic restructuring, particularly in rural and peripheral areas.

Network relationships are of great significance for tourism promotion and coordination. Coordination here does not mean any formal intervention, but identifying and working towards common objectives by tourism enterprises and by their support bodies in the public and private sectors. Similarly, Buhalis and Cooper (1998: 338) have observed that networking will allow small- and/or medium-sized tourism enterprises (SMTEs) to:

- pool their resources in order to increase their competitiveness;
- draw up strategic management and marketing plans;
- reduce operating costs; and
- increase their know-how.

Despite increasing recognition of the significance of networks, there is an absence of a common set of factors for describing and explaining the development of networks because the conditions which give rise to network formation are diverse.

However, one of the most significant aspects of networks is that not only do they represent flows of cooperation information, e.g. research and promotion, but, from a tourism perspective, they may also represent flows of tourists on the ground. In other words, the economic and social characteristics of networks may parallel the flow of goods and services including tourists. Communicative relationships therefore affect business, community, economic, social and political relationships and need to be much better understood in the process of tourism development (Hall, 1999).

The following invited collaboration examines in more detail the nature and significance of partnership approaches within rural development with particular reference to tourism and recreation-related organizations.

Invited Collaboration

Partnership Approaches in Rural Development

Lesley Roberts and Fiona Simpson

The tourism industry is characterized by political, sectoral and geographical fragmentation; the production and delivery of the tourism 'product' traditionally involves and impinges on the work of a range of diverse organizations (Bramwell and Lane, 2000). Peripherality, in relation to many policy foci, serves to worsen the business position of SMTEs. The problems arising from such fragmentation are as diverse as the industry itself, and range from incapacity at local levels to address inter-agency conflicts, to a lack of recognition of the benefits of collaborative working.

Partly in response to these problems, and linked with the policy focus on sustainable development, partnership building has become increasingly important throughout the rural regions of Europe. There has been a growing recognition of the need to establish diversified and integrated economies based on a more holistic approach than the traditional rural focus on agricultural policy matters has allowed.

Within the EU, national governments have taken up the theme of partnership working, partly in response to the emphasis within the European Commission's Structural Funding Programmes on alliances, collaboration and stakeholder participation. At local, regional and national levels, the administration of rural development programmes requires new institutional forms and ways of working that have been termed 'new rural govern*ance*', the nature of which differs from govern*ment* in its emphasis on the inclusion of groups and individuals from outside the usual political sphere and its focus on the relationships between these various groups (Stoker, 1997).

A number of terms exist to describe group interaction in the development and policy domains, including partnership, collaboration, alliances, community-based, stakeholder-centred, consultative and participatory actions. This short piece is concerned neither with definitions nor with the nuances of practice that distinguish one from another. Much of the research to date has confined itself to defining and analysing partnership approaches, overlooking the potential benefits to be gained. Furthermore, there is little analysis that determines the factors critical to success in the community development process (Joppe, 1996; Roberts and Simpson, 1999a). The following, therefore, analyses what is generically referred to as 'partnership approaches' and identifies prerequisites to successful collaboration.

The importance of partnership approaches to development is now well recognized. Such links establish longer-term, cross-institutional frameworks for integrated community working. In terms of their main characteristics, partnerships are often formal, based on a willingness of partners to cooperate, and the identification of explicit common goals (OECD, 1990: 18). They provide a platform for the articulation of needs by a number of groups in the interests of consensus and may promote strategic, long-term thinking resulting in flexible and innovative ways of working. The critical mass achieved through collaboration can contribute to more effective lobbying, allowing local issues to be afforded a higher profile in development processes. Although difficult to measure, the importance of links forged through partnership approaches can now be seen in the range of processes that contribute to rural development (Roberts and Simpson, 1999a).

The motivation to seek other organizations for collaboration varies. Recognition of a shared problem, opportunities for mutual benefit, strength in numbers, or the requirement of funding bodies will each provide the impetus for some form of cooperative venture. Indeed the motive(s) may be the key to success. A strong sense of mutual benefit, for example, is likely to support the frameworks and processes necessary to ensure such benefits are felt. Other factors critical to successful partnership working are identified by Jamal and Getz (1995) (Table 5.2). These criteria provide a framework for the evaluation of partnership approaches and result from the need identified by Simmons (1994), Jamal and Getz (1995) and Reed (1997) to further our understanding of partnership approaches from an analysis of practice rather than theory.

Aims, structuring and monitoring are political and administrative processes essential to good management of development projects and are likely to be an explicit requirement of a funding body. Their tangibility and measurability often make them the focus of evaluation processes and thus they have dominated measurements of 'success'. Clearly, partnerships need to achieve their aims and objectives. But partnership approaches can also have a range of longer-term benefits such as capacity-building and social capital enhancement, neither of which is directly assessed by the achievement of tangible goals.

Table 5.2. Factors critical to successful partnership working (source: Jamal and Getz, 1995: 195–199).

1	Recognition of a high degree of interdependence in planning and managing the domain/project
2	Recognition of individual and/or mutual benefits to be derived from the collaborative process
3	A perception that decisions arrived at will be implemented
4	The inclusion of key stakeholder groups
5	The appointment of a legitimate convenor to initiate and facilitate community-based collaboration
6	Formulation of aims and objectives

For a comparative study of partnerships in Bulgaria and Romania, Roberts and Simpson (1999a,b) used the Jamal and Getz framework and found that the criteria contained therein indeed represented essential prerequisites for success. However, while they found them to include critical success factors,

Continued overleaf

Roberts and Simpson contended that in order to apply the criteria in a meaningful way, the extent to which each can be defined and measured should also be taken into account. As a result they suggest a prioritization of the six factors that ranks them in order of their measurability (Table 5.3).

Table 5.3. Critical success factors revisited (source: Roberts and Simpson, 1999a, after Jamal and Getz, 1995).

Most measurable
6 Formulation of aims and objectives
4 The inclusion of key stakeholder groups
5 The appointment of a legitimate convenor to initiate and facilitate community-based collaboration
1 Recognition of a high degree of interdependence in planning and managing the domain/project
2 Recognition of individual and/or mutual benefits to be derived from the collaborative process
3 A perception that decisions arrived at will be implemented
Least measurable

This adds a further dimension to the already complex process of managing collaborative processes to ensure they are both effective in the short term, and sustainable in the longer term. Shifting the focus of analysis from tangible and measurable outcomes of partnership working to processes such as participant sincerity and the development of trust, which are less tangible and more difficult to measure, opens up new problems. However, broadening the debate on partnerships in this way, may ensure that the full range of success factors for collaboration is better understood.

No doubt the complex nature of partnership working will continue to challenge researchers and practitioners alike. However, in order to be useful for rural tourism development in the new millennium, the ongoing development of our theoretical understanding of partnership working needs to be translated into practice. More realistic guidelines for communities engaging in new forms of rural governance are required if collaboration is to become synonymous with sustainable partnership working.

Lesley Roberts and Fiona Simpson

Chapter Conclusions and Summary

It is generally well accepted that 'rural tourism' must be integrated with community-based development initiatives and not planned as a single sector. Tourism's role in integrated rural development is fundamentally an economic one. The question of how tourism and recreation's development may be integrated into wider rural development planning is critical to the success of both businesses and regions and communities in which they thrive. Collaboration and cooperation are required of businesses in the development of networks, partnerships and regional bodies that can work in collective interest. Both economies of scale and scope (i.e. gains to a firm as a result of expansion of the industry) are only likely to be achieved by collaborative practices, the effects of individual firms' marketing often being widely dispersed and relatively ineffective. Certainly, the critical mass required to attract visitors, and generate regional distinctiveness, from which a quality image can be derived, is best achieved through collaborative working practices.

This chapter has attempted to provide a critique of the notion of embedding recreation and tourism development processes within the rural 'community'. It has done this by:

- critically evaluating the notion, role and use of local 'community';
- assessing the concept of community-based tourism development within a rural context;
- examining the role of partnerships, collaboration and networks in embedding SME-based tourism and recreation development within rural 'communities'; and
- evaluating the implications of such processes for rural development.

The following chapter evaluates motivation and demand for recreational and tourism experiences and products in rural areas.

References

Amin, A. and Thrift, N. (1994) Living in the global. In: Amin, A. and Thrift, N. (eds) *Globalization, Institutions, and Regional Development in Europe*. Oxford University Press, Oxford, pp. 1–19.

Amin, A. and Thrift, N. (1995) Globalization, institutional 'thickness' and the local economy In: Healey, P., Cameron, S., Davoudi, S. and Mandani Pour, A. (eds) *Managing Cities: the New Urban Context*. John Wiley & Sons, Chichester, pp. 91–108.

Amirou, R. (1995) *Imaginaire Touristique et Sociabilités du Voyage*. PUF, Coll. Le Sociologue, Paris.

Bell, C. and Newby, H. (1976) Communion, communalism, class and community action: the sources of new urban politics. In: Herbert, D. and Johnson, R. (eds) *Social Areas in Cities*, Volume 2. John Wiley & Sons, Chichester.

Bessière, J. (1998) Local development and heritage: traditional food and cuisine as tourist attractions in rural areas. *Sociologia Ruralis* 38, 21–34.

Beynon, J. (2000) National parks in Hungary: developments post 1990. *Geography* 85(3), 274–279.

Blonski, K. (1998) *Krakow 2000: European City of Culture*. City and Voivodship of Kraków, Kraków.

Bognar, A. (1996) *Budapest's Protected Natural Heritage*. Municipality of the City of Budapest, Budapest.

Bowen, R.L., Cox, L.J. and Fox, M. (1991) The interface between tourism and agriculture. *Journal of Rural Studies* 2(2), 43–54.

Boyne, S., Williams, F. and Hall, D. (2001) Gastronomic tourism as a vehicle for rural development. In: Hjalager, A.-M. and Richards, G. (eds) *Moveable Feasts: Tourism and Gastronomy in a Globalising World*. Routledge, London (in press).

Bramwell, B. and Lane, B. (2000) Collaboration and partnerships in tourism planning. In: Bramwell, B. and Lane, B. (eds) *Tourism Collaboration and Partnerships: Politics, Practice and Sustainability*. Channel View Publications, Clevedon, pp. 1–19.

Bramwell, W., Henry, I., Jackson, G., Prat, A., Richards, G. and van der Straaten, J. (1996) *Sustainable Tourism Management: Principles and Practice*. Tilburg University Press, Tilburg, The Netherlands.

Buhalis, D. and Cooper, C. (1998) Competition or co-operation? Small and medium-sized enterprises at the destination. In: Laws, E., Faulkner, B. and Moscardo, G. (eds) *Embracing and Managing Change in Tourism*. Routledge, London, pp. 324–346.

Caalders, J. (2000) Tourism in Friesland: a network approach. In: Richards, G. and Hall, D. (eds) *Tourism and Sustainable Community Development*. Routledge, London, pp. 185–204.

Carter, F.W. and Turnock, D. (eds) (1993) *Environmental Problems in Eastern Europe*. Routledge, London.

Cloke, P. and Little, J. (eds) (1997) *Contested Countryside Cultures: Otherness, Marginalisation and Rurality*. Routledge, London.

Cohen, B. and Lipman, Y. (1998) Rural tourism: alternative strategies for income generation. *Shalom* 2. http://www.israel.org/mfa/go.asp?MFA07pm0

Cooke, P. and Morgan, K. (1993) The network paradigm: new departures in corporate and regional development. *Environment and Planning D: Society and Space* 11, 543–564.

Csergo, J. (1996) L'emergence des cuisines régionales. In: Flandrin, J.-L. and Montanari, M. (eds) *Histoire de l'Alimentation*. Fayard, Paris, pp. 823–841.

Dahles, H. (2000) Tourism, small enterprises and community development. In: Richards, G. and Hall, D. (eds) *Tourism and Sustainable Community Development*. Routledge, London, pp. 154–169.

Davidson, R. and Maitland, R. (1997) *Tourism Destinations*. Hodder and Stoughton, London.

de la Soudière, M. (1995) Dis-moi où tu pousses… Questions aux produits locaux, régionaux, de terroir, et à leurs consommateurs. In: Eizner, N. (ed.) *Voyage en Alimentation*. ARF-Editions, Paris, pp. 155–166.

Edwards, J. (1991) Guest–host perceptions of rural tourism in England and Portugal. In: Sinclair, M.T. and Stabler, M.J. (eds) *The Tourism Industry: an International Analysis*. CAB International, Wallingford, pp. 143–164.

Faulkner, B. (1998) Tourism development options in Indonesia and the case of agro-tourism in central Java. In: Laws, E., Faulkner, B. and Moscardo, G. (eds) *Embracing and Managing Change in Tourism*. Routledge, London, pp. 202–221.

Fleischer, A. and Pizam, A. (1997) Rural tourism in Israel. *Tourism Management* 18(6), 367–372.

Frank, A.G. (1967) *Capitalism and Underdevelopment in Latin America*. Monthly Review Press, New York.

Freeman, C. (1991) Networks of innovators: a synthesis of research issues. *Research Policy* 20, 499–514.

Getz, D. (1994) Residents' attitudes towards tourism: a longitudinal study in Spey Valley, Scotland. *Tourism Management* 15(4), 247–258.

Gilg, A. and Battershill, M. (1998) Quality farm food in Europe: a possible alternative to the industrialised food market and to current agri-environmental policies: lessons from France. *Food Policy* 23, 25–40.
Goluza, M. (1996) *Zagreb: the New European Metropolis*. Tourist Association of the City of Zagreb, Zagreb, Croatia.
Goodall, B. and Stabler, M. (2000) Environmental standards and performance measurement in tourism destination development. In: Richards, G. and Hall, D. (eds) *Tourism and Sustainable Community Development*. Routledge, London, pp. 63–82.
Gray, B. (1985) Conditions facilitating interorganizational collaboration. *Human Relations* 28(10), 911–936.
Gray, B. (1989) *Collaborating: Finding Common Ground for Multiparty Problems*. Jossey-Bass, San Francisco.
Grimes, S. (2000) Rural areas in the information society: diminishing distance or increasing learning capacity? *Journal of Rural Studies* 16(1), 13–21.
Hall, D.R. (1982) Valued environments and the planning process: community consciousness and urban structure. In: Gold, J.R. and Burgess, J. (eds) *Valued Environments*. George Allen & Unwin, London, pp. 172–188.
Hall, D.R. (1993) Ecotourism in the Danube Delta. *Revue de Tourisme* 3, 11–13.
Hall, D.R. (1998) Tourism development and sustainability issues in Central and South-eastern Europe. *Tourism Management* 19(5), 423–431.
Hall, D.R. (2000a) Cross-border movement and the dynamics of 'transition' processes in South-eastern Europe. *GeoJournal* 42.
Hall, D.R. (2000b) Evaluating the tourism-environment relationship: Central and Eastern European experiences. *Environment and Planning B: Planning and Design* 27(3), 411–421.
Hall, D.R. (2000c) Tourism as sustainable development? The Albanian experience of 'transition'. *International Journal of Tourism Research* 2(1), 31–46.
Hall, D.R. (2001) Central and Eastern Europe. In: Apostopoulos, Y., Sonmez, S.F. and Timothy, D. (eds) *Women as Producers and Consumers of Tourism in Developing Regions*. Greenwood, Westport, Connecticut.
Hall, D. and Kinnaird, V. (1994) Ecotourism in Eastern Europe. In: Cater, E. and Lowman, G. (eds) *Ecotourism: a Sustainable Option?* John Wiley & Sons, Chichester, pp. 111–136.
Hall, M. (1999) Collaboration, strategies and partnerships: perspectives on their relevance to tourism. In: Arola, E. and Mikkonen, T. (eds) *Tourism Industry and Education Symposium: Jyväskylä, Finland*. Jyväskylä Polytechnic, Jyväskylä, pp. 87–92.
Henderson, M. (2000) *Scottish Cheese? It's a Brie-z*. Scotland On Line. http://www.travelscotland.co.uk/features/cheese.htm
Hetland, P. (1998) Constructing technology in a social experiment: following the actors and controversies. In: Hetland, P. and Meier-Dallach, H.-P. (eds) *Domesticating the World Wide Webs of Information and Communication Technology*. European Commission, Luxembourg, pp. 59–78.
Hillery, G. (1955) Definitions of community – areas of agreement. *Rural Sociology* 20, 111–123.
Holland, J. (2001) Consensus and conflict: the socio-economic challenge facing sustainable tourism development in Southern Albania. *Journal of Sustainable Tourism* 9.
Howie, F. (2000) Establishing the common ground: tourism, ordinary places, grey-areas and environmental quality in Edinburgh, Scotland. In: Richards, G. and Hall, D. (eds) *Tourism and Sustainable Community Development*. Routledge, London, pp. 101–118.
Iglicka, K. (1998) The economics of petty trade on the Eastern Polish border. In: Iglicka, K. and Sword, K. (eds) *Stemming the Flood: the Challenges of East-West Migration for Poland*. Macmillan, London.
Ilbery, B. and Kneafsey, M. (1998) Product and place: promoting quality products and services in the lagging rural regions of the European Union. *European Urban and Regional Studies* 5(4), 329–341.
Ilbery, B. and Kneafsey, M. (2000a) Producer constructions of quality in regional speciality food production: a case study from south west England. *Journal of Rural Studies* 16, 217–230.
Ilbery, B. and Kneafsey, M. (2000b) Registering regional speciality food and drink products in the United Kingdom: the case of PDOs and PGIs. *Area* 32(3), 317–325.
INSEE (1996) *Les Vacances des Français: Tendances Longues et Résultats Détaillés de 1993 à 1994*. INSEE, Paris.
Ioannides, D. (1995) A flawed implementation of sustainable tourism: the experience of Akamas, Cyprus. *Tourism Management* 16, 583–592.
IUCN-EEP (World Conservation Union – East European Programme) (1990) *Protected Areas in Eastern and Central Europe and the USSR*. IUCN, Cambridge.

Jackson, G. and Morpeth, N. (2000) Local Agenda 21: reclaiming community ownership in tourism or stalled process? In: Richards, G. and Hall, D. (eds) *Tourism and Sustainable Community Development.* Routledge, London, pp. 119–134.

Jamal, T.B. and Getz, D. (1995) Collaboration theory and community tourism planning. *Annals of Tourism Research* 22(1), 186–204.

Janowitz, M. (1951) *The Community Press in an Urban Setting.* Free Press, Glencoe.

Jessop, B. (1998) Reflections on globalization and its (il)logics. In: Dickens, P. (ed.) *The Logic of Globalization.* Routledge, London.

Johnson, D., Snepenger, J. and Akis, S. (1994) Residents' perceptions of tourism development. *Annals of Tourism Research* 21(3), 629–642.

Joppe, M. (1996) Sustainable community tourism development revisited. *Tourism Management,* 17(7), 475–479.

Kappert, J. (2000) Community and rural development in Northern Portugal. In: Richards, G. and Hall, D. (eds) *Tourism and Sustainable Community Development.* Routledge, London, pp. 258–267.

Karpowicz, Z. (1993) The challenge of ecotourism – application and prospects for implementation in the countries of Central and Eastern Europe and Russia. *Revue de Tourisme* 3, 28–40.

Keane, M.J. (1992) Rural tourism and rural development. In: Briassoulis, H. and van der Stratten, J. (eds) *Tourism and the Environment: Regional, Economic and Policy Issues, Environment and Assessment,* Volume 2. Kluwer Academic Publishers, Dordrecht, pp. 43–55.

Kinnaird, V. and Hall, D. (1996) Understanding tourism processes: a gender-aware framework. *Tourism Management* 19(2), 95–102.

Kinnaird, V. and Hall, D. (2000) Theorizing gender in tourism research. *Tourism Recreation Research* 25(1), 71–84.

Klarer, J. and Moldan, B. (eds) (1997) *The Environmental Challenge for Central European Economies in Transition.* John Wiley & Sons, Chichester.

Koh, K.Y. (2000) Understanding community tourism entrepreneurism: some evidence from Texas. In: Richards, G. and Hall, D. (eds) *Tourism and Sustainable Community Development.* Routledge, London, pp. 205–217.

Konstantinov, Y. (1996) Patterns of reinterpretation: trader-tourism in the Balkans (Bulgaria) as a picaresque metaphorical enactment of post-totalitarianism. *American Ethnologist* 23(4), 762–782.

Lane, B. (1994) Sustainable tourism development strategies: a tool for development and conservation. *Journal of Sustainable Tourism* 2(1–2), 7–21.

Latour, B. (1997) *Science in Action.* Oxford University Press, Oxford.

Lukashina, N.S., Amirkhanov, M.M., Anisimov, V.I. and Trunev, A. (1996) Tourism and environmental degradation in Sochi, Russia. *Annals of Tourism Research* 23, 654–665.

MacDonald, S. (1997) A people's story: heritage, identity and authenticity. In: Rojek, C. and Urry, J. (eds) *Touring Cultures: Transformations of Travel and Theory.* Routledge, London, pp. 155–175.

MacLeod, G. (1998) In what sense a region? Place, hybridity, symbolic shape, and institutional formation in (post-) modern Scotland. *Political Geography* 17(7), 833–863.

Mandell, M.P. (1999) The impact of collaborative efforts: changing the face of public policy through networks and network structures. *Policy Studies Review* 16(1), 4–17.

Milbourne, P. (ed.) (1997) *Revealing Rural 'Others': Representation, Power and Identity in the British Countryside.* Pinter, London.

Milward, H.B. (1996) Symposium on the hollow state: capacity, control and performance in interorganizational settings. *Journal of Public Administration Research and Theory* 6(2), 193–195.

Morgan, N. and Pritchard, A. (1998) *Tourism, Promotion and Power: Creating Images, Creating Identities.* John Wiley & Sons, Chichester.

Morin, E. (1962) *L'Esprit du Temps.* Grasset, Paris.

Murphy, P. (1983) Tourism as a community industry: an ecological model of tourism development. *Tourism Management* 4(3), 180–193.

Murphy, P. (1985) *Tourism: a Community Approach.* Methuen, London.

Murphy, P. (1988) Community driven tourism planning. *Tourism Management* 9(2), 96–104.

OECD (Organisation for Economic Co-operation and Development) (1990) *Partnerships for Rural Development.* OECD, Paris.

Page, S.J. and Getz, D. (eds) (1997) *The Business of Rural Tourism: International Perspectives.* International Thomson Business Press, London.

Painter, J. and Goodwin, M. (1995) Local governance and concrete research: investigating the uneven development of regulation. *Economy and Society* 24, 334–356.

Pavageau, J. (1997) Imaginaire alimentaire, projet de voyage et pratiques touristiques. In: Poulain, J.-P. (ed.) *Pratiques Alimentaires et Identités Culturelles.* Etudes Vietnamiennes, Hanoi, Vietnam, pp. 599–622.

Peck, J. and Tickell, A. (1994) Searching for a new institutional fix: the after-Fordist crisis and global-local disorder. In: Amin, A. (ed.) *Post-Fordism: a Reader.* Blackwell, Oxford, pp. 280–315.

Petrin, T. (1996) *Basic Facts on Rural Women in Selected Central European Countries.* Food and Agriculture Organization of the United Nations, Rome.

Powell, W. (1990) Neither market nor hierarchy: network forms of organization. In: Straw, B. and Cummings, L. (eds) *Research in Organizational Behavior,* Vol. 12. JAI Press, Greenwich, pp. 295–336.

Raco, M. (1998) Assessing 'institutional thickness' in the local context: a comparison of Cardiff and Sheffield. *Environment and Planning* A 30, 975–996.

Ray, C. (1998) Culture, intellectual property and territorial rural development. *Sociologia Ruralis* 38, 3–20.

Redclift, N. and Sinclair, M.T. (eds) (1991) *Working Women: International Perspectives on Labour and Gender Ideology.* Routledge, London.

Reed, M. (1997) Power relations and community-based tourism planning. *Annals of Tourism Research* 24(3), 566–591.

Rhodes, P. and Marsh, D. (1992) *Policy Networks in British Government.* Oxford University Press, Oxford.

Richards, G. (1999) Cultural tourism. In: van der Straaten, J. and Briassoulis, H. (eds) *Tourism and the Environment,* 2nd edn. Kluwer, Dordrecht.

Richards, G. (2001) Gastronomy as a source of regional identity and tourism development. In: Hjalager, A.-M. and Richards, G. (eds) *Moveable Feasts: Tourism and Gastronomy in a Globalising World.* Routledge, London (in press).

Richards, G. and Hall, D. (2000a) Conclusions. In: Richards, G. and Hall, D. (eds) *Tourism and Sustainable Community Development.* Routledge, London, pp. 297–306.

Richards, G. and Hall, D. (2000b) The community: a sustainable concept in tourism development? In: Richards, G. and Hall, D. (eds) *Tourism and Sustainable Community Development.* Routledge, London, pp. 1–13.

Richards, G. and Hall, D. (eds) (2000c) *Tourism and Sustainable Community Development.* Routledge, London.

Roberts, L. (1996) Barriers to the development of rural tourism in the Bran area of Transylvania. In: Robinson, M., Evans, N. and Callaghan, P. (eds) *Tourism and Culture: Image, Identity and Marketing.* Business Education Publishers, Sunderland, pp. 185–196.

Roberts, L. and Simpson, F. (1999a) Developing partnership approaches to tourism in Central and Eastern Europe. *Journal of Sustainable Tourism* 7(3/4), 314–330.

Roberts, L. and Simpson, F. (1999b) Institutional support for the tourism industry in Central and Eastern Europe. *Tourism Recreation Research* 24, 51–58.

Ruukel, A. (ed.) (1996) *Estonia – the Natural Way.* Kodukant Ecotourism Association of Estonia, Pärnu, Estonia.

Sakertour Greenscape (1998) *Birdwatch Hungary 1998: Rewarding Birding Holidays on the Hungarian Steppe and in the Carpathian Mountains.* Sakertour Greenscape, Debrecen, Hungary.

Sassen, S. (1991) *The Global City.* Princetown University Press, Princetown.

Siiskonen, P. (1996) *Overview of the Socio-economic Position of Rural Women in Selected Central and Eastern European Countries.* Food and Agriculture Organization of the United Nations, Rome.

Simmons, D.G. (1994) Community participation in tourism planning. *Tourism Management* 15(2), 98–108.

Stocks, J. (2000) Cultural tourism and the community in Northern Ireland. In: Richards, G. and Hall, D. (eds) *Tourism and Sustainable Community Development.* Routledge, London, pp. 233–241.

Stoker, G. (1997) Public-private partnerships and urban governance. In: Stoker, G. (ed.) *Partners in Urban Governance: European and American Experience.* Macmillan, London, pp. 1–21.

Storgaard, K. (1998) Rural telematics – social networks, local rivalry and readiness. In: Hetland, P. and Meier-Dallach, H.-P. (eds) *Domesticating the World Wide Webs of Information and Communication Technology.* European Commission, Luxembourg, pp. 79–100.

Sylvander, B. (1993) Specific quality products: an opportunity for rural areas. *LEADER Magazine* 3, 8–21.

Taylor, G. (1995) The community approach: does it really work? *Tourism Management* 17, 487–489.

Urbain, J.-D. (1993) *L'Idiot du Voyage. Histoires de Touristes.* Plon, Paris.

Urry, J. (1995) *Consuming Places.* Routledge, London.

van der Straaten, J. (2000) Can sustainable tourism positively influence rural regions? In: Richards, G. and Hall, D. (eds) *Tourism and Sustainable Community Development.* Routledge, London, pp. 221–232.

Wood, D.J. and Gray, B. (1991) Toward a comprehensive theory of collaboration. *Journal of Applied Behavioral Science* 27(2), 139–162.

WTTC (World Travel Tourism Council) (1999) *Millennium Vision Competitiveness Report.* WTTC, London.

Yarwood, R. (1996) Rurality, locality and industrial change: a micro-scale investigation of manufacturing growth in the district of Leominster. *Geoforum* 27(1), 23–37.

Zarza, A.E. (1996) The LEADER programme in the La Rioja Mountains: an example of integral tourist development. In: Bramwell, W., Henry, I., Jackson, G., Prat, A., Richards, G. and van der Straaten, J. (1996) *Sustainable Tourism Management: Principles and Practice.* Tilburg University Press, Tilburg, pp. 103–120.

6

A Sideways Look at Tourism Demand

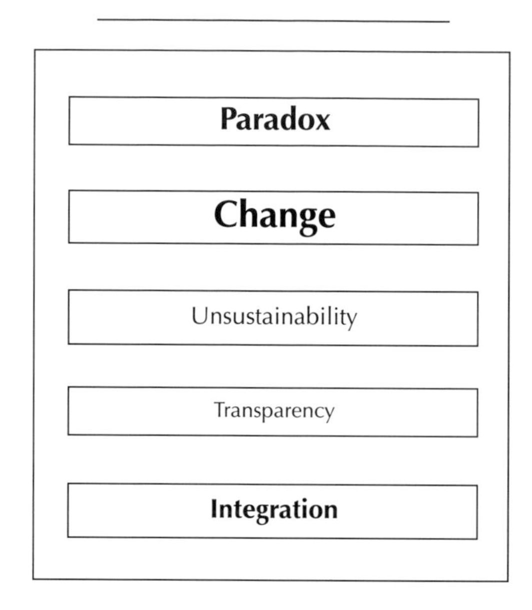

This chapter explores a number of ways in which meaningful market segments for tourism and recreation in rural areas might be identified, including demographic, psychographic and benefit segmentation, in an attempt to support marketing practice that may better suit the needs of new and changing markets, and the environments in which they operate. In response to a recognition of the declining usefulness of traditional forms of market segmentation, and an increasing demand for more individualized products (AEIDL, 1994: 31), the chapter analyses demand for 'rural tourism and recreation' consumption by:

- illustrating the limits of 'traditional' market segmentation for tourism and recreation consumption;
- analysing demand within the framework of Sharpley's consumption typology (Sharpley, 2000); and
- appraising potential opportunities for future segmentation of markets for tourism and recreation in rural areas.

Although all of the book's themes can be traced, three emerge particularly strongly in this chapter. *Change*, perhaps the strongest, is evident in the need to focus, not just on the processes of tourism consumption, but on the consumer culture in which they take place. *Paradox*, the pivotal theme, can be seen in the way that, despite the emergence of new consumption patterns, there is both stability and change. Finally, *integration* is required to combine tourism research with consumer research, and indeed behavioural research in general, to provide a more comprehensive understanding of tourism consumption.

As illustrated in earlier chapters, the increasing importance of rural tourism as one of the fastest growing elements of the tourism industry, an important agent within processes of rural restructuring, and key to the establishment of regional images, is well documented (see also Page and Getz, 1997; Sharpley and Sharpley, 1997; Butler *et al.*, 1998). Yet hard data on the size and growth of markets for tourism and recreation in rural areas are difficult to find. The measurement of demand is complicated by a number of factors. Even in Western Europe, where statistical collection and analysis are relatively widespread, it is impossible to gain an accurate picture of the volume of visits to and stays in the countryside (Edmunds, 1999). As discussed at length in earlier chapters, the difficulties of defining the terms 'rural' and 'tourism' separately, let alone the concept of rural tourism, render their accurate description and measurement difficult. Measures of accommodation occupancy often form the basis of statistical analysis but account for only one of the activities of rural tourists. The collection of data on visits to attractions is difficult and expensive given the fragmentation and geographical dispersion of facilities. And data collected often do not capture day visits to the countryside so that the importance of domestic tourism, a very large element of tourism in rural areas, may go unrecognized.

Where attempts have been made to measure demand, the data reveal that tourism in rural areas makes up over 20% of all tourism activity in Europe with an estimated 23% of European holidaymakers choosing the countryside as their holiday destination (EuroBarometer, 1998). Bessière, in Chapter 5, cited 370 million tourist days in the French countryside in 1994; in 1998, 1.25 billion visits were made to the English countryside (Countryside Agency, 2000). Throughout Europe generally, about a quarter of the population spend their main holiday in a countryside destination (Sharpley and Sharpley, 1997: 1).

Studies of rural tourism in Italy, Spain, Portugal and the UK indicate the importance of domestic markets for tourism and recreation in rural areas. In Italy, for example, in 1997, the extent of domestic visits to the countryside of one night or more by Italians was five times greater than that by foreign visitors (Euromonitor, 1998a). In France in 1993, while only 4 million trips of one or more nights were spent in rural areas by foreign visitors, 13 million were made by the French (Davidson, 1995). And in Finland, domestic tourists constitute over 80% of rural tourists (see Chapter 4).

Although statistics paint a picture of overall growth, they tell us nothing of regional or sectoral situations. Not all rural areas can benefit alike from increased interest in the countryside and/or the activities it has to offer. Those that do will have either notable natural or cultural resources, or a critical mass of attractions and amenities to be able to capitalize effectively on pre-identified markets.

To some extent, therefore, business diversification into, and developments in, tourism in rural areas are leaps of faith. There is little doubt, however, that while business success cannot be guaranteed, its likelihood is increased by a good understanding of the markets in which firms operate. Thus it is the *nature* of demand for tourism and recreation in the countryside that will provide the focus for this chapter. It is worth noting that although tourism and recreation are not synonymous – recreational motivations represent only one of many motivations to travel – from a consumer behaviour perspective both are consumption experiences and can therefore be studied together (Dimanche *et al.*, 1991). In both tourism and recreational settings, motivators are recurrent as needs for rest, escapism and novel social interaction, for example, are unlikely to be permanently satisfied by one experience.

Studies of motivation in tourism have identified a number of categories within the process. McIntosh and Goeldner (in Cooper *et al.*, 1993: 22), for example, identified four such categories as:

1. *Physical motivators*: needs for rest and recuperation or for sport and physical activity.
2. *Cultural motivators*: needs to visit and learn about new places and to experience new cultures.
3. *Interpersonal motivators*: needs to extend friendships and to meet new people, perhaps a search for spirituality.
4. *Status and prestige motivators*: the expression of self through tourism and the desire for recognition by others.

Clearly, travel for pleasure is insufficient to explain tourists' motivations. Tourists may experience a visit as a recreational experience, as a diversion from the norm, as a search for deeper meaning of life, an alternative lifestyle, and even as a pilgrimage (Cohen, 1996: 97).

The Development of Tourist Typologies

Motivation is only one of many variables that explain tourist behaviour. Although useful in the development of an understanding of why people choose to travel *per se*, by themselves theories of motivation may not explain the holiday and recreational choices people make. A provider may be able to differentiate motivations of a particular market such as adventure tourism, and segment according to the compatibility of needs identified (Fluker and Turner, 2000). In order to be able to operate optimally in a given market, however, tourism businesses need not only to be able to identify consumers who constitute their customers but also to understand their perceptions of different holiday products and services and formulate offers to attract specified markets to them. In other words, business operators need a knowledge of consumer behaviour. Businesses therefore need to be able to divide a large tourism market into segments that might be expected to have an interest in their products/services. Market segmentation is the process whereby a total market is divided into groups, members of each group sharing similarities in consumption patterns that reflect a common need or desire for a particular type of holiday experience. This is neither a simple nor a static process, and it is unwise to 'pigeon-hole' visitors. Tourists are becoming more individualistic and can only be characterized by a search for autonomy and a preference for more flexible holidays, leaving more space for personal initiative (Edmunds, 1999: 50). Rural visitors in particular form an 'unstructured pool of customers' who will be attracted to holidays offering 'content', intellectual discovery and contact with local people (AEIDL, 1994: 22).

Together, tourism and marketing research provide a rich analysis of tourism motivations, needs and expectations to aid an understanding of tourism markets. Tourism research has produced a number of tourist typologies that constitute market segments. Cohen's (1974) classification recognizing forms of institutionalized and non-institutionalized types of behaviour is perhaps one of the best known. Plog's 'psychocentric–allocentric' continuum (Plog, 1977) also constructs a classification around characteristics of the tourist, linking individual personality traits with holiday preferences. At one end of his continuum, 'psychocentrics' are unadventurous travellers who seek psychological safety in the familiarity of surroundings. At the other extreme, 'allocentrics' are adventurous and seek challenge in different cultures, environments and activities. Unsurprisingly, 'mid-centrics' fall somewhere between the two, representing the majority of tourists. More recently, and in response to recognition of potential tourism niches, Cochrane (1994) has set out a classification of foreign tourists likely to visit cultural or natural attractions in developing countries. Her classification, too, is multi-dimensional, accounting for psychological and socio-economic characteristics of foreign tourists, their holiday objectives and the level of facilities they require. Cochrane identifies the achievement of specific holiday objectives as the key motivator for a number of her groups; the demand for comfort and good facilities coming second to the tourist's primary motive for travel.

Market Segmentation: a Critique

Segmentation is merely a way of understanding the market for a product or service. It is a process whereby an overall market, the tourism market for example, is sub-divided into distinct groups according to personal or social characteristics or recognized buying behaviour. Thus 'rural tourists' may form a separate segment from 'sea, sun and sand' tourists, each with different purchase preferences. In present markets, subject to increasing fragmentation, 'rural tourists' present the potential for recognition of a number of smaller segments.

A useful segment is one that allows a business to match its product or service to the needs of target consumers; the aim of the process is to provide insight into consumers' tastes, preferences and buying behaviours in order to be able to position a product or service in an appealing manner.

Demographic data alone have been recognized as an inadequate means of identifying market segments (Mayo, 1975). Nevertheless, the most frequently collected data for identifying the characteristics of tourists are demographic data (Gladwell in Silverberg *et al.*, 1996). Since the 1970s, demographics, the use of simple social categories to explain general consumption patterns has given way to psychographics, a marketing technique that aims to measure intangible personal characteristics such as personality, values and lifestyle. Widely used in marketing generally, psychographics provides an understanding of tourists by looking at their activities, interests, attitudes, opinions, perceptions and needs (Gladwell in Silverberg *et al.*, 1996). The argument that the 'traditional' social categories and their related social constructs were no longer useful in explaining consumption patterns moved the analysis from the collective to the individual. It developed explanations for consumer behaviour based on individual traits, values and beliefs that were held to be influences on consumption (meaning both the selection and use of products and services). The marketing literature reflected this change of emphasis through the development and widespread use of psychographic typologies such as VALs (values and lifestyles) and LOV (list of values). Markets were segmented, for example, by values placed on the importance of education or community, social values that were considered to have a bearing on consumption decisions. Psychographic segmentation was held to be more comprehensive than demographic and socio-economic analysis in its ability to segment markets and provide useful information on the consumption patterns of the various typologies identified. Often, it was layered over socio-economic segmentation to provide a multidimensional approach.

In its turn, however, and in the light of recent changes, postmodern perspectives have challenged psychographic segmentation. A 'new age of tourism' has been identified characterized by super-segmentation of demand and the need for flexibility in supply mirroring changes in post-Fordian production systems (Fayos-Solá, 1996). Research has revealed new types of tourist creating varying demands for a range of experiences (Gunn, 1994). The 'new' term 'post-tourist' is equated with consumers whose socio-economic status, social tastes and lifestyles are now evident in their novel tourist experiences (Feifer, 1985; Urry, 1990; Poon, 1993). Consumption is paradoxically both an expression of collective identity and a statement of individualism. We use goods and services not only to satisfy material needs but also to create social ties and to display social status. In relation to the consumption of leisure and tourism, the cultural value of goods is often more important than their use value. The location and type of tourism experience has become an explicit fashion accessory. Such fundamental changes to meanings of consumption require us to review our definition of the consumer and to revisit our analysis of segmentation.

To reject social groupings *per se* as a means of analysing consumption just because the groupings themselves have become less useful is, in postmodern discourse, a fundamental error because the resulting emphasis on individual traits to explain our purchasing behaviour does not allow for analysis of consumption within its social context: clearly a critically important factor in contemporary tourism markets. The meanings that may be attached to our consumption patterns (either conscious or unconscious) can only be derived from the complex social settings in which they take place, and may be related to the emotional pleasures of consumption, especially in the cases of recreation and tourism. Psychographic segmentation therefore, by itself, is likely to be inadequate in explaining the consumption of many tourism and recreation products.

The term postmodernism is used here in the sense of state of mind, a perceptual condition, rather than to refer to a period in time. As such, the importance of its perspectives lies in the meanings we attach to holidays and holiday types. We may indeed take a holiday because we 'need a break'. Additionally, however, we may go on an ecotourism trip because we have an interest in the environment and our selection of such a holiday confirms our moral standpoint, conveys it to others and helps us to place ourselves in a particular social grouping. We may visit the countryside and stay in remote accommodation because we like the idea of a holiday that visibly sets us apart from 'the masses'.

Appreciating postmodernism in this way helps us to understand the apparent confusion that arises from complex and seemingly contradictory changes. As traditional distinctions between previously separate phenomena are eroded, we may no longer be able to separate work time from leisure time, or workplace from home. 'Old' ways of using time are disappearing. Permanent jobs, 'regular' hours, traditional divisions of labour and common patterns of leisure are changing in our endlessly flexible society. Marriage, work and retirement no longer follow the traditional life cycle. Such changes have made time another resource, the control of which has thus far not fallen to the individual (Mulgan, 2000). The term 'de-differentiation' (Lash in Featherstone, 1991: 11) encapsulates many of the changes we recognize in social and cultural spheres. Meanings now attached to our life experiences are inherently unstable and entirely dependent on the connections different individuals make with them in different circumstances.

Tourism consumption and general consumer culture

Postmodernism's demand on theories of consumption is, therefore, that they focus on the *culture* of consumption rather than the *process* that simply derives from production (Featherstone, 1991: 13). If, as identified above, our enjoyment of commodities we buy is only partly related to their physical consumption (Douglas and Isherwood in Featherstone, 1991: 17), then we must focus on their importance as social markers and the meanings we attach to the social spaces in which these signs appear, taking a broad sociological approach. Indeed, the 'tourism-centric' approach to tourism consumption studies has been criticized by Sharpley (1999: 173) who argues for the recognition of broader social and cultural influences that shape consumer behaviour as a whole. And the same criticism has been applied to the examination of consumer behaviour in isolation from other human behaviours resulting in lack of recognition of the ways in which consumption relates to other social practices (Belk, in Engel *et al.*, 1995: 265). In order to progress our understanding of contemporary tourism demand, therefore, it is essential to recognize the significance of general consumption, which is commonly related to personal identity and status in a broad sociological context.

But postmodernism has been described as 'at best a patchy phenomenon', its effects being more visible in some countries than others, and variable even where they can be identified (Brown, 1998: 125). 'To many people', Brown says, 'postmodernism must seem a complete irrelevance'. It is likely, therefore, that while adding further dimension to the question of tourism consumption, postmodernism has only a partial relevance for it. The extent to which its relevance relates to markets for rural tourism will be addressed later in the chapter.

Where does all this leave us in our quest for a useful means of market segmentation for tourism generally?

It is posited by Sharpley (2000) that the narrow focus of much tourism consumption research, by taking as its starting point either a type of tourist or a type of tourism, has oversimplified issues and not allowed for the fact that a tourism product may be consumed in a number of different ways by different tourists. Furthermore, it is understood that there are more differences between the same consumer making a brand choice on two different occasions than between two different consumers choosing the same brand on the same occasion (Valentine and Gordon, 2000).

Sharpley (2000) argues that it is no longer realistic to attach stereotypical labels to tourists and aim to relate them to stereotypical tourism products in the fashion of 'traditional' market segmentation. This 'new' approach classifies the consumer, not just as the person, but as the person *plus* the consumption process (Valentine and Gordon, 2000).

People's consumption of products and services is influenced by the product or service environment, the human environment, external factors (such as fashion), and physiological or emotional needs (Valentine and Gordon, 2000). Rather than a typology of tourists, therefore, Sharpley suggests a typology of tourist consumption practices that he derives from a general model of consumption practices from Holt (1995). In such a model, tourists may consume in four distinct ways:

1. *As experience*: with a focus on the affective domain and tourists' emotional responses to experience, tourism may be respite from stress, a spiritual experience or the hedonistic pursuit of pleasure resulting from the consumption of dreams. Consumption as experience reflects a subjective state of consciousness for which the countryside can provide a range of meanings such as peace and quiet, isolation or a good place for adventure.
2. *As play*: the object of consumption being a vehicle for the achievement of inter-personal goals thus emphasizing the social element of tourism and the importance of other tourists in the social composition of the holiday. Consumed as play, tourism is used as a vehicle for socializing and sharing experiences with other tourists. Tourism is frequently a social experience, fellow visitors being an important element of tourist satisfaction.
3. *As integration*: where tourists, in their adoption of its associated values and meanings, assimilate the symbolic qualities of the product/service. As tourists play an integral role in the production of their holiday, some degree of integration is automatic. As an instrumental action, integration occurs when a holiday's attributes are absorbed into the person's self identity, for example as an ecotourist.
4. *As classification*: where, by the consumption of particular holiday or recreational experiences, tourists signify social status and mark similarities to, or differences from, social groups and settings, thereby creating identities. As classification, tourists seek the display of social differentiation and status through different styles rather than values of consumption.

(After Sharpley, 1999: 180–186, 2000)

Sharpley maintains that by developing a consumer culture for tourism in this way, we can add an additional dimension to our understanding, knowledge and (importantly for rural tourism operators) to our prediction of tourist-consumer behaviour.

Since symbolic values of tourism have become considerably more significant to consumption, and use values less so, our understanding of tourism and recreation markets must adapt accordingly to take account of the wide range of motivations, desires and satisfactions that drive 'new' markets for rural products. Yet market analysts still almost universally refer to socio-demographic or lifestyle variables in their reports. Psychographic segmentation forms the basis of widely used tourist typologies, and is still the fundamental means of researching specialist sectors of the market such as for nature-based tourism (Silverberg *et al.*, 1996). However, the social foundations on which some long-established methods of defining markets were built are shifting, and their relevance is increasingly questioned (Moutinho, 2000: 132).

The limits of 'traditional' market segmentation

The third age market

If the 'first age' refers to childhood and the second, the age spent home-making and working, the 'third age' is the age of active retirement. Often used to identify those years between family and work responsibilities and the onset of 'old age', the difficulties of defining the latter have extended use of the term to mean anything over the age of 50. A number of changes have contributed to the identification of such a supposed market segment:

- a rise in the population aged 50 and over;
- increasing life expectancy (OECD, 1998: 17);
- increases in leisure time as the average age at retirement falls (OECD, 1998: 5);
- a concentration of wealth (over 45s in the UK own 80% of personal financial wealth and are responsible for an estimated 30% of consumer spending); and
- A propensity to travel (Smith and Jenner, 1997).

Together, these factors identify a demographic trend that provides a new focus for marketers: the needs and aspirations of older people who, in number at least, represent a large block of consumers. But this does not suggest, as countless marketers have assumed, that 'older people' constitute a typology or market segment that shares similar consumption patterns reflecting common needs and desires. Yet the 'grey market' is one that is repeatedly identified as a marketing opportunity suggesting that this may be the case (Smith and Jenner, 1997; Moutinho, 2000: 19).

One of the first difficulties encountered in an attempt to define the segment is how the terms 'old' or 'older' are defined. Age is a relative concept; the younger we are, the earlier old age is seen to begin (Age Concern, 1993). The age at which people become 'old' is therefore impossible to define. The word itself influences people's perceptions of ageing. The label 'old' is overworked, being the opposite of 'new' as well as 'young', with consequent connotations of decline and decay (Midwinter, 1991). Additionally, perceptions of age and ageing differ between European countries.

In general terms, however, European societies' expectations of old age are largely negative, giving rise to associated negative images. Loss of power resulting from reduced responsibilities, frailty of body and mind, sadness and loneliness become 'given' characteristics of age. Positive qualities such as kindness, affability, courage, wisdom and sense may also be attributed to ageing (Age Concern, 1993).

Apart from contact with older relatives, TV and radio are the most important influences on perceptions of old age. Popular culture confronts societies with outdated images of old people which, by being recognizable (if inaccurate), have the ability to reinforce prevalent negative perceptions. Such simplistic image formation relates closely to a process referred to as 'perceptual set and expectancy' where people see, not what *is*, but what they *expect* as a result of past experience (Seaton and Bennett, 1996: 76). Commonly, it results in simplistic stereotyping rather than segmentation, in this case, in the creation of an image of an 'old' person as someone who is slow and frail and thus in need of care, support and mobility aids. Based on very limited analysis, such a stereotype should not be confused with a typology. The rejection of a collective stereotype by older people is illustrated by recent research reported by the Henley Centre (1998a: 208). In the UK, a study for the companies Barclays Life & GGT Direct found that older consumers did not respond positively to British advertisements featuring sedate, white-haired people playing bowls, instead preferring American imagery showing older people in physically demanding and challenging roles. More active lifestyles clearly present images that today's older consumers see as reflections of their lives: busy, physically active and open to new learning and experiences (Plate 6.1).

Further research indeed presents a more dynamic picture of ageing across Europe. A combination of greater longevity, better health and greater expectations are together bringing about a social redefinition of the ageing process, and the chronology of 'traditional' life stages is changing. The gap year for university students and the notion of lifelong learning serve to alter the student life cycle. Average age at first marriage has been postponed as has the mean age of women at childbirth. 'Maturescence' (Attias-Dofunt in Maiztegui Oñate, 1994) describes the years between adult working life and the onset of 'old' age and represents a new life stage. Thus 'middle age' now represents two life stages, being preceded by 'middle youth'. The UK magazine *Red* is targeted at women who have 'grown up without growing old', and motorcycle culture, once the preserve of the young,

Plate 6.1. Active lifestyles for the third age.

has become a middle-aged past-time (witness the characteristics of visitors to the Isle of Man during TT race week).

The principal importance of these changes is that 'old age' has been deferred, and this demographic shift fits comfortably within a trend towards *agelessness* where the traditional characteristics of age no longer significantly define expectations, ambitions, beliefs and behaviour (Henley Centre, 1998a: 201) (see Plate 6.2). One theory to explain these potentially significant shifts in perception lies with the '47–53' group, Europe's 'baby boomers'. Born between these years and now similarly aged, their experiences of post-war economic prosperity and its accompanying social reconfigurations created high expectations of life. The 47–53 group contains some of leisure's fastest growing markets and constitutes the next generation of 'third-agers'. Its importance is twofold:

- Demographically, it is expanding; in the UK this age group has expanded from 6.5 million in 1990 to 8 million in 2000.
- In relation to its raised expectations, it influences attitudes that have the potential to change significantly the consumption patterns of older people.

Accumulated wealth and increases in disposable time stimulate demand for leisure, travel and recreational experiences, and it is not unreasonable to expect this age group to be of marketing significance in the future. However, it should be acknowledged that their increased affluence has accrued from a time of stable employment that supported both savings and pensions, and the ability of third age clients to participate in travel and recreation depends largely on such funds. The capital growth that characterized stock markets towards the end of the 20th century sustained pensions, and those who escaped problems of poor pension selling, endowment insecurity and lower interest rates may now be wealthy enough to spend widely on nonmaterial commodities. In the longer term, however, there are threats to this continued financial security. There is no guarantee that stock markets will continue to support pensions (and in the longer term it is unlikely that they will as demographic changes alter the balance of investments). Population ageing will therefore place unprecedented burdens on government expenditures as we move further into the 21st century (Hantrais, 1999).

There is another significance to these older age groups. Those over the age of 45 have matured as travellers throughout the early stages of mass tourism and are identified as one of the main catalysts in the drive towards higher quality in the tourism industry. Baby boomers were among the first to take advantage of expansion in the travel market. It was they who first experienced foreign travel as a leisure experience rather than a means of recuperation or other necessity. They are now experienced travellers and consumers, and their resulting confidence has created a critical approach to tourism consumption. Experienced travellers no longer need the security of the package, and independent travel is one of the fastest growing tourism sectors in Europe. More older tourists now look for high standards and imaginative holiday products; original sea, sun and sand packages have lost much of their appeal (Mintel, 1999b). Where attitudes have thus been shaped by past experiences, they influence the nature of current and future demand. People expect quality *and* value for money.

In some respects, therefore, age does influence consumption, and marketers have derived useful information from a focus on it. But while age may inform the product or service design process (in relation to quality for example), it is of little use in product or service conception. Fundamentally, it appears that traditional characteristics of age no longer define expectations, ambitions, beliefs and behaviour in a significant manner (Henley Centre, 1998a: 201) and age is therefore of limited use in defining consumer groups for leisure, recreation and tourism.

Yet ways must be found in which useful consumer segments can be identified because there clearly are 'mature' markets to be captured. The European Travel Commission (1999) reports growth in travel by older people throughout Europe. And worldwide, third age international arrivals exceeded 100 million, 65 million of which were in the EU (Smith and Jenner, 1997).[1] The estimate for EU arrivals into the 21st century suggests continued growth of as much as 30%.

Common needs and desires of consumers according to age may be identifiable in other economic sectors, in financial markets, for example, or in health care. Where tourism and recreation are concerned, however, the social trends analysed require that simplistic categorization of either tourists or tourism products and services is avoided. What if, as suggested by Sharpley (2000), a typology of tourism *consumption* is applied to the wide range of likely demands that result from the needs and desires of third age consumers? If needs or benefits-based segmentation identifies target markets according to people's reasons for choosing a particular holiday, Sharpley's (2000) classification of tourism consumption, as explained above, provides us with an analytical framework.

This framework identified that people consume tourism as: (i) experience; (ii) play; (iii) integration; and (iv) classification. The typology can be used to present an analysis of older consumers' likely needs as illustrated in Table 6.1.

Use of a consumption typology rather than one based on tourists provides a broader analysis of needs that may drive consumption. The predominance of *consumption as experience* is notable; *integration*, association with product values, registers a secondary importance.

A family market?

'Myths' about 'the family market' may be further explored using the analytical framework applied to the third age market. Across the EU changing patterns of family formation have made alternative, non-institutionalized family forms more widespread. Marriage rates have fallen, age at first marriage has increased for both men and women, and the average age of women at childbearing had risen to almost 29 years by the mid-1990s. Completed fertility rates have fallen to the lowest levels ever recorded and births of third and subsequent children have declined rapidly in those countries where larger families were prevalent (notably Ireland, Portugal and Spain). Unmarried cohabitation, prevalent among younger age groups, now represents approximately 25% of all couples (Hantrais, 1999).

Family restructuring and changes to the traditional family life cycle have contributed to the fact that by the mid-1990s, single person households were among the fastest growing

Table 6.1. Consumption preferences of older consumers.

	Formal consumption modes			
Likely needs of older consumers	Experience	Play	Integration	Classification
Challenge, as these may no longer be provided by work/family responsibilities	✔		✔	
Enjoyment, common to all age groups	✔			
Learning, The University of the Third Age exists to support the demand for lifelong learning	✔		✔	
Adventure, increases in disposable time provide opportunities for people to pursue long-standing personal goals	✔		✔	✔
Socializing, especially for older people who may live alone	✔	✔		
Social recognition, notably where this need is no longer met by occupational status			✔	✔
Mental and physical well-being, to achieve good health and, as age increases, maintain physical function	✔		✔	
For rest from routine, older consumers may still work or be carers	✔	✔	✔	

across Europe, reaching almost 35% in Finland, Sweden and the UK. Divorce with children in the family has helped to raise levels of lone parenthood to 10% of families across the EU; there are 7 million lone parents in Europe. Figures vary across the EU with the highest rates of lone parent families found in the UK and the lowest in Mediterranean states (Hantrais, 1999).

The number of women in full-time employment has also increased. In the UK, women now make up almost half of the workforce. Since 1980, the proportion of mothers with children under 5 who are in paid work has increased from 28% to 53%. To this is attributed an increase in discretionary consumer spending. Non-traditional household structures are growing so much faster than traditional family formations that new ideas about what is 'normal' are developing (Henley Centre, 1998a: 203). Figures 6.1 and 6.2 show the contrast between traditional and non-traditional family forms.

The effects of social and demographic changes can be expected to be both profound and wide ranging. Although care must be taken when speculating on direct relationships between emerging family formations and the nature of tourism demand, it is reasonable to explore the possibilities afforded by such change.

Hall (2000), for example, speculates that there will be increasing recognition by the tourism industry of the needs of single parent families, thus suggesting the existence of a potential market segment. To apply Fayos-Solá's theory of 'super-segmentation' (Fayos-Solá, 1996), we may recognize common needs of lone parent families within a larger 'family market' for access to cheaper travel and accommodation, although for travel to where and for what we could not say. The idea of 'social tourism' is one that is more familiar in some European countries than others. Between the Second World War and 1989, Comecon countries benefited from a range of reciprocal agreements that provided state-sponsored holidays for workers and their families. The need for social tourism is currently recognized in France where it is estimated that 40% of the population does not take an annual break of three nights or more. The problem is addressed with an imaginative idea that has been found to be of economic benefit across a range of tourist regions. *Cheques Vacances* can be set against expenditure on travel, accommodation, food and cultural and sporting activities and events. Funded by both employer and employee contributions to a tax-exempt holiday fund, the scheme is considered a great success, each *Cheque* generating three times its value in

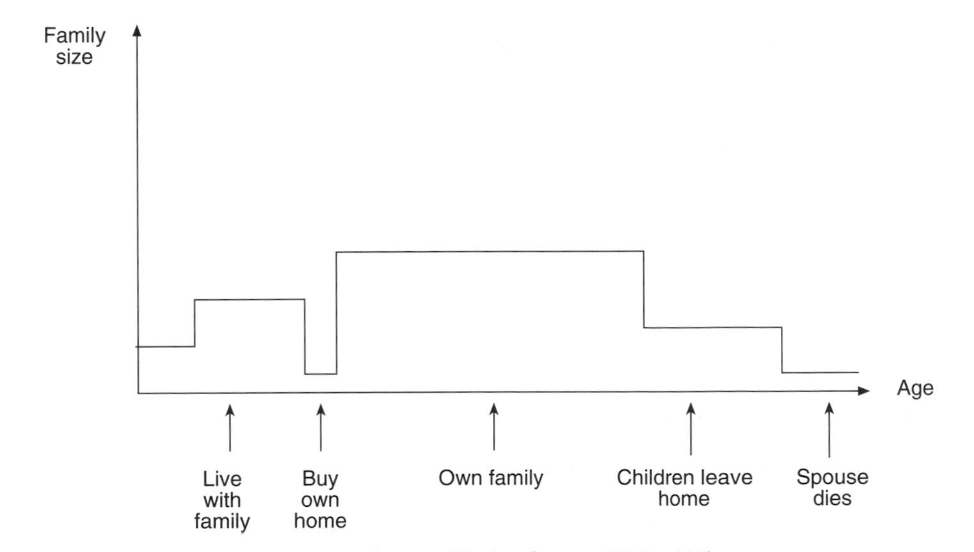

Fig. 6.1. The traditional family life cycle (source: Henley Centre, 1998a: 202).

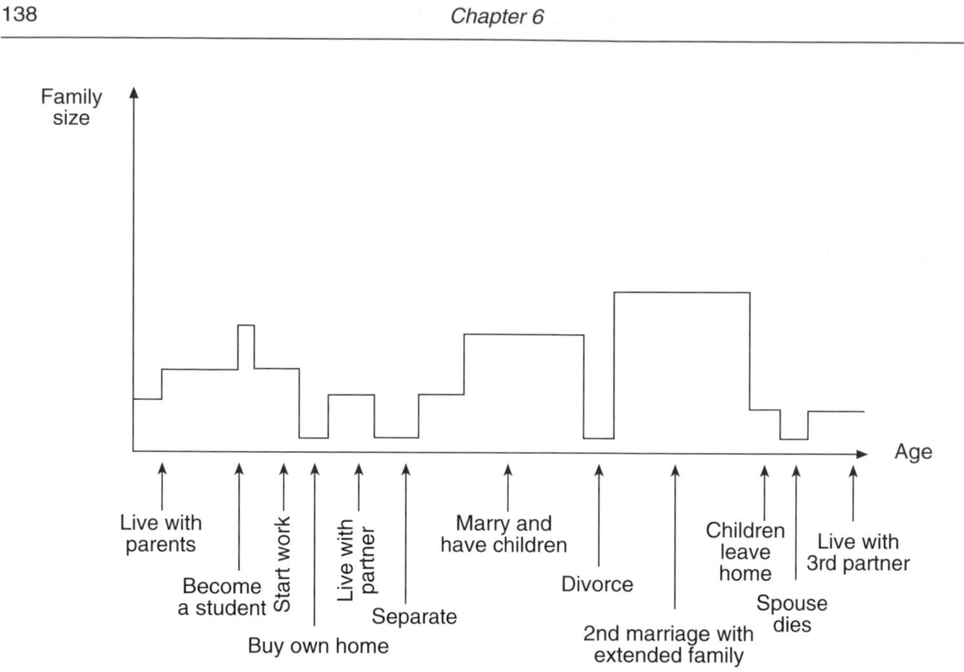

Fig. 6.2. The contemporary family life cycle (source: Henley Centre, 1998a: 202).

money spent on related goods and services. In 1997, 1 million employees were in receipt of a *Cheque* and when benefiting families were taken into account, there were 4 million beneficiaries of the scheme. Consideration is being given to its extension to more people (Euromonitor, 1998b).

Aside from potential 'super-segments' such as this, however, it is becoming increasingly difficult to see how the motives of different family groups can be found to coincide sufficiently to form a useful typology or market segment. Following the pattern of the contemporary family life cycle, families may express demand for holidays and recreational experiences both with and without children. Where children form part of the group, families may contain an above average number of children where the offspring of former marriages spend holiday and leisure time together. Family groups often span three or more generations (Plate 6.2), creating demand for a greater range of products and services. And demand from unaccompanied adolescents who do not wish to holiday with extended families may also be expected to rise. Such variables operate in addition to the wide range of motivations and aspirations that influence holiday preferences and consumption patterns of any consumer group. Applying a consumption typology, the needs of the family market may be identified as in Table 6.2.

As with the analysis of older consumers' needs, the resulting picture is a complex one reflecting a wide variety of consumption modes. The *consumption of experience* again dominates the analysis; an issue that will be

Plate 6.2. Agelessness: recreation for first and third agers.

Table 6.2. Consumption preferences of families.

Likely needs of families	Formal consumption modes			
	Experience	Play	Integration	Classification
Passivity, for socializing within the family, time to be *passed* together	✔			
Activity, for time to be *spent* together			✔	
Socializing with others		✔		
Adventure	✔	✔	✔	✔
'*Edutainment*', parents may like to use leisure time as learning time but learning has to be fun in a leisure context	✔		✔	
Freedom	✔			
Enjoyment and fun, rest from routine of work and of domestic chores	✔			
Rest from routine, from employment and domestic demands	✔			

addressed in the next chapter's analysis of tourism products and services. The consumption analyses presented here are not intended to represent prescriptive or static models and it is, of course, possible to recognize changing needs and argue against the categories identified. The aim of the process is to illustrate a fundamentally different way of viewing demand for tourism and recreational products.

The 'family market' like the 'third age' market therefore appears largely to be little more than the 'unstructured pool of customers' identified by LEADER programme experts (AEIDL, 1994: 22). It may, therefore, be preferable for 'alternative' characteristics of a client group to form the basis of market segmentation. Markets for recreation and tourism in rural areas appear not to be created according to age, gender or stage in the family life cycle, for example, nor are they determined solely by lifestyles and values (although these may contribute more to segmentation for some rural products than for others).

In both 'markets' analysed, the demand for *experience* appears to register as an important feature. For something to register as an experience, it must offer sensory differentia. To further complicate matters, experiences vary widely, and are intensely individual phenomena. However, rural environments, as the setting for tourism and recreation, have the potential to provide particular experiences relating to visitors' perceptions of rurality as discussed in Chapter 1. Tourism markets promote experiences as either loss-leaders or relationship building devices (Henley Centre, 1998b: 13) in order to attract custom. Experiences can be revenue streams in their own right, however, constituting a fourth phase in economic development after extractive, manufacturing and service economy stages (Pine and Gilmore, 1998) (see Chapter 7). More businesses are responding to this 'progression of economic value' by designing, promoting and charging for experiences in response to what they see as growing consumer demand.

A Market Segment of Rural Tourists?

Much of the analysis of demand thus far has related generally to tourism. Perhaps because of its diverse nature and its relatively recent recognition as a distinct form of tourism, 'rural tourism' research says little about types of 'rural tourist'. Predominantly, rural tourism research is characterized by a planning and development perspective rather than a marketing one, as a result of which there is little research relating to market segments in rural tourism.

So is there such a thing as a rural tourist? As it is asked here, the question relates to the environmental attitudes of rural visitors rather than simply their presence in rural space, the justification for this association being the vulnerability of natural areas in the face of the twin pressures of growth of, and change in, consumption. In part, an answer to this question lies within debates on the meaning of rural tourism (see Chapter 2 and Keane, 1992; Lane, 1994; Page and Getz, 1997: 7; Sharpley and Sharpley, 1997: 7). It is not the purpose of this chapter to add to this well-documented discourse, merely to extract from it that which gives us a better understanding of the ways in which people consume tourism in rural areas. Perhaps because commentators generally agree that definitions and thus the scope of 'rural tourism' are open to so much question, accounts largely fall short of identifying rural tourists.

Given the multidimensionality of people's social identities, rural tourism and recreation are likely to be consumed in different ways on different occasions. Sharpley and Sharpley (1997) point to the many different meanings of 'rural tourism' to those who participate thus broadening the concept to the European Commission's definition of it as 'all tourist activities in rural areas' (Sharpley and Sharpley, 1997: 8). Lane (1994) identifies the existence of what he refers to as a 'general interest' market for 'less specialized' forms of tourism. Such broad views of the rural tourism market suggest a mass rural market distinguishable by activity. The distinction between the activities that make up rural tourism and the environment in which they take place is indeed an important one, the significance of which may have major management implications; an issue addressed further in Chapter 8. One piece of research (Kastenholz, 2000) has identified market segments that are distinguishable, among other attributes, by a primary focus on either activities or the rural environment.

Conducted in Portugal and reported by Kastenholz (2000), the study has some important findings in relation to segmentation of rural tourists. The study was of demand for tourism in the Portuguese countryside. A questionnaire was designed to allow definition of tourists' profiles by analysis of demographics, attitudes and behaviour. Subsequently, segments were identified by analysis of importance ratings that respondents gave to a list of statements about potential benefits of tourism and recreation in the Portuguese countryside.[2] The following four typologies/segments were identified:

1. The *Want it all ruralists* are those who are interested in the wide range of activities and opportunities a rural environment may have to offer and value the benefit of a 'calm and unpolluted environment' less than others. For this group, therefore, what they can do in the countryside is more important than the countryside itself and this characteristic particularly differentiates the segment. These 'rural tourists' tend to travel in groups, and present medium expenditure levels. They are relatively young, mostly Portuguese (representing the domestic element of rural tourism) and Dutch. They tend to take more than one holiday per year and personal recommendations or their own previous visits influence their holiday choices. 'Want it all ruralists' made up 25% of the sample.

2. *Independent ruralists*, 24% of those surveyed, as the name suggests, value independent travel in a calm and unpolluted environment. They are interested in walking and hiking, eating out and discovering a region on their own initiative rather than the culture and traditions of the region visited. British, German and Portuguese respectively, they are likely to be couples in their early 40s. Also independent of commercial promotion channels, they too, like the 'Want it alls', rely heavily on word-of-mouth recommendations to make destination and holiday choice. They are both price and quality conscious.

3. The *Rural romantics* value culture and tradition and a calm and unpolluted environment as the most important benefits of holidaying in the countryside. With an emphasis on the importance of the rural environment and with the potential for an interest in conservation issues, they are more interested in the concept of rurality than in the activities or opportunities for 'doing things' that the countryside might have to offer. Mostly couples, the 'Rural romantics' are the highest spenders and were mainly British, Portuguese and German respectively. Perhaps because they placed less importance on independent travel there was a heavy reliance by this segment on tour operators and travel agents when selecting destinations and holiday types. The importance to this group of a previous visit may signify a degree of consumer loyalty to the destination. As the largest group, 'Rural romantics' constituted 30% of the sample.

4. The smallest of the segments, the *Outdoor ruralists,* value both a calm and unpolluted environment and social, active hedonism as potential benefits of holidaying in rural areas. They place less emphasis on culture and tradition and on independent travel. 'Outdoor ruralists' prefer outdoor activities such as horse-riding and cycling, and are relatively young (in their mid-30s), holiday in groups, tend to be the lowest spenders, and rely on personal recommendation to make their holiday choice. Portuguese, perhaps indicating the importance of the domestic market for this segment, was the dominant nationality.

It can be argued that the usefulness of these findings may be limited by the individualist approach to segmentation. Additionally the study itself identified some methodological shortcomings. Nevertheless, the conclusion that the overall sample was divisible into four clusters according to the main benefits sought by rural tourists may be important for sociologists and rural businesses across Europe. Its identification of market segments distinguishable, among other attributes, by a primary focus on either activities or the rural environment is a critical observation for rural tourism planners and managers. The work represents empirical study rather than abstract conceptualization and therefore provides some evidence for market analysis. The motivations the study identifies are both socio-psychological and cultural, both 'push' and 'pull', in that for some clusters, the destination is the attraction while for others, it is their own desire for challenge and means of self-exploration. The findings suggest that there is potential for a number of niche markets offering specialist activities in rural areas. The predominance of 'Rural romantics' in the sample suggests, however, that such provision should not be at the expense of the tranquillity and unpolluted environment that the countryside is seen to offer.

Other significant findings related to the importance for rural tourism of the domestic market. Both 'Want it all ruralists' and 'Outdoor ruralists' represented a high level of Portuguese compared with foreign tourists. While it is clearly possible that this fact represents only the findings of this case, it lends support to other studies that indicate the importance of domestic visitors for the rural tourism industry (Davidson, 1995; Euromonitor, 1998a: 193; Mintel, 1999a). It may also be significant that the two segments presenting high levels of domestic participation are those that expressed interest in activities, socializing, fun and sports rather than in the aesthetic qualities offered by rurality. It is suggestive of the possibility that the countryside as a resource for general activities is particularly important to the domestic market. Perhaps foreign visitors are more attracted by their expectations of the qualities of new and different landscapes. Also in line with other studies (Greffe, 1994; Cavaco, 1995: 131), the Portuguese research confirms the predominance of visitors to rural areas with higher than average levels of education and corresponding professional status. However, it may be important to note that in the area of Ponte de Lima, one of the research areas, the dominance of *turismo de habitaçâo,* may have influenced the nature of demand. *Turismo de habitaçâo* represent the highest level of rural accommodation registered with, and regulated by, the national tourist authority, DGT. Typically buildings with a high architectural value, they offer high standards of facilities and decoration.

As segments of the overall tourist market, typologies ascribe different styles of tourism and recreation consumption to different types of people according to selected personal characteristics. But the extent to which such abstract values play a role in determining consumption patterns is open to question. And the lack of evidence that express values give rise to changes in behaviour further lessens the usefulness of such segments.

Despite the problems of measurement and definition, however, businesses and developers generally put a great deal of faith in the existence of the 'green consumer'. But the idea of the 'green' consumer is ambiguous

(Plate 6.3). Is the 'green' consumer concerned about the environment? Probably: there appears to be a great deal of evidence that consumers are becoming more environmentally aware (Bramwell, 1994; Wight, 1994: 40; Ottman and Terry, 1997; Probasco and Heimlich, 2000). Does this mean that consumers are prepared to pay more for environmentally benign products? Possibly not: a Green Gauge Report in the USA in 1986 found that the number of consumers willing to pay a premium for environmental products was 11%. This figure had fallen to 5% 10 years later (Ottman and Terry, 1997). Even if someone is prepared to pay more, the question of how much more is a fraught one (see Ecotourism, Chapter 7).

Is the 'green' consumer someone who is prepared to alter consumption behaviour to avoid unsustainable practices? Probably not: although a small number of consumers seek out environmentally benign products in markets for items such as household and office consumables, there is little evidence that tourists are prepared to compromise their personal comforts in pursuit of the altruistic goals of sustainability. According to Swarbrooke (1999: 26) there is little indication that tourists are:

- switching from the use of private cars to public transport;
- demonstrating against the environmental impacts of developments; and
- insisting on sustainable management practices, in hotels, for example.

Swarbrooke goes on to identify possible levels of tourist behaviour change along a continuum that describes them in terms of *shades of green*. From *not at all green*, a position where no sacrifice is made because of environmental concerns, to *totally green*, showing considerable adaptation, the framework presents an inverse relationship between numbers of people and environmental concern. The higher the level of concern, the fewer the people likely to be associated with it. Thus 'it is clear that *dark green/totally green* tourists are a small niche only, in the UK at least' (Swarbrooke, 1999: 26).

Plate 6.3. Green wellington boots: but do the tourists' attitudes match?

Among tourists there appears to be a 'lack of self-criticism' that prevents them from recognizing the damage they cause (Becker, 1995: 209). Becker echoes the widely held belief that few tourists are consciously willing to change their behaviour on the grounds of environmental preservation. Worse still, many mass tourists appear to be ignorant of, or indifferent to, the needs of host communities with resulting stress placed on both host communities and environments (McKercher, 1993).

Evidently, the assumption that the rural tourist has an interest in the environment is a naive one. Consumers buy out of self-interest (Ottman and Terry, 1997). Even the supposed 'green' German tourism market has been revealed to be 'more about the vested interests of these consumers in the environment as a key determinant in the quality of their holiday experience, than their concern with the environmental impacts of tourism in general' (Swarbrooke, 1999: 26). Tourists are 'pleasure-seekers ... and above all, consumers' (De Kadt in McKercher, 1993: 12).

The evidence points, therefore, to the continuing unlikelihood of there being a rural tourism segment based on an interest in, and care of, the environment. This does not bode well for the growth and development of sustainable forms of rural tourism that are dependent on 'the adoption of a new social paradigm relevant to sustainable living' (Sharpley, 2000). Despite the fact that the claim has been made for tourism as an ideal medium of learning for environmentally conscious behaviour (Becker, 1995: 209) it seems more likely that reality is reflected in McKercher's (1993) assertions that tourism's very consuming nature rather militate against a role for it in the promotion of environmental concerns.

So how else may we identify a rural tourism segment? Sharpley and Sharpley (1997) question rural tourism's existence as a market sector, its nature, territory and meanings being subject to such ambiguity. Despite our theoretical misgivings, however, it is evident from the relatively scarce data that are available that the European countryside is an increasingly popular location for tourism and recreational activities. Development organizations and the business sector thus need to make some sense of the phenomenon, however labelled and measured, in order that rural businesses and communities may benefit from its presence.

Environmental concern currently provides no means of identifying a rural tourism market segment. Further, traditional segmentation, with its focus on demographic or stereotypical lifestyle characteristics, is unlikely to provide an effective way of looking at the demand and consumption of all forms of rural tourism.

Modal segmentation, however, identifies opportunities that may not be visible to businesses with a traditional focus, and lends itself to the marketing of experiences, clearly identified earlier as a motive for participation in recreation and tourism. Modal theory (Henley Centre, 1998b: 18) supports the view that people's identities are no longer only defined by characteristics such as sex, class, age or occupation for example, but are drawn from a wider range of influences such as social relationships, interest groups, travel and hobbies. Thus while family roles and those defined by occupation are significant, it is also important to recognize that an increasing sense of identity is drawn from people's individuality as well as their sense of 'social place', both capable of expression in leisure and recreational pursuits.

From this we may infer that:

- Tourists are likely to be inconsistent in their consumption patterns depending on the roles and settings in which they find themselves. For example, someone travelling as a business tourist may be more inclined to sacrifice personal comfort in the interests of sustainable practice than he or she would on a leisure vacation.
- In particular modes (i.e. on certain occasions), different types of people are likely to consume products/services more similarly to each other than would similar types of people in a different mode. A number of examples of this exist in 'customary' tourist behaviours such as the purchasing of souvenirs and the taking of photographs.

Modal segmentation requires no more than a shift of focus away from characteristics of individuals to the ways in which they consume products and services. The preferences of consumers change according to the influences of:

- the marketing environment: design, location, atmosphere, services;
- the personal environment: accompanied or alone, other consumers;
- external factors: fashion or climate; and
- psychological or emotional needs.

(Valentine and Gordon, 2000)

Although it has been possible to identify evidence of postmodern consumption patterns, undoubtedly, some traditional market segments continue to exist. Brown (1998: 125) points out that large numbers of people take what may be described as 'traditional holidays', and it is therefore likely that, across Europe, businesses will continue to identify traditional market segments to which their products and services appeal. Certainly, the institutionalized tourist, looking for sea, sunshine, and a culturally familiar (or at least neutral) holiday environment, continues to fund the operations of Europe's main tour operators.

The ideas explored here are complicated in themselves. Their extension to the regions of Europe has, therefore, not been attempted, although it is recognized that consumption patterns are unlikely to be common to the whole of Europe. It will be the task of analysts and policy-makers at national and regional levels to consider the implications of new concepts for different geographical and cultural settings.

Chapter 7 shifts the focus from demand to supply by analysing a number of rural tourism products in an attempt to identify the characteristics that appeal to motivations, meet needs, and give rise to satisfaction for tourists and recreationists in rural areas.

Chapter Summary

This chapter has analysed demand for tourism and recreation consumption by illustrating the limits of traditional market segmentation for providers of products and services in rural areas. Analysis of demand within the framework of Sharpley's (2000) consumption typology show how characteristics such as age or stage in the family life cycle, for example, have little predictive power for marketing purposes. The chapter has illustrated how the consumption of tourism is complicated by the symbolic values that have become attached to it. This is likely to be especially so with forms of 'rural tourism' where the countryside: (i) can be seen to reflect many aesthetic and spiritual values that stand in stark contrast to the relatively quotidian nature of urban life; and (ii) provides a suitable setting for the pursuit of a growing range of physical activities.

Notes

1 US statistics reveal an interesting trend that is reinforced by British figures. People over 55 make up only 20% of the US population yet account for 50% of long-haul trips (Smith and Jenner, 1997). Moreover, it may be that one long-haul trip is likely to stimulate the taking of further similar holidays. A US consulting group found that over a 3 year period, the 'vast majority' of older travellers took at least two trips out of the US and that almost 25% took four trips or more. In the UK, domestic holidays taken by the over 45s increased by little more than 5% between 1995 and 1999. For foreign trips during the same period, the increase was 22%. The extent to which this is true of other European countries is, however, questionable.
2 In relation to its analysis of segmentation, this study adopted a personality/values approach to segmentation. By placing respondents into lifestyle groups according to their ranking of a priori valued statements, the research appears to lend support to the values paradigm holding that lifestyles are structured by quantitative differences in universal values.

References

AEIDL (1994) *Marketing Quality Rural Tourism.* LEADER Co-ordinating Unit, Brussels. http://www.rural-europe.aeidl.be/rural-en/biblio/touris/art07.html
Age Concern (1993) *Reflecting our Age: Images, Language and Older People.* Age Concern, London.
Becker, C. (1995) Tourism and the environment. In: Montanari, A. and Williams, A.M. (eds) *European Tourism: Regions, Spaces and Restructuring.* John Wiley & Sons, Chichester, pp. 207–220.
Bramwell, B. (1994) Rural tourism and sustainable rural tourism. *Journal of Sustainable Tourism* 2(1/2), 1–6.
Brown, F. (1998) *Tourism Reassessed, Blight or Blessing?* Butterworth Heinemann, Oxford.
Butler, R., Hall, C.M. and Jenkins, J. (1998) *Tourism and Recreation in Rural Areas.* John Wiley & Sons, Chichester.
Cavaco, C. (1995) Rural tourism: the creation of new tourist spaces. In: Montanari, A. and Williams, A.M. (eds) *European Tourism, Regions, Spaces and Restructuring.* John Wiley & Sons, Chichester, pp. 127–149.
Cochrane, J. (1994) *Eco-tourism Surveys.* Expedition Advisory Centre, London.
Cohen, E. (1974) Who is a tourist? A conceptual classification. *Sociological Review* 22(4), 527–555.
Cohen, E. (1996) A phenomenology of tourist experiences. In: Apostolopoulos, Y., Leivade, S. and Yiannakis, A. (eds) *The Sociology of Tourism: Theoretical and Empirical Investigations.* Routledge, London, pp. 90–111.
Cooper, C., Fletcher, J., Gilbert, D. and Wanhill, S. (1993) *Tourism, Principles and Practice.* Longman, Harlow.
Countryside Agency (2000) *English Countryside Day Visits.* Countryside Agency, Cheltenham.
Davidson, R. (1995) Rural tourism in France. *Insights* 6/A-145, 145–152.
Dimanche, F., Havitz, M.E. and Howard, D.R. (1991) Testing the Involvement Profile (IP) scale in the context of selected recreational and touristic activities. *Journal of Leisure Research* 23(1), 51–66.
Edmunds, M. (1999) Rural tourism in Europe. *Travel and Tourism Analyst* 6, 37–50.

Engel, J.F., Blackwell, R.D. and Miniard, P.W. (1995) *Consumer Behaviour*, 8th edn. Dryden, Orlando.

EuroBarometer (1998) *Facts and Figures on the Europeans' Holiday*. EuroBarometer for DG XXIII, Brussels.

Euromonitor (1998a) *Travel and Tourism in Italy*. Euromonitor, Brussels.

Euromonitor (1998b) *Travel and Tourism in France*. Euromonitor, Brussels.

European Travel Commission (1999) *World Travel and Tourism Development*, Issue 6. ICM International Publishing, London.

Fayos-Solá, E. (1996) Tourism policy: a midsummer night's dream? *Tourism Management* 17(6), 405–412.

Featherstone, M. (1991) *Consumer Culture and Postmodernism*. Sage, London.

Feifer, M. (1985) *Going Places: the Ways of the Tourist from Imperial Rome to the Present Day*. Macmillan, London.

Fluker, M.R. and Turner, L.W. (2000) Needs, motivations and expectations of a commercial whitewater rafting experience. *Journal of Travel Research* 38, 380–389.

Greffe, X. (1994) Is rural tourism a lever for economic and social development? *Journal of Sustainable Tourism* 2(1/2), 22–40.

Gunn, C.A. (1994) The emergence of effective tourism planning and development. In: Seaton, A.V. (ed.) *Tourism: State of the Art*. John Wiley & Sons, Chichester, pp. 10–19.

Hall, C.M. (2000) The future of tourism: a personal speculation. *Tourism Recreation Research* 25(1), 85–95.

Hantrais, L. (1999) Socio-demographic change, policy impacts and outcomes in Social Europe. *Journal of European Social Policy* 9(4), 291–309.

Henley Centre (1998a) *Planning for Consumer Change: Trends*. Henley Centre for Forecasting, London.

Henley Centre (1998b) *Planning for Consumer Change: Issues*. Henley Centre for Forecasting, London.

Holt, D. (1995) How consumers consume: a typology of consumption practices. *Journal of Consumer Research* 22, 1–16.

Kastenholz, E. (2000) The market for rural tourism in North and Central Portugal: a benefit segmentation approach. In: Richards, G. and Hall, D. (eds) *Tourism and Sustainable Community Development*. Routledge, London, pp. 268–284.

Keane, M.J. (1992) Rural tourism and rural development. In: Briassoulis, H. and van der Straaten, J. (eds) *Tourism and the Environment: Regional, Economic and Policy Issues*. Kluwer Academic Publishers, Dordrecht, pp. 43–55.

Lane, B. (1994) What is rural tourism? *Journal of Sustainable Tourism* 2(1–2), 1–6.

McKercher, B. (1993) Some fundamental truths about tourism: understanding tourism's social and environmental impacts. *Journal of Sustainable Tourism* 1(1), 6–16.

Maiztegui Oñate, C. (1994) Ageing and mass media. In: Henry, I. (ed.) *Leisure in Different Worlds*, Volume 1: *Leisure, Modernity, Post-modernity and Lifestyles*. Leisure Studies Association, Eastbourne.

Mayo, E.F. (1975) Tourism and the national parks: a psychographic and attitudinal study. *Journal of Leisure Research* 14(1), 14–18.

Midwinter, E. (1991) *British Gas Report on Attitudes on Ageing*. Age Concern, London.

Mintel (1999a) *Activity Holidays*. Leisure Intelligence, London.

Mintel (1999b) *Tourism and the Over 45s*. Leisure Intelligence, London.

Moutinho, L. (2000) Segmentation, targeting, positioning and strategic marketing. In: Moutinho, L. (ed.) *Strategic Management in Tourism*. CAB International, Wallingford, pp. 121–166.

Mulgan, G. (2000) *Time Politics*. http:www.kingston.ac.uk/cusp/lectures/mulgan.htm

OECD (1998) *Maintaining Prosperity in an Ageing Society*. OECD, Paris.

Ottman, J. and Terry, V. (1997) Strategic marketing of greener products. *Green Marketing and Eco-Innovation*. Ottman Consulting Inc, New York. http://www.greenmarketing.com/articles/JSP1Apr98.html

Page, S.J. and Getz, D. (eds) (1997) *The Business of Rural Tourism: International Perspectives*. International Thomson Business Press, London.

Pine, B.J. and Gilmore J.H. (1998) Welcome to the experience economy. *Harvard Business Review*, July–August, 97–105.

Plog, S.C. (1977) Why destination areas rise and fall in popularity. In: *Domestic and International Tourism*. Institute of Certified Travel Agents, Wellesley, Massachusetts.

Poon, A. (1993) *Tourism, Technology and Competitive Strategies*. CAB International, Wallingford.

Probasco, I. and Heimlich, J.E. (2000) *Guidelines for the Environmentally Conscious Consumer*. Ohio State University, Columbus. http://ohioline.ag.ohio-state.edu/cd-fact/0180.html

Seaton, A.V. and Bennett, M.M. (1996) *Marketing Tourism Products: Concepts, Issues, Cases*. International Thomson Business Press, London.

Sharpley, R. (1999) *Tourism, Tourists and Society*, 2nd edn. ELM, Huntingdon.

Sharpley, R. (2000) The consumption of tourism revisited. In: Robinson, M., Long, P., Evans, M., Sharpley, R. and Swarbrooke, J. (eds) *Reflections on International Tourism: Motivations, Behaviour and Tourist Types*. Business Education Publishers, Sunderland, pp. 381–391.

Sharpley, R. and Sharpley, J. (1997) *Rural Tourism: an Introduction*. International Thomson Business Press, London.

Silverberg, K.E., Backman, S.J. and Backman, K.F. (1996) A preliminary investigation into the psychographics of nature-based travelers to the Southeastern United States. *Journal of Travel Research* Fall, 19–28.

Smith, C. and Jenner, P. (1997) The seniors' travel market. *Travel and Tourism Analyst* 5, 43–62.

Swarbrooke, J. (1999) *Sustainable Tourism Management*. CAB International, Wallingford.

Urry, J. (1990) *The Tourist Gaze*. Sage, London.

Valentine, V. and Gordon, W. (2000) The 21st century consumer: a new model of thinking. *International Journal of Market Research* 42(2), 185–206.

Wight, P. (1994) Environmentally responsible marketing of tourism. In: Cater, E. and Lowman, G. (eds) *Ecotourism: a Sustainable Option?* John Wiley & Sons, Chichester, pp. 39–55.

7

The Nature of Supply or the Supply of Nature?

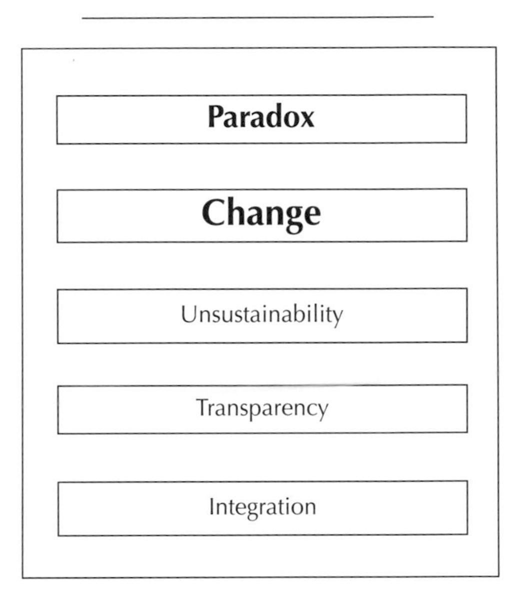

The supply of tourism and recreation in rural areas involves the public, private and voluntary sectors of a country's economy, and encompasses a wide variety of products and services. The purpose of this chapter, however, is not to provide a comprehensive analysis of the supply side of the industry; this has been done elsewhere (e.g. see Chapter 4 of Sharpley and Sharpley, 1997). Rather, it is to illustrate a range of products, services and experiences that:

- reinforce the countryside's role as a site of consumption rather than of production; and
- further develop the process of rural commodification.

Two of the key themes are particularly prominent in this chapter. *Change* is evident in the 'new' forms of tourism that can be found in rural areas, and each of the 'products' examined reflects this trend. *Paradox* is evident in the complexity of demand that provides both threat and opportunity to rural businesses and environments.

Earlier chapters have highlighted issues of consumption and commodification of the rural and discussed the implications for localities and their residents. By using the term 'product' to label aspects of rurality, association with processes of consumption is axiomatic (Burns and Holden, 1995: 73). Places become destinations, and crafts, souvenirs. Even communities become framed within images of their localities created by external forces.

Perhaps the most obvious 'product' of rural tourism is the countryside itself. But as was illustrated in Chapter 2, research shows that widely differing, and constantly changing, perceptions of rurality make meanings attached to the countryside, whether real or imagined, difficult to identify. Removed by distance from the countryside, visitors' perceptions of it as a rural tourism product emerge from complex interactions of facts and images that confer upon it idealized values. Such notions are of more than academic interest because the way people view rural areas is of fundamental importance for the way they use them (Butler and Hall, 1998: 115). This is a critical observation in the process of defining the term 'rural tourism' and viewing it as a 'product'.

Until the latter part of the 20th century, rural areas were attractive to visitors because of their inherent appeal as rural idylls (Butler and Hall, 1998: 116). However, the emergence of the countryside as a place of consumption, and the development of rural identities, images and themes, have created products and services evident in the range of visitor attractions and facilities that can now be found in rural areas. Participation in recreation in the countryside has become sufficiently widespread and diverse to require special facilities (Glyptis, 1992). Increasingly, therefore, the rural visitor's experience is derived from the consumption and commodification of rurality that are the result of the conversion of 'the rural' into the rural 'product'. Mindful of its connotations, therefore, the term 'product' is used here as a means of describing and analysing rural tourism and recreation activities as they are manifest in marketing terms.

Commodification is largely achieved by the marketing of 'place myths': images of rural areas as treasured landscapes, pastoral retreats and places of community (Hopkins, 1998: 154). This fuels the desire to *experience* rurality and results in demand for visitor experiences rather than merely the products and services that support them. The experience economy is based on an understanding that visitors' experiences derive from products and services that provide only the stage and props respectively, and experiences can be thus presented as 'a distinct economic offering' (Pine and Gilmore, 1998: 97). Figure 7.1 provides an example to illustrate this process.

Experiences have always played an important part in tourism and recreation markets, and those business operators who have escaped the 'commodity mind-set' (Pine and Gilmore, 1998: 99) will see little that is original in the experience idea. What may be new, however, is recognition of the experience economy as an opportunity to stage experiences that can be sold. The example in Fig. 7.1 is not a hypothetical one. It is an example of a product and service combined that can be sold at a premium because it is staged as

Product:

A nostalgic journey through the Bulgarian countryside by horse and cart. 1 day; lunch provided

Service:

Collection from accommodation; provision of a picnic lunch; stops at suitable viewpoints and places of interest; guided tour; return to accommodation

Experience:

Met en route by bandits, 'kidnapped' and taken to an outlaws' hut where participants share a meal of locally hunted and freshly cooked game around a camp fire

A chance to learn about the harshness and pleasures of rural life in 19th and 20th century Bulgaria

Fig. 7.1. The product, service and experience framework (source: Pirin Tourist Forum, 1998, personal communication, May 1999).

an experience. It is exciting, interactive and provides 'captives' with a role to play within their experience. Experiences can be placed into four broad categories as illustrated in Fig. 7.2.

The model in Fig. 7.2 is based on two dimensions:

- Participation: from passive to active; the extent to which consumers participate in the experience.
- Connection: from absorption to immersion; the extent to which consumers unite with the experience.

Experiences may be classified according to where they fall along the two dimensions:

- Entertainment (such as television viewing or spectating at an event) tends to be passive and absorbing.
- Educational events (such as attending a class or workshop) tend to require more active participation but still allow the participant to remain outside the core action.
- Escapist experiences (like participating in an event such as a harvest festival rather than merely observing it or hiking in the Grand Canyon) involve both active participation and immersion in the experience.
- Aesthetic experiences minimize active participation but retain the extent of immersion (for example, a visit to an art gallery or the viewing of the Grand Canyon without going down into it).

The richest experiences encompass something of each category, but the combination of possibilities appears to be endless (adapted from Pine and Gilmore, 1998).

The commodification of rural spaces and lifestyles in this way may be distasteful to those for whom authenticity of experience is paramount. The staging of rural experiences lends them 'an aura of superficiality' (MacCannell, 1999: 98). Whether perceived as such by tourists or not, this has the power to alter meanings attached to the environments, people, lifestyles and events so staged, potentially diminishing their significance as meaningful social or religious phenomena. It is perhaps no coincidence that MacCannell uses the same terminology as experience brokers when identifying the processes of 'stage-setting' associated with inauthenticity in tourism environments. Not all forms of rural tourism, however, can be similarly labelled, and as the following pages illustrate, even within 'product categories', experiences vary according to the meanings conferred upon them by participants.

The following pages describe a range of rural tourism products in the following categories:

- farm tourism;
- ecotourism;
- cultural tourism;
- adventure tourism; and
- activity tourism.

The selection reflects current themes and products within 'rural tourism' industries, and potential for future product, service and experience design. Although each is capable of translation

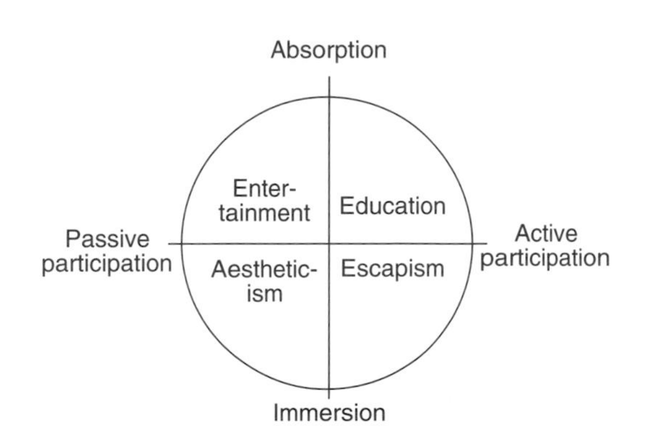

Fig. 7.2. The four realms of an experience (source: Pine and Gilmore, 1998: 102).

into a tourism form as illustrated, their selection does not suggest recommendation. The choice is intended to stimulate thought and discussion with regard to the economic potential that may exist within the reader's locality. It may be the analytical process rather than the product itself that directs the focus of an individual or group. Development opportunities are regionally and locally defined, and dependent on existing strategies as well as the preferences, skills and expertise of the local businesses and entrepreneurs involved. Different challenges require different strategies and actions, and these generally need to be tailored to local circumstances.

The 'product' descriptions illustrate the different forms that rural tourism and recreation products, services and experiences may take. In each case, examples are given and potential modes of consumption analysed in order to generate suggestions for marketing opportunities.

Farm Tourism

Reviews of the farm tourism sector are numerous (Dernoi, 1983; Frater, 1983; Opperman, 1995, 1996; Gladstone and Morris, 1998). For the purposes of tourism research, definitional clarity is required in order to collect meaningful statistics on the growth and development of the farm tourism sector (Page and Getz, 1997). Much of the research has been characterized by a lack of definitional clarity and a focus on economic costs and benefits (Evans and Ilbery, 1989). According to Page and Getz (1997: 13), this has resulted in an absence of accurate statistics on both growth and development of the sector.

For marketing purposes, too, it would be useful and convenient to be able to identify a clear and recognizable product. Nevertheless, the fact remains that, in common with 'rural tourism' and many of its components, simple definition remains elusive (see Chapter 1, page 15). Across Europe, the term 'farm tourism' may be used to refer to stays in a rural homestead, where subsistence farming supports off-farm employment, as well as on a full-time working farm. The generic term 'rural tourism' may include a stay on a farm. Agro or agritourism, often used interchangeably with farm tourism, may include off-farm activities in addition to on-farm accommodation, but may also include forms of rural tourism not associated with farming activities at all. Traditionally, farm tourism refers to rural tourism conducted on working farms where the working environment forms part of the product from the perspective of the consumer. It is thus a sub-sector of rural tourism (Clarke, 1999). In practice, the term is increasingly used to describe a range of activities including accommodation, farm visitor centres and museums, farm shops, farm trails, educational visits, and a range of other activities on farmland (Sharpley and Sharpley, 1997). These activities may have little in common with the farm other than that the farmer manages the land on which they take place.

In terms of farm tourism as a product, Page and Getz's comment that 'the focus on farm tourism has detracted from a more critical debate on the wider significance of rural tourism within an economic context' (1997: 14) has been overtaken by the nature of the sector's more recent development. As indicated above, farm tourism is now much more than a farm business with accommodation and farm-based attractions, and this broader base makes it less distinguishable from products that may be classified under the more general title of 'rural tourism'. This is illustrated by examples of tourism in farming areas in a number of countries across Europe. It is well documented that England, France, Germany and Austria currently dominate the European farm holiday industry with something like 20,000–30,000 enterprises in each country (Busby and Rendle, 2000). For this reason, a number of lesser-known destination countries and their more broadly defined farm products have been selected to further illustrate the scope of activities commonly on offer in the 'farm tourism' sector.

Farm tourism in Poland

Rural tourism in Poland has a tradition going back to the 19th century. Since 1990 it has been part of the country's national policy to support rural families adjusting to changes resulting from economic restructuring.

The most important resources identified as valuable for the development of Polish rural tourism are authentic rural lifestyles with traditional agriculture, a rich and unpolluted environment, and a high quality of food and hospitality, and it is estimated that 65% of Poland fulfils the criteria to develop rural tourism.

Recognition of the importance of rural tourism as early as the 1930s led to training courses for farm housewives to be instructed in matters of lodging, catering and related services, and the first guidebook for farming families receiving tourists was printed in 1937. After 1945, the 'industry' continued and was still significant in economic terms, if altered by the non-market economy. The 1990s, however, saw a considerable push to return rural tourism to its former status, through the medium of farm tourism. Today, its characteristics are high-quality accommodation and service levels. Although rural tourism has only a small share of Poland's tourism market, government and local authorities see it as an important factor for sustainable tourism development in the future. Still well below capacity, the country's rural areas are in a strong position to develop tourism strategies with long-term environmental objectives. By so doing, authorities hope to establish the country's reputation as a clean and relatively 'unspoiled' country in contrast with its negative image caused by previous industrial intensification.

Although rural tourism encompasses rural attractions such as traditional crafts and folklore, and accommodation of a number of different types (from manor houses to caravan sites), the greatest number of beds is provided by farmhouse accommodation. Specifically, the European Centre for Ecological Agriculture and Tourism (ECEAT) – Poland, a not-for-profit, non-government organization, was created to support small-scale ecological tourism to organic and traditional farms. Its aim is to preserve cultural and natural landscapes and the 'traditional' ways of life of rural communities while promoting the growth of organic farming and nature conservation. Members are mostly organic farmers who welcome tourists to their farms (Plate 7.1) (ECEAT, 1999).

Plate 7.1. A typical Polish organic farmstead.

Country holidays in Latvia

'Enjoy vacation travel in the Latvian countryside' is the advertising banner of Asociácijá Lauku Ceļotájs, the tourism agency for Latvian rural tourism. In the Latvian countryside, accommodation ranges from camping to guesthouses; the majority are bed and breakfast in farmhouses or summerhouses in rural areas. The products offered, described in Box 7.1, show a clear focus on farmhouse and country home traditions. It is not difficult to identify some of the 'place-myths' (Hopkins, 1998: 154) invoked by the prose of such descriptions. The senses of family, homeliness, warmth and comfort promise protection from the harsh realities of everyday existence, and nourishment of the soul as well as the body is implied.

Farm holidays in Iceland

In contrast to the importance of the Latvian home, and thus the accommodation element of farm tourism, it is the tours and associated activities that form the focus of farm holidays in Iceland.

Icelandic farm holidays are a well-established tradition and the Icelandic Farm Holidays (IFH) brochure offers a range of accommodation. This may be farmhouse

Box 7.1. Christmas in the Latvian countryside (source: Country Holidays in Latvia, Riga: Asociácijá Lauku Ceļotájs).

Christmas in the country

You arrive at the country home on Christmas morning where you are greeted by the hosts. After coffee or tea you can, together with the children, start baking gingerbreads or start wrapping Christmas gifts. In the evening, when the serenity of Christmas reigns everywhere, you relish the Yuletide supper, sing Christmas carols and await Santa Claus.

After breakfast the next morning, ride horseback or in horse-drawn sleigh. Eat lunch, and in the evening, sauna with birch boughs followed by supper and the sipping of herbal teas by the fireplace.

On the third day of Christmas, skiing, sleighing, snowball fights, building a snowman ... a true winter holiday. A nourishing meal awaits you back at the house.

Other holidays celebrated in a country home are equally enjoyable: St Martin's Day, when cooked goose is served, New Year's Eve, when fortunes are told, Easter with egg rolling.

accommodation (in either made-up beds or sleeping bag accommodation, with breakfast only, half board or full board), separate accommodation in renovated farm cottages (usually rented by the week), or camping. IFH can arrange fishing permits, horseback trips, glacier visits and boat trips. Tours and activities are varied as illustrated in Box 7.2. Icelanders promote the opportunities for adventure and challenge afforded by the harshness and remoteness of their landscapes.

Agrotourism in Greece

Agrotourism refers to various small-scale family and cooperative tourism activities conducted by people employed in agriculture in rural areas. Its aim is to provide supplementary employment and income for farming families. Encouraged by the Ministry of Agriculture, the following accommodation and facilities make up the agrotourism sector:

- furnished rooms or flats to let;
- family restaurants serving traditional local food;
- sports courts;
- recreation parks situated in regions of exquisite natural beauty;
- cultural events; and
- workshops of popular art and local food.

Vocational training is provided for families in order to raise standards of quality and service for tourism.

'Agrotourism is the sort of tourism which offers the visitor the opportunity to spend his holidays in a peaceful natural environment near the simple villagers who continue to be attached to land and tradition until today' (Ministry of Agriculture, 1994: 4). Apart from farm-based accommodation, the rural product

Box 7.2. Icelandic Farm Holidays (source: Icelandic Farm Holidays, Reykjavik: IFH Tours).

IFH tours:

'Adventure on a farmhouse based tour': travel around Iceland and activities including hiking, boat trips, horse-shows, sightseeing, whale watching, glacier walking, warm spring bathing
'See the sights in comfort': a condensed week of sightseeing by touring
'For outdoor people': hiking in the interior

Rather more closely related to farming, there is the 'Autumn round up tour', where tourists can participate in the collection of grazing horses and sheep and their return to sheltered ground for the winter.

Growing in popularity, specialized farmers' tours are both sightseeing and educational and can be tailored to the needs of the group; sheep farming, geo-thermally heated greenhouses, the Icelandic horse, organic farming, or sub-arctic corn cultivation are just some of the themes available.

is enhanced for visitors by opportunities to taste home-made preparations such as conserves, pastries, cheeses and to buy fresh farm produce to take home (and often to help in its harvesting); to participate in day-to-day farming activities; and to see (and in some cases join) local cultural customs and events where traditional dress, dance and music express the regions' cultures. It is also possible to visit the homes of craft workers and see them weaving and embroidering or making pottery and silver jewellery (see Plate 7.2). Opportunities to buy products are available.

Connotations of rural simplicity and innocence, and the goodness inherent in local produce, contribute to the development of a sense of place while opportunities to participate in activities and to buy produce reflect Bessière's description of 'cultural appropriation' (see Chapter 5). The sentiments conveyed by both product and product description are strongly suggestive of consumption as integration (as described in Chapter 6).

Rural tourism in Romania

Following political change across Central and Eastern Europe, the restoration of Romania's agrarian social and economic systems was seen as a priority, not only to restore adequate food supplies but also as an essential element in the country's cultural renaissance. The essence of rural life in Romania, *Spatiu Mioritic*, encompasses common rights to, and dependence on, land, and reflects the spiritual relationship rural communities have with it, especially in mountain regions. Literally translated as 'sheep space', the loss of its spiritual association is keenly felt by those who have moved to towns and cities. It may be this that provides the Romanian rural product with its bucolic authenticity. Rural accommodation (sometimes on farms; often in rural smallholdings) is plentiful, products providing activities less so. It is possible to arrange tailor-made trips through the Assoçiata Naţionala de Turism Rural, Ecologic şi Cultural (ANTREC) or private companies such as SC Ovi-Tours SRL. Readily available products, while in the planning stages, can be difficult to source.

Plate 7.2. A Greek lacemaker.

Those areas with natural or cultural attractions have a greater advantage in this respect, and Transylvania, as the home of Count Dracula, has an obvious theme for tourism marketing. But as with a number of other CEE countries, in Romania, the 'product' is the place, its rustic authenticity providing both the backdrop for a holiday and the holiday itself, such is the nature of its rurality. Opportunities abound, for example in the Carpathian Mountains, for activities and adventures with appeal to rural holidaymakers (Roberts, 1996).

For domestic tourists who form by far the greater part of the market for rural tourism throughout Romania, commodification of the rural is unnecessary. Most families are relatively recent urban dwellers and their return to the countryside is simply part of life's routine, perhaps to assist elderly relatives still living off the land. The attraction of foreign tourists, however, requires the provision of products and services that confer place identities reinforced by the signs of commodification (Urry, 1995) (Plate 7.3).

The preceding examples have illustrated ways in which farm tourism presents images to visitors, many of which represent illusory values, but values sought by rural tourists nevertheless. These require careful consideration and marketing if they are to result in visitor satisfaction for 'imagination and desire fuel place-myths, but familiarity and dashed expectations will dissolve them' (Hopkins, 1998: 154). It has been identified that few farmers with tourism

Plate 7.3. Commodification in the Romanian countryside.

enterprises take a comprehensive marketing approach to their management (Yells and Slee in Clarke, 1999: 28). Definitional difficulties and the resulting lack of reliable data make market analysis for the prospective operator a rather haphazard process. It may be possible to identify a feasible product and to match it with markets, but the extent of potential demand and appropriate levels of investment are difficult to evaluate.

In its 'new form', farm tourism is a relatively new product. The label 'new' results from two fundamental changes in the historical product:

- Farm tourism has undergone a structural change with tourists expecting a high quality of accommodation and service (Taguchi and Iwai, 1998).
- Farm attractions have expanded to include a wide range of activities (Sharpley and Sharpley, 1997).

Some farm tourism activities, such as farm museums, farm trails and guided walks, have a focus on the farm and its activities. Others, such as pony trekking, fishing, shooting or off-road quad biking, bear no relation to farm work but merely take place on farmland. This gives rise to a distinction between 'farm tourism' and 'tourism on farms'.

The distinction has also been made by Busby and Rendle (2000) who state that 'tourism on farms' labels tourism activities that represent a relatively small amount of household revenue. The transition from tourism on farms to farm tourism, they say, takes place when:

- tourism revenue exceeds traditional farm revenue;
- a farmer adopts a tourism business plan; and
- the enterprise is recognized by consumers as farm tourism.

(Busby and Rendle, 2000).

New consumption patterns in tourism, however, give an added dimension to this analysis. The distinction between farm tourism and tourism on farms is an important one because it may be seen to present two very different products. Consumers of farm tourism require the farming environment for satisfaction of their tourism motivations. Conversely, the activity focus of the latter may render its environment less significant. For example, the visitor participating in a four-wheel drive experience will be indifferent to the fact that it takes place on farmland. While the boundaries of the two products may be blurred, and they may therefore be combined for some research purposes, the analysis required of a marketing perspective demands that farm tourism and tourism on farms be recognized as discrete rural tourism products (see Plates 7.4 and 7.5).

The distinction may be less important in relation to the contribution the farm tourism sector makes to rural economies. Tourism income is vital to farms and helps to keep families in employment (Denman and Denman, 1993). Local spending is stimulated by farm visitors. Rilla (2000) suggests that local tourism authorities' estimates indicate two-thirds of farm guests spend twice as much again as they spend on their overnight accommodation.

In terms of local embedding, perceived positive factors for farm tourism businesses include:

- re-use of existing buildings;

Plate 7.4. Farm tourism: the 'traditional' product.

- providing an opportunity for local initiative and control;
- directly supporting the local economy and local people;
- able to be integrated with other economic and social activities;
- assisting the 'stewardship' of the countryside and drawing upon inherent nature of open space;
- being small-scale with little apparent environmental impact; and
- helping to provide (urban) visitors with a genuine feel for the area they are visiting.

(Denman and Denman, 1993; Rilla, 2000)

Plate 7.5. Tourism on farms: the 'contemporary' product.

Farm tourism provides one means of representing 'rural realities' to urban visitors.

Table 7.1 provides an example of a way in which a farm tourism product may be viewed and consumed by visitors depending on the theme(s) chosen. Potential marketing opportunities arise from the identified modes of consumption.

Ecotourism

Increasing global concern for the environment has served to highlight the unsustainability of travel and tourism (see Chapter 3), and has focused research on the ways in which tourism industries can conserve and protect the resources on which they are based. One response to such concerns has been the emergence of a 'brand' of tourism practice, namely ecotourism.

There are two prevailing views of eco-

Table 7.1. Farm tourism marketing.

Generic product	Farm tourism
Specific product	Farm trail
Market(s)	Possible 'farm tourism-loyal market', otherwise, special interest markets might exist depending on the nature of the farming undertaken
Consumption mode	Consumption as experience, play and integration
Product customization	The availability of guided trails, self-guided trails, open-days for special interest groups
Marketing focus	Understand farming: managing grazing, what shapes our landscape ... Family fun: sleep easily, learn to count sheep Health issues: how safe is your food?

tourism in the context of a growing public interest in environmental concerns:

1. Public interest harnessed to conserve the resources upon which tourism is based; that is, ecotourism as an approach to tourism operations.
2. Public interest in the environment perceived as an opportunity to design and market a product; that is, ecotourism as a product in its own right (after Wight, 1994: 39).

Ecotourism as an approach to tourism operations

Seen as a means to 'alternative tourism', ecotourism is a 'responsible' and 'sustainable' approach to tourism (Cater, 1994: 3), and represents 'the best intentions of an educated and affluent middle-class to travel without despoiling the environment' (Peattie and Moutinho, 2000: 25). Ecotourism emphasizes local ownership in order to optimize its local benefits, and a commitment to ecologically sustainable practices (McKercher and Robbins, 1998). As a process, ecotourism therefore has the potential to influence a range of tourism forms, rendering tourism practices and processes generally more environmentally benign (Blamey, 1997).

It is often said that consumers are becoming more aware of environmental issues, resulting in both increasing concern for environmental problems, and desires to act more sensitively as a result (Wight, 1994: 40; Ottman and Terry, 1997; Probasco and Heimlich, 2000). Evidence for such conviction is seen in expressions of environmental concern and the rise in popularity of 'green' political parties. The concern, however, does not appear to translate into effective demand for sustainable forms of tourism (McKercher, 1993; Sharpley, 2000). A survey for the Travel Industry Association of America in 1992 found that travellers, on average, would spend 8.5% more on tourism products and services provided by environmentally responsible suppliers (Wight, 1994: 41). Intention, however, does not always translate into action. For example, In the Balearic Islands, the introduction of an eco-tax, equivalent at the time of the debate to approximately 6.5, was fiercely resisted by tour operators and hoteliers on the grounds that, without popular consumer support, it would affect their competitiveness in international markets (Morgan, 2000).

Ecotourism's potential to influence environmental sensitivity in tourism generally must therefore be questioned. Given that numbers of tourists have increased since ecotourism was conceived, tourism's negative impacts generally are worsening. Indeed, given the scale of tourism at the start of the 21st century, it may be no more than idealistic to expect small-scale operations and practices to provide alternatives to those practised in mass tourism.

Ecotourism as a product

Evidence of the environmentally concerned consumer may be assumed from the increasing range of ecotourism products in what is reported to be one of the fastest growing tourism markets (Cater, 1994: 4; McKercher and Robbins, 1998). However, although it seems reasonable to assume that the majority of existing and potential ecotourists have 'green' values, it may be a mistake to do so. Research into the potential ecotourism market in Australia indicates a low level of environmentally sensitive values among such tourists (Blamey and Braithwaite, 1997; see also Chapter 6). Thus, it seems a market exists for this new tourism product based on tourists' motivations other than environmental concern. Perhaps this is explained by recognition of the social importance of tourism consumption and its role as an indicator of values and social status. In the case of ecotourism, the importance of self-alignment with environmentally sensitive philosophies represents an example of integrative and classifying consumption. It may be more important to be seen to be environmentally aware than actually to be so.

Nevertheless, there exists an increasing number of ecotourism and nature tourism products around the world, with the potential to benefit rural businesses and communities. As a product, ecotourism must take on a tangible or visible form that requires definition, clarification and the setting of parameters to establish the nature of activities encompassed by the 'eco' label. Although there is no one accepted definition of the term, the Canadian Environmental Advisory Council adopted the following at its 1991 conference on the topic: 'Ecotourism is an enlightening nature travel experience that contributes to conservation of the ecosystem while respecting the integrity of host communities' (Scace *et al.*, 1992, in Wight, 1994: 39). Box 7.3. lists the requirements for ecotourism operations/products. This rather challenging list helps to explain why it is difficult both to describe and to identify genuinely 'eco' products.

It has been suggested by Shores (1999) that the continuing use of vague definitions for products that are 'nature-based' or 'eco' products weakens the power of the concepts, contributes to ambiguity, and encourages misuse and abuse of the terms (see also Chapter 3). Ecotourism and nature-based products encompass a broad spectrum of activities and enterprises as illustrated in Table 7.2.

Shores's categorization is a useful one, offering distinctions between different levels of environmental sensitivity in ecotourism. Clearly, 'incidental' travel is a tourist trip that affords an opportunity to view nature. However, the passive and superficial nature of such viewing, likely to form a part of many tourist trips, denies it definition according to ecotourism's criteria. In line with its underlying concepts, only the last two categories, 'involvement' and 'ecological', would appear to qualify for an 'eco' label. Similar distinctions have been made between 'shallow' and 'deep' ecotourism, relating the terms to underlying philosophies of environmental issues.

Box 7.3. The requirements of an ecotourism product (source: Wight, 1994: 40).

An ecotourism product should:

- not degrade the resource and should be developed in an environmentally sound manner
- provide long-term benefits to the resource, to the local community and industry (benefits may be conservation, scientific, social, cultural or economic)
- provide first-hand, participatory and enlightening experiences
- involve education among all parties: local communities, government, non-governmental organizations, industry and tourists (before, during and after the trip)
- encourage all-party recognition of the intrinsic values of the resource
- involve acceptance of the resource on its own terms, and in recognition of its limits, which involves supply-orientated management
- promote understanding and involve partnerships between many players, which could include government, non-governmental organizations, industry, scientists and locals (both before and during operations)
- promote moral and ethical responsibilities and behaviour towards the natural and cultural environment by all players

Table 7.2. The rainbow of definitions for nature-based tourism (source: Shores, 1999).

The rainbow of nature-based tourism	
Incidental	Any travel during which the traveller views or appreciates the green environment
Nature-centred	Travel in which nature is the central value rather than an afterthought
Support	Travel organized to provide appreciable financial support for the protection of the green environment visited or enjoyed
Involvement	Travel in which the traveller personally engages in activities that support conservation or restoration
Ecological	Travel in which all activities are ecologically benign

'Shallow' ecotourism values nature according to its usefulness to humans and sees it as a resource to be exploited. Conversely, 'deep' ecotourism concerns an intrinsic value of nature, and reflects the principles cited earlier (Acott *et al.*, 1998).

Two other issues further complicate ecotourism as a tourism or recreational product:

- The product's inherently paradoxical nature.
- The responsible marketing of ecotourism products.

The predominance of ecotourism products in the fragile environments of developing countries requires travel to such destinations in order to consume the product. The environmentally benign nature of the product, therefore, should be balanced against the incompatibility of long-distance travel with the aims of environmentally sound tourism practices (Hall and Kinnaird, 1994: 111). At a global level, the contribution of the ecotourism product to environmental aims may be entirely negated by the demand it creates for travel to it. The lack of appreciation of such a paradox contributes to criticisms of 'eco-' and similarly labelled forms of tourism as a form of conspiracy, contributing to the hypocrisy of 'environmentally aware' tourists who wish to travel, but with a clear conscience (Wheeller, 1993, 1996).

The 'eco-' label is a neat and attractive prefix that finds itself attached to a range of products, sending to consumers a message of environmental concern and responsibility. Thus we can choose eco-body care products, do our shopping with biodegradable 'eco' credit cards, and invest in a socially responsible manner by buying 'eco-friendly' investment funds in socially and environmentally responsible corporations. By doing any of these things, we buy into a philosophy of sustainability. But a lack of clear definitions for terms used, together with consumer uncertainty, may provide opportunities for 'eco' labels to represent a form of eco-exploitation or 'environmental opportunism', especially in tourism (Carson and Moulden in Wight, 1994: 41). The 'eco-' label may thus be used, not to provide assurance of environmental sensitivity, but as a promotional tool for forms of pseudo-environmentalism. Where the motivation to supply ecotourism products is based solely on the desire to meet a perceived gap in an emerging market for individualized, nature-based special interest holidays, the eco-product's integrity may be at risk and the term open to misuse. Fears of misuse and abuse of the label may lead to consumer scepticism and a resulting devaluation of the term.

Wight's (1994) list (Box 7.3) shows how difficult it is to achieve the underlying principles of ecotourism, and the problems inherent in the travel process only add to the difficulties of designing and delivering a tourism product that is consistently environmentally sound. Additionally, questions of contested heritage, especially where they remain suppressed, can blight claims to environmental sensitivity. The product example in Box 7.4 suffers from drawbacks in each of these areas. Confined within geographical location and cultural boundaries, however, it may be said to illustrate many of the qualities of a good ecotourism product.

It is evident, therefore, that while opportunities exist for the design and operation of eco and nature products, a number of critical factors must be accommodated:

- The product must be well defined, and genuinely and visibly based on the principles of ecotourism.
- Although definitions of ecotourism exist, businesses may still experience problems when trying to use them for the purposes of marketing (Blamey, 1997). Treadsoftly, a mountain biking operator in Alberta, Canada, does not advertise itself as an ecotourism operation despite the fact that it has an environmental mission statement and a total commitment to ecotourism principles. Consumer confusion and the potential for misunderstanding led to this decision (Herremans and Welsh, 1999).
- The product must have a clearly defined market. The potential market is not restricted to those who are sensitive to environmental issues. A significant component of the latent market, many members of which would not undertake such tours independently, will participate in trips to learn about the culture or nature of an area

Box 7.4. Vägvisaren: an ecotourism product (source: Vägvisaren – samiska upplevelser (http://www.repisvare.co.gellivare.se)).

Vägvisaren – samiska upplevelser

Sápmi, the land of the Sami, stretches through four countries: Norway, Sweden, Finland and Russia. It is home to around 85,000 Sami people. The Sami see themselves as one people, and have their own language, culture, parliament, and common flag and national anthem.

About two years ago, a Sami tourist enterprise started in Gällivare, Lapland, Sweden, calling itself Vägvisaren – samiska upplevelser, The Pathfinder – Sami activities. The business is owned and run by Sami people. The founder of the enterprise, Lennart Pittja, is a young Sami, born and raised in a reindeer-herding family within the Sőrkaitum Sami village in the municipality of Gällivare. His upbringing in a reindeer-herding family means that the Sami culture is strongly present in everyday life, and this genuine picture of Sami life is what Lennart wishes to show tourists during their visit to Lapland.

The philosophy of Vägvisaren is to run a tourism enterprise that allows visitors to learn about sociocultural and environmental conditions in the area. In order to limit the adverse impacts of tourism in the area, the number of tours to each location is limited, and group sizes restricted to a maximum of 12.

Vägvisaren offers a number of ecotourism products:

Hiking with reindeer through Laponia: experienced guides accompany small groups hiking through alpine and primeval forest areas. In time-honoured fashion, baggage is carried by domestic reindeer. Skis and sleds are used in winter.

The Sami camp at Repisvare: in this accessible yet hidden location, visitors can see traditional Sami architecture, both contemporary and historical, and learn about their construction and uses. This is the place to learn about reindeer herding and to develop some of the skills required by herders. The Sami way of life is demonstrated everywhere.

Dinner in a Sami hut: dinner is served in a large turf hut while visitors sit on reindeer hides around the fireplace. A range of food can be served, from a simple meal to a three-course dinner, and the minimum number of guests is two.

Fishing in unspoiled scenery: Vägvisaren has a small fishing camp in a remote area at Sårkåjaur, very close to the Norwegian border. Salmon, trout and arctic char are catches in these almost untouched waters. Visitors stay in Sami or ordinary tents and access is on foot (1 day's walking) or by seaplane in summer, and by snowmobile in winter. Group sizes are limited to eight.

in the safety and comfort of an organized tour (Blamey and Braithwaite, 1997). It seems therefore that ecotourists do not form a market segment but are to be found within the ranks of mainstream tourism (Reingold in Blamey, 1997: 37).

- Many rural tourism businesses suffer financial difficulties, the failure rate is high, and of those businesses that do survive, many remain only marginally viable (see Chapter 8). In such circumstances, the need to allocate scarce resources to core business operations may mean that environmentally sensitive practices are compromised (McKercher and Robbins, 1998). Potential ecotourism operators, perhaps more so than other business start-ups, need therefore to evaluate their financial viability carefully, and build into business plans considered cash flow projections to allow for expenditure on essential environmental as well as operational requirements.

Table 7.3 outlines the marketing opportunities of what may be defined as an ecotourism product.

Cultural Tourism

> In terms of culture, there are few rural regions which are under-privileged. Full of history, traditions, forged by the work of generations of men and women, they usually possess a rich heritage or a strong cultural identity. Local culture, a source of activities, pride and well-being, can be a major asset to development.
>
> (AEIDL, 1994a: 1)

The term 'culture' represents a number of broad concepts and defies simple definition. It

Table 7.3. Ecotourism marketing.

Generic product	Ecotourism
Specific product	Wildflower nature walk
Market(s)	Unlikely to be one identifiable niche market
Consumption mode	Consumption as experience and integration
Product customization	Availability of guided and self-guided trails, information at different levels
Marketing focus	Nature classes, photography subjects, painting subject, 'edible flowers' tour, craft classes

is a complex interaction of human phenomena. In its broadest sense, culture is anything that is created by human interaction with the environment. It may be material, like landscape, architecture, language, dress and food for example; and it may be intangible, that is, inherent in societies' traditions, knowledge and skills, language and dialect, and values. Culture evolves and is inculcated over generations, developing local customs and practices that serve to distinguish one culture from another.

Culture contributes to visitors' sensory experience and may be the motive for travel. As tourists, we may be interested in the different ways in which other communities live and work, the foods they eat or the clothes they wear. The more different these are from our own experiences, the more fascinating the culture becomes as an attraction. While the tourist gaze (Urry, 1990) may have largely evolved from landscape appreciation, it now includes a wide range of cultural representations. Destination marketers harness all of these, and increasingly market destinations on the qualities of locality.

For many people, the term 'cultural tourism' summons images that relate to urban rather than rural settings. Cities are perceived and marketed as major cultural centres and many of Europe's major cultural sites are to be found in urban areas. Major museums, galleries and libraries of note position Europe's towns and cities as world cultural sites. The fact that cities throughout Europe have become known for their cultural icons and landmarks is no accident nor has the evolution of such cultural production been mere happenstance.

On the supply side, across Western Europe throughout the later years of the 20th century, the demise of traditional manufacturing industries presented major urban centres with significant challenges of diversification, and they turned to new industries to replace lost jobs and income. Tourism now forms an important part of most cities' economic development plans whether for cultural tourism in amenities, at special events or for business-related travel such as conferences and conventions.

On the demand side, a number of important influences now shape our perceptions of place, and the profession of destination management has created a whole new industry, the aim of which is to create and project images for the tourist gaze. Thus we know Barcelona for Antonio Gaudí's Church of Sagrada Familia, and Prague for its Charles Bridge. Mozart is synonymous with Vienna, and the Mona Lisa with Paris. We could not visit Rome without going to the Sistine Chapel, and a trip to Copenhagen would be incomplete without seeing the Little Mermaid. Such cultural icons and their destinations merge in the minds of tourists who then compare images and their attributes in order to make a holiday choice.

The catalysts to cultural tourism in cities now exist in rural areas. Declining traditional markets need to be replaced with viable alternatives. Jobs and incomes must be found to sustain rural communities, and viable new industries are required to support social networks and groups. Does a rural culture still exist, however, and if so, what is its nature and how does it manifest itself?

It would seem that a generic rural culture does exist today despite the fact that the population involved in agriculture across Europe has fallen, by over two-thirds in France since the late 1950s, for example (Kayser, 1994: 1).

Rural culture has been, and still is, characterized by special features including relationships with the land and the skills associated with agricultural work, as well as other influences that have helped to shape rural lifestyles and communities. Often, these lifestyles and communities possess marked and specific elements of local and regional identity. The natural environment, as the dominant characteristic of many rural areas, is an integral part of rural culture, and although the economic importance of agriculture is declining, farmers, as the custodians of so much of the land, still have an important part to play in rural community life (Kayser, 1994: 2). Architectural heritage, likewise, provides a rich source of evidence of rural culture; as well as their aesthetic value, rural homes and farm buildings reflect living patterns and local histories that have contributed to the formation of rural cultures over centuries.

The European Centre for Traditional and Regional Cultures (ECTARC) provides a typical list of sites that might attract cultural tourists for traditional and regional cultures (ECTARC in Richards, 1996: 22):

- archaeological sites and museums;
- architecture (ruins, famous buildings, whole towns);
- art, sculpture, crafts, galleries, festivals, events;
- music and dance (classical, folk, contemporary);
- drama;
- language and literature study, tours and events;
- religious festivals, pilgrimages; and
- complete (folk or primitive) cultures and sub-cultures.

One can see that each of the products listed is as applicable to rural as to urban environments. Many archaeological sites and architectural ruins exist in rural parts of Europe: Hadrian's Wall at the 'roof' of England and the theatre of Epidavros in the Peloponnese for example. Local crafts form the industrial basis of many rural areas. The 'Made in Pirin' project in Bulgaria branded a range of craft products such as hand-woven fabrics and hand-made bells for livestock. Music and dance, and drama as part of storytelling may constitute the basis of rural social life. Religious festivals and pilgrimages often take place in the countryside, the passion plays at Oberammergau providing perhaps one of the most famous examples. Indeed, it may be argued that rural culture in many European countries is sufficiently 'folk' to be a cultural product in its own right. Rural regions of Europe possess strong local identities not known in urban areas, and rich heritages of tradition and custom passed down over centuries have a currency that is valued throughout the continent.

Thus we have the stimulus, the products, and the potential demand for cultural tourism in rural areas. How do we translate these into meaningful ideas for those involved in rural development? Perhaps the main problem with cultural tourism is that it is such a broad concept and thus difficult to identify in business terms. Research conducted by the European Association for Tourism and Leisure Education (ATLAS) shows that there is no single 'cultural tourist', but a range of different cultural tourism markets arranged around different types of cultural production and consumption. Each market, therefore, is going to have different characteristics, creating varying demands, and the economic potential of cultural tourism can only be optimized by matching the right products with the right consumers (Richards, 1999: 14).

Rural cultural tourism differs from other products analysed in this chapter in that it does not lend itself to delivery as a discrete product by a single provider. Rather, cultural tourism provides themes on which may be based a local or regional strategy. Because of this, its successful development depends on collaborative strategic alliances involving a wide range of stakeholders. Effective public/private sector partnerships are essential to sustained development. But while the participation of the public sector is to be welcomed, innovation should, and often does, come from the private sector, from those who live and work in the area, those most familiar with the resources that will be mobilized in the interests of cultural tourism development (see Box 7.5). The role of the public sector will be that of enabler rather than provider and its participation in a project ought not to be viewed as leadership.

Box 7.5. The Valley of the Senses, Tyrol, Austria (source: Info LEADER July–August 2000, 80).

This project was initiated by a number of farmers from Virgen whose aim was to restore a specific cultural landscape, almost lost as a result of agricultural intensification. The 'Virgen Feldfur' was created by the removal of accumulated debris from field and path edges. An appreciation of the cultural value of this landscape led to the restoration of meadows surrounded by low dry-stone walls and paths. Community consultation generated more interest by local farmers, and the Tyrol Government agreed to contribute to the costs of the operation. The initiative in the National Park of the Upper Tauern gave rise to the first programme for cultural landscapes in Tyrol.

The link with tourism arose from an audit of the valley's natural and cultural heritage and the development of a 2.5 km long historic trail. The subsequent LEADER II project in the national park had as one of its aims the exploitation of the Park's marketing slogan 'Make Sense of your Senses'. But it was perhaps an opportune visit by an Australian tourist that provided the impetus for the project's focus. He explained how a local action group in Australia had set up theme-based trails for the visually handicapped. Further research via groups working with visually handicapped people confirmed the importance of such a product for the potential target group, and a working party was set up to manage the development process.

The new products developed were:

- a new trail specifically for the visually handicapped;
- information signs and brochures in Braille;
- special facilities in hotels and guesthouses to cater for the needs of visually handicapped guests (adaptation of accommodation, menus in Braille);
- facilities for those accompanied by sighted guests and by guide dogs;
- the production of a package holiday including guided tours by coach for both visually handicapped and general family markets;
- an integrated information system established by the tourist board; and
- new sites, itineraries and attractions to stimulate the five senses of all visitors such as an aromatic plant laboratory and a trail of smells and sounds.

Other benefits of the development have been:

- business through non-tourist activities such as seminars for guide dog instructors;
- better understanding of the realities of sight difficulties by sighted people;
- empowerment of visually handicapped people through the participatory process; and
- employment for visually handicapped people as guides, instructors and programme coordinators.

Promoting local identity is the cornerstone of the strategies of many LEADER groups, making it easier to mobilize local communities and enabling the full benefit of cultural originality to be realized. The Virgen example in Box 7.5 illustrates well the potential that can be realized by partnerships stimulated by private sector initiative and the ways in which the multidisciplinary nature of such partnerships can result in integrated development.

Products of cultural tourism

Cultural trails and itineraries

Over the last two decades, the growing demand for rural tourism and recreation has coincided with the general development and promotion of trails by the EU, national, regional and local authorities and agencies. Motives for so doing have included job creation, rural diversification, and tourism development and management (Lane, 2000).

Trails have become multi-purpose and multi-user products. The basic concept of the linear trail gave way to the circular route, enabling tourists to return to their starting point. More elaborate trails, such as the figure eight trail, offer a circuit and link two trails at once. And trails using multi-modes, part train and part foot, for example, have emerged. The speciality themed trail is now commonplace (Lane, 2000).

The establishment of *cultural itineraries* enables local heritage to be promoted and allows interesting sites to link together, thereby widening tourist appeal. Routes may be planned for walkers, cyclists or car drivers, and should be planned on a theme and with the involvement of all local stakeholders.

RURAL HABITAT CULTURAL ROUTES. These were developed to satisfy the needs of Europeans to trace their roots. The first rural habitat route was established in France, crossing the Lorraine region before going on to the Grand Duchy of Luxembourg, Wallonia (Belgium) and the German Länder of Saar and Rhineland-Palatinate. As an example, 'Architecture without Frontiers' routes comprise circuits, each of which corresponds to a particular type of landscape and habitat. Activities along the routes such as booklets, seminars, travelling exhibitions and competitions advise local people on restoration and engage visitors in the work of localities they visit. Rural habitat routes have been extended to countries of CEE, notably Romania, affording opportunities for cultural cooperation and exchange. Additionally, such collaboration can benefit from synergies created by the blending of different cultural forms. In the Maramureș region, for example, an annual festival celebrating the use of the violin in traditional music has been instituted in collaboration with Romanian promoters of rural habitat routes. The European Institute of Cultural Routes is currently preparing a publication explaining and promoting its various initiatives.

CULTURAL TEXTILE AND CRAFTS ROUTES. These were developed as part of the Eurotex project (see Box 7.6); textile and crafts routes are complete holiday routes that include stops at craft producers and also restaurants, hotels and sites of interest. While the complete route is designed to be of interest to special interest cultural tourists, parts of routes are accessible to general tourists visiting just part of a region.

The route concept can highlight the existence of a 'community' of craftspeople such as the women textile producers of Rethymno, Crete, who, as 30 single producers, two small firms and one cooperative, use their embroidery, weaving and knitting skills to make tablecloths, napkins, bedding, curtains and church vestments from wool, cotton, silk and linen (Tzanakaki, 1999: 80). The route emphasizes that each craft producer is part of a larger group.

In recognition of the inability of any one craft worker to promote her goods so widely, local producers welcomed the 'Textile Routes' promotional brochure produced as part of the Eurotex project. Local tour operators and travel agents were keen to include the tours within their itineraries and excursions both for cultural and general interest tourists, and very positive feedback was obtained from tourists themselves (Tzanakaki, 1999: 86).

FOOD TRAILS. As illustrated by Bessière (Chapter 5), food and drink are traditional elements of cultural heritage and have become affirmations of local identity. There is, therefore, a great deal of potential for cultural tourism strategies to be developed based on local food production, preparation and presentation.

Catherine Brown's *Isle of Arran Taste Trail* is not a trail in the sense of a physical route; rather it represents an audit of what is available, and 'an attitude towards the production and preparation of traditional ingredients' (Brown, 2000). An EU LEADER II initiative, co-funded by Argyll and the Islands Enterprise (AIE)

Box 7.6. The Eurotex project, developing and marketing crafts tourism (source: Richards, 1999).

ATLAS defines cultural tourism as: 'The movement of persons to cultural manifestations away from their normal place of residence, with the intention to gather new information and experiences to satisfy their cultural needs' (Richards, 1996: 24).

ATLAS's Eurotex project was conceived out of recognition of the potential for culture to become an important lever for local economic development, and the project explored the European Commission's statement that 'cultural measures are more effective where they form part of a strategic concept for sustainable development.' The pilot project, run in Alto Minho (in north-west Portugal), Rethymno (in Crete) and Lapland, tested the potential for local economic development of transnational cultural projects, including original know-how in crafts.

Continued overleaf

Box 7.6. *Continued*

One of the project's guiding principles was to enable each partner to develop activities that, while being place-specific, could be structured within a system in order to provide project coherence and allow comparisons to be made. The activities of the project were to:

- promote cooperation;
- establish local demonstration projects;
- develop skills transfer;
- promote textile-related tourism; and
- disseminate information via new media.

Information was gathered on visitors, their motivations and consumption patterns, and their levels of interest in crafts and textiles.

The tourists in the three pilot regions were broadly described as 'general cultural tourists' with a strong secondary interest in culture (including textile culture). They tended to be older and have lower incomes than cultural tourists surveyed in towns and cities in Europe (Richards, 1999). Although they make a considerable number of visits to cultural sites and attractions they are not particularly motivated by culture, primary motives being relaxation, curiosity and fun. Their activity patterns reflected a number of elements characteristic of the 'new tourist' (Poon, 1993).

Over 60% of visitors had bought crafts products during their stay in the destination, predominantly to have a reminder of the region visited and/or because the object was useful. A minor importance was attached to the decorative nature of crafts purchased, suggesting that crafts have much more than a symbolic significance. Local origin and a high degree of craftsmanship were important characteristics in the perception of product authenticity.

A further survey was conducted with the organizers of textile tours. Thirty per cent of those questioned had bought textile products during their stay, almost half of which had been clothing. Bags, handkerchiefs and towels registered as important purchases. Over 80% of goods bought were for direct personal or household use rather than for decorative purposes, again suggesting the importance of use value.

Textile tourists were found to form a fairly homogeneous group, with direct contact with textiles either though work or education, and for whom contact with other textile workers formed a key motive for participation. They were found to be of two kinds: regular and sporadic. Regular textile tourists tended to be active textile workers themselves and were involved with other crafts such as pottery or painting. Sporadic textile tourists, on the other hand, were more likely to be motivated by a general interest in creative activities.

As a pilot project, Eurotex pointed to the importance of the following:

- The need for design innovations, perhaps in terms of form and function of goods produced, especially for tourist markets. This adds value to products and supports a design profession. However, the tendency to produce 'pure' souvenirs should be resisted, and place names or similar need not form part of a craft product.
- Effective marketing has the leading role in the regeneration of crafts production. Education and training for individual producers in the effective marketing of their goods is essential if they are to be able to distinguish their products clearly from manufactured goods, and transmit the values of products to tourists looking for authentic goods.
- Networking. Many craft workers work in isolation resulting in a lack of organization, and under-representation at a level that enables them to make contact with tourist organizations and tourists. Local networks establish contacts between producers and can be used to provide essential marketing training and support.
- Training to meet the needs of the wide range of producers. Some crafts workers create their wares as a spare-time activity; others run full-time businesses with their crafts skills. Businesses will therefore require training at different levels.
- Training needs analysis. Unless the precise training needs of crafts workers are clearly identified, generic courses may fail to meet needs and result in a lack of progress in business skills development.

This project was made possible by the financial support of DGXVI of the European Commission.

and launched in 1998, the taste trail is represented in booklet form and on its web site (www.tastetrail.co.uk). The guide presents to visitors an unstructured yet rewarding way to experience a visit to the island of Arran off the coast of south-west Scotland.

Arran's larder, the natural produce of the island, is presented as one of the destination's key attractions. Produce such as the blackface sheep (distinctive for its flavour as well as its appearance), game, wild brambles, the famous Arran potato (from which the Maris Piper was bred) and Arran cheeses all contribute to the development of a sense of place. Fine foods and drink (the island has its own brewery and distillery) are available from producers, retailers and restaurants, all of which are included in the trail. In order to establish and maintain quality and authenticity, inclusion in the trail is dependent on author invitation rather than subscription. Many of the outlets featured are visitor attractions in themselves, the production and preparation of foods being visible to the customer. This is the case with cheese manufacture at the Island Cheese Company and at James's Chocolates, for example.

To enable visitors to immerse themselves further in their Arran experience, recipes include traditional fayre as well as contemporary dishes for minimalist cooking with local produce. Books can be ordered through the website to complete the visitor's preparations for a forthcoming trip.

Trails provide opportunities for visitors to learn about whole regions, and as the above examples show, they can be unstructured and self-guided, allowing those who prefer the freedom of exploration to do so as individuals. Well planned, they are a good vehicle for the marketing and promotion of a region's other facilities, with the potential to lengthen the time spent in an area. Examples of other trails that may be developed are:

- heritage/commemoration trails;
- nature trails;
- health and fitness trails;
- youth challenge trails;
- partnership trails forging links between people, regions and countries;
- river trails; and
- combination trails (after Lanc, 2000).

'Composite' cultural products that reflect a number of a region's cultural attributes may provide some of the most rewarding cultural experiences. Thus we may theme cultural routes on local food and drink yet include a number of other cultural attractions:

> 'Sample the wines on a walk through Hungary: taste the cream of Hungary's wines, walk through rolling countryside, visit thermal baths and simple café life.' In addition to visits to local vineyards, the itinerary includes a stay in a castle, a visit to a stud farm, and a number of traditional Hungarian meals.
>
> (http.//www/unmissable.com/)

> 'Take a ramble in Rioja's wine region.' This 9-day walking tour crosses beautiful countryside, explores medieval towns and visits hilltop monasteries 'all washed down with tastings of Rioja's excellent wines'.
>
> (http.//www/unmissable.com/)

Identification of a 'cultural product' is complicated by the fact that there is neither a single form of cultural tourism nor one category of cultural tourist. While patterns of cultural production and consumption may tell us a great deal about our social histories, they may not provide a useful conceptualization for marketing tourism products based on them. As a result, many cultural pursuits are classified as 'special interest' holidays or excursions despite the fact that they are based on cultural themes. Examples may be military history weekends including visits to battlefield sites, gardening enthusiasts' weekends in the grounds of stately homes, and traditional craft workshops. Table 7.4 shows an example of the way in which one such cultural product may be marketed.

Adventure tourism

What is adventure tourism?

Exhilaration, challenge, thrill and fantasy represent some of the experiences sought by those opting for adventure tourism as their holiday choice. Imagination appears to be the only limit to the increasingly diverse and exciting activities that make this one of the

Table 7.4. Cultural tourism marketing.

Generic product	Cultural tourism
Specific product	Food/drink trail
Market(s)	General tourism market
Consumption mode	Experience, play, integration, possibly classification
Product customization	Ability to access whole or part of a trail, particular food type, e.g. cheese or wine, or the foods of a particular region, gourmet foods, healthy foods, food preparations, e.g. bottling or pickling
Marketing focus	Mediterranean foods, Burgundy wines Foods that heal Healthy eating, eat to your heart's content Nostalgia, the way grandma used to do it Preserving foods, capture the taste of summer all year round

fastest growing tourism sectors. Like rural tourism, of which it forms a sub-segment, it is difficult to define and therefore presents problems for the business operator who needs to establish its core characteristics for marketing purposes.

Invited Viewpoint

Adventure Tourism: a Journey of the Mind

David Grant

The adventure tourism industry is a developing market that is predicted to grow in the next decade (Smith and Jenner, 1999: 43). The adventure experience itself is as diverse as the individuals who take part in it. To a person with limited experience, a 2-day canoe trip on a slow moving river may be adventurous. For a rather more hardened adventure seeker, however, the product would have to provide greater challenge, perhaps through the existence of potential danger to increase the apparent hardships or risks being undertaken. 'Adventure' therefore is a personal construct, something unique to the individual and created in the mind.

Worldwide, travel identified as making up the adventure tourism market is growing. Evidence suggests that such travel from major European markets has grown by around 15% annually since 1995 (Smith and Jenner, 1999: 47), over three times as much growth as for tourism generally. This growth, however, is from a very small base. Adventure tourism represents a niche in rural tourism, accounting for only 0.5% of the tourism market in Western Europe. Importantly, the product offered by European adventure tour operators is based on packages offering experiences worldwide, and predominantly outside Europe.

It is the intention of this piece to contextualize adventure tourism and to identify the core features that distinguish it from other similar tourism forms, most notably activity tourism and ecotourism. As will be seen, the distinctions are not at all clear, and both activity and ecotourism have characteristics that overlap with those of the adventure sector. On a practical level this may provide problems when attempting to market a product which specifically sits in the adventure tourism arena. This analysis therefore aims to present adventure tourism as a discrete product with clearly distinguishable characteristics that can be marketed to existing and potential consumers.

Distinguishing the three tourism types

It is apparent that there are more similarities than differences between adventure, activity and ecotourism. A structured analysis is achieved by looking at the elements common to all three in order to eliminate similarities and identify the significant unique elements offered by adventure.

PHYSICAL ACTIVITY. Activity tourism, as the title suggests, involves participation in some recreational form. Ecotourists, likewise, often must access their ultimate destination on foot, and participate in treks and climbs. And adventure tourists' perceptions of adventure usually arise from participation in some form of physical activity. In fact, activity tourism often provides the building blocks, for example technique, experience and fitness, required for future participation in adventure tourism. The different products cannot, therefore, be distinguished by reference to activity types or levels.

ENVIRONMENTAL SETTING. A major component of adventure tourism is that it takes place in a natural environment, often remote, and sometimes of a wilderness nature. With its focus on the (often-endangered) natural environment, ecotourists too, require rurality to pursue their goals. And in rural settings, most activities require something of their natural environment to contribute to the overall experience. Moreover, each of these groups is required to adhere to environmental guidelines thus making environmental setting a common rather than distinguishing characteristic.

CULTURAL EXPERIENCE. In its broadest sense, this, too, may contribute to both adventure tourism and to an ecotourism holiday. The cultural experience may result from interaction with host communities and environments or from intra-group interaction. Intra-group interaction is important in activity tourism. Cultural experience therefore does not allow us to identify the core of the adventure tourism product.

FOCUS. Perhaps it is the focus of the adventure tourism experience that distinguishes it from others? Clearly an interest in the natural environment as the focus of an ecotourism trip is an easily understood concept; likewise activity as the focus of activity breaks. But is not adventure *through activity* the focus of an adventure tourism holiday? And must not the adventure tourist take a sufficient interest in the environment not to affect it adversely? Confusion therefore remains.

RISK. May the perception of risk be a factor that sets adventure tourism apart from other forms? It is widely accepted that risk is an integral part of defining adventure, and there are those who seek out adventurous activities because of the associated risk. Quite often, the higher the risk, the greater the appeal of the activity. Why else would people participate in whitewater rafting rather than flatwater canoeing on a calm lake? Various authors (Priest, 1992; Fluker and Turner, 2000) focus on this aspect as being the sole differentiator for adventure tourism. However, there are elements of activity tourism that have risk as a major focus, for example whitewater rafting on an artificial course.

The above characteristics, although part of the product, do not help us to identify what sets adventure tourism apart from other similar activities. By focusing on the relationships between *adventure* and activity, environment and risk, we fail to recognize the element of *tourism* involved, and tourism, by definition, involves a journey.

A JOURNEY OF THE MIND. In fact, the main factor distinguishing adventure tourism from all other forms is the planning and preparation involved. While something of this characteristic may be present in all forms of travel and tourism, it is essential in the adventure tourism setting. The 'journey of the mind' (*The Times*, 2000) refers not to the administrative planning required of all trips but to that part of planning and preparation which allows for dreaming of the passion, excitement and fear that might be experienced, and the risks that may be encountered, much of this framed by accounts of journeys of past explorers. Essentially, each person's mind journey is unique; importantly, it is a strong enough element to characterize the product. This is well illustrated in the following example.

Everest in your sleep

Kieron MacKenzie, director of New Heights Adventure Travel, recently returned from a trip to climb Everest's north ridge, yet it was not the first time that he had been there. Granted, it was the first time for his body but in his mind he had been there many times before. The dream of many mountaineers is to

Continued overleaf

stand on the summit of the world's tallest mountain. The many books that have been written by past explorers, such as Hunt, Hillary, Boardman, Tasker and Bonnington further fuel this dream.

A few months before Kieron was due to head out to Kathmandu, I asked him how his preparation was going. He pulled out a big book full of photographs of Everest. He showed me the route that he would be taking and explained in graphic detail what he would expect at each stage. I asked whether he was nervous in any way and whether it was affecting his sleep. He said he was not nervous but excited, and that even in his sleep he was visualizing himself summitting the mountain. Up until that point he had summitted Everest numerous times, though he did have a slight concern in that on the previous night's summit bid he had arrived to find it covered not in snow and ice but green grass and heather. Global warming has a lot to answer for!

Figure 7.3 illustrates the characteristics of activity, eco- and adventure tourism, and highlights the unique offerings of each. Figure 7.4 shows how an adventure tourism business will operate most effectively where products offered have a low actual risk but a high perceived one (in the dotted zone); for example summer whitewater rafting on the river Tay in Scotland. In contrast, some adventure tourism companies offer products in the high-risk category (such as Everest expeditions) but such trips demand a high premium. Much adventure tourism takes place in between these two with activities and in terrains that offer varying degrees of actual risk, and careful management is required to ensure adequate safety measures are taken. The model in Fig. 7.4 is adapted from Christiansen (1990) and illustrates the relationship between perceived risk and actual risk.

A successful trip may be put down to good planning, or the absence of bad luck. Planning for client safety must be one of the business's primary objectives. Even where this is the case, accidents will occur.

The Interlaken Gorge walking tragedy

On 27 July 1999 21 people died while taking part in a gorge walking activity in the Interlaken area of Switzerland. There was a great deal of media interest and much speculation about what happened and where the fault lay. An unfortunate aspect of adventure activities is that, in the event of an accident, there is high media interest, seeking sensationalism and somewhere to lay blame.

In the case of Interlaken there was no culprit to whom blame could be apportioned. What happened was tragic and unforeseen. Some time before the trip, an ice bridge farther up the valley had collapsed, damming the river and creating a massive head of water that had been increased by more recent heavy rainfall. Occurring in an uninhabited area, this had gone unnoticed. Tragically, the dam broke when there were people in the gorge. Had it done so earlier or later in the day, there may have been no fatalities and casualties.

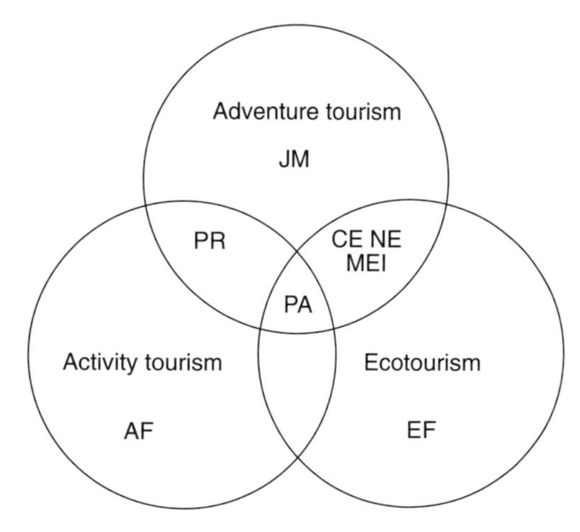

Fig. 7.3. Characteristics of activity, eco- and adventure tourism. PR, perceived risk; PA, physical activity; JM, journey of the mind; NE, natural element; CE, cultural experience; MEI, Minimum environmental impact; AF, activity as the focus; EF, eco-activities as the focus.

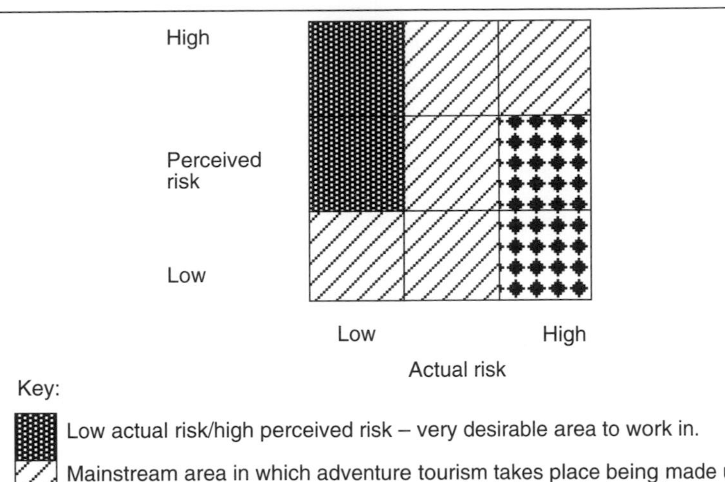

Key:

Low actual risk/high perceived risk – very desirable area to work in.

Mainstream area in which adventure tourism takes place being made up of areas of low perceived (soft adventure) and high actual risk (in need of careful management) as well as average amounts of each respectively.

High actual risk but low perceived risk – an unattractive area in which to operate.

Fig. 7.4. The relationship between perceived and actual risk (after Christiansen, 1990).

Accidents happen; the only way to stop them happening in adventure tourism is to desist from undertaking adventurous activities. Given the nature of demand for them, however, this is unlikely to happen. What operators must do is ensure that safety procedures are as effective as possible and currently acceptable at a national level for that or a similar activity. Professional operations management in adventure tourism involves making participants aware of:

- personal levels of competence required to undertake adventures safely;
- risks they are taking; and
- their part in avoiding hazards they may encounter.

Where risk forms part of the product's attractions, it may be used as a marketing tool. As more and more businesses are established, rather than lower their visibility, there is a need to make safety procedures more visible to clients. Reference to national guidelines and good practice often make good selling points. Those operators who use safety issues as a marketing device may, in time, govern the rules of supply. Demand may dictate safety but supply has to ensure it. In highly competitive business environments, where competitive edge is sought, this is likely to be the case, but problems may remain in those areas where competition is low and where good practice may not be in operation or overly visible.

Being aware of the risks does not mean that clients have less of an expectation of operators to manage them on their behalf. What assurance do they have that this is actually the case? In the UK there is a mandatory licensing scheme in place for adventurous activities entitled the 'Adventurous Activities Licensing Bill'. This, however, applies only to children under the age of 18 and currently covers certain activities only (watersports, caving, climbing, trekking). Thus it legislates only for a small part of the adventure tourism market.

Seasonality

Seasonality has a major influence on the provision of adventure tourism and careful planning is required to match the adventure with appropriate climatic conditions in order to optimize the experience for clients, within the bounds of safety. Not all adventures require extreme conditions, however, and mild conditions need not be a deterrent to offering adventure tourism packages. The use of themes for adventures (such as 'in the footsteps of Hannibal') means that they can be planned and marketed as experiences of hardship and toil irrespective of season.

Continued overleaf

Marketing

Marketing an adventure tourism package poses a number of problems, not least of which is defining the product. An understanding that adventure tourism is a blend of factors differentiated by the 'journey of the mind', allows an operator to define a product clearly and position it to meet the needs of a target market, however these are recognized. Fluker and Turner (2000), for example, identify the need to differentiate marketing between first time whitewater rafters and repeat whitewater rafters, suggesting that risk motivates first timers more than experienced customers who focus more on the social aspects of the experience.

For a European tourism generating market the thought of adventure 'in your own back yard' may be a hard product to sell. Activity tourism in Europe is understood but adventure tourism is perceived as being a Middle and Far-Eastern phenomenon. Yet there are opportunities for adventure tourism within Europe, and remote areas do exist, for example in the Slovenian Alps and northern Norway. With a focus on characteristics other than the geographical in adventure, it may still be possible to create desire for the adventurous journey. For example, routes that have historical significance, such as Hannibal's journey across the Alps or the Vikings' North Sea crossings create images for clients that denote the start of their 'journeys of the mind'. That such activities will be physical and cultural and have an element of risk is undeniable; the main focus, however, remains 'the journey'.

In conclusion we can say that 'pure' adventure tourism is a niche tourism product that can be distinguished from others by its nature as 'a journey of the mind'. The quality of the adventure experience is a combination of different factors including:

- a package that allows a client to start the journey well before they actually go, and has the perception of participating in the planning, preparation and possibly even design;
- the perceived risk involved;
- a niche product that focuses on like-minded individuals seeking adventure;
- product enhancers such as good food, unusual accommodation, good guides, etc.;
- unplanned enhancers: the sighting of a rare animal or natural phenomenon; and
- visual safety procedures.

David Grant

David Grant provides a good analysis of the adventure tourism product that clearly identifies characteristics that can be built on by rural tourism businesses. Certainly, his account of the 'pure' product places adventure in remote parts of the world that, largely, lie outside of Europe, in regions such as Nepal, Bhutan and China, for example. There are, however, a number of issues raised that illustrate ways in which the European operator may capitalize on this growing[1] sector in the development of new products and services.

The world's remote regions are few and becoming fewer. As wild places lose that which essentially sets them apart from the mapped and the familiar, then 'true adventure' in the sense of pioneering and exploration – loses some of its meaning, or rather results in changes to meanings of adventure that rural operators may be able to use to their advantage. Europe clearly has its own remote regions, centrally as well as at the northern and eastern fringes of the continent. It must be reasonably safe to assume that adventure may be experienced in European locations that offer considerable challenge and that may be perceived to be no less remote than many long-haul destinations with their improved means of access.

Unsurprisingly, adventure tourism is on offer across Europe (although perhaps not of the 'pure' variety, offering journeys of the mind only to varying degrees). In Iceland, adventurers are offered river-rafting, snowmobiling and trekking, snowscape safaris and whale watching trips. They can even join the annual livestock round-up; 'serious horseback adventures' not merely being the preserve of the Americans. Tourists can explore the remoteness of Greenland with a pack of huskies, go polar kayaking in Norway at Europe's most northerly point, or snowshoe through the Pyrenees. Farther south, in Bulgaria, if backpacking through the Rhodopi Mountains does not appeal then whitewater rafting in spring melt on the Mesta River may. And the Carpathian Mountains, with their largely unexplored spaces, offer wilderness, remoteness, scarce wildlife, and challenge to be revealed throughout a journey.

It is likely that adventures further afield, experienced as events planned in the long term and priced at a premium, are relatively rare events in people's lives. Whetted appetites for adventure may be satisfied by challenging activities closer to home and thus more easily accessible in terms of disposable time and income. Where remoteness is a problem, therefore, in England, for example, adventure may be provided by activities such as off-road driving, hot air ballooning or seaplane flights. In such instances, adventure is defined by a focus on the product itself rather than by the environment in which it takes place. The idea of the 'journey', however, becomes a little blurred. Additionally, this raises the question of people's capacity for adventure; just how much of it can one consume before the experience negates itself? Research by Fluker and Turner (2000) identified differences in expectation between first time whitewater rafters and those with experience. This suggests that previous experience lessens adventure's impact, perhaps through the process of learning, and the consequently reduced need for imaginative planning that constitutes the journey of the mind.

If this is the case then the overlap between adventure tourism and activity tourism may be a fortunate one. Grant identifies that activities often provide the experiences, competencies and levels of physical fitness required of adventure tourism trips and this may provide activity tourism businesses with a niche in which to operate, in conjunction with adventure tourism providers. Acorn Activities, the UK's leading activity holiday company claims a 50% increase in holiday activities over recent years with growing demand for diverse and exciting recreational opportunities. Such demand may be able to be channelled into purposeful rather than random experiential activity. Crossing the boundaries of adventure and activity tourism therefore represents market opportunities for businesses that wish to design their activities either as adventures or as preparatory skill-building activities (see Plate 7.6).

Because of the difficulties in identifying adventure for different participants, products may offer adventure labelled in a number of ways. Some challenge, both physically and mentally. Some offer opportunities for spectacular sights of rare species or natural phenomena. Others are based on unusual destinations and landscapes, still little known. Some combine softer adventure with a cultural experience, while others simply aim to thrill. 'Soft' adventure (easy trekking, rafting or kayaking) and 'hard' adventure (challenging activities in hostile terrain) may cater for different modes of consumption in attempts to match products with their appropriate markets. Table 7.5 illustrates the ways in which an adventure tourism operator might position a core product.

Activity Tourism

This term is yet another that describes widespread forms of tourism with varying meanings for different people, rendering precise definition difficult. Most literature and market analyses apply the label activity holiday to tourism and recreation involving some kind of sport or physical activity, and special interest holidays to theme or hobby holidays that exclude physical activity. For both markets,

Plate 7.6. Recreational kayaking trips build the skills required for more demanding adventure tourism.

Table 7.5. Adventure tourism marketing.

Generic product	Adventure tourism
Specific product	Dog sledding in Greenland
Market(s)	Fit, 'wintered' tourists, thoroughly prepared via pre-planning
Consumption mode	Consumption as experience, integration, classification
Product customization	Involvement in expedition planning. The availability of experienced guides, good interpretive material to enhance the journey, flexible itineraries
Marketing focus	Remoteness Challenge Communing with local people Nature watching

the importance to the rural context arises from increases in the range of leisure activities available to groups and individuals, and the use of the countryside as a recreational resource. The previous section identified activity tourism's core characteristic as a focus on a chosen activity; the potential for challenge and skill development, and the qualities of the natural environment have the potential to contribute to the experience.

The word 'activity' may be used to refer to a range of special interest holidays and recreational activities:

- physical activity: active pastimes, usually outdoor such as walking, cycling, climbing, watersports, pony trekking;
- hobbies and practical interests such as photography, painting, crafts, cookery;
- nature tourism: wildlife watching, ecotourism (including conservation activities), garden tours; and
- cultural and intellectual pursuits such as archaeology, architecture, language learning, religious themes.

Ecotourism and cultural tourism have been analysed as discrete products rather than as part of the activity and special interest tourism markets. Only the first two categories, therefore, are further considered in this section.

In 1997, the UK activity holiday market was estimated to be worth £2 billion with forecasts for growth to £2.5 billion by 2002. In the domestic sector, activity holidays are estimated to make up 17% of the market, and in the overseas sector, 14.3% (Henley Centre, 1997). Research conducted by Mintel into 1998 markets shows that 14 million activity holidays were booked in the UK, of which 11 million were domestic trips. This represents a growth of 10% since 1994. A modest increase in this growth to 11% is forecast for 2003 (Mintel, 1999).

Research suggests that at least 20% of Europeans are looking for more active, health-orientated holidays and would like to find some kind of health and fitness facilities integrated into their holiday resorts or even to take their holidays in a dedicated health resort (Cockerell, 1999). In much of Western Europe, a general lifestyle trend towards decreased participation in physically active pastimes is evident as the demands of family and work dominate. Forty-three per cent of UK adults take no sport or exercise in an average week. The trend to lower participation is most marked in men from social classes ABC1, older parent families and families with young children suggesting further that people cut back on commitments outside the home in order to support family life. Nevertheless, 20% of UK women aged 25–34 believe that physical activity is an important lifestyle factor, a higher percentage than for any other female age group. This is attributed to an increased desire to maintain a healthy lifestyle before and after childbirth. All of this points to a latent demand for activity tourism holidays that may be converted by the right products. The evidence suggests that these figures are relevant for a number of Western European countries.

Special interest holidays are described as a holiday for the minority (Mintel, 1998); at 8% of all holidays taken by the British, sales are only half the level of those for activity and sporting holidays. Special interest holidays are largely a domestic phenomenon; 16% of long holidays (four or more nights away from home) and 24% of short breaks in 1998 were based around a particular theme or interest. There is no conclusive evidence of market growth. That which is anticipated is expected to come from demographic changes that will see increases in 'empty-nesters' and early retireds, key purchasers of such products (Mintel, 1998).

The strength of activity and special interest tourism markets is their versatility; new activities, new routes and itineraries, and variations on a theme are all good for repeat business, building customer loyalty and the establishment of long-term relationships with visitors. In order to illustrate activity and special interest holidays (and to show how they may be combined), two products have been further analysed, one to represent each.

Invited Viewpoint

Cycling Tourism

Les Lumsdon

Recreational cycling or cycle tourism has caught the imagination of recreation and rural planners because, in theory, it offers a healthy, inclusive and sustainable form of activity, which also brings visitor spending to rural economies. There are associated social and environmental impacts, but an evaluation of the research suggests that these are minimal (Woods, 2000).

Definitions

Cycle tourism, which encompasses the activity of recreational cycling, can be defined as: 'recreational visits, either overnight or day visits away from home, which involve leisure cycling as a fundamental and significant part of the visit' (Sustrans, 1999: 1). The cycle tourism offering is essentially intangible and brings benefits such as 'having fun' or viewing 'beautiful countryside'; it involves a wide range of service and societal elements.

Cycle routes take three forms: linear trails, circuits and networks. They use mainly existing assets, many of which are capable of re-use with modest investment. These include quiet back roads, forestry tracks, canal towpaths, disused railways and greenways. Some are developed entirely on highways and others involve partly, or totally segregated infrastructure. Off-road mountain biking is primarily site-based, with circular routes radiating from a visitor centre, café and cycle hire facility.

The level and mix of use on any route or network depends on location, design standards, the level of tourism appeal, and access from nearby populations. This work focuses on casual and touring cyclists rather than opportunities for mountain bike facilities.

Market volume and trends

Two core market indicators illustrate the potential of cycle tourism:

1. Ownership of bicycles. There are now approximately 200 million bicycles in use in the EU (European Commission DGVII E-1, 1997) and the trend in increased cycle ownership has been a sustained one in the past two decades.
2. Use of cycles for recreation. Recreational cycling is increasing. Adult participation in recreational cycling in the UK is 11% – up from 8% in the previous survey (Office for National Statistics, 1996). A

Continued overleaf

survey undertaken in Scotland indicated that 55% of adults mentioned leisure as one of the main reasons for cycling (Scottish Natural Heritage, 1998, personal communication). There are several other trends in favour of cycle tourism, such as the move to less packaged holidays (Brady, Shipman, Martin, 1993), and towards activities. In Germany, for example, healthy living is a key motivating factor for recreational cycling. Thus, one survey revealed that 52.7% of the German market indicated a desire to cycle while on holiday (Datzer, 1998). The major deterrent to cycling, however, is fear of traffic (Snelson *et al.*, 1993).

The best current estimate of market size and value of cycle tourism in the UK is 16,683,000 trips, which yield £285 million in visitor spending. This excludes local recreational trips of less than 3 hours in duration, which are estimated to add approximately 102,500 million additional trips, and visitor spending of £350 million (Sustrans, 1999). This represents a sizeable market.

Case study: C2C route

One well-documented route is the C2C (Sea to Sea) route, situated in the north of England, which crosses the 'roof' of England, the Pennine hills. It forms part of the National Cycle Network that will offer a 12,800-km network by the year 2005. The C2C route was opened and promoted in 1995, the year in which it won the British Airways Tourism for Tomorrow Award and hence generated extensive media coverage. The pattern of demand was high in the first season, then declined slightly in the second year but has since stabilized at approximately 10–11,000 entire route cycle trips per year. Visitor spending amounts to £1.1 million per annum (Cope, 2000).

Cope and Doxford (1998) undertook an initial study in 1996 and repeated the exercise for a full summer season in 1997. Data collected in 1997 highlight a much wider age spread than in the previous year. An increasing number of older cyclists used the route although the gender balance was 73% male and 27% female in both years. In 1997, the average duration of trip extended to 3.4 days. The route continues to attract a larger proportion of casual cyclists than lifestyle/dedicated cyclists.

A study by Brown (1997) investigated the perceptions of managers and proprietors of 72 bed and breakfast and hotel providers, five camp site managers, 15 visitor attractions and 15 cycle shops offering visitor facilities on or near to the route. It concluded that there is a high level of business confidence, which is attributable to the C2C route. In particular, there has been a significant increase in interest from small enterprises, especially accommodation providers, in the central, very rural section of the route.

Opportunities for enterprises

The main market for cycle tourism in the UK will be the 'near to home' day visitor. This segment will bring additional revenue to the hospitality sector but there are also opportunities for cycle hire, repair and support services situated on or near the route.

For rural areas, situated some distance from urban areas, the key market segment is short break cycle tourism. This involves visitors either taking a day ride from holiday accommodation or cycling for 2–3 days. There is a need for light packaging, or the opportunity to purchase individual components: cycle hire and repair, luggage transfer, information packs and maps, plus accommodation where the needs of cyclists are met.

A second market segment is the holiday cyclist, riding a section of the National Cycle Network or similar routes. While smaller in number, this segment is likely to seek a wide range of visitor services. The segment can be sub-divided into independent and package users. With regard to the latter, there are real opportunities for small tour operators who are able to network with agents to develop overseas markets.

Most commentators suggest that recreational cycling is set to grow in the first decade of the 21st century. However, in order to satisfy the market, there will be a need to improve the cycle tourism offering in the UK if it is to compete effectively with destinations such as Denmark, parts of France and the Netherlands, Germany, Switzerland and upper Austria.

Les Lumsdon

Les Lumsdon identifies a number of experiences sought by recreational cyclists:

- having fun;
- viewing beautiful countryside;
- a desire for independent travel with support services (safe adventure); and
- development of a healthy lifestyle.

Recognition of these needs and the nature of demand permits a continued focus on the product and the number of ways in which it is consumed. Clearly there are different markets. Some off-road participants seek adventure in difficult terrain. Others may be cycling in order to take physical exercise for purposes of health and fitness, while others may wish to tour, perhaps seeking a cultural experience but with the freedom provided by independent travel (see Plate 7.7).

The web pages of 'Go Europe', an on-line travel site, provide information for those contemplating activity holidays, including cycling trips. Questions it recommends tourists ask themselves provide some insight for providers and potential providers of cycling products and services. These are outlined in Box 7.7.

As with cultural tourism products, perhaps the richest experiences are provided by composite products that blend activity with culture as illustrated by the following example:

Plate 7.7. Cycle touring in Belgium.

> 'Saddle up to sip your way through Bordeaux' – an 8-day cycling holiday in the largest wine-producing region in the world's leading wine producing nation, France. With cycling as the mode of transport, it is possible to explore the region's less well-trodden paths, 'along picturesque riverbanks, within fields of poppies, between fruit orchards, woods and pasture and even, in the case of Margaux, on an island.' Visits to wineries and regular tastings promise to add interest to the tours! Local gastronomy too provides an additional cultural element to the trip. With only two to four hours in the saddle each day and a route of 20 to 40 miles, the holiday is not a strenuous one. It is a fully supported, guided tour, combining the cultural experience of food and drink with leisurely, independent outdoor travel, and is a holiday for those seeking to learn about and enjoy good foods and wines and their nurturing environment and culture.
>
> (www.unmissable.com)

Box 7.7. Insights into provision for cyclists (source: Go Europe (http://goeurope.about.com/travel/goeurope/library)).

'Do I want an all-inclusive package?' Accommodation providers able to provide additional accommodation and services for cyclists, outdoor clothing, packed meals, etc. may contact tour operators rather than try to market directly to customers. In order to promote customer loyalty and generate repeat business, tour operators constantly seek new regional destinations, new routes within popular destinations, and new types of accommodation on popular routes.

'Do I want to travel with a group or on my own?' Those who do not wish to travel as part of an organized group may require self-guided packages. Information will be required on routes, terrain and distances, accommodation, places to eat and drink, sites of interest en route, local customs, traditions, stories and myths.

'Do I need a bike?' Bicycle hire is common and it might be possible to provide special facilities for families (if there is demand) by hiring out child seats, trailers and trailer bikes.

'What are my bicycling interests and skills?' Routes that offer little challenge are likely to bore the experienced cyclist while arduous climbs and remote terrain may be unsuitable for beginners or leisure cyclists. Regional cycle travel guides that can be bought in advance of trips provide both useful information and an effective marketing tool. Additionally they may include information on the region's attractions, hospitality and services, costs of production being offset by the inclusion of advertising.

Lumsdon identifies opportunities for businesses in cycle hire. Table 7.6 provides an overview of the way in which such a marketing opportunity may be developed.

Painting holidays

Holidays and leisure time provide people with opportunities to pursue hobbies and interests for which too little time may be available in everyday life (Plate 7.8). The provision of instruction and tuition, moreover, permits skill development in, for example, painting, drawing or photography. A growing number of businesses focus on such special interest markets as illustrated by the example in Box 7.8.

It is not uncommon for larger providers of such special interest holidays to offer a range of products such as painting holidays, writing holidays and cultural tours. In the heart of Alpi Apuane in Tuscany, Il Collegio Artists and Writers Retreat runs painting holidays that include visits to local art galleries for art appreciation sessions and to beauty spots for sketching and painting workshops. It offers creative writing holidays and even a gastronomic tour entitled 'A taste of Tuscany'.

Table 7.6. Activity tourism marketing.

Generic product	Activity tourism
Specific product	Cycle hire
Market(s)	Cycle hire that is not pre-booked is likely to be for a casual cycling market, e.g. couples, family groups and social groups for half or one-day hire
Consumption mode	Consumption as experience; good health, fun as play: families spending time together as integration: exploring an area
Product customization	The provision of sturdy, off-road cycles, children's cycles, the availability of child trailers, guided tours, self-guided trails, cycle delivery to accommodation, general tourist information provision
Marketing focus	Cycle treasure hunts, bark rubbing trails, hill climbs to viewpoints, life cycle health trails

Box 7.8. Paintfrance.com (source: David and Sally McEwen, personal communication, October 2000).

David and Sally McEwen moved from England to Lodève in the South of France in 1997 in order to set up their holiday business as a way of achieving a blend of career and lifestyle objectives. As a painter and former art teacher, David saw an opportunity to apply his skills in a setting that would lend itself to the creation of a personalized holiday experience. Painting courses can be tailor-made to suit the needs of the client and include tuition in techniques and approaches to painting and drawing. Visitors live 'en famille' with David and Sally. Food is prepared from fresh, local produce, further enhancing the quality of the holiday experience.

That visitors are on holiday while with David and Sally is an important element of their marketing. The needs of accompanying partners and families can be catered for, and the website provides information on local activities and places to visit. A wide range of links to other websites of interest, and not just in relation to a stay in France, suggests that David and Sally know their market well.

They view their product as a special interest holiday rather than as a cultural pursuit and differentiate it from those of other providers by the personal contact it involves. Guests live with David and Sally, sharing their dining room at home and eating with them in local restaurants. And David works alongside his guests rather than merely demonstrating to them in a purely tutorial role.

Already, about one-quarter of their clients represent repeat business, and word of mouth is an important source of business. Apart from the website, advertisements are placed in artists' magazines. In part, David and Sally attribute their early success to the fact that their business is part of a number of other local tourist attractions so that their clients will visit other nearby locations as part of a longer holiday.

Plate 7.8. The countryside as a subject.

The earlier section on cultural tourism identified that culture is often more important as a secondary motive for tourism than a primary one, the majority of cultural tourists being part of a general market that participates temporarily in a cultural pursuit. While a special interest has the potential to create a 'cultural tourist' it may be wise to follow the example of David and Sally McEwen (Box 7.8) and market such special interest holidays as part of a wider experiential trip. Table 7.7 provides a marketing analysis for a cultural tourism product.

From the examples in this chapter, it would appear that the scope of tourism and recreation products in rural areas is extremely broad, their nature varying according to:

- the natural and cultural resources available;
- geographical location;
- the nature of existing products and services (whether viewed as competitive or complementary);
- the skills of local people;
- local entrepreneurship; and
- regional competitive advantage.

As part of a major policy response to the need for diversification within Europe's rural regions, the EU has developed a number of mechanisms that support restructuring and change. For the past 10 years, tourism has been identified as having an important role to play in these processes. Through the LEADER initiative, one of its most significant rural development strategies, the EU identified a number of problems with the supply of rural tourism products across Europe (AEIDL, 1994b: 21):

- There is a shortage of rural tourism products.
- The range of products on offer is limited, particularly in southern Europe.
- Structured supply is rare, resulting in incoherence in the sector and difficulties in identifying, branding and marketing coherent experiences of geographical regions.
- Its seasonal nature reduces rural tourism's attractiveness as an investment opportunity.
- Rural tourism is a low valued-added product. In France, where the consumption of tourism in rural areas represents 25% of domestic tourists, the revenue derived from it equals only 10% of total receipts.

Table 7.7. Special interest tourism marketing.

Generic product	Special interest tourism
Specific product	Stained glass making course
Market(s)	Those interested in craft working Interior design and DIY fans
Consumption mode	All categories. 'Play' may be significant due to the importance placed on meeting fellow craftspeople
Product customization	Tuition at different skill levels, raw materials availability, imaginative tours to demonstrate design principles, competitions, accommodation, visiting speakers, extension of the craft/design interest to other contexts, e.g. printing, fabric design
Marketing focus	Learn and maintain a traditional craft Make your own door panels 'Stories in stained glass' tour Visits to other craft workers' studios

These observations reflect a number of assumptions about 'rural tourism', namely that it is:

- identifiable as an industry (or as a number of related industries);
- still in the early stages of development, with underdeveloped structures, systems and networks; and
- reliant on strategic coordination and collaborative working to realize the full benefits of tourism development.

In its recognition of the need for a product strategy, AEIDL identified a market trend towards demand for customized holidays, different from mass tourism products in the way that they provide opportunities for tourists to explore and experience the cultural environments they visit. As a result, it recommended that products developed:

- can accommodate independent tourists/visitors;
- provide an authenticity not possible in the mass industry; and
- constitute holidays with 'content', intellectual discovery and contact with local people.

(AEIDL, 1994b: 22)

The increasing diversity of markets is of paramount importance. 'The system of market segmentation aimed at targeting well-defined client categories in relation to specialized, structured products of the package type is less able to meet the new customer characteristics' (AEIDL, 1994b: 31).

LEADER tourism products have been divided into two categories:

- 'Supple' products: customized products that can be created to meet the individual needs of different tourists or tourist groups. Such supply matches demand for freedom from organization rather than a desire or willingness to follow pre-determined itineraries and schedules. Many of the trails described in this chapter fall into this category.
- 'Theme' products: intended for groups that seek planned and prepared experiences created around a cultural topic or attraction, and that are more structured, thus corresponding to the needs of tour operators rather than individual tourists (AEIDL, 1994b: 26).

Some early LEADER products failed to adopt a market-led approach to product development, and product descriptions did not lend themselves to effective marketing. It is important, therefore, that products developed should:

- provide a new type of satisfaction or experience;
- send the appropriate message(s) to consumers with regard to quality or service levels, for example; and
- stand out from those of competitors.

Chapter Summary

The complexity of contemporary tourism markets may be seen as both threat and opportunity. Business planning and stability may be threatened by fickle demand in competitive markets. Conversely, the demand for new and rewarding experiences is an opportunity to attract different forms of consumption. There seems little doubt, however, that better success rates will be achieved by those businesses that understand how their products serve their markets.

Such understanding is complicated by both growth and change in rural tourism markets, and this chapter has identified what may be a significant distinction within many of the product categories analysed. As noted earlier in the chapter, farm tourism, one of rural tourism's 'oldest' forms, has expanded to provide products that may be more usefully described as tourism on farms. There is evidence that tourists buy new and distinctive holidays for reasons other than might reasonably be assumed. Ecotourism holidays, for example, are bought by people with low levels of environmental sensitivity, and markets for them, therefore, are found in the ranks of mainstream tourism. Many cultural tourists, it appears, are not particularly motivated by culture. And the increasing range of rural activities that are available serve to disaggregate the activity tourism market and to blur distinctions between activity and adventure tourism so that the consumption of an experience may satisfy a myriad of needs. Thus traditional forms of rural tourism now appear to be shadowed by contemporary forms of tourism in rural areas. This theme is further developed in the next chapter.

Note

1 Research by Smith and Jenner (1999) identified growth in the sector that is expected to continue in the foreseeable future, underpinned by increasing demand for adventure and 'journeys of the mind'. A cautious calculation of 15% growth in a market with 0.5% penetration across EU member states indicates increased participation by only about 25,000 people. This does not account for participation in other European countries where growth may also be strong.

References

Acott, T.G., La Trobe, H.L. and Howard, S.H. (1998) An evaluation of deep ecotourism and shallow ecotourism. *Journal of Sustainable Tourism* 6(3), 238–253.

AEIDL (1994a) Culture and rural development. *LEADER Magazine* 8. http://www.rural-europe.aeidl.be/rural-en/biblio/culture/art05.htm

AEIDL (1994b) *Marketing Quality Rural Tourism.* LEADER Co-ordinating Unit, Brussels. http://www.rural-europe.aeidl.be/rural-en/biblio/touris/art07.html

Blamey, R.K. (1997) Ecotourism: the search for an operational definition. *Journal of Sustainable Tourism* 5(2), 109–130.

Blamey, R.K. and Braithwaite, V.A. (1997) A social values segmentation of the potential ecotourism market. *Journal of Sustainable Tourism* 5(1), 29–45.

Brady, Shipman and Martin (1993) *Urban Environment: the Problems of Tourism, Final Report.* Commission of the European Community, Directorate General XI Environment, Brussels.

Brown, C. (2000) *Isle of Arran Taste Trail.* Argyll and the Islands Enterprise, Lochgilphead.

Brown, E. (1997) The economic impact of the C2C route. Unpublished undergraduate thesis, University of Sunderland, Sunderland.

Burns, P. and Holden, A. (1995) *Tourism, a New Perspective.* Prentice Hall Europe, Hemel Hempstead.

Busby, G. and Rendle, S. (2000) The transition from farm tourism to tourism on farms. *Tourism Management* 21, 635–642.

Butler, R. and Hall, C.M. (1998) Image and reimaging of rural areas. In: Butler, R., Hall, C.M. and Jenkins, J.M. (eds) *Tourism and Recreation in Rural Areas.* John Wiley & Sons, Chichester, pp. 115–122.

Cater, E. (1994) Introduction. In: Cater, E. and Lowman, G. (eds) *Ecotourism: a Sustainable Option?* John Wiley & Sons, Chichester, pp. 3–17.

Christiansen, D. (1990) Adventure tourism. In: Miles, J.C. and Priest, S. (eds) *Adventure Education.* Venture Publishing, State College, Pennsylvania.

Clarke, J. (1999) Marketing structures for farm tourism: beyond the individual provider of rural tourism. *Journal of Sustainable Tourism* 7(1), 26–47.

Cockerell, N. (1999) Short term trends and key issues in the tourism industry. *Travel and Tourism Analyst* 6, 65–79.

Cope, A. (2000) *Monitoring Cycle Tourism on the C2C Cycle Route during 1999.* University of Sunderland, Sunderland.

Cope, A.M. and Doxford, D. (1998) *Visitor Monitoring of the C2C Cycle Route; Analysis of the Results from 1997.* University of Sunderland, Sunderland.

Datzer, R. (1998) Fahrradtourismus – wirtschaftliche Bedeutung und Perspektiven für die Tourismusentwicklung in Nordrhein-Westfalen. *Proceedings: Workshop Qualitätsoffensive für den Fahrradtourismus in Nordrhein-Westfalen,* ADFC, Marl, Germany, 16 May, ADFC, Brennen, pp. 9–11.

Denman, R. and Denman, J. (1993) *Farm Tourism Market: a Market Study of Farm Tourism in England.* The Tourism Company. Hereford.

Dernoi, L.A. (1983) Farm tourism in Europe. *Tourism Management* 4(3), 155–166.

ECEAT (1999) *Holiday on Organic Farms in Poland, 1999–2000.* ECEAT, Stryszow.

European Commission DGVII E-1 (1997) Bicycle Transport. *European in Transport: monthly information.* Brussels.

Evans, N.J. and Ilbery, B.W. (1989) A conceptual framework for investigating farm-based accommodation and tourism in Britain. *Journal of Rural Studies* 5(3), 257–266.

Fluker, M.R. and Turner, L.W. (2000) Needs, motivations and expectations of a commercial whitewater rafting experience. *Journal of Travel Research* 38, 380–389.

Frater, L.M. (1983) Farm tourism in England: planning, funding, promotion, and some lessons from Europe. *Tourism Management* 4(3), 167–179.

Gladstone, J. and Morris, A. (1998) The role of farm tourism in the regeneration of rural Scotland. In: Hall, D. and O'Hanlon, L. (eds) *Rural Tourism Management: Sustainable Options.* The Scottish Agricultural College, Auchincruive, pp. 207–221.

Glyptis, S. (1992) The changing demand for countryside recreation. In: Bowler, I.R., Bryant, C.R. and Nellis, M.D. (eds) *Contemporary Rural Systems in Transition* Vol. 2, *Economy and Society.* CAB International, Wallingford, pp. 155–165.

Hall, D. and Kinnaird, V. (1994) Ecotourism in Eastern Europe. In: Cater, E. and Lowman, G. (eds) *Ecotourism: a Sustainable Option?* John Wiley & Sons, Chichester, pp. 111–136.

Henley Centre (1997) *Market Assessment: Activity Tourism.* Henley Centre for Forecasting, London.

Herremans, I.M. and Welsh, C. (1999) Developing and implementing a company's ecotourism mission statement. *Journal of Sustainable Tourism* 7(1), 48–76.

Hopkins, J. (1998) Commodifying the countryside: marketing myths of rurality. In: Butler, R., Hall, C.M. and Jenkins, J.M. (eds) *Tourism and Recreation in Rural Areas.* John Wiley & Sons, Chichester, pp. 139–156.

Kayser, B. (1994) Culture, an important tool in rural development. In: Culture and Rural Development. *LEADER Magazine* 8, 1–4. http://rural_europe.aeidl.be/rural-en/biblio/culture/art05.htm

Lane, B. (2000) *Trails and Tourism: the Missing Link. Issues in Partnering with the Tourism Industry: a European Perspective.* http://www.outdoorlink.com/amtrails/resources/economics/tourismUKecon.html

MacCannell, D. (1999) *The Tourist. a New Theory of the Leisure Class.* University of California Press, Los Angeles.

McKercher, B. (1993) Some fundamental truths about tourism: understanding tourism's social and environmental impacts. *Journal of Sustainable Tourism* 1(1), 6–16.

McKercher, B. and Robbins, B. (1998) Business development issues affecting nature-based tourism operators in Australia. *Journal of Sustainable Tourism* 6(2), 173–188.

Ministry of Agriculture (1994) *Agrotourism, Holidays in the Countryside.* Directorate General of Agricultural Extension and Research and Directorate of Rural Extension Home Economics, Athens.

Mintel (1998) *Special Interest Holidays, Special Report.* Mintel International Group Limited, London.

Mintel (1999) *Activity Holidays, Special Report.* Mintel International Group Limited, London.

Morgan H. (2000) A taxing time. *In Focus* 37, 6–7.

Office for National Statistics (1996) *Living in Britain: Results from the 1996 General Household Survey.* The Stationery Office, London.

Opperman, M. (1995) Holidays on the farm; a case study of German hosts and guests. *Journal of Travel Research* 33, 57–61.

Opperman, M. (1996) Rural tourism in southern Germany. *Annals of Tourism Research* 23, 86–102.

Ottman, J. and Terry, V. (1997) *Strategic Marketing of Greener Products.* Green Marketing & Eco-innovation, Ottman Consulting Inc., New York.

Page, S.J. and Getz, D. (eds) (1997) *The Business of Rural Tourism: International Perspectives.* International Thomson Business Press, London.

Peattie, K. and Moutinho, L. (2000) The marketing environment for travel and tourism. In: Moutinho, L. (ed.) *Strategic Management in Tourism.* CAB International, Wallingford, pp. 17–37.

Pine, B.J. and Gilmore J.H. (1998) Welcome to the experience economy. *Harvard Business Review* July–August, 97–105.

Poon, A. (1993) *Tourism, Technology and Competitive Strategies.* CAB International, Wallingford.

Priest, S. (1992) Factor exploration and confirmation for the dimensions of an adventure experience. *Journal of Leisure Research* 24, 127–139.

Probasco, I. and Heimlich, J.E. (2000) Guidelines for the environmentally conscious consumer. Ohio State University, Columbus, Ohio. http://ohioline.ag.ohio-state.edu/cd-fact/0180.html

Richards, G. (1996) *Cultural Tourism in Europe.* CAB International, Wallingford.

Richards, G. (1999) Culture, crafts and tourism: a vital partnership. In: Richards, G. (ed.) *Developing and Marketing Crafts Tourism.* ATLAS, Tilburg, pp. 11–35.

Rilla, E. (2000) *Unique Niches: Agrotourism in Britain and New England.* Small Farm Center, University of California at Davis, Davis, California. http://www.sfc.ucdavis.edu/agritourism/printer.html

Roberts, L.A. (1996) Barriers to the development of rural tourism in the Bran area of Transylvania. In: Robinson, M., Evans, N. and Callaghan, P. (eds) *Tourism and Culture: Image, Identity and Marketing.* Business Education Publishers, Sunderland, pp. 185–196.

Sharpley, R. (2000) The consumption of tourism revisited. In: Robinson, M., Long, P., Evans, N., Sharpley, R. and Swarbrooke, J. (eds) *Reflections on International Tourism: Motivations, Behaviour and Tourist Types.* Business Education Publishers, Sunderland, pp. 381–391.

Sharpley, R. and Sharpley, J. (1997) *Rural Tourism: an Introduction.* International Thomson Business Press, London.

Shores, J.N. (1999) The Challenge of Ecotourism: a Call for Higher Standards. Washington, DC. http://www.txinfinet.com/mader/planeta/0295/0295shores.html

Smith, C. and Jenner, P. (1999) The adventure travel market in Europe. *Travel and Tourism Analyst* 4, 43–64.

Snelson, A., Lawson, S. and Morris, B. (1993) *Cycling Motorists: How to Encourage Them.* Automobile Association, London.

Sustrans (1999) *Cycle Tourism.* Sustrans, Bristol.

Taguchi, K. and Iwai, Y. (1998) Agri-tourism in Austria and its implications for Japanese and rural tourism. In: Hall, D. and O'Hanlon, L. (eds) *Rural Tourism Management: Sustainable Options.* The Scottish Agricultural College, Auchincruive, pp. 527–538.

The Times (2000) Journeys of the mind, where 21st century travellers tread. *The Times* 29 February.

Tzanakaki, K. (1999) Crafts tourism in Crete, Greece. In: Richards, G. (ed.) *Developing and Marketing Crafts Tourism.* ATLAS, Tilburg, pp. 73–87.

Urry, J. (1990) *The Tourist Gaze.* Sage, London.

Urry, J. (1995) *Consuming Places.* Routledge, London.

Wheeller, B. (1993) Sustaining the ego. *Journal of Sustainable Tourism* 1(2), 121–129.

Wheeller, B. (1996) Here we go, here we go, here we go eco. Sustainable Tourism: Proceedings of the Conference, Newton Rigg College, Cumbria, pp. 17–19.

Wight, P. (1994) Environmentally responsible marketing of tourism. In: Cater, E. and Lowman, G. (eds) *Ecotourism: a Sustainable Option?* John Wiley & Sons, Chichester, pp. 39–55.

Woods, M.J. (2000) The National Cycle Network – Ways for wildlife. *Countryside Recreation News* 8(2), 18–20.

8

Where Demand Meets Supply: Markets for Tourism and Recreation in Rural Areas

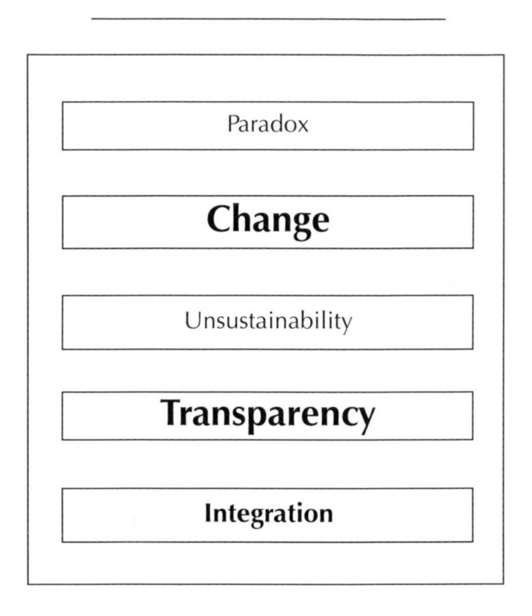

As illustrated in Chapter 1, issues of tourism's development in rural areas attracted an increasing interest in the 1990s, and a growing literature has had much to say about its potential within processes of integrated rural development. This chapter aims to explore some of the ideas that have emerged by analysing them within the broader contexts of:

- tourism consumption generally rather than for 'rural' tourism; and
- market structures and the market conditions within which small rural tourism businesses operate.

In particular, the chapter questions perceptions of 'rural tourism' as niche rather than mainstream tourism, and investigates its role as a vehicle for integrated development.

As with earlier chapters, all of the key themes are reflected in the following pages. The culmination of the book's analysis, and the ideas it generates, however, place a focus on the need for *transparency*. Recognition of tourism in the European countryside as a mass rather than a niche activity requires a different approach to development and conservation. It also requires a new lexicon that removes the disguise created by terms such as eco-, green, soft and niche. *Change* is evident in the move from traditional to contemporary patterns of consumption, old to new kinds of activity, and in the shift from rural tourism to tourism in rural areas. Finally, it is critical for rural development that tourism, as a form of economic development, is *integrated* into rural development through its ability to contribute to the vitality of a region.

The complex nature of the products and markets that constitute tourism industries in rural areas is self-evident, and it is clear that the processes relating to their convergence require further analysis, in particular, the market*ing* of such tourism. In the context of this chapter, the term marketing refers to the 'analytical orientation' (Seaton and Bennett, 1996: 5) that involves understanding and achieving the development and organizational needs of tourism's management. Within 'rural tourism', the subject of marketing is often marginalized, regarded as the task of the individual provider, and often confused with promotion (Clarke, 1999). The potential benefits of successful marketing therefore elude many tourist areas, with social and financial consequences for the families and communities that rely on tourism as a means of diversifying local economies.

The task of understanding marketing is further complicated by fundamental changes in global consumption patterns that have an impact on tourism markets as illustrated in Chapter 6. Twenty-first century consumers present a complex picture of demands that question old assumptions and are difficult to understand and use in operational terms. Of market segment evaluation, Moutinho (2000: 132) says 'Only one overriding trend is clear: that old assumptions are being swept aside. New thinking on the subject is urgently needed.' The pressing need to mobilize and coordinate resources for tourism industries in order to capitalize on the inputs of individual businesses makes Moutinho's comment particularly relevant for rural areas. It is the intention that this chapter should help to provide some new thinking in relation to the development and marketing of tourism products and services in the countryside.

The Nature of Tourism in Rural Areas

In his seminal article on rural tourism, Lane (1994) presented the concept of a rural–urban continuum as a way of understanding issues of rurality where they are complicated by non-rural qualities and characteristics (see Chapter 1). Analysing rural tourism in this way, Lane identifies types of tourism and recreation that are predominantly urban in nature (although they may take place in rural areas), those that are rural (and therefore must take place in the countryside) and those in between (that may be urban or rural in nature and based in either).

The increasing need for analysts to focus on tourism *consumption* as a better explanation of contemporary forms of demand (see Chapter 6) requires a framework within which the analysis can be conducted. One such framework is suggested here as a useful adjunct to Lane's (1994) analysis of the rural–urban nature of activities. A continuum to measure the relative importance of the countryside to the consumption of tourism in rural areas is used to explain something of the motivations of tourists in rural areas.

Lane (1994) identified the characteristics of *rural tourism* in its 'purest form'. He also pointed to the emergence of a large, general-interest market for less specialized forms of rural tourism. This type of tourism will be referred to as *tourism in rural areas*. The importance of the countryside to the tourist may be used to evaluate tourists' motivations for visiting rural areas and to distinguish the two tourism forms (see Table 8.1). A high importance suggests participation in rural tourism. A relatively low importance indicates that the tourist's focus is primarily on participation in an activity and that the nature of the environment is of secondary relevance.

Figure 8.1 shows how the *importance of the countryside* factor may be used to evaluate whether or not a market niche (or market niches) might exist. A relatively low importance indicates participation in general tourism activities in the countryside (kite flying, for example, or a visit to a historic site). A relatively high importance suggests participation in a 'pure' form of rural tourism such as hillwalking.

Research to date indicates that there may still be identifiable market segments and products with which they may be targeted at the 'pure' end of the scale (Greffe, 1994; Clemenson and Lane, 1997; Herries, 1998). Where consumers' focus is placed on a wide range of activities that may satisfy a number of personal needs, it becomes increasingly difficult to identify a product's core value. As a result, the identification of a niche market is much less likely.

Table 8.1. The characteristics of rural tourism and tourism in rural areas (after Lane, 1994).

Rural tourism	Tourism in rural areas
Essentially located in rural areas	Not essentially located in rural areas
Functionally rural, i.e. built on the special features of the countryside	Not functionally rural, i.e. built on the special features of the chosen activity
Rural in scale (i.e. small scale)	Rural in scale (i.e. small scale)
Traditional in character; organic growth, local ownership	Traditional in character; organic growth, local ownership: but possibilities for expansion via alliances/partnerships may alter the locus of control
Varied, representing the complex pattern of the rural environment	Varied, representing the breadth and volatility of demand
High importance of the countryside for consumer satisfaction	Relatively low importance of the countryside for consumer satisfaction

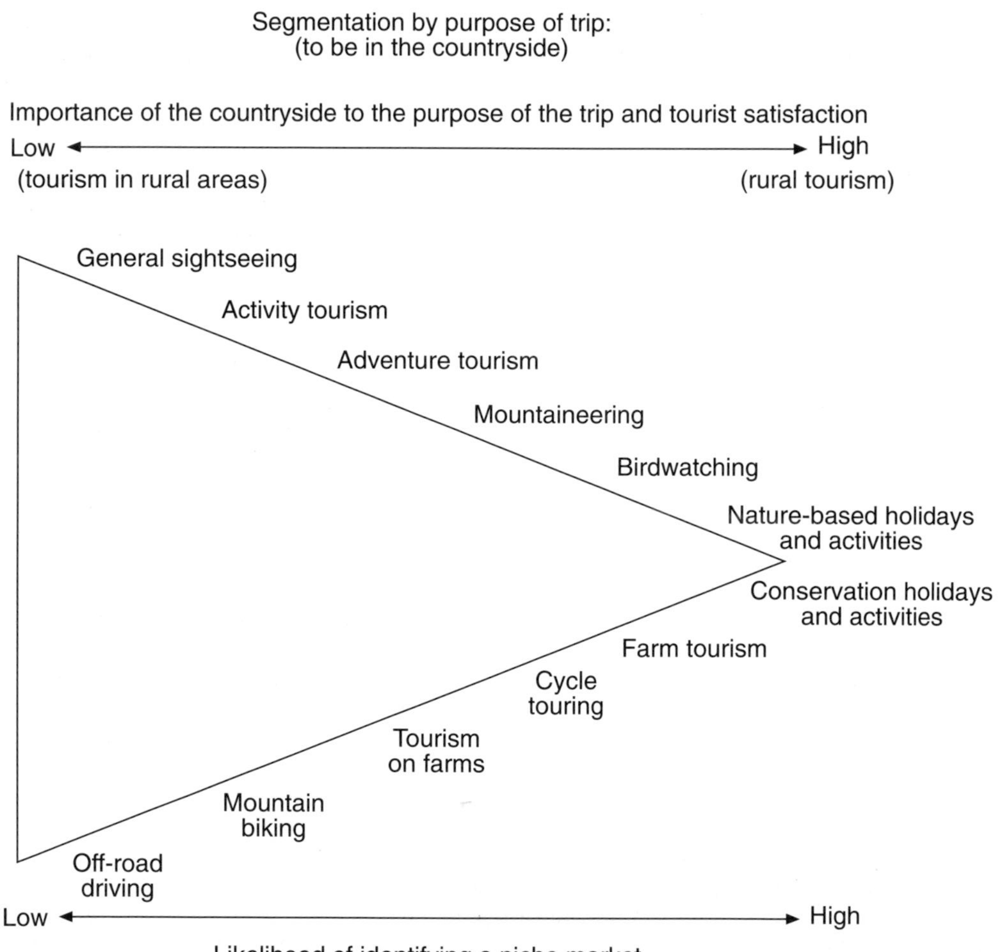

Fig. 8.1. The importance of the countryside to the purpose of visit.

Figure 8.1 also attempts to identify types of activity that fall into the category of rural tourism in its broad sense, and to position them on a continuum indicating the importance of the countryside to the purpose of tourist trip and thereby the extent to which activities may be classed as rural tourism or tourism in rural areas. It is not always possible to draw clear distinctions. However, as Lane's (1994) continuum allows for change over time, this model, too, is capable of accommodating change, according to mode of consumption. For example, it is recognized that cycling may represent the challenge of off-road adventure for one person and a means of sustainable transport to view rural landscapes for another (and, of course, both for the same person on different occasions). This requires cycling as an activity to move along the continuum according to the way in which it is consumed, or indeed to be categorized twice but labelled accordingly.

As with models generally, it is acknowledged that the concept of the importance of the countryside to consumer satisfaction is a simplification, and its application may not be as simple as the link with activity implies. Of tourists in the countryside, Grolleau (1994: 7) has said:

> We should not ... allow ourselves to be deluded; city dwellers are primarily in search of themselves and of a personalized response to their need for emotional and social appreciation. The countryside, nature, and the rural way of life just provide a suitable and reassuring setting giving a sense of security.

While this still implies a primary consumer focus other than on the countryside, the dependency of the experience on a sense of rurality makes it rather more difficult to separate the rural visitor's satisfaction from the vehicle for it. Nevertheless, Grolleau's comment does imply that a 'suitable and reassuring' setting for such tourists might be found in a number of rural spaces. Honeypot sites across Europe have been successful in drawing large numbers of rural visitors to prime managed sites where impacts can be contained and better managed, thus reducing visits to threatened and vulnerable areas.

The narrowing of the scale from left to right Fig. 8.1 indicates the assumption that niche markets in rural tourism are relatively small in number as well as size. Those for tourism in rural areas, stimulated by, among other things, increases in leisure time and private car ownership, are likely to involve larger numbers of visitors. In a sense, therefore, rural tourism is a relatively small sector of the much larger market for tourism in rural areas. Expressed differently, mass tourism is alive and well in the countryside.

Applications of the model

Empirical research is clearly required to test the widespread usefulness of this model, but one of its key strengths is the direction it can give to operational as well as policy and management decision making (see also Chapter 9). At an operational level, the model reflects Sharpley's (2000) assertion that tourism *consumption* should form the basis of an understanding of tourism demand, and it can be seen to be helpful in making sense of theories of niche marketing. Niche markets may be identified as having two key characteristics:

- On the demand side, they are capable of segmenting their consumers into identifiable groups for targeting purposes.
- On the supply side, they are able to differentiate their products and services from those of competitors.

It appears to be a given characteristic of 'rural tourism' that it constitutes a number of niche markets (AEIDL, 1994: 22; Lane 1995a, b; Clemenson and Lane, 1997; Wanhill, 1997; Scottish Executive, 2000: 2). Certainly, rural tourism businesses are small, usually local and regional operations that lie outside the mainstream of the travel industry (McKercher and Robbins, 1998), and this may help to explain the perception of them as niche operations. Indeed, the development and marketing of niche products is recommended in the Scottish Executive's (2000) tourism strategy specifically in relation to rural tourism. The idea of niche markets has considerable appeal. Like other labels that have been applied to types of tourism development such as 'alternative', 'soft', 'green' and 'eco-', the idea of a niche implies small-scale and, by implication, low impact. It thus conveniently avoids association with the problems of mainstream tourism development. But there is a practical appeal too, and where a niche can be found, it has clear operational advantages:

- the cost advantages of targeting a smaller market;
- the scope they offer for premium pricing and above-average profit margins; and
- a starting point for businesses that may subsequently enter a larger market.

(Moutinho, 2000: 130)

By developing and labelling their products within ecotourism, nature tourism or activity tourism markets, rural businesses may perceive themselves to be operating in market niches. In its analysis of rural tourism products, however, Chapter 6 illustrated how a significant element of demand for allegedly 'niche' products has been found among the ranks of mainstream tourists. The question of niche markets, therefore, is a critical one and there is hidden danger in looking at what appears to be a niche product but is, in reality, merely a vulnerable sector in a mass market (Moutinho, 2000: 130). Clarification of a niche's existence may be achieved by answers to three questions, the responses to which must be positive if a niche exists in terms of commercial reality:

1. Is the niche or segment recognized by consumers and distributors or merely a figment of imagination?
2. Is the niche product distinctive and does it appeal to identified groups of consumers?
3. Is the product premium-priced with an above-average profit margin?

(Davidson in Moutinho, 2000: 130)

As illustrated in Chapter 6, the assumptions on which many market segments are based have lost much of their validity as motivations underlying consumption have changed. Inappropriate targeting, therefore, can be a very costly mistake, and careful consideration is required in order to evaluate the process of target marketing against the time and expertise required in order to manage it successfully. Even where a niche can be found, the cost of serving it may prove prohibitive for a small business (Wanhill, 1997).

The characteristics of the ideal niche are that:

- it is of sufficient size to be profitable;
- it offers scope for the provider to be able to demonstrate the distinctiveness of its products and/or services; and
- it shows some stability over time and has the potential for growth.

(Moutinho, 2000: 130)

Businesses might use the importance of the countryside model to establish where on the continuum their product is placed and the likelihood of establishing a niche in which to operate. Where no niche exists, businesses work within undifferentiated or mass markets with opportunities for *mass customization* of products, services and experiences. Mass customization is the term used to refer to a process of swift response to the changing needs of individual customers. Where change is turbulent, long-term growth is dependent on economies of *scope* rather than of *scale*; that is, by offering of a range of products and services to meet individual needs cost-effectively (Moutinho, 2000: 133) rather than by targeting a more limited range to a smaller market.

The rather contradictory notion of mass customization emerged as an alternative to mass production in the world's largest corporations, but its principles are highly relevant to the needs of some of the world's smallest businesses. Stimulated by consumers' changing needs and wants, market saturation levels, and a range of uncertainties outwith businesses' control (Pine, 1993: 54), it represents a way of working that may be familiar to a number of small tourism operations. Customization may occur at a number of points in the 'production' process. For example, a standard farm tour may be offered to school groups, with time allowed afterwards for pupils to ask questions specific to their information needs. This represents customization at the point of delivery. Customization at the design stage, on the other hand, would require the development of a wholly different farm tour and this might be done to meet the information needs of a particular interest group. An alternative approach would be to develop one standard trail and prepare a number of leaflets for self-guiding – in farming methods, the conservation needs of agricultural land and disease prevention, for example – in order that visitors may customize for themselves the standard trail provided.

For rural businesses, whose growth is restricted by human and financial capital, time and resources, customization can be a less profitable option as premium pricing may not always be possible. Conversely, it may offer the responsive and flexible small business a means of demonstrating its operational strengths *vis-à-vis* large, low-cost producers who are often unable to respond to market needs as effectively or efficiently. In this respect, although they may not have niche products or be able to sell to niche markets, many small businesses can exploit an operational niche to their advantage. Economies of scope, however, are not achievable by small businesses working in isolation.

The case study of Reivers of Tarset Ltd, situated in the north of England (Box 8.1), illustrates the distinction between niche and non-niche markets and the customization process in practice. Established just over 25 years ago, the company has diversified from its original form, offering activity holidays for families, to operate in two distinct yet complementary markets: corporate training and corporate hospitality (Plate 8.1). Yet despite this level of specialization, Paul Hodgson, the company's Training and Development Director, does not believe that the markets in which he operates are true niches.

Box 8.1. Reivers of Tarset Ltd (Paul Hodgson, Training and Development Director, personal communcation, November 2000).

The creation of a reservoir is a serious disruption to the local people for whom the flooding of valleys means loss of homes, businesses, communities and landscapes. So it was for Bob Hodgson, the teacher who ran the Kielder Field Studies Centre for Northumberland County Council Schools in England's north country. But as well as the threat of total disruption, the plans to build Kielder reservoir presented an opportunity for Bob and his family, for he and his wife Pat had always wanted to set up their own business.

Reivers of Tarset Ltd was registered in 1976 as a family activity holiday centre, offering hotel accommodation and activities such as river canoeing, climbing, hiking and nature walks. The reservoir, available for recreational use in 1981, extended opportunities for water-based activities as well as providing a new recreational landscape.

In the 1980s, UK Government measures for managing unemployment provided an opportunity for the company to diversify. Youth Training Schemes (YTS) involved a compulsory residential element that included training in personal, social and vocational skills such as team-building and problem-solving, and Reivers was positioned well to be able to serve the demand for outdoor training that emerged as a result.

The training role the company developed has become its core product; the family holidays element of the business was replaced by training activities in the mid-1980s. Since then, Reivers has gradually moved into the corporate market. Using skills first acquired serving early training markets, the company has developed a customized performance management role primarily in the UK corporate market.

Operating as Reivers Development, Bob and his son Paul, Training and Development Director, work in partnership with their clients, developing people at all levels of their organizations. The on-site hotel accommodation is positioned as a dedicated management training and development centre and the company runs residential development courses for clients. The design of courses depends entirely on the clients' needs. Some outdoor activities may be included in a programme by request. Predominantly, however, courses currently run include a significant indoor element, and Reivers has developed a formidable programme of complex cerebral challenges for team building, leadership development, and innovation and change management.

Despite the fact that the services offered are targeted at a clear market segment, Paul does not think that the company operates in a niche market:

> There is a great deal of competition in this market in the UK, and it is quite difficult to differentiate our courses from those provided by others. Fundamentally we believe that we have the ability to deliver a much broader

Continued overleaf

Box 8.1. *Continued*

development programme than our competitors using experiential learning. Among the further competitive advantages of our product , we stress:

- the attractive rural location;
- the on-site residential facilities;
- exclusive use of our training centre by any client.

Many other training and development companies offer the same sort of service as we do but operate out of hotels. We can do so if required, but we can also offer confidentiality in our exclusive facilities where clients can work without fear of distraction or interruption.

As well as its UK operations, Reivers Development operates in two other European countries, Romania and Turkey. Expansion into Europe was one of the company's objectives, and it was achieved, in the first instance, through customer satisfaction. In the Romanian venture, the company was approached by a past delegate who had subsequently established a marketing company in Romania and identified training needs for which he thought Reivers a suitable partner. Initially, in the mid-1990s, Reivers staff conducted the training themselves. Following the establishment of a foothold in the market, they went on to train Romanian trainers. Largely, the company now collects royalties for training conducted under the Reivers badge. The Turkish link was established following a meeting at a training and development conference in London. The approach to the company resulted in the development and delivery of training programmes based on the Romanian model.

In September 2000, under the management of Rory, Paul's brother, Ultraventure began trading. Another wholly owned subsidiary of Reivers of Tarset, Ultraventure makes use of the 24 ha of land owned by the company, and offers a distinctly different, yet complementary product. The demand for corporate entertainment is growing, and Ultraventure has leased and bought a range of equipment from quad bikes to ex-MOD tanks, and offers a wide range of corporate entertainment activities such as four-wheel driving, clay pigeon shooting, paint-balling and hot air ballooning (see Plate 8.1). Although the corporate market is an obvious target, Ultraventure activities are also targeted at social groups such as stag parties.

The facilities also permit the operation of special events such as 'dealer days' when four-wheel drive dealers can advertise new models, display vintage ones, and allow customers the opportunity to test drive vehicles on Ultraventure's four-wheel drive course.

The complementary nature of the two different products means that companies can use Ultraventure's facilities to reward staff for their hard work on a residential training course. And the proximity of the two acts as a form of promotion, clients of each company being made aware of the services of the other.

Self-application of its training and development principles means that Reivers is hardly a company to let the grass grow under its feet. Asked about the future, Paul had plenty of plans: 'We're very busy with our newest developments, and still training new staff, in special events operations for example. But we have considerable plans for the future.' Bob and Pat's retirement and the sons' formal succession creates no breaks in forward planning:

The recent management buy-in has strengthened our management capability considerably. In relation to our training and development operations, we aim to become Europe's premier supplier of training. In the long-term, we expect this to involve the acquisition of other training companies. With Ultraventure we plan to secure other operational sites and work with partners, such as hotel owners, to bring the product to a wider audience.

It has taken 25 years and a great deal of hard work to develop a two-person business into one that now employs over 20 people and is still growing. But this case study of Reivers illustrates ways in which remote rural businesses can operate effectively in large markets, using their rural location to advantage. It provides a practical illustration of process, product and design innovations, and represents a good example of a family-run business that has been able to blend personal and lifestyle objectives with those of a successful business.

Clearly, some rural niches do exist, and recognition of a niche provides an opportunity for an operator to select one or more consumer groups within it, and develop a target strategy. By example, one such niche is recognized within the equine tourism industry. Horses have a number of roles to play in tourism. Horse shows throughout Europe draw large crowds. Equine centres such as Vindheimamelar in Iceland and the Spanish

Plate 8.1. The countryside as an attraction for the corporate sector.

Riding School in Vienna are world famous as equine centres of excellence. Horse riding, whether for trekking or eventing, is an increasingly popular rural activity. As a result of growth in the above markets in the UK, and a resulting diversity of demand, the British Horse Society recognized a need for B&B accommodation to include accommodation for the horse. Their 'Bed and Breakfast for Horses' scheme is outlined in Box 8.2.

A further example serves to illustrate the way in which a niche can be created within a general market. As a Bulgarian tour guide, Pandelia Pandeliev accompanies visiting groups around Bulgaria. Each year his services are sought by the same tour operators because of the way in which he has tailored his programmes to the perceived needs of visitors of different nationality. Box 8.3 contains his account of the requirements of visiting Japanese tourists.

The importance of the countryside model may be seen as the culmination of a number of related issues within the realm of tourism in rural areas relating to:

- traditional vs. contemporary patterns of consumption;
- traditional vs. new types of activity; and
- 'pure' rural tourism and mainstream tourism in rural areas.

From the perspective of the individual provider, however, it may appear to have little relevance. Mass customization is not a

Box 8.2. Bed and Breakfast for Horses (source: British Horse Society, 2000).

The millennium edition of the *Bed and Breakfast for Horses* directory is the seventh, and contains over 400 entries comprising providers of accommodation for horses. For the British Horse Society, the directory provides an enhanced service for members, complementing other publications such as horseback trail guides. For the accommodation providers listed, it is a means of targeting advertising at a niche in the equine tourism market, people travelling with horses.

Customers may be tourists travelling to an area for the purposes of trekking. They may be travelling to an event such as cross-country, dressage or show jumping. Or they may be going to an approved training centre for advanced tuition. The purpose of the trip is not the defining characteristic of this niche. In order to be able to serve it, providers must be able to accommodate visitors' horses. This may be done in a number of ways. Some providers accommodate horses but not people while others lodge both horse and owner. Advertisements variously offer services such as grazing, stabling, hard standing for box trailers, security lighting, and other 'domestic' facilities. Some providers are equine centres and offer tuition and training. Some advertise hacking, cross-country courses, and endurance rides. Many people promote the locality as one of the attractions with suggestions for activities other than equine tourism.

The niche is readily recognizable by its need for a clearly definable product. It is of sufficient size to justify repeat production of a directory of providers. Its relative stability derives from the fact that it contains a number of market segments. A decrease in demand from one may be able to be offset by a marketing focus on another. Operators have flexibility in that their core product, accommodation (whether for horses or people, or both) can be made available to markets other than equine bed and breakfast. Finally, an appropriate marketing programme can be designed to meet the needs of each segment, maximum service flexibility increasing the range of needs that can be met.

Typically, advertising may be placed in specialist publications, with a range of equine centres, vetinerary surgeries, and with tourist boards. But the directory enables accommodation providers to target the niche directly. Its geographical organization of entries permits some degree of regional marketing, and the directory itself encourages a form of 'product loyalty'. Although entry into the directory does not imply recommendation (quality accreditations are listed where appropriate), association with the directory may be a marketing benefit.

Box 8.3. The requirements of Japanese visitors to Bulgaria (Pandelia Pandeliev, personal communication, July 2000).

Tourists from Japan are very attentive and never tire. They can travel from morning until night without complaining. If I say that the sightseeing tour of Sofia is at 9 o'clock, then at 8.55 everyone is in the lobby ready to go. They follow very carefully, with great interest in every gesture of the guide, from a respect for his wisdom. I remember a warm day at Rila Monastery when, before entering the museum, I stopped at one of the water fountains. I washed my face and exclaimed 'Hu, hu!' at the cool and fresh pleasure of the experience. The tour leader asked about my ritual and I replied that washing the face with clean mountainous water and breathing fresh mountain air is good for one's health. When I returned from paying for our entry tickets, the whole group had queued by the water fountain to share my experience. Everybody was washing their faces and exclaiming: 'Hu, hu!'. The Japanese have an interest in matters of health.

The visitor from Japan has great expectations about two things. The first is yogurt. In Japan there are factories for the production of Bulgarian yogurt. As visitors to Bulgaria, Japanese tourists do not only want to taste the original product but also have it contribute to their well-being so they eat it in copious amounts. My duty as a guide is to explain why Bulgarian yogurt is such a quality product. On the one hand, yogurt absorbs unwanted substances produced by digestion, on the other, it kills harmful bacteria. In order to summarize it all I declare that if you eat yogurt and you breathe the fresh air of the Bulgarian mountains you will live to be 100. In the ears of the Japanese, this is like Turkish delight in the mouth!

The second thing our Japanese visitors want to know about is the rose. Every year, on the first Sunday of June, our famous Rose Festival takes place, and thousands of tourists from Japan come to Bulgaria for it. The rose was brought originally from Persia, now in the boundaries of Syria, but here in Bulgaria it found particularly favourable conditions. Rose oil is produced in neighbouring countries, too, but the price of Bulgarian rose oil is higher because of its premium quality.

We have a special tour for Japanese visitors particularly interested in roses. We wake up early in the morning to join the local population picking the flowers. The best time for picking is between 4 and 10 a.m. This is a great deal of fun and many pictures are taken in the fields. Then we go to the Museum of the Rose. Here, visitors are offered fresh rose products for sale such as rose oil, rose perfume, rose water, rose jam, rose cream and rose liqueur. This is the pleasant moment to think about presents for relatives and friends, and our guests buy them in great quantities. The visit to the ethnographic complex is well enjoyed. Among the guests are dancing girls in folklore dresses offering typical Bulgarian cheese pastry, rose liqueur and rose jam. There are two distilleries, where tourists can have freshly prepared rakia (the local hard drink). They can sit in the shade of linden trees or watch folk programmes on a stage in the yard. This is the starting point for the carnival. Hundreds of people from the town and nearby villages arrive in folklore dress on donkey carts, singing and dancing on the way to the central square, where on a large stage the Queen of the Festival meets them. The Queen is the most beautiful girl from the graduating classes in the town of Kazanluk, the capital of the Valley of the Roses. An airplane sprays rose water over the crowds. Pleasantly tired, we make our way to a picnic restaurant by a lake where, for goodwill, the owner makes a gift to everyone of a small bottle of original rose oil. To end a beautiful (if long) day, we stop at the golden church at Shipka and attend special choir religious singing.

comfortable idea for the micro-business that has neither the time nor the resources to achieve the economies of scope demanded of such markets. And the idea of lower prices due to increased competition also holds little appeal. Denied the existence of (perceived) niches, rural tourism operators require support, guidance and assistance in order to plan business operations. Box 8.4 provides an account of a self-analysis of business needs of the Australian nature-based tourism sector.

While some training needs identified may be able to be tackled at provider level, a considerable number of issues raised by McKercher and Robbins's study in Box 8.4 point to the inability of any provider, in the long term, to operate in isolation from others in the sector and indeed, the industry as a whole. The need for product development to evolve with the market is suggestive of a level of knowledge at market rather than provider level. And understanding of the nature of competition requires a focus that goes beyond

Box 8.4. Nature-based and ecotourism operations in Australia: a study of business practices (source: McKercher and Robbins, 1998).

The comparative relevance of this research for European rural tourism industries is twofold:

- The nature of businesses referred to as nature-based and ecotourism concerns are those such as bushwalking firms, four-wheel drive centres, horse-riding businesses and boating enterprises. As such, they fall within most definitions of 'rural tourism'.
- The identified business dilemmas they face are identical to those of small rural businesses around the world.

Two facts were the catalysts to the study, the purpose of which was to establish the skills and knowledge required by those seeking to enter the nature tourism market.

- Although nature-based tourism in Australia is one of the industry's most dynamic sectors, with estimates of growth between two and five times as fast as for tourism generally, the failure rate of nature tourism businesses is high. Many companies that survive operate at the margins of viability.
- Generally, nature-based tourism operators are people with little or no business or marketing background and no prior experience in the tourism industry. Without the capital to buy in the required expertise, many business operators suffer unnecessary losses and delays in business growth and development.

A survey was conducted of current business operators who were asked to identify either: three things they wish they had known before they entered the nature-based tourism industry; or three skills they felt every prospective nature-based tourist operator must have. The results showed four main areas of concern. No one area dominated, reflecting the breadth of skills and knowledge required of operators in this field. Findings can be summarized as follows.

Business planning, financial management, and research

The need to develop formal business plans including realistic goals and marketing strategies. These to be prepared for a 3-year period and revisited and revised regularly as necessary
Existing operators felt that new entrants failed to identify clear goals for the business, had unrealistic sales and profit expectations, and assumed strong performance in development stages.

The need for accurate costs analysis, sound financial backing, good terms, and wise management of financial resources; the ability to remain enthusiastic while the business is building
Existing operators felt that new entrants under-estimate the time taken to achieve profitability, over-estimate demand resulting in high sales forecasts, and thus over-capitalize on plant and equipment. There is insufficient recognition of 'hidden' business costs such as membership fees, permits, tour operator accreditation, and ongoing advertising costs. Such problems are exacerbated by a financial sector that has difficulty recognizing forms of collateral other than property, and is therefore unsupportive of the sector generally. A number of operators agreed that costing, cash flow and break-even analysis are the most important business skills needed.

The need to research markets thoroughly in order to identify the most appropriate business opportunity(ies)
New entrants should learn as much as possible about the tourism industry in general as well as their chosen product market. A valid market opportunity together with the way(s) in which products will be differentiated must be clearly identified.

Marketing

The need for new entrants to develop a variety of marketing skills, and to understand the dynamism of the marketing process and the changing nature of tourism; the importance of conducting a feasibility study
Existing businesses cited the difficulties of segmenting markets, and positioning speciality products at small, operable niches. A strategic approach to marketing was felt to be desirable in order to:

Continued overleaf

Box 8.4. *Continued*

- define product markets;
- evaluate the level of investment required;
- determine the functional strategies of the business; and
- capitalize on strategic assets and skills.

It was felt that the high media profile of the industry had resulted in a number of unqualified operators entering the sector with new but undifferentiated products.

The need for product development that evolves with the market
The product development challenge is to provide a service that suits a wide range of skills and levels, but still gives a high quality result every time while not degrading the environment. Good product development includes a wide range of skills from providing opportunities for birdwatching or photography to organizing lunch or setting up camp. The marketing approach that delivers what clients want requires constant product modification. The ecotourism label may be becoming difficult to manage (see Chapter 7, p. 155). One operator expressed the belief that ecotourism was 'normal' tourism in a nature setting and that the 'normal' requirements of tourists must be met.

The need to charge a price that reflects the true value of the product
Existing businesses tend to operate a cost plus pricing strategy that does not reflect the true value of the product offered. The true value of nature-based tourism should reflect the level and quality of personalized service offered rather than just the costs of the holiday's sub-components of food, accommodation and travel.

The need to assess the business's promotional needs, to be professional in the approach to advertising, and to track the success (or otherwise) of advertising and promotional campaigns. In short, the need for a strategic approach to promotion of the business
Existing operators stressed the high costs and ineffectiveness of much advertising and the problems this causes when resources are scarce. The inexperience of most new operators results in wasted resources and the inability to create an operational niche.

The need to understand how the travel trade works and to minimize the fees and commissions paid to intermediaries
Agencies that sell trips and tours on behalf of nature-tour companies charge increasing levels of commission. Businesses that will not (or cannot) pay such fees are not advertised, and customers who specifically request their products may be steered towards those of another provider where fees to the agent are higher.

Operational skills

The need to be able to manage day-to-day operations
Time management emerged as an important skill and this included the need to understand and manage the effects of external constraints imposed on business operations. For example, the contribution of other organizations to the delivery of the product needs to be accounted for. Where businesses seek permission or permits for access to land, for example, they must learn to understand and tolerate the nature of the bureaucracy with which they must deal. This includes making allowance for the time it takes bureaucratic organizations to deal with simple applications. Similarly, operators had been surprised at the lead-time required to develop tours for inbound markets through the international travel trade; anything up to 10 months is required for negotiations.

The need to be able to do everything, from assessing and managing risk to lighting fires and cooking
Operators identified a wide range of skills required to cope with the rigour of running both businesses and the tours themselves.

The need for effective customer care skills
As tourism is predominantly a 'people business', it is essential that the operator can deliver what the consumer wants as this is the basis of good customer service. One operator suggested that the best way to deliver good customer service was to 'under promise and over deliver'. A significant part of the ecotourism product is the interpretation that underpins it. Effective communication skills are, therefore, essential.

Box 8.4. *Continued*

Personal attributes

The need for patience, courage, knowledge, drive and determination, enthusiasm and a love of hard work
It was identified that a number of new operators find it difficult to operate in a competitive, commercial setting when they have been accustomed to the casual low pressure situation of leading friends or other informal groups. Professionalism is essential as is the ability to be relaxed and friendly and to respond to the needs of different groups. Strength of character also appeared to be an essential requirement, the intensive nature of the work leaving little time for rest, relaxation and personal recreation.

The need for a good knowledge of, and affinity for, natural areas
Such knowledge extends to the natural history of an area, its flora and fauna, its ecological balance and its socio-cultural context.

Summary

There was a feeling that the nature-based sector was only as strong as its weakest members. While a healthy sector can contribute to the tourist experience in an area, and optimize the social, economic and ecological benefits of nature-based tourism, a weak sector is unlikely to achieve such objectives. There should be an onus on new operators, therefore, to prepare well for market entry. The strengths of the existing industry might otherwise be eroded.

'the farm gate'. That the sector is only as strong as its weakest link is a crucial observation, pointing to the responsibility of all businesses to contribute to the development of a strong and economically sustainable sector. But the combined needs of a number of businesses (especially of those perceived to be direct competitors) are unlikely to register as a priority for individual providers struggling at the margins of viability. As advice, the need for collaboration must be tempered by an understanding of the individual's perception of their survival needs.

The following invited viewpoint focuses on the needs of the rural tourism business at provider level. Written by an 'academic practitioner', the advice is well balanced, providing a good blend of local business and local development needs. Targeted at the start-up, it contains a great deal of useful advice and some excellent references and contacts for the existing rural tourism business.

Invited Viewpoint

Letter from an Academic Practitioner

Bernard Lane

Bernard Lane gives advice to his two perhaps imaginary nephews who are about to venture into the field of rural tourism. Ben has married into a farming family, and is considering new uses for surplus buildings. His wife ponders the idea of traditional B&B business. They have two small children. Basil has moved to Norfolk to go freelance as a writer. He and his partner are keen cyclists: they think cycle hire and cycle holidays might be an easy and attractive way to assist their cash flow. Both Ben and Basil have asked their elderly uncle if he has any tips. The following are extracts from his letters to them.

My dear Ben and Basil,

I was so pleased to hear that you are both thinking of going into rural tourism businesses as part of your future life plans. I was also more than a little concerned; the majority of all small businesses fail in the first 5 years. Remember, I did warn you!

As neither of you has any knowledge of tourism apart from having been on holiday yourselves, you have a lot to learn (like most rural tourism start-ups). Tourism is about giving service. You will not be working with a forage harvester or a keyboard, but with people, people who may be difficult, and who

Continued overleaf

like and demand service, often at inconvenient times. So you have to learn to please, to talk with them when they want to, and not to be offended by their outlandish views.

And rural tourism is a fashion industry; it's not like producing crops of standardized wheat. You'll have to have the right bedroom furniture and wallpaper, Ben, and the right food for your guests. It's all about fulfilling their holiday dreams, projecting the rural image they seek. You too Basil; cyclists want to hire trendy bikes, and feel they have had a real and full countryside day out on their rides. It's going to be a steep learning curve for both of you. (Have a look at Countryside Recreation Network, 1993 for more about customer service in rural tourism.)

First, start reading. You know my work on rural tourism (Bramwell and Lane, 1994; Lane, 1994; Long and Lane, 2000). Remember that you have to differentiate yourselves from resort experiences. Remember that personal contact is your big selling point. And remember that short breaks – and often out of season breaks – are the growth area. Do you recall Bob McKercher, that jovial Australian working in Hong Kong who I introduced you to in Sheffield? Bob has co-written a great paper about why small tourism businesses fail (McKercher and Robbins, 1998). I'm sending you a copy of it. Read it at least twice. Its message is that most people like you have terrible cash flow problems. In short, their business takes much longer to become profitable than they realize; typically, it can be several years. And so they run out of money to live on. That wonderful woman from New Zealand, Julie Warren, found the same universal problem (Warren and Taylor, 2000). And why? Read Bob's work about how you need to understand your market, work on effective small-scale marketing, work with others in the area, and get your prices right; and that does not mean cheap. You should also read the new edition of *Community Tourism Developent* due out of the University of Minnesota any time now (Tourism Center, 2001). It's got some great practical tips. Fax 001–612–624–4947 to reserve your copy. Try *The Business of Rural Tourism: International Perspectives*, edited by Don Getz and Stephen Page (1997), too: it's a little academic but it has some interesting ideas.

Ben and Penelope: you certainly have accommodation potential. Read the English Tourist Board (ETB) book to look at the many types of accommodation you could set up (ETB,1990). Yes, Penny, I know that you see yourself as an earth mother with a frying pan, always cheerful at breakfast, but B&B businesses have their problems. You may get low occupancy rates (often only 25–30%), and you have to be careful not to allow guests to take over all your personal space. If you like talking to people, you'll have a great time. If not, careful demarcation is the rule; keep both time and areas of your house for yourselves. Luckily, you have enough German to work through the greatest manual on rural accommodation ever written (edited by Monika Deubzer, 1992).

You should also consider self-catering. Your simplest properties could become camping barns. You will never grow rich that way but at least it will cover some basic building maintenance costs for now, ensure a good roof, and keep the property viable. Then, when you have the money to invest, good quality self-catering conversions can get occupancy levels up to 75%, and excellent returns. Self-catering visitors don't bother you with too much chat either. But whatever you do (apart from your camping barns) you must ensure that conversions are completed to a high standard. You need to provide en suite facilities all the time nowadays. It's cheaper to do this from the outset, and you'll get better returns, and increase the value of your property. Talk to your local authority tourism officer to see if you can get any grant aid in your area, perhaps from EU sources.

Have you thought about how you will market your property? Good signposts help, but the real key to success lies in joining a local group. The Farm Holiday Bureau (FHB) has lots of them; look at their website (www.farm-holidays.co.uk), and read Jackie Clarke's really splendid paper on the subject (Clarke, 1999). Get into your local authority brochure; it's always good value. Keep a list of all your guests, and stay in touch with them, at Christmas or whenever. They often come back, and they are likely to tell their friends (see LEADER, 1994, too, for more ideas).

Basil: I know that you love bikes. Experience shows, however, that you need to add to your enthusiasm some good business sense; liking bikes can actually be a drawback! But you've got space in that little shed of yours for perhaps 30 bikes, and luckily you have great local off-road potential. Remember that using an old rail track, quiet byways or country lanes is a powerful market attraction. You need to contact two good friends of mine. Susan Achmatowicz runs Country Lanes – the leading cycle hire and holiday company in Britain – perhaps the best in Europe. Get her website on your screen (www.countrylanes.co.uk). Then there is Nigel Wiggett, way down in Wadebridge in Cornwall, hiring 400 bikes on the Camel Trail. He's on www.cornwall-online.co.uk/bridgebikehire. Nigel is a treasure trove of information on the nitty-gritty of cycle hire, and he can get you good fleets of bikes at keen prices. Have a long weekend out west to sample their wares, but remember it has taken them both many years of work to get where they are now.

The keys to success are good, interesting, quiet and safe routes, good bikes, good marketing and great personal service. It will be especially hard for you in your first year because you are a little off the beaten track. However, you are near an Anglia Railways station, and they – like a number of rail companies nowadays – are keen to go into joint promotional deals with quality cycle hire businesses. For an overview of the whole subject, look at Les Lumsdon's latest paper on cycle tourism (Lumsdon, 2000). He's the guru in the field (see Chapter 7). And all those things I said to Ben about working with others apply to you too: working with local hotels, guest houses and B&Bs to get your brochures out, delivering bikes to them as necessary, and offering special deals, etc. It's important for accommodation and attractions to work together for best results for both parts of the rural tourism equation.

Don't forget to cultivate the local and regional press to get publicity. They love well-written press releases; it saves them so much work. Set up a series of events, visits and other news items. Get your MP on to one of your bikes, have a fund raising day for a good charity: the list of possibilities is endless. Always put out a press release in good time. You have to stay in the public eye. You have to be good at what you do, and you must not be shy of publicity.

Both of you, Ben and Basil, know that in my spare time I edit the *Journal of Sustainable Tourism*. I expect you, therefore, to have a good environmental policy for everything you do, from loos to local food and more (Herremans and Welsh, 1999, will give you some ideas). Your markets are very middle class and they expect you to be green even if they are not! *The Green Tourism Audit Kit* is a useful start (ETC/Countryside Agency, 2000, see the UK's Countryside Agency web site about how to obtain this kit at www.countryside.gov.uk).

Finally, the exciting thing about rural tourism is that it's not boring. Indeed it's a treadmill – you have to get better every year. Ask your customers what they think about your product regularly. Find out about what they read, where they live and who their friends are. Find your market niches, and work on them. (I'll write to you again about niche marketing, meanwhile consider my old chestnuts on the subject (OECD, 1995; Clemenson and Lane, 1997) in the light of what you've read in Chapters 6 to 8 of this book.) And keep track of the competition, not just locally, but across the world. It's the far-flung destinations that are your real competitors in fact, not the locals. Check out those websites in the USA that I told you about; try the Aspen Institute's rural newsletter for starters, to keep you in touch with wider events (www.aspeninst.org/csg/csg_newsletter.asp). In Europe, Austrian Farm Holidays is the website to watch; their Chief Executive, Hans Embacher, is always up to the minute with new ideas, and has a keen eye for good graphics: (www.farmholidays.com). It comes in English or German so you can have a fun evening updating your German by comparing the two.

Good luck !

Your ever-loving Uncle Bernard

Your bedtime reading

Bramwell, B. and Lane, B. (eds) (1994) *Rural Tourism and Sustainable Rural Development.* Channel View Press, Clevedon.

Clarke, J. (1999) Marketing structures for farm tourism: beyond the original provider of rural tourism. *Journal of Sustainable Tourism* 7(1), 26–48.

Clemenson, H. and Lane, B. (1997) Niche markets, niche marketing and rural employment. In: Bollman, R.D. and Bryden, J.M. (eds) *Rural Employment: an International Perspective.* CAB International, Wallingford, pp. 410–426.

Countryside Recreation Network (1993) *Customer Care in the Countryside.* University of Wales, Cardiff.

Deubzer, M. (1992) *Handbuch: Gaeste auf dem Bauernhof, Beratungshilfe 8–92.* Staatliche Fuehrungsakademie für Ernaehrung, Landwirtschaft und Forsten, Landshut.

English Tourist Board (1990) *Developing Rural Accommodation: a Good Practice Guide.* English Tourist Board, London.

ETC/Countryside Agency (2000) *The Green Audit Kit.* Countryside Agency, Cheltenham.

Continued overleaf

Getz, D. and Page, S.J. (eds) (1997) *The Business of Rural Tourism: International Perspectives.* International Thomson Business Press, London.
Herremans, I.M. and Welsh, C. (1999) Developing and implementing a company's ecotourism mission statement. *Journal of Sustainable Tourism* 7(1), 48–76.
Lane, B. (1994) What is rural tourism? *Journal of Sustainable Tourism* 2(1/2), 7–22.
LEADER (1994) *Marketing Quality Rural Tourism,* Leader Technical Dossier. LEADER/AEIDL, Brussels.
Long, P. and Lane, B. (2000) Rural tourism development. In: Gartner, W.C. and Lime, D.W. (eds) *Trends in Outdoor Recreation, Leisure and Tourism.* CAB International, Wallingford, pp. 299–309.
Lumsdon, L. (2000) Transport and tourism: cycle tourism – a model for sustainable tourism. *Journal of Sustainable Tourism* 8(5), 361–379.
McKercher, R. and Robbins, B. (1998) Business development issues affecting nature based tourism operators in Australia. *Journal of Sustainable Tourism* 6(2), 173–189.
OECD (1995) *Niche Markets and Rural Development: Workshop Proceedings and Policy Recommendations.* OECD, Paris.
Tourism Center (2001) *Community Tourism Development.* University of Minnesota, Minneapolis.
Warren, J.A.N. and Taylor, C.N. (2000) *Developing Rural Tourism in New Zealand.* Centre for Research, Evaluation and Social Assessment, Wellington.

Bernard Lane

In line with the recommendations of development agencies, Bernard Lane's advice stresses the need for rural tourism businesses to work together, and to differentiate their products, not only from each other, but from *resort* experiences; that is, from other locations and types of experience. He makes the critical point that competition comes from farther afield than local providers, demonstrating the extra-parochial nature of competition in rural tourism markets. Lane's advice demonstrates well how the synergy from collaboration can be a constructive business management tool for individual firms.

But in this 'bigger picture of things', what is the place of the individual provider? This chapter has presented the importance of the countryside model as a means by which business operators can identify the nature of the markets in which they operate, and it is clear that these are changing. The McKercher and Robbins (1998) study identifies a need to understand the dynamism of markets and for constant modification of products and services provided for visitors. Lane (above) describes rural tourism as a 'fashion industry'. Again, the focus on dynamism is clear. Perpetual change requires a preparedness to accept new ideas and the demands these place on individual businesses and 'rural tourism' industries as a whole.

Acceptance of the idea that mass tourism is now a countryside phenomenon poses a range of challenges. While the success of product and service providers is critical to the achievement of a successful rural tourism industry, the issues embraced by changes in countryside consumption and commodification require a broad, multi-sectoral approach that involves the full range of economic, environmental, political and social stakeholders. Within such a development community, rural tourism businesses have a vital role to play. Currently, the market conditions under which they operate largely direct their focus towards individual rather than collective action. Should this continue, we are likely to witness:

- lower likelihood of tourism's integration with other forms of rural development;
- a reduced potential for businesses to contribute to dynamic economies and communities; and
- continued exploitation of the natural environment as a 'free' resource.

As identified in Chapters 4 and 5, tourism is widely regarded as an agent for stimulating economic development and redevelopment. As a form of economic development, rural tourism has a place within the broader concept of rural development, which seeks to balance social, economic, institutional and environmental goals in a holistic manner. The evidence is compelling that the benefits of growth and changes in rural tourism markets cannot be harnessed by businesses and communities working in isolation. In order for rural tourism to be the effective vehicle for rural development that is often claimed of it, it needs to function as a collective activity and within the framework of a strategic development plan that coordinates the inputs of different actors, and promotes effective application of resources at a regional level. But what is the likelihood of this happening? The answer may lie in an exploration of the context in which the rural tourism business sector operates.

The Nature of the Business Sector

Data and information on small businesses in Europe are difficult to find. Much that is written relies on EU data that classify businesses into very small (0–9 employees), small (10–49 employees) and medium-sized enterprises (49–250 employees). Collectively referred to as SMEs, this group of businesses makes up 99.2% of all EU enterprises. Due to the size of, and range within, the SME category, information and data on the sector are of limited value to very small (micro-) businesses.

More than 90% of the EU's total enterprise population (approximately 15 million businesses) falls into the 'very small' category, employing less than ten people. Of these, on average, approximately half are one-person businesses, employing no salaried staff. (An intra-country comparison shows notable variations. Self-employment is much more prevalent in the south of Europe, particularly in Spain, with The Netherlands, Germany, Luxembourg and Austria at the other end of the scale (Eurostat, 1997: 39).) As detailed in the invited viewpoint below, micro-businesses' impacts on the EU economy, therefore, are significant. The micro-business sector employs one-third of EU workers and accounts for one-quarter of business turnover. Increasing recognition of this economic power helps to explain the EU funding shift away from large grants to attract inward investment towards small firms and indigenous development (Wanhill, 2000).

The 'recreational and other cultural services' sector of the available data that most closely relates to tourism businesses is dominated by very small businesses (Eurostat, 1997: 38). On average, they represent almost 97% of the total. Relatively little is known of the behaviour of these firms. The following viewpoint, from Victor Middleton, adds considerably to our knowledge and understanding of the sector.

Invited Viewpoint

The Importance of Micro-businesses in European Tourism

Victor T.C. Middleton

> At their best, small businesses reflect most of the features and characteristics that are unique to the tourism destinations in which they operate. The sector has vibrancy and originality and can play a vital leading role in delivering excellence with personality that big business cannot replicate. At worst, however, small businesses make survival decisions that physically degrade the attractions of the local environment, damage the destination image, and draw in the lowest spending clientele, boosting short run numbers but not the revenue on which long run tourism futures depend.
>
> (Middleton, 1997: 13)

Context

There is a broad consensus in Europe that SMEs already play a vital part in the economic, social and environmental life of EU Member States. Their future role in providing employment and underpinning the economic and social life of local communities, especially in the tourism and recreation context, is well recognized, in principle. The issue for all European countries is how best to recognize, measure,

Continued overleaf

Table 8.2. Indicators[a] of the volume and value of tourism SMEs in Europe.

	Europe	UK (1)	UK (2)
Estimated number of SMEs	2.6 million	72,000	170,000
Estimated jobs generated by SMEs	10.5 million	290,000	500,000
Potential for job creation at 20% growth	2.1 million	60,000	100,000

[a] There are no definitive statistical estimates for these data. However, research undertaken for an EC supported conference on SMEs in tourism in 1998 (Wales Tourist Board, 1998), estimated the volume of SMEs for Europe as a whole and the UK in particular. Using data accepted by the EC as valid for their purposes, UK (1) is an estimate based on data that are broadly comparable across Europe. UK (2) is based on alternative data for the UK from several national sources that provide a more accurate picture, and a volume estimate that is around twice that produced by the EC-agreed methodology.

appreciate, support and regulate the sector so that it may play its full potential role in achieving national and EU tourism objectives.

Within the broad economic sector of SMEs in tourism (less than 250 employees) there is growing evidence that the group representing the smallest employers (those employing less than ten people) have unique characteristics that require special attention in policy terms. Identified as 'micro-businesses' to distinguish them within the SME sector, the smallest employers are by far the largest numerically, estimated at more than nine out of ten SMEs (e.g. see Table 8.2). In fact the majority of them employ less than five people and many comprise only the proprietor and immediate family. There were estimated to be some 2.4 million such enterprises actively trading within European tourism at the end of the 1990s, although this may be a significant under-estimate (as indicated in Table 8.2).

Individually, micro-businesses are insignificant as players in international and domestic tourism and recreation and in practice they are often ignored in national and regional tourism policy developments. Collectively, however, they provide the bulk of the essentially local ambience and quality of visitor experiences at destinations on which the future growth of overseas and domestic visits depends. They also comprise a seedbed of entrepreneurial and enterprise 'culture' on which much of the profit and employment prospects of big businesses ultimately depends.

Airlines and railways, with their national and international linkages, may provide the best of public transport. Global hotel groups may provide the highest standards of branded accommodation. But it is small, single enterprise businesses that deliver the bulk of the visitor experiences that define a visitor's perception of a destination. It is likely that nine out of ten domestic or overseas leisure visitors will encounter micro-businesses at some point during their stay in a destination. Those encounters will influence their perception of sense of place, quality and value for money, and their wish to revisit, or recommend friends to visit.

A focus on micro-businesses

Micro-businesses typically operate in a very local context, motivated by a mix of personal, quality of life and community goals as well as the normal business/commercial rationale. In the UK, for example, there are many semi-retired people who operate small accommodation businesses to support an alternative lifestyle rather than for profit. Numbered in their hundreds of thousands, micro-businesses are as unique as individuals. Unfortunately this makes them amorphous and difficult to measure and to 'badge' as a coherent sector. It is often very difficult to access the sector through any of the existing processes of tourism policy consultation. Many prefer to be left alone and they are not natural 'joiners' of organizations. The sector comprises:

- guesthouses and B&Bs;
- self-catering in cottages/holiday parks;
- farmhouses;
- museums and other small attractions;
- cafes, inns and restaurants;
- operators of sports equipment;

- artists and others involved in cultural provision;
- souvenir shops;
- taxi drivers; and
- coach operators.

The value of micro-businesses to European tourism

Their value can be viewed along three dimensions.

1. In economic terms, micro-businesses:

- make up 95% of businesses operating in tourism, generating perhaps a third of total tourism revenue;
- earn income, which tends to stay in the local community; they typically purchase locally and are part of the fabric of the local money circulation cycle;
- are a vital part of new job creation, especially in areas of rural and urban regeneration;
- perform an important economic stability role in fragile areas by sustaining their businesses, even without new job creation;
- are increasingly required to play an important role in public policy implementation, for example payroll operation and good environmental practice, although the costs to them are proportionally far higher than for larger businesses; and
- have a potential that is currently under-utilized and, with support, could be much enhanced.

2. In social terms, micro-businesses:

- are part of the lifeblood of local communities – as local residents, neighbours, taxpayers and employers – even where they may be part of the unofficial or 'grey' economy; many micro-business proprietors are also found in local politics;
- often provide local employment to people with lower skills/poor qualifications and offer flexible working arrangements;
- therefore have a social as well as an economic impact which is especially important in rural and economically deprived areas;
- are often seen by visitors as the 'friendly locals'; they may represent all that most visitors will ever encounter of real local character and individuality at destinations, reflecting the special values of 'place'; and
- provide leading edge small businesses which can act as entrepreneurial role models of success and may inspire young people in their communities by example.

3. In environmental terms, micro-businesses:

- typically express through their operations the local character of a destination, and in many ways also help to sustain that character and communicate it to visitors;
- influence the perceived visual quality of the built and natural landscape by their actions;
- undertake operations which impact daily on local sustainability issues, and they are obliged to implement government requirements for health and safety and environmental good practice, again bearing proportionally higher costs than larger businesses; and
- need to be embraced by LA21 programmes if the latter are to achieve their targets.

Measurement issues

In line with normal EC practice for statistics, SMEs are estimated from the supply side basis (for DGXXIII in the Annual Report of the European Observatory for SMEs; ENSR, 1997). Not surprisingly, there is, of course, a major definitional issue in deciding exactly which sectors of economic activity should be counted as 'tourism'. Within any agreed definition, a secondary issue is how can small and micro-businesses be estimated. Estimates of tourism SMEs are generally based on NACE Rev 1 (European

Continued overleaf

standard for employment sector statistics) in which tourism is assessed as the HORECA (hotel, restaurant and catering) category (NACE 55), plus travel agencies and tour operators (NACE 63.3). In other words tourism is deemed to include hotels and other accommodation; camping sites and 'short stay' accommodation; restaurants and similar outlets; bars and similar outlets; canteens, catering and similar outlets; travel agents, tour operators and similar outlets (Middleton, 1998).

It will be obvious that many of these businesses included as tourism are not in practice significantly engaged in tourism at all, or only as a very minor part of their total turnover. Many other vital businesses for tourism, such as transport, visitor attractions, cultural attractions, sporting and recreational enterprises, and tourism-focused retailing are excluded. The exclusions may to some extent be balanced by the over-generous inclusions, but the UK evidence for UK 1 and UK 2 (Table 8.2), suggests that SMEs are currently significantly under-estimated in European tourism.

Another major measurement issue is that business numbers across Europe are estimated primarily from value-added tax (VAT or TVA) returns, from surveys of business operations carried out by national statistical and related agencies, and from databases based on registration of businesses, for example for accommodation. In all such cases the methodology varies between countries and the probability is that thousands of the smallest businesses are simply not counted. In the UK and other countries, the lack of legal registration requirements for accommodation businesses is the source of major gaps in the data.

The need for explicit strategic recognition and action by government

- Numbers of micro-businesses make them a core, rather than a peripheral part of almost every tourist experience in all countries.
- Micro-businesses are not the same as SMEs. They are not scaled down versions of bigger businesses. Many may not seek to grow, but that does not invalidate their role. At the leading edge, they embody the entrepreneurial spirit and fully merit specific support in tourism policy terms.
- They form an important part of community life, especially in rural, mountain and environmentally fragile destinations.
- They offer the best opportunities for low-cost job creation, especially, but not only, in economically fragile areas.
- They are often highly independent operators, often preferring minimal contact with bureaucracy and tourist boards, and it requires special measures to communicate and consult with them. At present, they often 'slip through the net' of provision and support and some can avoid regulation.
- They are an important and cost-effective tool for the delivery of EU and national government policies such as minimum wages, working hours, parental leave, human rights, collection of PAYE data, environmental requirements, and health and safety regulations.
- They are made up of people from all backgrounds and cover a wide cross-section of the population. Many have no formal management education or training.
- Collectively, micro-businesses have the capacity to underpin and deliver government objectives for tourism, or to seriously undermine them.

Main policy issues

There appear to be eight key issues surrounding very small businesses in tourism that warrant policy development.

1. Developing product quality assurance schemes to maintain, enhance and communicate competitive standards in the sector, and to prevent incompetent micro-businesses from damaging the reputation of their location.
2. Support with information and communications technology in the sector and access to e-commerce and the use of the Internet.
3. Support with marketing and financial management – many micro-businesses have no formal training in these disciplines – and management training generally.
4. Developing more functional links with larger businesses that now dominate tourism marketing and development in all countries.

5. Development of more functional links with local authorities, not least in the application of LA21 programmes.
6. Review of the disproportionate impact of the increasing regulatory burden that affects micro-businesses.
7. Better research for the sector and its component parts on a European basis, ideally using demand-side as well as supply-side methods.
8. Development and communication of good practice models for supporting the micro-business sector. These will be typically private/public sector partnerships but the variety of options is large.

The available evidence generated by the EU-sponsored 1998 conference on tourism SMEs held in Wales and the evidence available at that time from DGXXIII suggests that, with the possible exception of countries such as Austria and Switzerland, the particular importance of micro-businesses in tourism is generally unrecognized in practice across Europe. That SMEs is a current buzzword universally popular with politicians is not in dispute. The key issue is that the sector has to be appreciated in its own terms, recognizing that it comprises only about one in ten operators who can be classified at the leading edge of good practice. The trailing edge, many of whom are collectively damaging the prospects of the destinations in which they are located, may be a third or more of the total operators and they cannot safely be ignored. Above all, it is not an option simply to adapt the traditional mechanisms and approaches used to support larger businesses over recent years.

Victor T.C. Middleton

The nature of the environment within which micro- and small businesses work

Perhaps because of the difficulties of identification and measurement described by Middleton, rural tourism and recreation businesses across Europe work in something of a tourism policy vacuum. Within the EU, little policy is directed specifically at tourism development, the most important industry impacts deriving from generic policies and measures directed at business generally (Davidson and Maitland, 1997: 117; Wanhill, 1997). While the needs of small rural tourism and recreation businesses converge to some extent with those of businesses in general, a range of factors serve to differentiate their requirements and create the need for a specific policy focus and tailored support. These may be related to two broad areas, as illustrated in Table 8.3, the rural context and the tourism context.

Conditions such as those listed in Table 8.3 offer both threat and opportunity to tourism businesses in general and rural ones in particular. The decline of mainstream agricultural industries provides an impetus for the design and delivery of a range of new products and services in rural areas ranging from organic or specialist livestock production to fishing, fruit-picking and four-wheel driving. Increasing demand for tourism and recreation in the countryside, together with the promotion of possibilities in the field, appear to make tourism an attractive option. But business failures among rural tourism businesses are high (see Bernard Lane's letter). Peripherality, remoteness, small business structures and a lack of necessary business skills all militate against success. Many of those businesses that survive are only marginally profitable. Those that have diversified from farming may find that their returns from new ventures (especially in terms of time invested) are less efficient than those from traditional agriculture (Hjalager, 1996).

Nevertheless, as identified by LEADER (AEIDL, 1994: 15), opportunities exist within coordinated development plans to service growing tourism markets in rural areas. Opportunities may be perceived in two main ways as shown in Fig. 8.2. Some start-ups may represent the totality of an operator's business; others may be diversified activities to support core agricultural businesses; and further examples may be found in operators who diversify into recreational activities in the hope that they will ultimately replace traditional agricultural activities. Fundamentally, the strategy of those businesses diversifying into rural tourism and recreation activities is one of recovery. Recovery is about the management of businesses in crisis: businesses that are, or may become, insolvent unless actions are taken to address their situations. Symptoms of such a position may be expressed in:

Table 8.3. Special needs of 'rural tourism' businesses for policy focus.

The rural context	The tourism context
Decreasing labour-intensity in agricultural industries Falling returns from many agricultural products The need for diversification to create and support dynamic economies A speed of change uncharacteristic of rural areas The emergence of new and specialized uses of rural space and resources Conflicts arising from competition over resource use The potential for information and communication technologies to reduce physical isolation Demographic changes that have blurred the distinction between rural and urban Changes in consumption patterns that require the acceptance of cultural symbols attached to the rural idyll The predominance of micro- and small businesses	A tourism economy that has failed to adapt to changing circumstances and is low value added (Wanhill, 1997) Increasing fragmentation of markets for tourism Increasing dispersion and diversity of supply Product delivery through SMEs that lack capital and resources and suitable organizational structures (Wanhill, 1997, 2000) Minimal research base (Wanhill, 1997) Minimal interest in sustainable business practices Problems of seasonality

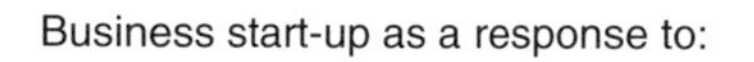

Perceived market gap:	Perceived market decline:
(an opportunity to move towards a new market)	(an opportunity to move away from a declining market)
An opportunity to operationalize a hobby	An opportunity to diversify
A lifestyle search decision	A lifestyle maintenance decision

Fig. 8.2. Perceptions of opportunity.

- declining market share;
- falling sales;
- falling profits;
- increased debts; and
- decreases in liquidity.

Any (or all) of these serve as indicators of the need to look to new products and markets in order to improve business prospects. The term usually used to describe this process is diversification.

Development beyond present product(s) and market(s) but still within the broad confines of a familiar industry is referred to as related diversification. An example of this might be farm sales of produce from the farm gate directly to the consumer rather than to an intermediary to process, package and sell on. Unrelated diversification, on the other hand, refers to the development of new products and services in markets that are distinctly different from existing ones. Many rural businesses enter into such undertakings; for example when farm households offer bed and breakfast accommodation or farmland is turned over to campers and caravanners for accommodation and recreational use.

Whether related or unrelated, rural diversification requires a critical review of new market opportunities. Opportunities vary within and between localities and regions as well as between regions and countries, and it is commonplace to identify products or services that take advantage of local product strengths as well as markets whose needs they meet. Markets and products should allow businesses to meet locally defined objectives, examples of which may be:

- to maximize receipts from tourism;
- to generate low volume visiting (depending on the locality's carrying capacity);
- to attract high-spending visitors;
- to extend the season;
- to contribute to the quality of life of rural residents; and
- to respond to local issues of sustainability, for example to include more stakeholders in initial planning processes.

Operational opportunities open to businesses must be analysed within the context of national or international markets within which they will operate. Markets for tourism and recreation in rural areas are highly competitive ones, where market forces influence both supply and demand. Table 8.4 lists the characteristics of competitive markets generally and their relevance to markets for rural recreation and tourism in particular. The analysis reveals a number of market imperfections and failures, conditions that indicate the inability of the private sector to operate at optimum effectiveness and efficiency without intervention in some form. These failures are defined in Table 8.5, and the challenges to the industry that arise as a result are identified.

Although Tables 8.4 and 8.5 provide a useful synthesis of market conditions, there is little new in the detail of what is said. Middleton (above) highlighted the varying goals of small tourism businesses. The inability of individuals in the private sector to work together to co-ordinate a strategy to protect the natural environment is stressed by Hall and Jenkins (1998: 21). And the lack of structure across the rural tourism sector is well documented (Wanhill, 1997; McKercher and Robbins, 1998; Edmunds, 1999). Less attention has been paid, however, to the changing nature of consumption and its effects on demand. The effects are both profound and wide-ranging, with the potential to alter business and development issues in fundamental ways. However, while the 'failures' identified arise from the private sector's inability to optimize the benefits of rural tourism development, it is not suggested that such development is the responsibility of individual entrepreneurs and the preserve of the private sector. In fact, it has long been accepted that the most successful outcomes are obtained from public/private sector partnerships. In France, for example, the 'Pays d'Accueil' policy has operated successfully for 25 years. State assistance is provided to rural areas that can show three things:

1. A willingness to implement an inclusive and concerted tourist development programme.
2. Possession of a number of tourist assets.
3. An ability to meet the costs of accommodation and activities provision (Keane, 1992: 49).

Table 8.4. Characteristics of competitive markets and their relevance to markets for rural tourism and recreation.

Market characteristic	Relevance to rural tourism and recreation products
Supply and demand characterized by large numbers of sellers and buyers, none of whom are in a position to influence market price	Price is a given factor: individual businesses internalize only their own costs and benefits and price accordingly, and the whole is therefore no more than the sum of its parts. Positive externalities are ignored, individual targets dominating community or regional aims that may represent a local or regional synergy, widen access to participation and provide a platform for integrated development. Negative social and environmental externalities such as crime and littering, crowding and congestion become the preserve of the public sector. The public sector also fills gaps in provision relating to, for example, national and regional promotion and tourist information provision, public goods outwith the private producer sphere.
Relative ease of customer access to information for price comparisons and resource decisions	Both the availability of information and people's potential to access it (via increased use of the Internet by small businesses for example) mean that businesses must assume customers are in a position to make well-informed decisions. In reality, however, individual firms' abilities both to maintain market awareness and to make up-to-date product information widely available is constrained by time, cost and limited marketing expertise. And consumers' ability to handle the vast amount of literature available is limited by time and cognitive processing ability.
The product(s)/service(s) sold are similar enough to be substitutable	The emergence of the consumer society and a new consumer behaviour related not to the use-value of purchases but to their social identity and status messages has complicated our understanding of both markets and products. It has become increasingly difficult to identify a product's core value as it may be perceived by customers. A tourist in search of challenge may find this in both whitewater rafting and mountain biking, thus rendering the two interchangeable. In this way, products lose their former distinctions, acquire more substitutes, and may become more homogeneous (like those of competitors).
There are low barriers to entry for new suppliers of the product(s)/services(s)	High levels of competition are catalysts to innovation and enterprise. However, fragmentation of rural tourism activities and poor information flows can reduce this effect. Moreover, diversified businesses and/or those run by families often lack the business and marketing expertise to innovate in the ways required of the market. The result may, in fact, be lowered standards. A business sector is only as strong as its weakest members, and new business entrants with insufficient business training and preparation may risk the reputation of a whole sector.
Firms aim to maximize profits and customers aim to maximize benefits	The rural tourism market is characterized by a large number of family businesses and by businesses for whom tourism is primarily a way of supporting other rural activities such as farming. Other enterprises may have entered the tourism market because of an interest in the activity offered. Personal, family and lifestyle objectives may mean that such businesses often accept lower returns on investment and longer payback periods than would be expected according to rational business theory.

Table 8.5. Market failures and the challenges they present to 'rural tourism and recreation' industries.

Failures in 'rural tourism and recreation' markets	Industry challenges
There is no costing of negative externalities accruing from the activities of rural businesses. Price therefore reflects merely the sum of costs of physical sub-components such as accommodation and food rather than the value placed on the specialized product, service or experience, or on the environment	Development of value-based pricing strategies to reflect: (i) the full costs of service and experience provision; and (ii) the consumption of the countryside
A lack of business and marketing experience in small businesses in the sector makes it difficult for operators to manage businesses efficiently and prepare and distribute marketing information effectively	Identification of training needs and the subsequent development of useful, targeted and recognized training programmes
Successful competitive strategies derive from individual providers' abilities to differentiate products or service elements. Where market niches do not exist, and the marketing of experiences makes products or services interchangeable and thus more homogeneous, businesses may lose their competitive advantage	Better understanding of product characteristics and values, and the way these relate to the needs of consumers Increased acceptance of the benefits derived from cooperative rather than competitive marketing strategies at local and regional level
The diversity and dispersion of rural tourism businesses makes it difficult to establish effective coordinating structures to support business development. Low entry barriers to product markets allow entry to those with limited preparation and experience, and unrealistic expectations of business performance, with the potential to damage existing market sectors	The establishment of quality standards in business practice, and the creation of professional associations with the legitimacy to implement and monitor them The provision of informal, on-the-job training and mentoring
The predominance of family-operated businesses in the sector results in start-up goals that have less to do with economic objectives than important personal goals such as economic independence and enjoying a particular lifestyle. Thus the sector as a whole suffers from sub-optimal use of resources, inadequate returns on capital, and input (i.e. time) disproportionate to outputs (i.e. profits)	The need to analyse the extent to which lifestyle objectives are met by businesses with such an input–output imbalance. It may be that lifestyle objectives can be better met by the application of financial goals, e.g. the way in which a profit orientation or a premium pricing policy may contribute to better cash flow, reductions in personal stress, and increases in the quality of free time

The scheme provides for support to such areas in the development of a high degree of local participation.

Investment incentives throughout the EU are based on a requirement for tourism SMEs to work within partnership arrangements (Wanhill, 2000). But while examples can be found to illustrate successful partnerships, it remains true that rural tourism and recreation industries, as part of integrated rural development plans, remain poorly understood, haphazardly planned and under-funded. They are thus still identified as being low value-added products (AEIDL, 1994: 21; Wanhill, 1997). In short, aside from its broader development potential, rural tourism is not yet realizing its economic potential, and the failures and challenges identified are those of the public as well as the private sector.

The challenges identified in Table 8.5 may be seen to set an agenda for research into rural tourism's role within rural development to question the roles of issues such as:

- entrepreneurship and innovation
- marketing
- quality
- collaboration and partnership.

The interlinked nature of these issues is obvious in the following pages. Nevertheless, each is addressed separately.

An entrepreneurial economy encourages people to seek opportunity and embrace creative approaches to exploiting it. Thus, entrepreneurship is defined by how firms and people behave, rather than by what they produce. And it is concerned as much with the environment within which they operate as it is with entrepreneurs and companies themselves. This requires the following:

- An environment that encourages spin-offs from established businesses and research institutions; this, in turn, raises three issues: (i) the ability of employees to start their own companies; (ii) the willingness of employers to help employees spin off; and (iii) the role that universities and research institutes play in turning research into marketable commodities.
- An educational system that stimulates and prepares entrepreneurs with skills which can transcend business issues and be applied to community and public life, such as managing change and risk, creative problem solving, and the ability to see opportunities in problems.
- A culture that values and celebrates entrepreneurship.

(Aspen Institute, 1996)

The paucity of information on the behaviour of small tourism firms means that entrepreneurial activity in the tourism sector is poorly understood. Studies that have been done have focused on the impact of large firms at the expense of SMEs (Shaw and Williams, 1990: 79). Even less is written on entrepreneurship in rural tourism businesses, with some notable exceptions that will be discussed below.

Enterprising businesses

Research into local and regional competitiveness identifies three types of successful SME producer (Leat *et al.*, 2000). The typology is outlined in Box 8.5. Across all 12 regions of

Box 8.5. Successful Scottish SMEs (source: Leat *et al.*, 2000).

What constitutes 'success' is open to interpretation and dependent on the objectives of the enterprise. In the context of the RIPPLE* project, the term reflected a business's ability to derive competitive advantage through quality and the use of regional imagery. Three types of successful business emerged:

1. *Survivalists* seek to survive and maintain the status quo. Satisfactory personal income and non-monetary rewards, such as a good local reputation, satisfy their ambitions. Within the Scottish sample, survivalists made up 25–30% of the sample.
2. *Profit satisficers* seek a 'satisfactory' level of output, market share and profit, but value the quality of their lives as much as financial rewards or prestige. Profit satisficers represented between 40% and 50% of the Scottish sample.
3. *Accumulators* have major growth ambitions, and plan and act accordingly. In addition to stated growth intentions, they had either changed scale, and/or developed their products or services, and/or changed their employment levels, and been profitable over a period of 5 years or more. Accumulators represented 25% to 30% of the Scottish sample.

* RIPPLE is an EU (FAIR) project researching production, marketing, consumption, and regulation of quality products and services in 12 lagging European regions in six EU states: Finland, Ireland, Greece, France, Spain and the UK. Research was conducted into a range of business sectors of which tourism was only one. The findings, reported above, relate only to Scotland, one of the UK regions.

the 'RIPPLE' project, there was a high proportion of family-owned businesses. This finding may add to the belief that family-based structures can contribute to a lack of expansionist ambitions among small rural businesses (Dunn, 1995; Wanhill, 1997; Getz and Carlsen, 2000). Family businesses do not, however, form a homogeneous group. Distinct types have been identified as: family-centred businesses (where business is a way of life); and business-centred families (where business is a means of livelihood) (Singer and Donahu in Getz and Carlsen, 2000).

Research conducted by Getz and Carlsen (2000) in rural Western Australia examined the business goals of family and owner-operated businesses in the rural tourism and hospitality sectors. The aim of the research was to improve understanding of the motives of rural tourism entrepreneurs, and the impact their values and goals might have on the nature and performance of relevant business sectors. By far the most important reason given for starting the business was 'lifestyle' (almost 35% of those sampled); 'challenge' and 'independence' were also of significance. In fact, only 1.6% of the sample claimed to have started their business because they saw a market need for it. Living in the right environment, and enjoying a good lifestyle were therefore the strongest goals of many family businesses surveyed.

In relation to business operation goals, the RIPPLE project identified two 'types' of business: 'family first' and 'business first' (corresponding with Singer and Donahu's typology above). About half of the respondents had no formal business goals (Getz and Carlsen, 2000), providing something of an explanation for the high degree of business failures, and suggesting a training need in skills of management planning. There appears to be evidence, therefore, to support the theory that family firms have objectives other than profit maximization that drive business decisions.

From the rural development perspective, it is likely that the greatest contribution to output will come from *satisficers* and *accumulators*. Given this expectation, the interests of economic development will be better served by the targeting of assistance at such businesses (Leat *et al.*, 2000). It is notable that the emphasis of the LEADER+ programme has shifted away from support for areas of need towards targeted support for those areas that demonstrate an understanding of the need to reinforce the local economic environment in order to contribute to job creation (see Chapter 4).

Alongside the business entrepreneur, however, in rural contexts, the 'civic entrepreneur' (MAF, 1999) has been recognized as having a key role to play in local tourism development through mobilizing collaboration. Civic entrepreneurs are people who help communities collaborate, so they can develop and organize their economic assets and build effective relationships across the public, private and voluntary sectors (Box 8.6).

In relation to tourism development, one criticism of rural areas is that they demonstrate low levels of entrepreneurship (Keane, 1992: 46; Wanhill, 1997; McKercher and Robbins, 1998), although there may be

Box 8.6. The common traits of civic entrepreneurs (source: Aspen Institute, 1996).

- Economic optimism: they understand new economic realities, and are compelled to act on an optimistic vision of how their community can be successful in the future. They believe the new global economy provides opportunities and helps communities make positive choices about their future, building the relationships and specialized resources for success.
- A 'classic' personality type: as people of vision, they see possibilities and work creatively and persistently to make possibilities real.
- Collaborative leadership style: they know how to work with people to get results, to bring together diverse parties, identify common ground, and take joint action. Often, civic entrepreneurs lead with no formal power or authority, just their personal credibility.
- Enlightened self interest: they believe that their personal long-term interests, and those of their organization, are to some extent tied to the health of the local economy and the community.
- Team players: they play different roles on a team, contributing their unique skills, experience, personalities and connections. Only by combining roles and developing more and more new leaders are civic entrepreneurs effective (see also Chapter 5).

evidence of higher degrees of innovation in those firms in accessible rural locations (Page and Getz, 1997: 29). In the development literature generally, reflecting a recent re-emphasis on the importance of locality, there is increasing interest in the nature of regional economic vitality and its role in regional economic development (Williams *et al.*, 2000). Research provides evidence of 'success factors', and while these vary between regions (because of various inherent advantages, for example) it is possible to discuss them in general terms as:

- integrated and diversified rural development;
- community development (Murphy, 1985; Keane, 1992: 47);
- the need for cooperative and collaborative working practices (Peebles, 1995);
- targeted public sector support of private sector initiatives; and
- development of economies of scope (Greffe, 1994).

Each of these is embraced by the concept of 'economic vitality'. The term 'vitality' is used to include levels of entrepreneurship as well as rates of innovation. It is influenced by the local milieu: the 'soft' environmental characteristics of regional development that are difficult to identify. Studies relating to milieux include themes such as:

- social capacity and local capital, concepts that stress the skills culture and attitudes of local people;
- institutional networks and their role(s) in effecting community-based development;
- clusters of businesses, 'agglomerative economies'; and
- the importance of the 'knowledge economy': the roles of, and access to, information.

(Williams *et al.*, 2000)

Almost all that has been said of local milieux and their roles in regional development has been based on qualitative, case study material from which theories of 'success factors' have been derived. Box 8.7 outlines the findings of two important empirical studies. Each of the factors relates closely to the industry challenges identified in Table 8.5 and to the characteristics of success factors. Points 1 and 2 clearly show that successful development is linked to principles of association.

Collaboration and partnership

Networks and collaborative agreements provide support and contribute to a better understanding of business and marketing environments within which firms operate. The synergy of a business cluster working together produces outcomes not possible of any indi-

Box 8.7. Characteristics of high levels of economic vitality (source: Williams *et al.*, 2000).

Two quantitative studies of local milieux seek to explain geographical variations in economic vitality between regions that have broadly similar resources and potential yet demonstrate differing entrepreneurial cultures.* Findings in relation to two Scottish regions, Orkney and Caithness were that:

1. Economic vitality is higher in areas that have relatively dense and active informal networks facilitating the diffusion of various kinds of information within the business community.
2. Economic vitality is higher in areas where the local network of SMEs has effective links with markets and sources of information outside the area. They are lower where the networks have a more local focus.
3. Economic vitality is influenced by the quality and density of links between local development agencies, supporting institutions and business networks.
4. Variations in economic vitality are in part related to the local development of an 'entrepreneurial culture' which in turn is influenced by various aspects of the recent economic history of the area.
5. Rivalry at local and regional scales is an effective stimulus to economic vitality.

* 'Milieux', a 1-year study was funded by the EU Northern Periphery Programme. The Scottish Executive Rural Affairs Department (SERAD) funded 'Success Factors', a 2-year programme.

vidual provider. And collaboration encourages recognition of the benefits of an entrepreneurial region whose 'dynamic economic and social characteristics' may, to some extent, compensate for the disadvantages of rural locations (Williams *et al.*, 2000).

While association and collaboration are recognized for their importance to the development function generally, they are essential to the development of a tourism region. The importance of a regional approach to rural tourism development is well recognized. According to Fagence (1993), a failure to achieve 'critical mass', that is a sufficient concentration of visitor attractions, facilities and amenities, means that a rural area lacks the ability to draw visitors to it for anything more than a few hours. Critical mass is required in order to:

- develop the capacity to serve and satisfy an increased market with a more diverse range of tourism experiences;
- encourage longer visitor stays;
- develop mutually supportive attractions and services; and as a result
- market, promote and package tourism opportunities for themed attractions and associated services.

(Fagence, 1993)

Clearly, an understanding of each of these benefits is essential to an agreement to work towards the development of a regional tourism base. The latter two points are, perhaps, particularly important in order to change understanding of the nature of competition in rural tourism and recreation markets. If it is the case that it is critical mass that attracts visitors for a period from which economic benefits can be achieved, and not the products or services of one particular provider, then it is in the interests of local providers to work together. Where the market is characterized by small-scale providers, economies of scope will only be derived from a collaborative and cooperative approach to market development. Individual providers and small communities must, therefore, surmount the barriers created by short-term and small-scale thinking and parochial perceptions of development that attempt to exclude others from development processes.

Point three of the 'milieux' research focuses on the importance of links between private and public sectors and the partnerships that result. Local development agencies and municipalities can provide assistance and finance for small businesses. Partnerships that result can be influenced by the extent of coordination between public sector agencies. Other influences may be the conditions attached to business support that affect operators' development plans (Williams *et al.*, 2000). Nevertheless, such partnerships are likely to be the most effective way of mobilizing and coordinating the resources required to develop a regional distinctiveness, and create the infrastructure to support a tourism that in its turn contributes to regional development. Factors critical to the success of partnerships include a high degree of interdependence and a perception that decisions made will be implemented. Trust, sincerity and honesty are therefore a critical element in the regional development process (Roberts and Simpson, 1999).

It will be difficult for firms to work together in a cooperative manner where regional institutions do not. The idea of 'institutional thickness' is, therefore, of critical importance. Although the term may be used to include the cooperation of businesses, 'institutions' more often refer to agents such as financial institutions, development agencies, local authorities and industry associations. Thus 'institutional thickness' refers to the presence of such organizations, the level and nature of inter-institutional interaction, the extent of a culture of collective representation, and the resulting 'social atmosphere' of a particular locality (Amin and Thrift, 1995, unpublished). Opinions differ as to whether a high level of inter-institutional activity is a positive quality and an indicator of dynamism and collective initiative. While it may be interpreted as a good thing, the need for simplification, integration, partnership and the elimination of redundancy within systems have been cited as negative qualities of inter-institutional working (Copus *et al.*, 2000, unpublished). More empirical research is required to improve understanding of such linkages.

Marketing

To be sustainable as individual enterprises, and to sustain their communities and cultural landscapes, rural businesses have a great deal to gain from understanding and adopting effective marketing practices. Better use of marketing can:

- reduce the isolation of small rural businesses;
- use resources more efficiently; and
- enable rural tourism industries to work within frameworks that will give them access to foreign tourist markets.

(Clarke, 1999)

Both niche and customized marketing are expensive processes that require a level of marketing expertise often not possessed by small rural tourism businesses (Hjalager, 1996; McKercher and Robbins, 1998; Clarke, 1999). As agricultural commodity producers, farmers and others have traditionally worked within regional or national networks, and with large organizations supporting the range of agricultural production types from processing to marketing and financing. Conversely, in relation to their tourism activities, rural providers tend to work as individuals thus losing the benefits of cooperative structures and coordinated programmes (Hjalager, 1996). The conscious need to re-establish such marketing channels has been slow to emerge but there is no doubt that cooperative practices and joint ventures, where they have been established, have generated marketing synergies at all spatial levels.

The case study of the English Farm Holiday Bureau (FHB) detailed in Box 8.8 illustrates the effectiveness of collaborative marketing for individual providers and tourism regions. Clarke (1999) stresses that the case study is not intended to represent a model for strategic marketing, the characteristics of individual cases requiring place and people-specific responses. It does, however, illustrate the benefits of collaborative over individual attempts at marketing. It is a good example, too, of the ability of the private sector to overcome its marketing problems with little recourse to public sector organizations. This will not always be possible, however; nor is it necessarily desirable. The fate of many small businesses is determined by market factors outwith their control, and public/private sector partnerships can help to shape improved responses to adverse market conditions in a number of ways.

Competition

Issues of marketing are closely linked to concepts of competitive advantage (Leat *et al.*, 2000) and enterprise. The milieux research (Box 8.7) highlights the significance of an enterprise culture and the importance of rivalry. It identifies that rivalry has a direct role in the stimulation of product improvements and innovation (after Porter, 1990, 1995). Significantly, it highlights two main sources of influence on innovation – 'competitors' and 'other' – and finds that 'a greater dependence on competitors as sources of the innovative idea ... may suggest more of a tendency to lag behind the competition' (Leat *et al.*, 2000). The adoption of 'other' sources of inspiration – customers, consultants, development agencies and research institutes, for example – demonstrates understanding of the extra-parochial nature of competition in rural markets and leads to competitive advantage. Chapter 4 showed how the LEADER+ programme is intended to promote transnationalism through inter-area cooperation and the exchange of experiences.

Perceptions of competition appear to lie at the heart of many of the challenges faced by rural tourism businesses. On the one hand, firms operate in highly competitive environments where small businesses vie for custom within poorly understood markets. On the other, they are required to work in partnership (often with those whom they view as their closest competitors) in order to develop the critical mass required of a dynamic tourism region. In order to make sense of the apparent paradox, individual providers must recognize the significance of external factors that have influenced demand for rural tourism and recreation products. These include the following:

- The emergence of consumer behaviour related to the non-use value of holiday and

Box 8.8. Strength in number: a case study of the Farm Holiday Bureau (FHB), England (source: Clarke, 1999).

The FHB is a member-owned consortium of farm accommodation providers. Originally formed in 1983, the FHB achieved autonomy from its founding members* in 1989 and established itself as a cooperative organization, run by members for members. The bureau has over 1000 individual farm members organized into 17 local area groups (LAGs), and is funded almost entirely by membership subscriptions.

Fundamentally, the Bureau aims to counteract the marketing problems of small, isolated rural businesses by:

- making marketing practice more effective through collective expertise and financial resources; and
- reducing the psychological isolation caused by remoteness of physical location through the professional contact and social cohesion of local area groups.

The model is essentially democratic, demonstrating grassroots control, power being retained by the collective voice of individual providers.

The FHB structure has three levels:

- *Head office:* primarily responsible for structured and planned research, marketing plans, PR, literature production and distribution, promotion.
- *Local area group:* primarily responsible for development of a local sense of place, local advertising, brochure policy, distribution, quality control.
- *Individual provider:* primarily responsible for market targeting, the formulation of individual products, pricing decisions, individual advertising and brochure production where appropriate, booking mechanisms.

The Bureau's synergy is partly attributable to the creative tension between these levels, the formality of strategic work at head office supporting the self-help of LAGs, and the individuality required at provider level. Thus each level has a different primary function and a complementary approach. With regard to marketing, local providers tend to act instinctively and informally, head office providing planned and formal structure. A further characteristic of the FHB model is its intra-level variety. Different LAGs operate in different ways and want different outcomes from their cooperation, for example continuity of group or dynamism of purpose.

Quality control

In the case of FHB, service quality was a supply- rather than demand-led initiative. It became operational through the membership recruitment process which demanded examination of:

- the extent to which the product reflected life on a working farm;
- the tangible product elements such as might form the basis of an accommodation classification scheme; and
- the intangible product elements such as host personality and local group 'fit'.

Additional measures to ensure product quality and consistency included:

- the provision of training opportunities: many of which were informal, 'on-the-job' training schemes within LAGs;
- local area group meetings: held in members' properties encouraging both best practice demonstration, and the sharing of ideas; the scrutiny to which host accommodation was subjected acts as further incentive to quality provision;
- the implementation of a customer complaint system at LAG level; and
- the threat of membership termination.

Further study of the groups' operations identified the following recommendations for continued good practice:

- In order to emphasize product authenticity, the level of the individual operator should seek to maintain and improve links with agriculturally affiliated organizations and allow evidence of such affiliation to form part of the product. Although product definitions did not result in watertight membership, for maximum effectiveness, definitions should be as tight as is feasibly possible in order to allow a clear product image, product differentiation and market positioning.

Continued overleaf

Box 8.8. *Continued*

- Local area identity (sense of place) becomes integrated with the product at the level of the local area, and should be emphasized by LAGs. This helps to counteract the trend towards the homogenization of tourism destinations and to retain the image of farm holidays as specialist, differentiated experiences.
- The national head office should build and maintain links with other organizations in the global tourism systzem, notably members of the travel trade. FHB has fostered links with Gîtes de France and the European Federation of Farm and Village Tourism, and has designed a web site to provide worldwide trade access for members on an individual basis.

Marketing

Marketing via a national framework creates the opportunity to generate repeat business. Within the FHB framework, three types of repeat usage are identified:

- Traditional: re-booking the same accommodation, that is repeat of a previous experience.
- Variety-seeking: booking another product but within a known local area.
- Generic product repeat booking: booking another farm stay but in a completely new geographical area.

FHB data analysis revealed that two out of every ten visitors were 'traditional' repeat visitors to an individual farm, demand created by product quality at individual operator level. The three-tier system allowed the FHB to capitalize on the marketing opportunities afforded by access to a group referral system at local area level. Additionally, a focus on generic product repeat usage, researching loyalty, not to a provider or local area, but to farm tourism generally, showed that 70% of consumers were repeat buyers of farm holidays. Attempts to capitalize on this include the strengthening of links with quality organizations at a national level.

In summary, the potential benefits of a successful collaborative marketing structure can be summarized as:

- increased benefits from limited marketing resources (such as finance, time and marketing expertise);
- an improved competitive position in the global marketplace for providers that may have been geographically remote;
- strengthened product authenticity and local identity retaining the individuality and distinctive character of rural tourism;
- mechanisms for improving product quality and consistency without loss of distinctiveness; and
- a number of different forms of repeat business.

* Royal Agricultural Society of England, ETB, Agricultural and Development Advisory Service (ADAS), and the trade magazine *Farmers Weekly*.

recreational products. As well as growing in size, rural tourism markets are changing in nature. Thus visitors may be in search of the rural idyll, peace and tranquillity, fresh air and good food as 'traditional' rural products, or wilderness, challenge, excitement and fun from participation in some new activities. And they may be in search of a combination of any of these experiences.

- The inability of any one provider to meet all of a visitor's needs.
- The benefits to all businesses in a region from the increased spending of visitors who stay overnight (who may spend four times as much as day visitors (Leones, 1995)).
- The need to provide a range of goods, services and experiences for visitors, and for ongoing innovation in product development in order to stimulate repeat visiting.

In order to participate in a regional initiative to meet the emerging needs of 'new' rural tourism and recreation markets, individual operators need to view competition from a new perspective that influences their perceptions of it in two ways:

- Competition should not be perceived only in those businesses operating in the same field. A farmer who develops a farm trail, for example, may be just as much competition for an operator with rowing boats for hire on a local river as she is for other farm

trail providers. At the product level, therefore, competition should not be viewed as activity specific.
- Competition should not be perceived as a parochial phenomenon, that is between providers at a local level. Small-scale perceptions of competition stifle strategic thinking and the subsequent development of business and marketing strategies on which integrated development can build. Furthermore, its narrow focus minimizes opportunities for collaboration and renders regional distinctiveness difficult to achieve.

The search for experiences in the countryside blurs the distinction between a range of activities, and renders them interchangeable. From a regional perspective, the existence of an increasing number of activities represents complementarity rather than competition; the range of experiences available, if of sufficient quality, will add to the area's attractiveness as a place to visit. Instead of viewing competitive edge as the appropriation a share of an existing regional market, for example by aggressive pricing, local providers should see it as a means of increasing the overall size of the regional market by improving regional competitiveness. Clarke's (1999) account of the FHB illustrates how a national marketing initiative provided access for individual members to worldwide markets, and identified opportunities for repeat business generation at provider level, within a region, and for farm holidays in general.

Value adding

It is only concerted effort that will tackle the problems of the low value-added character of rural tourism. Competitive markets and the existence of rivalry intensify businesses' reactions to market forces (Williams *et al.*, 2000). Aggressive pricing policies usually drive market prices down, eventually diminishing product quality. In an increasingly competitive market it is preferable to compete by differentiating product or service. Differentiation can create a competitive edge that may even permit premium pricing. There is a clear need to increase the value of the rural products, services and experiences that make up rural tourism and recreation markets, and quality is emerging as a key means of differentiation with commercial benefit for producers (Leat *et al.*, 2000). If a farmhouse accommodation provider can offer service and hospitality that exceeds that offered by others, they have added value to their product and can reflect this in the price they charge. Research has shown that diversification from agriculture into tourism requires a greater investment in terms of time (Hjalager, 1996). Why should this not be reflected in the price the consumer pays?

Clearly, in order to be able to achieve a quality advantage in practice, businesses must relate the quality they are offering to the satisfaction of consumer needs. In their analyses of markets for rural tourism and recreation products and services, Chapters 6 and 7 explain why this might be difficult in practice. Nevertheless, clear ways exist by which value can be added to rural products as Boxes 8.9 and 8.10 show.

The boxes show how value has been added by the addition of elements other than the threshold benefits of price, quality and value for money. Increasingly, value is reflected in intangible benefits such as experiences, a sense of authenticity and nostalgia. Figure 8.3 illustrates this process.

What does a focus on added value through quality mean for the marketing function? Marketing emerged as a discipline when consumerism was driven by the purchasing of tangible goods at a time when it was relatively easy to identify their core benefits and position them in relation to competition. At the start of the 21st century, standards have risen to the point where consumers can see little difference in the threshold benefits of products and services. Differentiation lies in the anticipation of people's desires, whether or not these have been articulated (Henley Centre, 1998: 23).

As identified by the Henley Centre, and described overleaf by Williams, the intangible elements that represent quality permit three key development processes.

1. They provide the qualities to create regional images and distinctiveness.
2. They create opportunities for the identification of distinctiveness at regional, local and individual level.

Invited Viewpoint

Quality Rural Tourism, Niche Markets and Imagery: Quality Products and Regional Identity

Fiona Williams

This section briefly addresses five issues:

1. The nature of quality in tourism.
2. The nature of rural quality products.
3. Trends towards a commodification of the rural.
4. Integration and promotion of imagery.
5. The role of quality products in promoting regional identity.

When applied to a service context, quality is a particularly subjective notion and there is no generally agreed definition of what constitutes quality. However, a number of indicators exist which may characterize a quality product or service. Such indicators can be categorized into two groups: (i) those relating to attributes which can be externally verified and controlled, for example certification and specification; and (ii) those of a subjective nature, in that they are experiential and lie in the eye of the beholder, for example establishing association or generating attraction.

Day and Peters (1994) refer to these various characteristics as the static and dynamic dimensions constituting service quality. The static dimensions refer to expectations of a basic level of facility or service, whereas dynamic dimensions are those that occur during the service delivery process and allow the provider the opportunity to exceed consumer expectations. The nature of the rural tourism product raises a number of issues relating to product quality and service delivery. For example, because characteristics of the rural tourism sector can include remote locations, a large number of relatively unorganized small businesses, resource constraints, and often a lack of management skills (Dolli and Pinfold, 1997), an indifference to marketing by SMEs comprising the rural tourism product can result. Given such an environment, linking supplier to buyer can be problematic. The heterogeneity of consumer preferences adds to the complexity of the service delivery interaction.

The adoption of marketing principles can provide a structured approach for the management and promotion of destinations in order to increase revenue for a destination while protecting such areas from the adverse impacts of tourism development. More recently, rural areas have sought to differentiate themselves (and their products and services), in an increasingly competitive marketplace, through the use of quality and regional imagery. With the acknowledgement that a symbiosis between place and product may exist which can add value to local resources (OECD, 1995), a policy direction has evolved which seeks to build on existing skills and rural resources and the encouragement of niche markets based on those assets.

An EU EC Agriculture and Fisheries Research Programme (FAIR) research project entitled 'Regional Images and the Promotion of Quality Products and Services in Lagging Regions of the European Union' (RIPPLE) investigated how the potential of rural resources through the use of quality and imagery in marketing could be realized. The project examined the production, marketing, consumption and regulation of quality products and services (including rural tourism providers) in 12 'lagging' regions of six EU states. RIPPLE sought to identify how the competitiveness of quality products and services could be improved and thereby inform policy decisions, strategies and structures.

The research identified quality as an important determinant of choice and highlighted that new ways to the construction of quality were being sought. However, a plethora of influences need to be considered when adopting quality as a new competitive tool. As summarized by Leat *et al.* (2000), some of the issues involved in deriving competitive advantage through quality can be considered in terms of:

- Supply side differentiation: the ability to add uniqueness to the services provided; for example level of customer service, quality of management activities including marketing, quality design, production and approach.
- Demand side differentiation: the firm's ability to understand customer or consumer demand and match a demand for difference with its own service and the associated marketing mix. This can be gained through formal or informal market research.

A quality image can be created through the use of subtle signs and symbols ('branding') which consumers use to judge quality and forge links between a product and a region's landscape. Culture and heritage can assist in reinforcing this message. The use of imagery in promotion is characteristic of the tourism industry in that the intangible nature of the product means that potential customers place greater importance on the image of a destination, in order to inform their purchasing decision. The branding of rural destinations (in comparison with their urban counterparts) is a more contemporary development, although currently there are many examples of rural areas seeking to develop images and to promote themselves in an integrated fashion.

There are a number of difficulties in creating imagery to promote a place:

- there is the problem of distinctiveness when so many rural areas have comparable attributes; and
- it is difficult to assess the effectiveness of the strategic promotional element when perceptions are formed by so many different influences, many of which are outside the control of individual businesses.

With reference to other product and service differentiation, the value of linking product to place is a more recent development, though the use of regional imagery to promote quality products, most notably food items, is now prevalent. In a number of cases, for example beef and salmon, an effective link between quality and regional imagery has been built, and has proved lucrative, with some regionally branded products demanding premium prices in the market place. With greater integration between rural sectors, the tourism industry can also benefit from a raised quality profile in other sectors and from the identity generated by the sale of regionally branded goods. More obvious examples include the link between Scottish whisky and tourism in the Grampian Highlands or wine tourism in the vineyard regions of France. Rural areas are now beginning to experience the proliferation of food trails and craft trails and industrial attractions based on the production of quality produce. Examples include creameries, factory outlets, for example Baxters of Speyside, distilleries and breweries. Many of these developments are characterized by:

- being set in a rural heartland;
- utilising local resources and regional imagery; and
- contributing to the rural tourism product.

Regional imagery can add to the differentiation of regional quality products and services but the images developed and projected must link regional characteristics with consumer perceptions and values. Differing products and services may utilize particular aspects of imagery deemed most suitable for the promotional message; however, the images portrayed need to form a cohesive whole. To ensure that consumers are not bombarded with conflicting information that complicates the purchase decision (e.g. competing advertising or potentially conflicting websites), the approach to the use of regional imagery requires coordination and consensus among interested parties.

Rural tourism providers need to consider their own products in terms of consumer expectations and to develop them accordingly. The quality message needs to be communicated and to involve all aspects of the product and all levels of the purchasing process. Increasingly, there is a need for tourism forums and consortia to develop a quality image and achieve consistency in terms of the regional product. This approach needs to encompass other actors in the rural arena and to bring together those interests that are adjacent but have traditionally remained distant.

Fiona Williams

Box 8.9. James's Chocolates, Arran (source: Brown, 2000; also see Cultural tourism, Chapter 7).

The *Isle of Arran Taste Trail* is a visitor's guide to good food and good eating on the Isle of Arran.

James's Chocolates at Invercloy, Brodick are chocolate makers you can watch 'weaving their magic' as you stand in the shop as the hand-made chocolates are manufactured on site. In the interests of market research (and, probably, repeat visiting!) there is a tasting tray on the shop counter which are James's latest flavour experiments. While making your selection, therefore, you can try out the Lochranza whisky truffle, after which a visit to the Isle of Arran Distillers might be in order. Buying chocolates thus becomes, not an activity, but an experience.

Box 8.10. Souvenir production in Lapland (source: Miettenen, 1999: 95; see also Cultural tourism, Chapter 7).

Through the Eurotex project (see Chapter 7), crafts producers in Lapland were encouraged to consider the nature and purpose of souvenirs:

- As a memory, a souvenir represents a traveller's experiences and feelings about places visited. As such, it has the power to return her or his thoughts to that place many years later. A good souvenir strengthens the traveller's positive experiences about the destination.
- As a gift, a souvenir's significance lies in its ability to give pleasure as well as some idea of the place visited.
- As an object of use, a souvenir has a function but may also carry connotations of tradition.

Recognition of the importance of the souvenir industry to crafts producers had led to the decoration of products with Lapland stickers or traditional Sami decorations rather than concentrating on the production of good crafts products.

An understanding was achieved that local materials and traditional techniques were in themselves representations of Lappish and Sami crafts that produce innovative, functional products with good design and semantic information about Lapland as an area with natural materials, using techniques that can make good use of modern technology. One purpose of the project was to increase the value of gifts and souvenirs bought by visitors to the region.

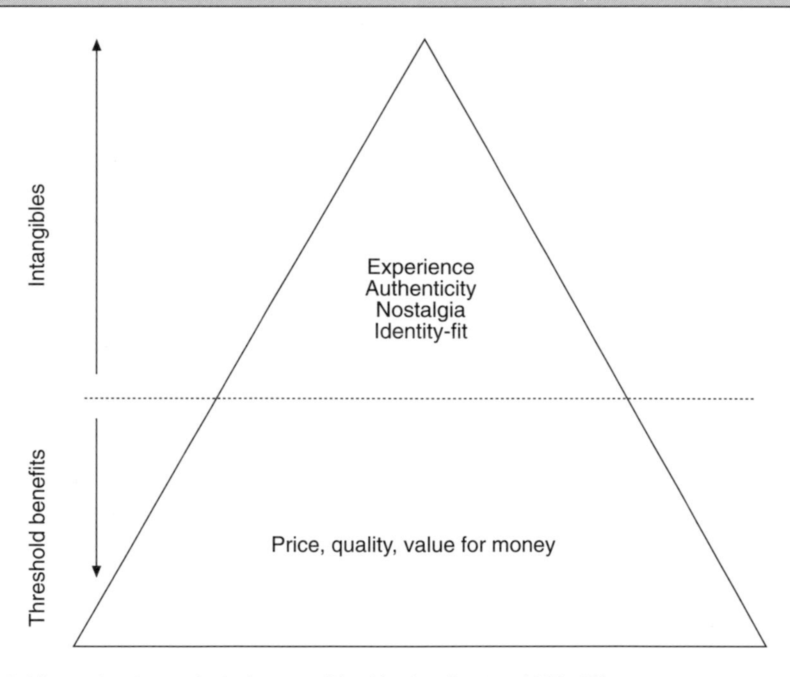

Fig. 8.3. Adding value to products (source: The Henley Centre, 1998: 23).

3. They generate the experiences sought by both rural tourists and tourists in rural areas.

Chapter Summary

Earlier in the chapter, Table 8.5 presented a number of market failures that require public sector intervention if they are to be overcome. The subsequent debate has outlined a number of areas of research that contribute to an understanding of both market conditions and potential remedies, and further inform the development process.

It is clear, however, that 'rural tourism and recreation' industries do not provide a panacea for declining rural areas. The aims of rural development (as set out in the Cork Declaration, see Chapter 4) require a holistic approach and are centred around the well-being and perpetuity of rural communities. The requirements of rural tourism development, dissimilarly, focus on the needs of a fragmented private sector with some degree of profit orientation. Beyond the enablement of the market conditions for successful business operation, therefore, one of the public sector's main roles in tourism development is to maintain the integrity of the rural communities on which development is based.

The analysis in this chapter has shown that issues such as entrepreneurship and innovation, economic vitality and an understanding of markets and marketing, all contribute to a region's ability to benefit from tourism development. It is also clear that for micro- and small businesses to thrive, they need to play a cooperative role within a regional initiative. Above all, however, the analysis has shown that, while the conceptual frameworks on which rural tourism communities can build their futures exist, their development potential has yet to be realized.

References

AEIDL (1994) *Marketing Quality Rural Tourism.* LEADER Co-ordinating Unit, Brussels. http://www.rural-europe.aeidl.be/rural-en/biblio/touris/art07.html

Amin, A. and Thrift, N. (1995) Globalisation, institutional thickness and the local economy. In: Healey, P., Cameron, S., Davoudi, S., Graham, S. and Madna-Pour, A. (eds) *Managing Cities, the New Urban Context.* John Wiley & Sons, Chichester.

Aspen Institute (1996) *Developing Entrepreneurial Economies in Rural Regions: Lessons from Kentucky and Appalachia.* Aspen Institute, Washington, DC.

British Horse Society (2000) *Bed and Breakfast for Horses, the Millennium Edition.* The British Horse Society, Kenilworth.

Brown, C. (2000) *Isle of Arran Taste Trail.* Argyll and the Islands Enterprise, Lochgilphead.

Clarke, J. (1999) Marketing structures for farm tourism: beyond the individual provider of rural tourism. *Journal of Sustainable Tourism* 7(1), 26–47.

Clemenson, H. and Lane, B. (1997) Niche markets, niche marketing and rural employment. In: Bollman, R.D. and Bryden, J.M. (eds) *Rural Employment: an International Perspective.* CAB International, Wallingford, pp. 410–426.

Copus, A., Gourlay, D. and Williams, F. 'Holding down the global': regional milieux, innovation and economic vitality in the periphery. Unpublished report.

Davidson, R. and Maitland, R. (1997) *Tourism Destinations.* Hodder and Stoughton, London.

Day, A. and Peters, J. (1994) Rediscovering standards: static and dynamic quality. *International Journal of Contemporary Hospitality Management* 6(1), 81–84.

Dolli, I.N. and Pinfold, J.F. (1997) Managing rural tourism businesses: financing, development and marketing issues. In: Page, S. and Getz, D. (eds) *The Business of Rural Tourism.* International Thomson Business Press, London, pp. 38–58.

Dunn, B. (1995) Success themes in Scottish family enterprises; philosophies and practices through the generations. *Family Business Review* 8(1), 17–28.

Edmunds (1999) Rural tourism in Europe. *Trade and Tourism Analyst* No. 6, 37–50.

ENSR (1997) *The European Observatory for SMEs,* 5th Annual Report for DGXXIII. EIM Small Business Research and Consultancy, The Hague.

Eurostat (1997) *Enterprise in Europe, 4th Report.* Eurostat, Luxembourg.

Fagence, M. (1993) Regional tourism strategies: the 'critical mass' as an optimisation tool in rural areas. In: Bruce, D. and Whitla, M. (eds) *Tourism Strategies for Rural Development.* Mount Allison University, New Brunswick, pp. 1–15.

Getz, D. and Carlsen, J. (2000) Characteristics and goals of family and owner-operated businesses in the rural tourism and hospitality sectors. *Tourism Management* 21, 547–560.

Greffe, X. (1994) Is rural tourism a lever for economic and social development? *Journal of Sustainable Tourism* 2(1/2), 22–40.

Grolleau, H. (1994) Putting feelings first. *Marketing Quality Rural Tourism.* LEADER Technical Dossier, LEADER Co-ordinating Group, Brussels, p. 7.

Hall, C.M. and Jenkins, J. (1998) The policy dimensions of rural tourism and recreation. In: Butler, R., Hall, C.M. and Jenkins, J. (eds) *Tourism and Recreation in Rural Areas.* John Wiley & Sons, Chichester, pp. 19–42.

Henley Centre (1998) *Planning for Consumer Change: Issues.* Henley Centre for Forecasting, London.

Herries, J. (1998) *Glen Shiel Hillwalking Survey 1996: report of findings.* Scottish Natural Heritage, Perth.

Hjalager, A.M. (1996) Agricultural diversification into tourism. *Tourism Management* 17(2), 103–111.

Keane, M.J. (1992) Rural tourism and rural development. In: Briassoulis, H. and van der Straaten, J. (eds) *Tourism and the Environment: Regional, Economic and Policy Issues.* Kluwer Academic Publishers, Dordrecht, pp. 43–55.

Lane, B. (1994) What is rural tourism? *Journal of Sustainable Tourism* 2(1–2), 1–6.

Lane, B. (1995a) *Niche Markets and Rural Development.* OECD, Paris.

Lane, B. (1995b) *Niche Markets as a Rural Development Strategy.* OECD, Paris.

Leat, P., Williams, F. and Brannigan, J. (2000) Rural competitiveness through quality and imagery across lagging regions of the European Union. In: *Proceedings of the Conference on European Rural Policy at the Crossroads.* The Arkleton Centre, University of Aberdeen, Aberdeen, 29 June–1 July.

Leones, J. (1995) Tourism trends and rural economic impacts. In: AREC (eds) *Direct Farm Marketing and Tourism Handbook.* Agricultural and Resource Economics, Arizona, pp. 15–18.

McKercher, B. and Robbins, B. (1998) Business development issues affecting nature-based tourism operators in Australia. *Journal of Sustainable Tourism* 6(2), 173–188.

MAF (Ministry of Agriculture and Food, New Zealand) (1999) *Civic Entrepreneurs: Community Builders.* MAF, Wellington. http://www.maf.govt.nz/MAFnet/publications/

Miettenen, S. (1999) Crafts tourism in Lapland. In: Richards, G. (ed.) *Developing and Marketing Crafts Tourism.* ATLAS, Tilburg, pp. 89–103.

Middleton, V.T.C. (1998) SMEs in European tourism: the context and a proposed framework for European Action. *Revue de Tourisme* 4, 29–37.

Moutinho, L. (2000) Segmentation, targeting, positioning and strategic marketing. In: Moutinho, L. (ed.) *Strategic Management in Tourism.* CAB International, Wallingford, pp. 121–166.

Murphy, P.E. (1985) *Tourism – a Community Approach.* Routledge, London.

OECD (1995) *Niche Markets as a Rural Development Strategy.* OECD, Paris.

Page, S.J. and Getz, D. (eds) (1997) *The Business of Rural Tourism: International Perspectives.* International Thomson Business Press, London.

Peebles, M.S. (1995) Cultivating the tourist: farm tourism. *Tourism* 86, 20.

Pine, B.J. (1993) *Mass Customisation.* Harvard University Press, New York.

Porter, M.E. (1990) *The Competitive Advantage of Nations.* Macmillan, London.

Porter, M.E. (1995) The determinants and dynamics of national advantage. In: Drew, J. (ed.) *Readings in International Enterprise.* Routledge, London.

Roberts, L. and Simpson, F. (1999) Developing partnership approaches to tourism in Central and Eastern Europe. *Journal of Sustainable Tourism* 7(3/4), 314–330.

Scottish Executive (2000) *A New Strategy for Scottish Tourism.* Scottish Executive, Edinburgh.

Seaton, A.V. and Bennett, M.M. (1996) *Marketing Tourism Products: Concepts, Issues, Cases.* International Thomson Business Press, London.

Sharpley, R. (2000) The consumption of tourism revisited. In: Robinson, M., Long, P., Evans, M., Sharpley, R. and Swarbrooke, J. (eds) *Reflections on International Tourism, Motivations, Behaviour and Tourist Types.* Business Education Publishers, Sunderland, pp. 381–391.

Shaw, G. and Williams, A.M. (1990) Tourism, economic development and the role of entrepreneurial activity. In: Cooper, C.P. (ed.) *Progress in Tourism, Recreation and Hospitality Management,* Vol. 2. Belhaven, London, pp. 67–81.

Wales Tourist Board (1998) *Recommendations Arising from the Agenda 2010, European Conference on SMEs.* Wales Tourist Board, Cardiff.

Wanhill, S. (1997) Peripheral area tourism: a European perspective. *Progress in Tourism and Hospitality Research* 3, 47–70.

Wanhill, S. (2000) Small and medium tourism enterprises. *Annals of Tourism Research* 27(1), 132–147.

Williams, F., Gourlay, D. and Copus, A. (2000) *Something in the Water? Local Milieux as an Explanation for Geographical Variations in Economic Vitality.* Discussion Paper, The Scottish Agricultural College, Aberdeen.

9

Synthesis and Conclusions

'By themselves, people and scenery are not enough to form the basis for good, steady, stable tourism. What Ireland is now engaged in is grafting on a whole range of products which will be built on environmental excellence to make it a more attractive destination. It is necessary to get away from the "green desert" image of a nice country of friendly people and poor weather with not much to do' (Convery and Flanagan, 1992: 146).

The processes of nature's appropriation, representation and commodification for tourism purposes could hardly be more succinctly put. Inclusion of the term 'environmental excellence' permits continued refuge behind the rhetoric of sustainability, yet the thing most sustained is the dichotomy between principle and practice. The 'implementation gap' (Pigram, 1993; Butler and Hall, 1998: 254) remains. We need, therefore, to move on from protracted debates about the sustainability of 'alternative' tourisms (of which rural tourism has been considered a part) to issues regarding the management of the material consumption of the European countryside by substantial tourism markets.

Within tourism generally it is well accepted that exogenous values can significantly influence the social character of destination areas. Susceptibility to social change in the rural sector was examined in Chapter 2 where the challenges of counter-urbanization and its often anachronistic rural values were examined. Chapter 3 analysed rural sustainability conflicts, and Chapter 8 illustrated the ways in which the countryside, as a site for consumption, may merely provide a convenient setting for recreational pursuits regardless of its intrinsic qualities. Change is inevitable but it is preferable as the result of informed decision making made possible, in the first instance, by the removal of the linguistic and perceptual barriers created by terms such as green, eco-, soft and niche. Chapter 8 revealed a 'rural tourism' reality more accurately interpreted with labels such as mainstream, mass and hard.

By accepting that there is a 'rural crisis in Europe' (Swarbrooke, 1999: 162), we recognize the unprecedented pressures from a wide range of sources including tourism development. As a result, we argue that:

- 'Pure' forms of rural tourism constitute a lesser part of the 'rural tourism phenomenon' than does tourism in rural areas. Tourism and recreation in the European countryside are, therefore, predominantly forms of mass tourism.
- Forms of mass tourism, with their emphasis on the consumption of experiences, are incompatible with the principles of sustainable tourism development.
- The importance of the intrinsic values of the countryside is likely to be lower for those 'rural visitors' for whom the focus of their trip is an activity such as off-road cycling or driving or windsurfing.
- It is important to recognize that 'rural tourism' is not a small-scale, low impact phenomenon. Views of it as such divert attention away from critical development

issues of the reality. The demands and likely impacts of tourism's development should be openly acknowledged within decision processes regarding the acceptable limits of likely changes. The simplicity of this statement, however, is not meant to imply that harmony will necessarily be achieved in the process. Conflict is an inherent characteristic of development. But Chapter 5 showed how the term 'community' can be used to convey false notions of consensuality revealing yet another example of the linguistic sophistry that prevents us from dealing with the realities of tourism development in the European countryside.

The preceding chapters have revealed a number of tensions that complicate an understanding of the changes being experienced within the rural realm, many of which are paradoxical in nature. The final chapter explores the extent to which these paradoxes reflect dichotomy, divergence and distinction, or present opportunities to manage coexistence and complementarity. This exploration is conducted by revisiting the book's recurring themes.

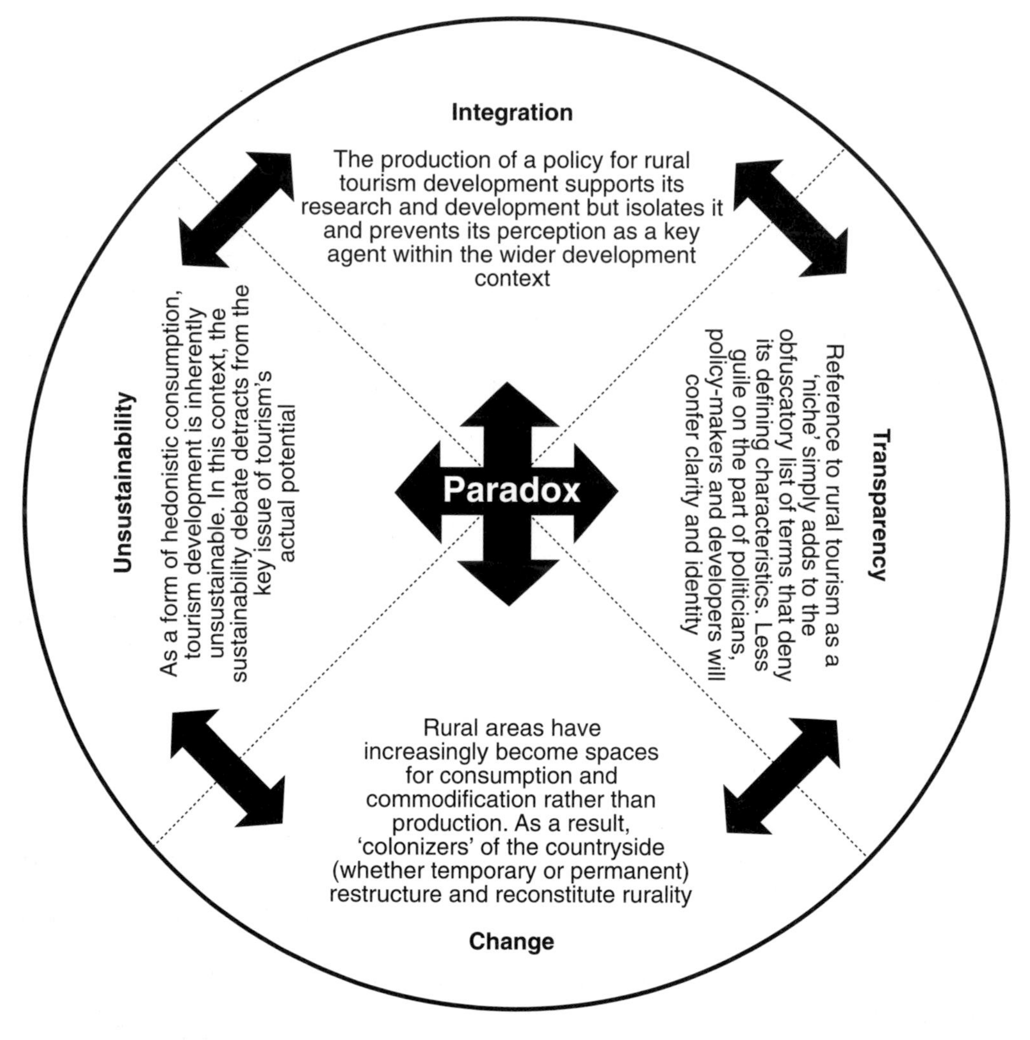

Fig. 9.1. Key themes.

Paradox

As the pivotal theme, paradox permeates each of the others as illustrated in Fig. 9.1. A number of paradoxes have been identified throughout the book:

- continuity and change;
- old and new forms of tourism in rural areas;
- heterogeneity and homogeneity;
- myth and reality;
- sustainability and unsustainability;
- competition and cooperation;
- mass and niche;
- the notion of mass customization; and
- principles and practice.

Tourism studies generally expose tensions within production and consumption processes, and the rural context presents no exception. But while paradox represents apparent contradiction, it does not necessarily imply irreconcilability.

For example, although popular images of the rural idyll may be largely fabricated, it has been argued by Sørensen and Nilsson (1999) that the dualism between myth and reality can be used to advantage in the marketing of tourism and recreation in rural areas (see Chapter 2). Although tourists' perceptions of rurality are often described as being in conflict with the realities faced by rural areas, interviews with tourists in rural areas in Denmark suggested a high degree of awareness of farming methods, animal rights and issues of land ownership. It is claimed that the visitor to rural areas has a high degree of 'reality awareness' but that this in no way lessens the demand for visitor enjoyment of the rural idyll. The suggestion is that tourists in rural areas understand and accept the inauthenticity, or the 'virtual rurality' they are offered where it provides a sufficiently rewarding experience of a 'rural reality'. Chapters 6 and 7 outlined the developing experience economy. Given the need to focus on demand rather than supply-led products in the rural sector (AEIDL, 1994; Swarbrooke, 1999: 169), the question of consumer behaviour and the consumption of tourism generally might be addressed by research in the rural context.

Further, the suggestion that rural tourism in its 'pure' form consists of a relatively small number of modestly sized markets while tourism in rural areas is a mass phenomenon, may not represent irreconcilable differences. That people appear to have multiple (and sometimes contradictory) perceptions of the countryside clearly renders its management much more difficult. But skilful use of marketing, de-marketing, commodification, education and interpretative materials may permit shared, if different, forms of consumption. Especially where policy direction is lacking, a framework for the development of management practice is required.

Change

Because the pace of change in rural areas is accelerating, its impacts may be felt more precipitously than in the past. The restructuring processes common to most industrialized countries have wrought significant economic, social and political change in rural areas, of which tourism and recreation development have been both agent and subject.

The shift from rural depopulation to counter-urbanization was identified in Chapter 2, together with an associated research focus on the integration of the relations of property and occupation with those of consumption and commodification. The reversal in the trend of rural-to-urban migration results from a number of influences, perhaps most notably the aspirations of many people to adopt a rural lifestyle. Where this involves the expression of values representative of past rather than present rural milieux, it can result in opposition by newcomers to any form of development that will mar the rural idyll they have achieved for themselves. The receptivity of old and new rural residents to tourism development and, in turn, such communities' attractiveness to tourists in rural areas, adds further dimension to issues of tourism's social sustainability and is worthy of further research.

Questions of social exclusion, exacerbated where development reinforces prevailing power relations, were raised in Chapter 2.

Attempts to quantify and map rural well-being are thwarted by the concept's subjectivity. Rural residents' perceptions of their well-being may be at odds with a generally held view, and further research may establish new indicators with which to measure qualities of rural life.

Socially constructed countryside is dangerous territory. Subjective, emotional attachments to imagined place and/or community may bear no relation to objective reality yet may influence the ways in which people behave. Representations of rurality, even those known to be false, may actively structure rural spaces. The demand for pretty villages comes to shape the appearance of rural settlements in order to satisfy the needs of visitors. Awareness of such processes should be raised during the development consultation stage.

Unsustainability

Sustainable development, with its demands for the holistic and equitable, and its long-term focus, may limit the potential for economic development which often takes a short-term and rather more sectoral approach. Local needs, and the stimuli for economic growth, are essentially incompatible with the aims of sustainable development as explained in Chapter 3. Chapter 8 pointed to the need for tourism development to form a part of regional development. But the planning and coordination required to achieve this are unlikely to arise from grassroots initiatives and thus another unsustainable element of tourism development must be accepted. Future research should focus on the means by which development objectives can be achieved with minimum adverse impacts. Better models for the measurement of physical, social, cultural and psychological carrying capacities are required, and an understanding of the opportunity costs of tourism development is essential. Regions marketing themselves as destinations should promote a prior understanding of the limits to change they will accept, and develop a means of measuring the quality of environments that are placed at risk by intended tourism development processes.

> The uneasy combination of new and traditional forms of tourism and recreation casts increasing doubt on their sustainability in the changing rural environment. One of the major aims of research on tourism and recreation in rural areas should be the identification of new frameworks for applying the principles of sustainability and long-term economic viability of tourism. Only in this way can rural tourism fulfil its long-vaunted economic potential as an effective tool of rural regional development.
>
> (Butler and Hall, 1998: 249)

Chapter 8 introduced the *importance of the countryside* model as a tool for evaluating the extent to which consumer satisfaction depends on the rural environment, and its marketing implications were analysed. The model also has applications for policy and management purposes.

At a policy level, the importance of the countryside model is useful for focusing attention on the ways in which the activities of rural visitors may provide insight into the importance they place on the countryside for consumer satisfaction. While the value judgements attached to many countryside access policy decisions are questioned (see Shoard, 1987), they may become increasingly recognized to be based on the premise that the countryside, as both a finite resource and a contested space, will be unable to support the capacity required of the projected growth of tourism and recreation. Some areas will support some activities. Fragile areas may be unsuitable for most recreational forms. Many types of tourism and recreation may be better managed in dedicated resorts and spaces (where these may be contained within rural environments, e.g. Center Parcs).

Notions of selection, restriction and exclusion in rural tourism and recreation clearly conflict with the principles of social inclusion analysed in Chapter 2. However, the importance of the countryside model may have greater appeal than one based on the payment of entry fees, which excludes on the grounds of ability to pay for access (see Chapter 4). While entry fees can be designed to reduce subsidization to groups that may be seen to receive unfair advantage (Laarman and Gregersen, 1996), their inherent inequality may be the basis of their unpopularity. Research conducted by Fyall and Garrod (1998) found little evidence that pricing is used as a device for limiting visitor demand or as a means of applying the 'user pays' principle.

The European countryside has an existence value as well as a use value, however, and some means of permitting use without threatening viability must be found. There is little doubt, therefore, that increasing restrictions will be placed on future access to areas such as national parks due to the negative impacts of large numbers of visitors (Hall, 2000). Selection, restriction and exclusion may be the future tools of tourism management in rural areas in coming decades, where the resource base is threatened. The importance of the countryside model adds further dimension to processes by which such tools may be implemented.

Principles of social *inclusion* require access to potentially fragile resources by those who may have little experience in such settings. The extent to which the development and use of interpretative materials can assist in the management of rural tourism and tourism in rural areas is yet to be explored. Is there scope for re-evaluation of consumer values through tourism provision in rural areas or is the countryside merely another resource for consumption? What is the role of interpretation? Does it help people to understand and therefore benefit more from a countryside visit? Or, in 'putting it on a plate' does interpretation prevent people from exploring and interpreting the countryside for themselves, removing the challenge of discovery? And is this sacrifice less than that which accompanies habitat and landscape damage, and lifestyle acculturation? The focus of future research may address any (or all) of these issues.

Transparency

The differences between the terms 'mass' and 'niche' are more than a mere question of semantics because the labels used influence perceptions that shape the nature of policy issues and management practices. There is a fundamental need for transparency in recognizing the essential nature of 'new' forms of tourism in rural areas, and to label these different forms so that they are seen for the phenomena they are: often large rather than small-scale, and with consumption patterns that demand a high degree of place commodification. This need not imply that they are 'bad' forms of tourism; the negative connotations carried by the pejorative use of the term 'mass' are not always justified. Appropriate policy approaches and management strategies cannot be devised, however, until the nature of the industry is acknowledged and its implications fully understood.

This raises questions about the consumers of tourism and recreation in rural areas as analysed in Chapter 6. Who essentially are tourists in rural areas? Are they: (i) 'rural tourists' for whom the earnest quest for authenticity (MacCannell, 1999) is essential for their enjoyment of the countryside? or (ii) 'tourists in rural areas' whose trivial, frivolous and superficial pursuit of vicarious and contrived experiences (Boorstin in Cohen, 1996) drives their consumption?

There is a focus on the increasing heterogeneity of demand for different activities in rural areas, but this change, too, may reflect the paradox of postmodern forms of consumption. In developing products and services for consumers, many 'new' forms of tourism in rural areas offer experiences that, although they may be manifest differently, offer similar sensations, of adventure, thrill or fun, for example. In this way, the increasing heterogeneity of demand may be seen to be satisfied by products that are interchangeable and increasingly homogeneous. The concepts of 'traditional' and 'contemporary' types of rural tourism were introduced in Chapter 1, 'traditional' representing 'passive' activities including landscape appreciation, and 'contemporary', more 'active' pastimes such as whitewater rafting and horse-riding.

Yet again, the labelling of tourism's forms is significant. While it is the case that many of the 'new' tourism and recreational forms involve more physical activity than some 'traditional' rural pursuits, contemporary forms may be perceived to be passive in the sense that their enjoyment relies on the input of intermediaries to plan and deliver the consumer experience. Hillwalking or birdwatching, on the other hand, is achieved by the individual who communes with, and interprets, nature as a result of an active involvement with the rural environment. The role of interpretation may be important in generating involvement with the countryside as a cerebral activity where this is a desirable policy and/or management objective. Activity and passivity therefore refer to dimensions other than the physical and require clarity in their use to avoid misunderstanding.

It seems to be widely accepted that 'new' forms of tourism and recreation in rural areas are changing the nature of the industries that collectively make up what are referred to as 'rural tourism' (Butler and Hall, 1998: 249; Swarbrooke, 1999: 169). Increasing visitor numbers and the changing nature of consumption combine to force significant change in terms of both scope and scale. The suggestion that tourism in the countryside is dominated not by niche markets, but by a form of non-coastal mass tourism may be an uncomfortable one. Its existence as such may be less obvious because, despite congestion in popular areas such as the Alto Minho in Portugal and the French Alps, for example, pandemic car use allows for the widespread dispersion of tourists throughout Europe's countryside rather than their concentration along accessible stretches of coastline. If the suggestion is uncomfortable, it is because the recognized problems of mass tourism clearly threaten its development in rural areas as currently practised. Mass tourism and recreation in rural areas will require particular policy and management measures in order to avoid a repetition of coastal tourism's worst excesses (Plate 9.1).

Plate 9.1. Stop! By what criteria will we decide our future countryside management policies?

Under such circumstances, the motives of tourists become all-important. What needs and wants is the rural setting to satisfy? Is the rural environment important or are visitors drawn by the activities the commodified countryside now offers? Do people visit the countryside because they want to or because they can? Do the stresses of urban and suburban living drive people out of their pressured environments in search of an alternative? If the countryside becomes a vehicle for the satisfaction of a range of egotistical motivations as suggested by Grolleau (1994) (Chapter 8) we may witness the pursuit of leisure and recreation at the expense of nature, the unique qualities of special places not registering as important to the visitors' experiences and satisfactions, yet still being consumed and commodified within consumption processes. Rural tourists require something of the natural environment for their consumption of it. For tourists in rural areas, the countryside may have very little intrinsic significance.

Integration

Paradoxically, the discrete study of tourism development may militate against this central theme. Chapter 4 presented an account of the Finnish national policy for 'rural tourism' and questioned the wisdom of isolating it for research and policy purposes thus removing it from its wider developmental context. The Cork Declaration on rural development (see also Chapter 4) stresses the need to integrate agricultural adjustment and development, economic diversification, the management

Principles	Theme	Practice
'Pure' rural tourism and recreation characterized by a 'traditional' context of relatively passive recreation. 'Contemporary' patterns of consumption whereby the countryside provides merely the setting for more physically active forms of recreation	← Change →	Growing demand for tourist attractions, amenities and services in rural areas more closely resembling mass forms of general tourism consumption than specialist forms of 'traditional' recreational activity. The countryside not necessarily a key component in consumer satisfaction
Myths of the rural idyll draw residents, tourists and recreationists to a countryside that barely exists in reality but that is created and maintained through the imposition of urban perceptions of rurality	← Transparency →	Manufactured images of the rural idyll – pretentiously pretty cottages and twee landscapes, wholesomeness, and community – are actively harnessed in the development of marketing campaigns to attract urban dwellers to rural areas for holidays and recreation
In theory, the concept of sustainable tourism development has been absorbed into policies and plans for rural tourism's development despite the fact that there remains an 'implementation gap'	← Unsustainability →	In practice, the prescriptive characteristics of tourism development, the top-down nature of planning required for its integration with rural development, and the nature of its consumption all militate against it meeting the requirements of sustainable development
Partnerships are likely to be the most effective way of mobilizing and coordinating the resources required to develop a regional distinctiveness. Tourism development can contribute more to a locality by its integration within rural development plans	← Integration →	Inter-business rivalry tends to dominate the principles of partnership and collaboration. Competition is a parochial phenomenon. Lack of understanding of the need to develop regional as well as business distinctiveness and local politics often render collaborative working difficult

← P A R A D O X →

Fig. 9.2. The continuing implementation gap between principles and practice.

and enhancement of natural resources, and the promotion of culture, tourism and recreation. The LEADER programme, too, focuses on the need for integrated schemes conceived and implemented by active partnerships (again, in Chapter 4). It is generally well accepted, therefore, that 'rural tourism' must be integrated with community-based development initiatives and not planned as a single sector (Keane, 1992: 53).

Tourism's role in integrated rural development is fundamentally an economic one. 'For almost all countries the economic significance of tourism has been the driving force in encouraging its development' (Burns and Holden, 1995: 64). The question of how tourism and recreation's development may be integrated into wider rural development planning is critical both to the success of businesses and of the regions and communities in which they thrive. The work of the Rural Policy Group at the Scottish Agricultural College, Aberdeen is contributing to an understanding of regional vitality (see Chapter 8), an integrated concept, and critical to the harnessing of funds for development purposes.

The term 'integration' applies at another level. Collaboration and cooperation are required of businesses in the development of networks, partnerships and regional bodies that can work in collective interest (see Chapter 5). Both economies of scale and scope (i.e. gains to a firm as a result of expansion of the industry) are only likely to be achieved by collaborative practices; the effects of individual firms' marketing are inadequate, widely dispersed and relatively ineffective. Certainly, the critical mass required to attract visitors, and regional distinctiveness, from which a quality image can be derived, will only be achieved through cooperative working practices.

But, as has been identified, although the conceptual frameworks exist for tourism's integration with rural development, their usefulness has not yet been translated into practical terms on any scale and the 'implementation gap' (Pigram, 1993; Butler and Hall, 1998: 254) still exists in relation to a number of development principles as illustrated in Fig. 9.2. The problem lies not with what has been achieved, but with what has not. Many 'islands of best practice' can be found, not least among the many successful LEADER initiatives. But this presents us with a further paradox, for the widespread application of good practice is inconsistent with the place and people specificity of 'rural tourism' development. We need a comprehensive and persistent application of 'appropriateness'; the type of development that meets local needs.

The explanation for the continuing implementation gap may lie in the narrow focus of much current research. In their 1997 publication *The Business of Rural Tourism*, it was recognized by Page and Getz that 'the continued debate and focus on farm tourism have detracted from a more critical debate on the wider significance of rural tourism within an economic context' (Page and Getz, 1997: 14). In its aim to translate development principles into practice, this book may, perhaps, claim to be a sequel to Page and Getz's introduction to the business of rural tourism. As such it may be deemed appropriate to conclude with a parallel statement that builds on their observation. It is the contention here that the continued focus and debate on issues of 'rural tourism', largely in isolation, have detracted from the more critical debate on the wider significance of *tourism* within a rural development context. A 'rural tourism'-centric focus, while important for issues of physical environment and the particular needs of rural people and place, limits consideration of tourism's essential nature, detracts from issues of consumption, and fails to appreciate the whole into which tourism development fits.

References

AEIDL (1994) *Marketing Quality Rural Tourism.* LEADER Co-ordinating Unit, Brussels. http://www.rural-europe.aeidl.be/rural-en/biblio/touris/art07.html

Burns, P. and Holden, A. (1995) *Tourism, a New Perspective.* Prentice Hall, London.

Butler, R. and Hall, C.M. (1998) Conclusion: the sustainability of tourism and recreation in rural areas. In: Butler, R., Hall, C.M. and Jenkins, J.M. (eds) *Tourism and Recreation in Rural Areas.* John Wiley & Sons, Chichester, pp. 249–258.

Cohen, E. (1996) A phenomenology of tourist experiences. In: Apostopoulos, Y., Leivada, S. and Yiannakis, A. (eds) *The Sociology of Tourism: Theoretical and Empirical Invesitgations.* Routledge, London, pp. 90–111.

Convery, F.J. and Flanagan, S. (1992) Tourism and the environment – impacts and solutions. In: Briassoulis, H. and van der Straaten, J. (eds) *Tourism and the Environment, Regional, Economic and Policy Issues.* Kluwer Academic Publishers, Dordrecht, pp. 145–153.

Fyall, A. and Garrod, B. (1998) Sustainability and rural heritage. In: Hall, D. and O'Hanlon, L. (eds) *Rural Tourism Management: Sustainable Options.* The Scottish Agricultural College, Auchincruive, pp. 153–168.

Grolleau, H. (1994) Putting feelings first. In: AEIDL *Marketing Quality Rural Tourism: Technical Dossier.* LEADER Co-ordinating Unit, Brussels, p. 7.

Hall, C.M. (2000) The future of tourism: a personal speculation. *Tourism Recreation Research* 25(1), 85–95.

Keane, M.J. (1992) Rural tourism and rural development. In: Briassoulis, H. and van der Straaten, J. (eds) *Tourism and the Environment, Regional, Economic and Policy Issues.* Kluwer Academic Publishers, Dordrecht, pp. 43–55.

Laarman, J.G. and Gregersen, H.M. (1996) Pricing policy in nature-based tourism. *Tourism Management* 17(4), 247–254.

MacCannell, D. (1999) *The Tourist, a New Theory of the Leisure Class.* University of California Press, Berkeley.

Page, S.J. and Getz, D. (eds) (1997) *The Business of Rural Tourism: International Perspectives.* International Thomson Business Press, London.

Pigram, J. (1993) Planning for tourism in rural areas: bridging the policy implementation gap. In: Pearce, D. and Butler, R. (eds) *Tourism Research: Critiques, and Challenges.* Routledge, London, pp. 156–174.

Shoard, M. (1987) *This Land is Our Land.* Paladin, London.

Sørensen, A. and Nilsson, P.A. (1999) Virtual rurality versus rural reality in rural tourism – contemplating the attraction of the rural. Paper presented at the *8th Nordic Symposium in Hospitality and Tourism Research, 18–21 November, Alta, Norway.*

Swarbrooke, J. (1999) *Sustainable Tourism Management.* CAB International, Wallingford.

Key Texts

Books

Butler, R.W., Hall, C.M. and Jenkins, L. (eds) (1998) *Tourism and Recreation in Rural Areas.* John Wiley & Sons, Chichester.
Sharpley, R. and Sharpley, J. (1997) *Rural Tourism. An Introduction.* International Thomson Business Press, London.
Page, S.J. and Getz, D. (eds) (1997) *The Business of Rural Tourism: International Perspectives.* International Thomson Business Press, London.
Swarbrooke, J. (1999) *Sustainable Tourism Management.* CAB International, Wallingford.
Richards, G. and Hall, D. (eds) (2000) *Tourism and Sustainable Community Development.* Routledge, London.

Conference Proceedings

Hall, D. and O'Hanlon, L. (1998) *Rural Tourism Management: Sustainable Options.* The Scottish Agricultural College, Auchincruive.

Journals

Journal of Sustainable Tourism, Channel View Publications, Clevedon (published bi-monthly)
Journal of Rural Studies, Elsevier Science Ltd, London (published quarterly)
Countryside Focus, Newsletter of the Countryside Agency, Cheltenham (five publications per year)
Insights, Tourism Marketing Intelligence Service, English Tourism Council, London (published bi-monthly)
The Tourist Review, Official Journal of the Association of Scientific Experts in Tourism (AIEST), St Gallen, France (published quarterly)

Useful Web Sites

InfoRurale, The online gateway for rural development: www.nrec.org.uk/inforurale/register.htm
Rural Europe, website of the EU LEADER initiative: www.rural-europe.aeidl.be/
The Scottish Agricultural College farm diversification database: www.sac.ac.uk/diversification
The Countryside Agency, England: www.countryside.gov.uk
The Ministry for Agriculture, Fisheries and Food (England and Wales) (MAFF): www.maff.gov.uk

Index

Browse
Read
and Buy
www.cabi.org/bookshop
ANIMAL & VETERINARY SCIENCES
BIODIVERSITY CROP PROTECTION
HUMAN HEALTH NATURAL RESOURCES
ENVIRONMENT PLANT SCIENCES
SOCIAL SCIENCES
CABI Publishing
A division of CAB International
Online BOOK SHOP
Subjects
Search
Reading Room
Bargains
New Titles
Forthcoming
Crop Pollination by Bees
A DICTIONARY OF Entomology
G Gordh and D H Headrick
Order & Pay Online!
MasterCard
VISA
AMERICAN EXPRESS
Principles of CATTLE PRODUCTION
C.J.C. Phillips
Seeds
THE ECOLOGY OF REGENERATION IN PLANT COMMUNITIES
2nd EDITION
Michael Fenner
FULL DESCRIPTION
BUY THIS BOOK
BOOK OF THE MONTH
Tel: +44 (0)1491 832111 Fax: +44 (0)1491 829292